Secular Devotion

Secular Devotion
Afro-Latin Music and Imperial Jazz

TIMOTHY BRENNAN

VERSO
London • New York

First published by Verso 2008
© Timothy Brennan 2008
All rights reserved

The moral rights of the author have been asserted

1 3 5 7 9 10 8 6 4 2

Verso
UK: 6 Meard Street, London W1F 0EG
USA: 20 Jay Street, Brooklyn, NY 11201
www.versobooks.com

Verso is the imprint of New Left Books

ISBN-13: 978-1-84467-290-5 (hbk)
ISBN-13: 978-1-84467-291-2 (pbk)

British Library Cataloguing in Publication Data
A catalogue record for this book is available from the British Library

Library of Congress Cataloging-in-Publication Data
A catalog record for this book is available from the Library of Congress

Typeset by Hewer Text UK Ltd, Edinburgh
Printed in the USA by Maple Vail

He is contemplative and relaxed [qualities that people] confuse with laziness because he is not hard at work drilling, blocking the view of the ocean, destroying the oyster beds or releasing radioactive particles that will give unborn three-year-olds leukemia and cancer. PaPa LaBas is a descendant from a long line of people who made their pact with nature long ago . . . The essential pan-Africanism is artists relating across continents their craft, drumbeats from the aeons.

Ishmael Reed

For Danny

Contents

List of Illustrations — xi
Acknowledgments — xiii

Introduction — 1
1 World Music Does Not Exist — 15
2 Surrealism and the *Son* — 49
3 Face Down in the Mainstream — 83
4 Rap and American Business — 117
5 Global Youth and Local Pleasure — 146
6 The War of Writing on Music: *Mumbo Jumbo* — 182
7 Imperial Jazz — 213

Notes — 247
Illustration Credits — 275
Index — 277

List of Illustrations

1.1	Images on Putumayo CD covers	25
1.2	*Flying Down to Rio* (1933), dir. Thornton Freeland	38
1.3	*Written on the Wind* (1956), dir. Douglas Sirk	40
1.4	Gigi (Ejigayehu Shibabaw)	45
1.5	Koffi Olomide	47
2.1	The *cinquillo* rhythmic phrase	59
2.2	The rhythm for the *cinquillo*, the *tresillo* and the clave and pulse	65
2.3	The notation of the habanera rhythm in the *contradanza*	77
5.1	*National Geographic* cover picture	166
5.2	Image from Pedro Coll, *El Tiempo Detenido*	168
5.3	Image from René Burri, *Cuba y Cuba*	170
6.1	The Masonic "Egyptian Rite"	193
6.2	"The elements of Western metaphysics as represented by Masonic symbols"	195
6.3	"*Vévés* (images) of Haitian Voodoo"	196
6.4	"St. James, the Warrior Spirit (Ogu)"	202
6.5	Image from Ishmael Reed, *Mumbo Jumbo*	204
6.6	A Dionysian celebrant depicted on a Greek vase	205
6.7	Image from Vachel Lindsay, *Collected Poems*	209
7.1	Painting by Kdir (Kadir Lopez)	221
7.2	"Lt. Europe Stirring Up the Band"	231
7.3	"Regimental band, 13th Minnesota Volunteer Infantry, Manila, P.I."	232

PLATES

1	"Son," Argeliers León	242
2	"Danzon," Argeliers León	243
3	"Solace: A Mexican Serenade," Scott Joplin	244
4	"La Celosa," Ignacio Cervantes	245

Acknowledgments

My thanks to the State University of New York at Stony Brook for a Provost's Research Grant that supported my study of Afro-Cuban musical practices in Havana and Matanzas (Cuba) in December and January of 1993; and to the University of Minnesota Grant-in-Aid for supporting a research trip to Havana and Santiago de Cuba in the summer of 2000. My gratitude to Lilia Carpentier for a helpful interview on her late husband's research, and to the staff at the Biblioteca Nacional "José Martí" and at the Museo de Música in Havana, who helped me with bibliographies and access to photographs. I would like to thank Columbia University for a President's fellowship that led to my field research in Nicaragua where I worked as a correspondent during the summer of 1986, and again to Stony Brook for a small grant that helped support a research trip to Haiti and the Dominican Republic in the summer of 1994. Many of my ideas benefited from my year at the Society of Fellows in the Humanities at Cornell University (1997–8) where I worked on the project "Protocols of the Boardroom: Music and Corporate Style." I am grateful as well to the University of Minnesota Press and to the editors of *Transition* for aiding me in my co-translation and edition of Alejo Carpentier's *Music in Cuba* – a project that led to this one. My gratitude to Ronnie Baró of Charanga América and percussionist Luis Benetti for the education in Afro-Latin ensemble performance; to Lillian Manzor and Ángela María Pérez for so many conversations on any number of topics relevant to this book; to Elizabeth Ruf for introducing me in the 1980s and early 1990s to the New York and Chicago Latin dance scenes; to Nalini Natarajan for allowing me to present some of this material at the University of Puerto Rico-Rio Piedras (and to benefit from the comments of Ángel Quintero Rivera); to Tobin Siebers and S. Shankar for inviting me to speak on imperial jazz at the University of Michigan and the University of Hawaii-Manoa, respectively; to Dean Charles C. Stewart who invited me to speak to the freshman class of the

University of Illinois – Champaign-Urbana on "world musics"; to Sumanth Gopinath and his music theory workshop for reading and extensively commenting on an early version of the manuscript; and to Tim August, my research assistant in the summer of 2007. I would like to mention Tony King as well – my jazz piano teacher at the Wisconsin Conservatory of Music, who often spoke about "classical clichés." And finally, Keya Ganguly for her constant and invaluable comments and insights. In much shorter versions, part of Chapter 1 appeared in the journal *Discourse* (2001), part of Chapter 2 in *Guaraguao: Revista de Cultura Latinoamericana* (2002); part of Chapter 4 in *Critical Inquiry* (1994), and part of Chapter 5 in Daniel Fischlin and Ajay Heble, eds., *Rebel Musics* (2003).

Introduction

Popular music in the Americas, although derived from a number of Arabic and European (especially Spanish and French) influences, is overwhelmingly neo-African – even in genres like ballroom, disco and Broadway where the African elements are far from obvious.[1] Once angrily denied, this observation is now a commonplace. It is not only that musicians of African descent throughout the Americas have had a lavish presence on the pop charts or that the instrumentation, voicing and percussion of the African diaspora flow everywhere through the rivulets of popular song. The observation can be put much more strongly: there is a massive African subtext to American everyday life and leisure.

Although not unheard of, this sort of point is still finessed in many of the tributes to U.S. forms like jazz and blues, which are rightly seen as valuable reserves of the black contribution to American culture. A similar avoidance has often been true in Latin America as well, although for demographic and political reasons, much less so, especially in recent decades. This is not to say, of course, that ballroom, disco, Broadway, or other North American genres could have taken their distinctive shapes outside the unique setting of U.S. culture, or that they did not depend on many interactions with white musicians in urban and rural settings, above all Tin Pan Alley and the popular theater. All the same, the idea that there is an African unconscious to our most unguarded moments is still too disturbing for many to admit, and the redefinition of self too disorienting for many to accept in any but the most abstract way.

Even less conceded, I would argue, is the claim that I take as the point of departure for this book: namely, that New World African music extending from northern Brazil to the southern United States is hostile to the dominant religious impulses of modern life, to forms of Western labor, and to the commercial assault on demotic traditions and other types of unscripted human contact. I am not appealing here, though, to the widely used idea (taken from W. E. B. du Bois) of an African-

American "double consciousness" – which is a familiar way of rendering the matter. On the contrary, it is more accurate to say that popular music offers its listeners a coded revenge on the modern, and that this is *why it is popular*.

By saying this I am not linking popular music to youth rebellion, which is an argument that has been something of a cottage industry for at least two decades.[2] For some time, in fact, this has been the political angle of most critical writing on mass culture. It was not hard for later writers to explode this doubtful thesis based on celebrating market openings and seeing racial minorities and working-class teenagers as revolutionaries who were subverting official categories through transgressive forms of art.[3] The youth rebellion critics (U.S. rock and, later, rap were the examples of preference) tended to take musical forms at their literal word, confusing marketing with high hopes for social change, and failing to guard their flank against the inevitable evidence of co-optation where yesterday's revolt was quickly turned into the gimmick of today's ad campaign.

African New World music is political not because it is always, or even usually, a carrier of political messages (it isn't) but because the saturation of New World sensibilities by African religion and philosophy is, by its nature, political – an aspect more difficult to co-opt since the African presence is part of leisure and entertainment in the Americas at a cellular level, so to speak. For historical reasons, the African presence was expressed very differently in the United States than in other parts of the Americas – the Caribbean and Latin America – and these differences are highly revealing of the political culture of both regions, at once culturally alike and fatally opposed. Many of my observations set out from this division, exploring the richness of Afro-Latin art given its relative escape from the burdens of living in a country with imperial ambitions and a salvational sense of religious mission.

In this book, I have given this counter-monotheism and pre-modern embrace the name "secular devotion." By this I mean the resilience in contemporary popular music of African religious elements that are not perceived by listeners religiously, but to which they are, often unconsciously, devoted.[4] The degree to which works of popular music are neo-African varies a great deal, of course (Nat King Cole's "Ramblin' Rose" not so much; Carlos Santana's version of "Oye Como Va" a great deal more). But that is not the key issue. It is rather that the disproportionate presence of neo-African musical elements in the popular music of the Americas has a political meaning. The popularity of popular music is grounded in aesthetic choices traceable to Africa, a fact that suggests that

INTRODUCTION 3

apart from being an immense continent of great complexity, it is also an idea – an idea that haunts the West given its unasked-for role in the West's development. It has become the ethical destination of those who want to flee all associations with that earlier and tainted relationship, the embodiment of an unacceptable status freely taken on.

How can one speak, though, so generally of "Africa" and "African religion" in popular music? Let me make three points.

First, despite the variety of African ethnic groups forcibly brought to the New World (in Cuba alone, these include the Arara, Lucumí, Congo, Mandingo, and Ñañigos), the great productive centers of New World music drew on a relatively small body of divinities and theological notions.[5] The worldview emerging from them was manageably similar. In Cuba and in northeast and southern Brazil, for example, Yoruba culture predominates.[6] In Haiti – the third great source of African New World creativity – the deities of Haitian *vodun* derive from the Fon and the Yoruba, especially the Fon, although many of these deities (Legba, Ezili, Ogu, and Shango) are shared with the Yoruba pantheon as well, and appear often in the lyrics of popular Caribbean songs.[7] What this means is that the religious motifs acquired a coherence that was partly *made so* in the streamlining of religious belief by diasporic Africans themselves. This condensing was the result not only of syncretisms, but was an attempt to achieve a unity impeded by colonial policies designed to keep African ethnicities separate.[8]

Second, the experience of capture, transport, forced labor, and death lent itself to a social vision antagonistic to the market. This antagonism, in fact, was already well marked in the relationships and structures of the African societies that the slave trade disrupted. The economic historian Anne Phillips, for example, points to communal (non-commercial) forms of land-tenure and small commodity production as being among those social structures of African societies that led to long-established resistance to Western "development." Looking both to the past (in their loyalties to tribal chiefs) and to the future (in their resistance to colonial intrusions), many of these societies were inimical to capitalist forms of production and pacification, particularly as it concerned free labor. So despite trying for centuries, European and U.S. companies never succeeded in making Africa properly capitalistic – one of the reasons for its pariah status today in world economic business projections.[9] The imposed economy's fiercest opponents in the New World were, moreover, revolutionaries of religious stripe. In Haiti, Macandal, Jean-François Biassou, Romaine Rivière, Hyacinthe Ducoudray, Halaou, and Boukmann all won large and enthusiastic followings based on religious and magical performances used to inspire and unify the local population in the decades preceding independence.[10]

Third, African music in the New World tends to operate (although obviously not exclusively) at the level of social allegory – one, moreover, expressed in musical structure and performance practices rather than the verbal content of messages alone. This was not just part of its secret life under conditions of repression but of an original African value system that made art and social commentary one and the same. These formal, sonoric features (not only the words and incantations sung) were capable of passing more easily from one social context to another, and so they retained their original meanings in the secular setting of a modern urban entertainment that was, and is, for that reason ritually significant. These features go beyond the well-known commonplaces about African music – namely, that it is rhythmically complex, that it relies heavily on percussion (especially that of the hide drum), and that it is syncopated. The matter is more complicated than that.

In Western music the rhythms of the bass and treble clefs generally unfold in the same meter. Music is divided into standard units of time, always actually or implicitly *written*.[11] As a number of specialists have observed, our very concept of syncopation is premised on the idea of a departure from the "normal" accents of regular rhythm. In African music, by contrast, there are always at least two rhythms in play to the point where, were the music written, more than one meter would be required.[12] I will look in more detail at these differences in Chapters 2 and 7 (and the examples I have just given are only preliminary). For now let me say that the meaning of form can be said to emerge in a differential emphasis on beat and tone as well as on the plural and the singular. To a large extent, neo-African music carries on that aspect of its original African setting where music never merely accompanies a social context. It is not just aurally taken in by a community but involves them as participants since music is not meant to be listened to passively.[13] Much more than random aesthetic taste lies behind the fact that in African music the stress of the measure is typically on the offbeat. Musicians play "around" the beat, so that understanding African music means being able "to maintain, in our minds or our bodies, an additional rhythm to the ones we hear."[14]

This formal feature not only can be, but usually is, understood by listeners in a substantive social and ethical way – in this case, where the implied or phantom beat is a striving or escape that is also and at the same time a complaint. In the chapters below, I examine in some detail how actual pieces from New World African music create a sonoric environment that amounts to a vision of society that is attractive in the West for being a not-West. The degree to which these neo-African formal elements apply to mixed forms like early jazz and blues, Cuban *rumba* and *son*, the *calenda* of Trinidad, or Jamaican reggae is very well-established and uncontroversial. With a great deal more cultural mixing, it has been repeatedly shown that these elements are found as well in pop R&B, 1960s and 1970s rock, some film music, *nueva canción*, and a variety of less obviously African forms. But there has been no systematic attempt to demonstrate the link between these forms and what I am calling secular devotion.

In this book I treat neo-African music of the Americas as a unity. Afro-Latin and African-American music are to a substantial degree part of a single complex, and the unwillingness in most writing on popular music to treat them this way has, among other things, prevented people from appreciating the message of neo-African form and its secular rituals. For a number of reasons, though, my primary focus is Afro-Latin music, especially the Cuban *son*. We notice something striking and significant about Afro-Latin music from the outset that separates it sharply from the various black musical genres of the United States. The degree of the latter's deeply Christian and revivalist surroundings is an obvious difference, and it certainly mitigated the more overt African-ness of the popular idiom – partly overcome, though it was, by the constant influx into the United States of Latin forms under assumed identities. But there is another factor I would like to highlight at this point.

The global spread of Latin music took place without occupying armies, high-tech distribution networks, or a well-developed advertising apparatus. It did so, some have argued, because of the pathways laid down by the publicity networks of North American jazz between World War I and the late 1930s (the United States being in those years, as now, highly skilled at training foreign ears). But there is at least one important reason to modify the view that jazz played this leadership role or that the United States paved the way for commercialized global popular music by establishing itself as the model for everything that followed. For it could only have been a highly developed outlook, a coherent body of thought and feeling, that gave Latin music its global reach and staying power without any of the assistance given jazz by Madison Avenue, military occupation, and a media mobilized to instruct the global public in matters of taste. It needed a worldview in order to be passed on and to circulate intact.

From a variety of angles, this book is an attempt to describe and assess that worldview. In the last decade or so, various Caribbean musical forms (what Ángel Quintero Rivera and others have called "Tropical Music") have enjoyed unprecedented critical attention. Suddenly, a number of excellent books on salsa, *samba*, calypso, and *rumba* began to appear. Almost nothing of this caliber, in English at any rate, existed even as recently as the 1980s. Even the popular "music-as-subversion" trends in various works of cultural studies and pop-music criticism mostly overlooked Latin music until very recently. With a few exceptions, until a decade or so ago, an actual tradition of first-rate writing on Latin music could be found only in Cuba. This was the direct result of the pioneering work of the novelist and musicologist Alejo Carpentier after World War II as well as the encouragement by the Cuban government of the critical apparatus he inspired, which led among other things to an entire generation of critics in the Carpentier mode of very high quality (explored in more detail in Chapter 5). A few precursors ahead of the curve could also be found outside Cuba, although they were conspicuous by their small numbers.[15]

In all of this, what went under-reported was what might be called Afro-Latin music's guilty popularity based on a counter-Christian allegory working through symbolic form and sonoric structure. Buried within its sounds was the architecture of African religion preserved at various levels of intensity. It was popular given its ability to mount a protest that was not just mixed with fun but in which fun was the protest itself. Stalked by a highly disciplined and militant Christianity, the Americas adopted popular music as an underground religion that found its cathedrals in the communal sites of dancehalls, ballrooms, and the street, publicly sharing an agenda of ideas that did not seem religious to the Western mind at all: animism, polytheism, political satire, transcendence through sex, and a secular humanism indistinguishable from all of them. This was not just a matter of youth breaking out of their parents' conservative straitjackets. The historical memory of a bad colonial inheritance was embedded in the leisure-form, and had continually to be exorcized by a cultural conversion. In a manner that the guardians of order sensed, popular music was a rival and nemesis of the Judeo-Christian tradition.[16] In many places and times, it was so deliberately.

Behind the concept of secular devotion is also a broader, arguably more consequential, claim. In this form, the argument will be more recognizable since it is more widely found and, in that sense, I am offering a view that only helps substantiate a colloquial version of an already shared public understanding. In the United States, it was Abolition, Reconstruction and the early Civil Rights movement; in the Caribbean, it was the invention of *mestizaje* (the idea of mixed race as a desired, even patriotic, destiny) during the independence struggles against Spain, and later of *negrismo* ("black-ism" as a common social ideal) during the independence struggles in early twentieth-century Cuba, that made it possible to say that the ethical core of civic life in the Americas is inseparable from the African presence. This is so first of all because, in case after historical case, public ethics tend to express themselves as an embattled response to the scandalous fact of Africans being in the Americas against their will. The very beginning and end of ethical public life for that reason tends to be defined by this issue first and foremost. But it is true also because African-American and Afro-Latin men and women, in response to hard times, were inspired to provide models of ethical conduct and truth-telling – a kind of anti-cynicism that is on the whole very un-American in the U.S. sense.

These qualities permeate the best of New World African popular music as a whole not only in its Afro-Latin guise. It is no coincidence, for example, that rap rose to prominence during the age of Reagan or that the *son* in Cuba found its voice during a particularly depressing hiatus in the independence struggle against Spain. The rejection of political extremes was also an ethical revamping and re-direction, often opposing the Christian revival that accompanied the rise of the new conservative power. In black culture, a peace treaty is signed with the body and sensuality is cast in the warm colors of the human in its divine manifestation. Self-mortification, denial, and abstinence are left behind. It is not simply as release or play, in other words, that popular music saves society from its routine murders; it is not just relief from the long day's work or the joy that comes from cutting loose or the affirmation of community that makes it attractive, although all of these play their parts. In the Americas, popular music is a mission and strategy of recovery with deep theoretical roots that extend far into the past and constitutes nothing less than an alternative history of Western civilization.

Under a firestorm of abuse, forms like rap, the *son*, *rumba*, and calypso staked out a position of morality in a society drunk with the hollow virtues of corporate greed. These types of music were for much of their audience a moral center, even though in every instance, and despite the different decades when they arose, they were attacked as immorality incarnate. For its part, as some very good scholarly work has shown, Latin music has been a vibrant player in the democratic national movements of Latin America.[17] But again, its politics typically do not lie in this overt dimension. Its naivety, its happy promotion of unfashionable ideas like heroism and sociability are fused with its ideas of self-expression and leisure – a rare coupling in mainstream North America.

The recent U.S. revival of traditional Cuban music inspired by *Buena Vista Social Club* has struck many commentators as novel – as though the music were finally getting its due. Actually, the film and the phenomenon that followed it are only the latest stage in a long history of affection and forgetting. The global circulation of these traditions dates from at least the mid-nineteenth century, sprang again curiously to life at the turn of the century during the Spanish-American war, rose up once more in the Parisian and Mexican nightclubs of the 1920s and 1930s, and achieved its golden age in New York and Havana during the 1950s.[18] Once these facts sink in, they have the power to affect our thinking about many other aspects of New World African music. Despite the detailed work by scholars like John Storm Roberts, Thomas Fiehrer, Isabelle Leymarie, Leonardo Acosta, and others, accounts of jazz (for example) still tend to be based on the thesis that the Caribbean and the United States exist in different musical zones – a position that seems to run up against everything we know about artistic exiles, maritime traffic, and what has lately been called "trans-border cultures." New Orleans plays the same iconic, and largely fictional, role in jazz criticism that Athens plays in accounts of the origins of Western civilization: the absolute origin that is not (an issue I return to in Chapter 7).

Hard national-cultural categories do not seem to have weakened very much despite the explosion of writing today dedicated to transnationalism and hybridity. The fact is that nation-centered assumptions are often as strong in that criticism as in older or more conventional studies. In any research library, one can find hundreds of books and articles on ragtime, delta blues, New Orleans jazz, swing, big-band, bebop, rock & roll, R&B, doo-wop, Motown, soul, gospel, and hip hop. There are little more than a handful on *samba, beguine, soca, son, bolero, tango, foró, charanga, merengue, danzón, calenda, tejano, conga, bachata, vallenato, plena, cumbia, norteño, pachanga* or *reggaeton*. Latin America and the Caribbean continue to be segregated from U.S. cultural reality. To read the American composer George Antheil from the late 1920s is to get the sense that this segregation has had a very long career:

> From 1920–1925 we see one definite trend . . . no matter how absolutely Latin the Latins might become . . . or how Germanic the Germans might become . . . deep down (or perhaps not even concealed at all) . . . is *ever* present the new *note* of the Congo. This *note* has erroneously been called "American," but this note belongs no more specifically to the North American Negro than to those of the West

Indies or South America. It is *black* ... not white, nor yellow. It is strongly marked and recognizable, never to be mistaken, even by the musical illiterate.[19]

This denial of a common cultural destiny of the Americas exists on the U.S. Left as well as the Right, and is as strong in literary criticism as in theories of popular and classical music.[20] Despite the recent excitement about globalization and the supposed transcendence of the nation-state, for instance, many still seem to think of the world in strictly cartographic terms. The U.S. border is not just a legal demarcation written about in news features and documentaries on Arizona and southern California. It is more like a sovereign mental space, as true of south Florida and the Louisiana delta as the American Southwest, and just as sharply drawn in the 1980s as the 1890s.

The reasons for these fissures are partly obvious. They have to do with the barriers of language, the ignorance of history and context, the desire of the North to portray its own national character as unique despite broad similarities in the way the Americas were cultivated and developed as colonial settler states, and finally (it must be said) the desire to get something for nothing. But there are deeper reasons too. In any discussion of culture, we are never far from the war over the comparative value of civilizations. When we study culture, what are we studying? Is it even remotely clear to most students of "English," for example, that African-based popular music plays a similar role in Latin American and the Caribbean that literature does in Europe and the United States? Is it appreciated that the popular and national sense of self – of being Colombian, Jamaican, Cuban – is bound up with musical expertise, musical style, the power of exerting musical influence that seems to be every bit as strong as the urge for political dominance, scientific prowess, or literary skill (in which the Caribbean and Latin America have also excelled, of course)?

The European struggles waged in the seventeenth and eighteenth centuries against monarchy and religious absolutism (which took place at the apex of imperial expansion), guaranteed that intellectuals would define civilization in terms of reason, logic, and the mind – qualities more closely associated with literature than the other arts. Foreign cultures defined by popular or folkloric music were considered, like sound itself, ethereal, transitory, and unsubstantial. Where a music from below was the predominant expressive mode of a people, only atmosphere or diversion were possible, not history. Ignoring the authors of inspiration and discounting attribution were invitingly easy for Europeans, and the revolt against modernity by secular devotion largely invisible. Writing is, after all, as much a technology as a technique. As a weapon, it aided invasion by way of the fabulous narrative accounts of travel that encouraged foreign adventures, in the justifications of conquest issued by the royal courts, and in the legal documents that dispossessed the illiterate from their lands.

As the earliest European travel narratives to the Americas show, music was described from the start as writing's other. Apart from being the vehicle for a strange and compelling sexuality – all travelers either were, or pretended to be, appalled by this aspect of native life – music was poorly designed for staking out a clearly bordered territorial possession. It was and is too ubiquitous, it flows, is everywhere, is atmospheric – although not necessarily borderless since it also marks space and claims territory. Popular music, moreover, is taken to be pre-intellectual and nebulous; one is supposed simply to absorb it, to like or dislike it, but (it is assumed) not as the result of a calculated judgment. On the other hand, music is audible form: the structuring of time as well as structured by time, and therefore on those terms attractive to the European values encoded in the age of the conquering Mind.

These observations bear on devotion in a specific way. As Régis Debray points out in *God: An Itinerary*, the divine was always bound up with technological invention.[21] Monotheism derives from the invention of writing and the wheel (the two discoveries that began a long-term mastery by humans over time and space). Debray then touches on an idea already underlined in the novel by Ishmael Reed from which I took the epigraph opening this book (and which I examine in Chapter 6): "Whatever their differences, the Jewish, Catholic and Protestant Gods share the Holy Book as their source within a civilization dominated for 2,500 years by the authority of writing."[22] As Janheinz Jahn observes, despite the immense accomplishments of sub-Saharan African societies, they typically did not excel in two of the areas identified as signs of civilizational greatness: architecture and writing. On the other hand, as a number of music critics have observed (most recently, Cheryl L. Keyes), the inherited concept of the Word in neo-African practices is non-literary in the sense of being unwritten as well as being indifferent to the purely aesthetic properties of verbal invention. Jahn puts the matter clearly: "*Nommo* is the magic power of the word ... the life force which produces all life ... Only through the effect of a *muntu*, a man, living or dead ... can 'things' become active and in their turn influence other 'things.'"[23] He explains further:

> The European poet is an individual and expresses what *he* feels, thinks, has experienced, and wants. The African poet is a person, and that means sorcerer, prophet, teacher. He expresses what *must be*. His 'I' is not therefore 'collective' in the European sense; it is not non-individual. He speaks *to* the community and *for* them. He has a social task which raises him above the community.[24]

This dedication to an animating rather than a recording or expressing word – one not dependent on writing – is also a difference from literature.

African New World music, but particularly, I think, the Afro-Latin forms, challenges this European monopoly on *technique*. For European literary values for the most part consist of novelty, complexity, innovation, and irony – a list that comes out of literary modernism and gives us the aesthetic outlook that still governs the general public sensibilities of the concert hall and museum. These aesthetic norms are challenged in the neo-African practices of secular devotion. Their "classical" (which is to say venerated, disciplined) approach to technique is based on a set of counter-values. Among these are repetition, sincerity, personality, and voice, which set out to explode the older hierarchies – or better, reassert them by going back to older practices.

There is a war between literature and music. Any moderately well-educated college student in the United States or Britain takes a few courses in literature, and these are identical in their minds with studying "culture" and the humanities. Far rarer for them to have gotten anywhere near a course in music, and far rarer still a course on Afro-Latin music. Meanwhile, outside the university walls, the culture with which almost everyone is "literate" is overwhelmingly musical. What they are devoted to – their time, their emotions, their sharing are all invested in it – is popular music. Broadening the canon with more course offerings, or requiring more music appreciation courses, does not begin to get at this unforgivable absence in our cultural training.

To get a sense of the severity of the divide, consider a contrast made by the Barbadian poet Edward Kamau Brathwaite between what he calls the "culture of the circle" transported from Africa to the Caribbean during the slave trade, and "Europe: that great vast ice-eroded plain" which "formed itself into a missile" (a different shape entirely).[25] This admittedly polemical view, which some might write off as arbitrary, suggests at least the fundamental nature of the rift. Just as circle is opposed to missile in Brathwaite's imaginative iconography, orality, communal performance, and polymeter are set against the European Word in popular music. Both sides recognize the other as its other, and know that the very media of expression (literature, music) – rather than any particular form they take – are symbolically associated with peoples and civilizations whose past hostilities never ended. To teach "English" faithfully today, one has to teach popular music, which is to say (among other things) neo-African music.

My starting point in "World Music Does not Exist" (Chapter 1) is the observation that the music that really is "world" in the sense of being globally familiar and admired is European classical music and jazz – two forms never included under the term's rubric. As a place rather than a style of music, world music grows out of earlier colonial relationships. I dwell on the fact, first of all, that the greatest cultural influence on the West by the global periphery is in music, and that the idea of world music structures the reception of these sounds and styles not unlike trade embargos do, or the filtering of foreign news by government spokespersons. The music disseminated internationally never attains the status of the international; it remains a transported locality. If the exoticism of early colonial travel narratives was erotic, that of world music is aesthetic, expressed in the suggestive titles and opulent CD covers of boutique collections of world music. By exploring early American film and theater, I identify a long history of "world music" that existed in the 1930s and 1950s before the term was ever coined. World music is not simply appropriative, though; it demonstrates an escape from the American self.

In "Surrealism and the *Son*" (Chapter 2), I test my thesis that Latin music thrived in an anti-modern outlook. By tracing the trajectory of success that Cuban music found in interwar Europe and in the World War II era in the United States, I develop the ideas formulated by Ángel Quintero Rivera, for example, that Latin music's otherworldliness had to do with its reorientation of Newtonian time; or, as Ruth Glasser has argued, with a form of ethnic reassertion camouflaged to appear as European melody. If the European avant-gardes have been understood almost exclusively through painting, sculpture, and literature, its musical sources are seen clearly in the avant-garde's use of the medium of radio. The Cuban *son*, however, is a musical genre that is largely about itself, where self-reflexivity is a basically modernist gesture. And yet, very much unlike the market detours of a surrealism already commercialized by the mid-1920s, the *son* moved rather in the direction of offering a formal allegory of the indigenous: just the opposite of the contemporary focus on "hybridity." The compositional mechanics of what later became salsa was based on a delayed merging of cultural elements that existed side-by-side in an intentionally unresolved state.

In "Face Down in the Mainstream" (Chapter 3) I revisit an issue that has been debated repeatedly in popular music theory: the problem of "authenticity." I offer a defense of this idea, which has been mostly ridiculed in writing on music in recent decades. Appeals to what is authentic or genuine are usually thought deeply suspect since they indulge in a myth of origins and rely on a notion of inviolable essence. While conceding that point, I argue that the question has been misposed. An authentic work is one that knows its own history of making, and is able to map the traditions of sound that made it possible. I explore these ideas by looking at the work of Fernando Ortiz, eventually turning to developments in Nicaraguan rural music during the Sandinista revolution and in contemporary salsa.

"Rap and American Business" (Chapter 4) takes as its starting point the coincidence in the 1970s of the birth of hip hop in the Bronx and the rise of salsa in neighboring barrios, often with the same personnel. These two forms offered diametrically opposed alternatives to the then-dominant rock scene. The chapter argues that co-optation is the *goal* of rap, and commercialization its final realization. It is a music that conforms well, for all its nonconformity, to the market, for it blurs the relationship of consumer to producer. Rap lionizes the lumpen rather than the bohemian (rock) or the working-class man or woman (salsa). This paradoxically paves its way to the mainstream. The mainstreaming of rap was also accomplished through the creation of (1) the female mack and (2) the R&B/rap duet. I look at the reception of Cuban rap and those Latin forms of music that most closely resemble U.S. rap.

In "Global Youth and Local Pleasure" (Chapter 5) I look at the paradoxes of world music in contemporary Cuba and Puerto Rico. Inasmuch as U.S. marketers have always targeted youth (and not only in music), it is not surprising that the Caribbean island considered a pariah nation would be portrayed as cramping the style of youth, pushing a stale vision of a venerable older Cuban music onto those who really just want to write rap and listen to *música romántica*. I show the weaknesses of this view, and by insisting on the importance of Cuba's role in the dissemination of New World African music generally, try to make a related case for the particular kinds of pleasures available in Cuban society. I contrast this milieu with the music of the "pisto-locos" of Colombia and Mexico to discuss criminality and the marketing of youth rebellion.

"The War of Writing on Music: *Mumbo Jumbo*" (Chapter 6) is a reading of the most important African-American novel about popular music in the postwar period. This chapter takes up Ishmael Reed's provocative thesis that African New World music is a search for the lost "Text" of African religion. His key moment of 1920s U.S. history for Americans of African descent is not, as usually advertised, the Harlem Renaissance but the occupation of Haiti by U.S. troops, which was simply a continuation of a millennia-long effort to cut off African religion at its source (a religion disseminated by way of New World popular dance). Reed offers a confirmation of the thesis of secular devotion which is relayed by him in a retelling of the history of the rise of Western civilization.

"Imperial Jazz" (Chapter 7) opens by reminding us that New Orleans between 1880 and 1910 was primarily a Caribbean city, its eyes trained on Port au Prince and Havana rather than Chicago or St. Louis. It is just as significant that the first acts of U.S. empire in Cuba and Puerto Rico at the turn of the century created the cultural contacts (often in the form of the recruitment of musicians) that helped create the viability of jazz. And yet, against this story, what was originally the artistic creation of an outcast and enslaved people was transformed overnight by U.S. journalists and music critics into proof of what was most liberating about the society that did the enslaving. The national mythology of jazz has always been deeply redemptive, broadcast by black and white scholars alike as the signature cultural creation of the home country characterized by improvisation, self-fulfillment, and social mobility. I conclude this chapter by reflecting on the tragic separation in jazz from its blues influences: a situation that stands in contrast to Latin music whose commercialized forms in salsa retain close and ongoing connections to the *son*.

I have tried to make an argument about musical form that does not limit itself to a discussion of genres or playing styles. I am less interested in insider knowledge, or the jargons and terms of practicing musicians, than the relationship of musical form to representative peoples and worldviews. If jokes are among the first things that do not translate from one language to another, it is also the case that whatever is culturally untranslatable appears as a joke to outsiders. There is nothing more outlandish than a situated signifier cut loose from its moorings: one of the reasons Latin devotion is misrecognized or, worse, rendered as corniness, kitsch, or nostalgia. Music criticism has been very effective at providing the lost cultural contexts of a genre's creation, but less so the imperial imagination in which culture is learned. To understand that imagination is to begin to understand what is classical about Afro-Latin music, and it is in the name of that understanding that I have written this book.[26]

1

World Music Does Not Exist

It takes an era advertised as having a "world culture" for world music to exist – despite my title – as an idea in the mind of journalists, critics, and the buyers of records. It is real if only because it is talked about as though it were real. When so much of the world seems accessible without our ever having to leave home, and our experience of things is really an experience of the representation of things, the idea of world music is arguably as important and as real as a world music that really existed.

By way of television and film, most people have access to a bewildering array of music from around the world. In Germany, where I lived in 1997 and 1998, one could find rock, rap and pop from France, Italy, Britain, and the United States on MTV or the Viva channel without having to buy a CD or download an MP3 file. A visit to any movie theater brought one into contact with soundtracks of an even more varied scope. There most audiences, even without looking for them, heard South African township music, Latin salsa, West African rock, Hindi pop, Moroccan *chaabi*, Brazilian samba, Colombian *cumbia*, and Algerian *rai* – music that over time actually becomes familiar, although the film-goers didn't know the names of the styles or where they originated or anything about what they mean in other locales. In stores, metropolitan listeners find a whole section of shelves with CDs grouped alphabetically by country in a bin labeled "world music."[1] And there, in the altogether normal place that is a record store, world music is born and becomes real. The everyday act of marketing suddenly coalesces into an idea or, rather, clarifies an idea that already exists. In the countries of Europe and North America, the idea is what hearing music from other parts of the world must be, the only thing we can make of it: namely, not a specific *form* of music (symphonic, choral, written, improvised, rural, or ritual) but a *place* of music – the music of everywhere else.

Think of world music in terms of trade. If we set aside the recording and electronics industries, which produce discrete objects known as compact discs, iPods, and software for downloading, we can say that world music often enters U.S. borders effortlessly, infiltrates sound environments unregulated, penetrates hearts and minds without having to contend with import duties, GATT accords, or business quotas. It arrives in travelers' luggage, in mix-tapes made by Brazilian friends, over Internet radio, and in the form of the scores of Iranian films at local college festivals. Much more than t-shirts and cocaine, it is harder to impound at customs – a point not lost on the frightened recording executives mulling over the Napster era.

But it would be wrong to suppose that the intangibility of the product endangered American business (as if it were uncontainable like fallout from a dirty bomb). To see world music against the backdrop of trade is to be reminded of the imperial underpinnings of trade itself, whatever the commodity. And that brings us to the problem of unequal trade, which is always about dependency – although it is a dependency that goes both ways. Just as there are no high-performance fighter jets without Saharan phosphorous (since the high-tech metals used in their construction require phosphorous) American musicians, just as much as U.S. and European audiences, heavily rely on the creativity of foreigners. For them, the explosion of world music has been a buffer against the mind-numbing effects of recycling, play-charts and niche marketing.

World music, then, is at least partly about a longing in the metropolitan centers for what is not Europe or North America. It represents much more than an encouragingly positive interest in the cultural life of other parts of the world. It is, among other things, a flight from the self at the very moment that one's own culture is said to have become the global norm, as though people were driven away by the image stalking them in the mirror.

This hunger for the cultural practices of peripheral parts of the world is occurring just when one finds declarations far and wide that a single global culture is emerging, that nation-states are an obsolete political form, and that a common cultural currency already exists – or has begun to exist – among teenagers from Beijing to Santiago de Chile. Two sides of a contradiction come together without being recognized as contradictory: the appeal to difference and the announcement that differences are happily disappearing. People are horrified rather than happy at that prospect, and so set about proving to themselves that it is not so, staking out a foreignness that, although safely consumed in metropolitan surroundings, is a kind of commitment to the *not-here*.

Take, for instance, Cesaria Evora. No one is more recognizable as world music than she is. Her singing is heard in every bar and grill from

Hawaii to Dubrovnic. If there is one artist who symbolizes the universality of world music, and who demonstrates its appeal as a genre, it is Evora. And yet she comes from an archipelago (Cape Verde) marked by recent revolutionary and anti-colonial change. Is there a connection between her popularity and this historical setting? Or is the observation merely worth a few ironic comments about the minstrelsy that is warmly welcomed from societies the public would probably not embrace were it not for the incomprehensibility of the language and the cultural misunderstanding that comes with it? Maybe her runaway fame, after all, has to do with nothing more than her sadness, maternal endurance and strength.

This safer sort of argument, though, begs the question. For even if we accept that her success has to do with the intangibles of taste – which would mean making no argument at all – we are still left with figuring out how much the form of Evora's art was the product of an historical experience from an unusual and formative time in Cape Verde. It is not out of the question, then, that her popularity today is part of a shared public understanding – that her audiences sense in her music the political mood she was capturing there, which involved (among other things) the longing for independence from the world eventually made by "globalization."

I am not saying, obviously, that Evora is distributed and heard outside a market, or that her records are not bought and sold according to the usual calculus, or that she performs without any consideration for money. I am saying that the attraction of her music partly lies in its evocation of a form of life divorced from, and antagonistic to, everyday business. The languorous melodies and sincere lyrics capture a lifestyle dedicated to conversation, emotion, and the simple art of living (without cut-throat ambition, fear, or the cynical competition of the bottom line). But even more, her creativity takes place in a national-popular environment with specific political associations which she inherits and which her audience knows (or if they do not know, senses) in the act of listening.

Evora's own relationship to Cape Verde's political past, at least, is well established. When Amilcar Cabral, the intellectual leader of the independence of Cape Verde and Guinea-Bissau, was assassinated in 1973 (two years before freeing itself from Portuguese rule), Evora was thirty-two, a rising star and a product of her time. A popular performer of *morna* music on the piano bar circuit, with several hit singles on national radio, her ballads were sung in support of that "progressive national culture" that Cabral had called for, and one of its intentions was to help unify Cape Verde's ten arid islands in images of longing for their familial topography and common traditions of the "dignified poor" (as she also describes herself).[2] Although derived from the lamenting tones of Portuguese *fado*, *morna* in her hands and that of others played a role in carving Cape Verde out of the Portuguese imagination, and making it theirs. For one thing, unlike *morna*, *fado* could not take on a political dimension given the close scrutiny of its lyrics by the Salazar dictatorship in Lisbon. When re-discovered by a French émigré in the late 1980s, her music was just as nationalist as it had been in the early 1970s, although now after the disappointments of the decades following independence, they nostalgically elicited its earlier dreams.

One complaint with this line of reasoning, of course, is that it seems to assume a Western consumer. Only for that kind of listener would it make sense to appeal to a "not here." Actually, this complaint is misdirected, as is clear if one considers a fairly representative cultural venue like the "3 Continents Film Festival" in South Africa in 2003. There, South African director Bridget Thompson and Somalian director Abdulkadir Ahmed Said presented their *Rhythms from Africa: Zanzibar – An Ocean of Melodies*.[3] The film contrasts scenes of bare-breasted women dancing to traditional music with images of African pre-teens in front of a Coca-Cola sign listening to hip hop. The narrator ironically intones: "Africa faces two illnesses: progress and tradition." What is most interesting about the film, however, is that despite this obligatory ambiguity the narrative is framed by an exposure of the dangers of globalization for traditional societies. This danger is registered by a series of interviews with young South African musicians discussing Kwaito music, post-apartheid township rap, and the influences that 1970s protest music has on the music of today.

The film perceptively portrays a recent music star, who is shown saying that all he cares about is being wealthy. In that comment, the director captures a very different and more interesting kind of hybridity than the one typically invoked in the world music concept – a much less-discussed political hybridity. For the star goes on to say that he wants to become once again an African king, buy his way back to his pre-colonial roots. Immersed in the game of commerce, this locally famous musician is at the same time sickened by a post-heroic vacuum in the South African struggle. The anti-apartheid heroes may be out of jail, but the (black) president drives a Mercedes.

The persistent lament of the narration is that South African youth opts for U.S. mass culture over traditional music not because they freely choose a form but because they are seduced by a more effectively distributed one from afar. They were simply overwhelmed. The styles devised by the youth of Zanzibar consist of blending traditional *Taraab* music with rap. But this is a hybridity that has less to do with brainstorming or with the strengths of a collage aesthetic than pure bricolage. They are, the film suggests, not unlike the builders of huts on empty lots surrounded by plastic sheeting and soggy chipboard. The house gets made by what is at hand not because the resourceful makers do not know that their grandparents used locally made clay bricks and rough-sawn timber but because they have no choice. The closing images of Fiats, ATMs, and Kentucky Fried Chicken cannot conceal the directors' anger at being involved in an unfair fight. The despised ticky-tacky of another's profit motive damages and delimits the prospects of a society even if it cannot entirely wipe them out.

Whether the endangered "traditional" musical practices are already a mixture of past impurities, intrusions or mixings is not really the most interesting point, although it is the one that current world music theory is constantly emphasizing. The much more vital issue is the plain and overpowering fact of people wanting and *needing* tradition, above all in former colonial territories, and what this tradition in all of its shifting faces is protecting them from. And this is another dimension of world music criticism that has been passed over in relative silence. In Zanzibar traditional musical cultures live on now in a hybridity that is pure make-do, unasked for, mostly unwanted, and valuable above all for managing to preserve at least some of what had been destroyed.

None of these observations means that the metropolis has not waged its own counter-insurgency. As above, Africa appears all too often in musical connoisseurship under the sign of *utility*: the rendering of a venerated cultural artifact into an object for use, which is the predictable fate of all activity, feeling, and event in the culture industry. In this tension between the progressive fantasy world of music from abroad and the violent forcing of local and traditional meanings into a concept taken from the lexicon of European empire, world music marches on, creating a number of misunderstandings that are not all unintentional.

The tyranny of a concept

The many articles and books written on world music give us a sense of what is actually at issue in claims to hybridization – which is a more dubious idea, at least as it is presented, than it at first appears. A fairly representative case is the book *World Music: A Rough Guide* by Simon Broughton, Mark Ellingham, David Muddyman and Richard Trillo, which is a beautifully produced compendium, complete with texts, photos, and maps acquainting readers with the variety and richness of folk and popular musics from literally everywhere.[4] It has entire chapters with several subheadings devoted to the Celtic world, the Balkans, the Maghreb, the Gulf, the Indian subcontinent, and the Far East. We are taken on a fact-filled journey through bhangra music, Sufi devotional music, Siamese bikers rock, Transylvanian metal music, and the political pop of Southern Africa – *Chimurenga* and *Soukous*. Each of the sections is written by someone who is either from the region or has lived there continuously, and the renditions are accurate and sensitive to detail.

If one had reservations about such a book, it could not be that it was ill-informed. Its problem is rather a categorical one, which is to say a phenomenological one. World music, although not real, becomes real in the mind of the audience by being presented vigorously as a commercial concept. Here we can see the contradictions in commerce itself, which in this case is expressed as the progressive act of cosmopolitan promoters eager to bring the cultural riches of other lands into Western homes so that people might appreciate their brilliance and humbly learn from their compelling and alien lesson.

At any rate, to take (as this book does) the *Qawwalis* of Pakistan and place them alongside the Benin rock of Angelique Kidjo is to get a false sense of both, regardless of what is said about them. One is a form of devotional music that has no desire to become *of* the world, for example, while the other is a music based on American models, altered by the addition of local rhythms and instrumentation, and produced in European recording studios for global distribution and consumption. Albanian epic, to take another example, has a primarily narrative content whereas Ethiopian groove is dancehall music. The categories on display, quite apart from the intentions of the authors to inform their public, force them into offering a training that can only misinform. Its subtitles, in order to prompt interest, cannot help flattening all this variety out into a series of manageable clichés. The section on Turkey, therefore, is called "Rondo à la Ataturk"; the section on flamenco, "A Wild, Savage Feeling"; on Zaire, "The Heart of Darkness"; and on Indian classical music, "From Raags to Riches."

This last example may be the most instructive, since anyone who knows the complexities of, and millennia-long commentary on, Hindustani classical music would be stunned to see it placed in the company of Irish folk music. It would be unimaginable, I think, for the authors, to place European classical music into such a context, since it quite rightly would be seen as requiring a training in a whole array of specialist skills and historical understandings that simply could not be captioned this way. Paradoxically, what is found in this book is precisely *not* world music, but rather local or regional music that either does not travel well or has no ambition to travel. An ethnographic impulse to study the foreign here confuses those protecting their art from invasion with music seeking to enter a transnational youth culture of entertainment. The specimens of the first, tacked to a musical wax board like a butterfly's wings, are placed alongside the work of immigrants who want nothing more than to enter the display-case rooms.[5]

But there is more to the paradox. What *is* world music – in the sense of being globally disseminated and popularly, even reverently, internalized almost everywhere – is precisely what is *not* "world music," which is to say included in books like these: namely, European classicism and American jazz, blues, rock, and (now) rap. In spite of the enormous transregional popularity of Hindi film songs, for example, or Quranic religious music, only select genres of U.S. neo-African music and European classicism are the traditions that can be called with any justification "world." Only they have circulated globally, and have managed, due to the legacy of imperial education systems, to create a caste of aficionados reproducing a vast international taste for them with all the trappings of significant cultural capital.[6] In the film *The Quiet American*, it is not surprising to find the British journalist Thomas Fowler listening to jazz on a turntable in his 1950s Saigon apartment, whereas hearing *chaabi* music there would only seem like an idiosyncrasy. Meanwhile, as the popularity of classical music steeply declines on U.S. and European radio and in its concert halls, it has taken off in China, which along with Korea is producing many of its performance virtuosos. A similar fate for *soca,* or any other "world music" would be, at least for the moment, unimaginable.

This is not to say that forms of music cannot or should not be exported globally or enjoyed out of their contexts; or that it is impossible *really* to understand music if one is not from the culture producing it. But circuits of leisure and relaxation like those involved in consuming music are also distractive and therefore adept at slipping arguments past us without our noticing or criticizing them fully. Despite its welcome cosmopolitan energies, the concept of world music is a loaded one, even an offensively narrow one, and yet it is hard to see the matter this way in a record store because having to consider the ideological nature of the category runs up against the simple pursuit of enjoyment. If it is true, as Herbert Schiller and others have argued, that leisure is a form of work, and recreation a form of consumer labor, it is also the case that ideological persuasion is more effective in relaxed minds where resistance may gnaw at the soul but rarely prompts one to destroy the moment in the name of principled thinking. The collective displeasure elicited by bothering with such ethical quibbles is all too palpable, and so usually silences the one who initiates the inquiry.

What world music means to those under the sway of its concept is nevertheless alarming to those who would like to see a genuine international cultural respect. In 1995, *Attitude: The Dancers' Magazine* carried a section dedicated to the then-new World Music Institute in New York. The magazine ran a list of reviews of recent dance performances sponsored by the Institute that included a Cajun/Zydeco Festival at Symphony Space, Simon Shaheen's Near Eastern Music Ensemble at the Brooklyn Museum and (again at Symphony Space) The Whirling Dervishes of Turkey, the Navaratri Celebration, the Indigenous People's Celebration, a Hungarian Folk Song Celebration featuring works from the north-eastern Transylvanian region of Bukovina and Moldavia, the Kuchipudi dance of Mallika Sarabhai, and the Black Umfolosi dance of Zimbabwe.[7]

It never occurs to the editors of *Attitude*, though, that the performers under review might object to being part of such a smorgasbord. This arrangement ensures that a thick line will be drawn between the guests at this cultural feast and the hired dancers assembled for the delight of the audience. The fawning would likely please the performers except for the fact that the Turks are as far from the Zimbabweans as both are from the Usonians.[8] *That* difference, however, is not foreseen by, and even seems uninteresting to, the reviewers. Against the apparent intentions of the hosts, a dividing line between America and non-America is brutally drawn: "It has been a glorious season for the World Music Institute [which is at] the forefront of celebrating the tapestry of both American & world cultures that we are privileged to have access to."[9]

Intoxicated by regard for a style of art they realize could only have been imported, world music fans of this variety exhibit a naivety that can be more disrespectful than disarming. At times the attitude of *Attitude* connects abject reverence with "them-and-us" differences in startlingly clear terms:

> You can't help but learn to appreciate and absorb both the peoples and musical heritage of the various sub-sets that delineate Middle Eastern Culture. Also dancing in this program was the recently seen spectacular Husni Shahata from Egypt . . . Mind you, this all goes on while he is turning in the dervish whirl and removing layers of clothing. His movement, mystery and magic bring to mind all the tension and

excitement of a combustible soul in communion with eternity... While our brethren turned on their axis and traveled around the stage, we were given an opportunity to embrace their individual states and collective symmetry.[10]

This didactic new age-ism choreographs a dream where anything-but-here-ness acquires a peculiarly suburban authority:

Born in Brooklyn, Cesar has Mohawk and Filipino ancestors. For this concert he had a Mohawk spiritual leader, Tom Porter, give a traditional Mohawk Thanksgiving address ... This was a lovely and gracious offering, profoundly respectful of the Earth and all upon it, in which he repeatedly asked all gathered here to bring our minds together "and our minds is agreed" to thank the waters, animals, plants, birds, winds, Brother Sun, Grandma Moon, and the Creator, and to tie it all up with our compassion and our love.[11]

It is therefore hard to work through the claims implicit in a category like world music. One has to consider, for example, the forces of market selection on the transformation of the material. The example of "salsa" is a clear one in this respect. Although many are unaware of this history, "salsa" was born from a 1960s and 1970s studio sound developed by Latin musicians in New York in order to compete with rock music and to pry away from rock a share of its youth audience.

The explicit attempt of salsa impresarios and connoisseurs like Jerry Masucci in that era was to recapture the commercial success that Latin music had in the U.S. and Mexican *mambo* craze of the 1940s and 1950s. The point is not that salsa was therefore simply a dilution of Afro-Cuban *batá* drumming or the *a cappella* songs of devotion – the cantos to the *orishas* – or even of the early *septetos* in Cuba of the 1930s, even though salsa originally grew out of all of these musical sources as well as others from Cuba and elsewhere in the Caribbean. The point is that the direction in which salsa developed was increasingly dictated by a world music *concept*, which is to say a joining in sound of already established American popular and commercial forms. It had to take that road, which meant there were other roads it could not take, or that it even did take in Cuba (a country partially, although not completely, protected from the world market).

The degree of innovation that continued in isolated Cuba – that continued *because* Cuba was isolated – met general bewilderment abroad until being borrowed by musicians in Miami, Los Angeles, and New York and then transformed into local variants of an older same. These borrowings continued, although more circuitously and anonymously, even after the legal isolation of Cuba following the revolution represented by the passage of the "Trading with the Enemy Act." The continued celebratory reception for world music (even if some have quibbled with the term in print) dictates that in this structure of creation and reception, the message audiences take away from such cases is distorted. The conclusions drawn are not (as they should be) about the North Americanization of the Cuban *son* but about the inviting openness of the market to non-Western forms of music.

Cuba was the embarkation point to Europe for ships from throughout the Spanish empire for centuries, the meeting place of adventurers, intellectuals, entrepreneurs, and misfits from all over the Caribbean. The island enjoyed a cultural centrality in the parts of the Americas colonized first, and it was the hub from which the rest of the greater Caribbean took shape (that is, all of the southern United States and South America north of Bahia). Cuba, moreover, had a special relationship to the United States. Its offshore life as investment opportunity, money-laundering outpost, and training-ground in vice was well established already during Prohibition and continued into the 1950s. It had been the source of a steady stream of disgruntled political refugees seeking a bigger paycheck from throughout the latter half of the nineteenth century (Cuban exiles are not a unique feature of the Castro era).

It has been argued that salsa and Dominican *meringue* have been largely excluded from "world beat" categories, in part because the desire for African authenticity in those circles was stymied, salsa being a form that represented the tendency by some in the Spanish Caribbean to "ignore or deemphasize the region's African heritage."[12] But there is scant evidence in the musical structure or lyrics of such a de-emphasis, particularly in the *sonero* allusions of the Fania All-Stars era, where a conscious homage is paid to the *son* as well as to the creativity of those earlier generations of black and white Latin émigrés to U.S. metropoles (see Chapters 2 and 5). The neo-African dimensions of the music have, moreover, been pronounced, and remain so to a surprising degree – certainly more than most pop R&B of the Zhané, Tony Braxton, or Chanté Moore variety, which as I argued above, is not perceived as world music by virtue of being Usonian. If salsa fits uncomfortably under the world beat rubric it is not because of racial inauthenticity but because it has an identity that pre-dated the world music category. The tenor of its original entry into the music markets was one that underlined its minority assertiveness, its pride in the uniqueness and flavor of the community's cultural achievements, and its strongly marked pan-*Latinidad*. All of these collide with the idea of a new world community transcending borders.

The world music concept has lately been refined to the point of seamless beauty. The Putumayo record label has put out a whole array of world music albums in the form of what one could call "boutique music." These are the brilliantly colorful CDs one finds at cashiers' counters in clothing stores like Banana Republic or Gap.

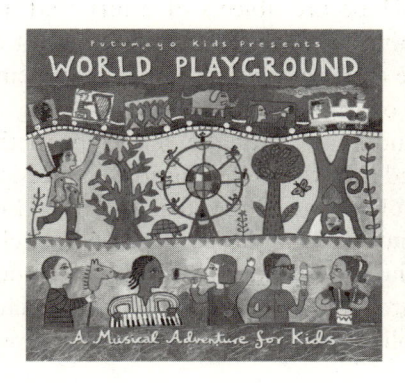

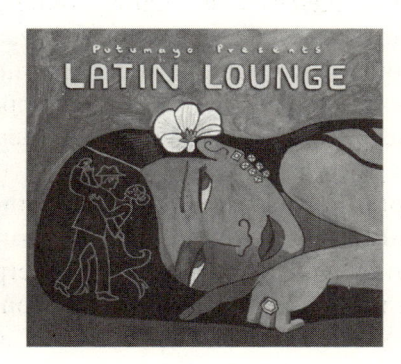

Figure 1.1 Images on Putumayo CD covers.

The desires tapped by this marketing genius are revealed with a bluntness that is often missing in world music circles. Here the repertoire of colonial imagery is on full display: for example, the corralling of divergent countries from diverse continents into an ensemble devised by the one thing "we" know them by – the commodity they export ("coffee") (another Putumayo offering is "Music from the Chocolate Lands"). Or the unconscious desires of the tourist found lurking in the idea that the world is a "playground." Or, more subtly, the labeling of music created by artists from over a dozen separate countries in sites that remain untranslatable not only to "us" but to each other by terms borrowed from an explicitly North American market terrain ("lounge," "soul," "groove," and so on – terms that have less to do with actual musical techniques or established genres than with atmosphere).

People buy these CDs to perform a service, to provide a particular niche that ensures by the selections made that they never have to leave a certain well-designed mental space. These are objects of utility that are meant to correspond to the establishing of a mood ("I feel like a bit of 'lounge' today"). But they are, in the end, ambiguous rather than being merely objectionable. Having spent over twenty-five years listening to Cuban music, I had to admit, begrudgingly, that the selection on the album "Margarita Mix" by a related world music boutique collection (Pottery Barn) was impeccable, tasteful, balanced – exquisite really.[13] For decades, in order to hear this music most fans had to depend on scratchy cassettes from friends from Colombia or Venezuela, who had recorded them off LPs inherited from their parents. The collectors and musicians who advise Putumayo and similar collections are obviously very knowledgeable.

But themes like "Latin Lounge," "Arabic Groove," and "Global Soul" are debilitating as well. Arguably designed to set at rest a restless audience by folding strange music into familiar categories, the strategy is also proactive. When a record company creates a niche, many underpaid artists from, say, India and Yemen will rush to create the very thing imagined in a Western publicity office. Instead of Putumayo sagely capturing an exciting new reality, they are really initiating a process that leads the people they are "discovering" to make their invented concept a reality. And of course, for the underpaid artists from India and Yemen to get it right – that is, to win attention for Putumayo and so find their way into the exclusive company of the selection, they have to bone up on the already existing lounge and soul music produced in the United States – that is, if they had not already been overly familiar with it from Karachi or Parisian radio. Into this vessel – the process is analogous to the prefabricated walls, roofs, and floors of the housing industry – the artist is asked to pour his or her phrasing, instrumentation, or harmonies, giving it the place-ability of a postcard, like that inevitable camel or palm tree in a Steven Spielberg film which tells us all immediately, without saying a word, that we are in the Middle East. In Putumayo's packaging of CDs with the suggestive names "Dreamlands," "Caribbean Party," "Mediterranean Odyssey" and so on, we are seeing an unflattering but accurate reflection of our own faces in a warped cultural mirror: a hopeful sign that now on display like this, the metropolitan ego will at least be under scrutiny.

The circuits of leisure, for the very reason that they do not seem to be where arguments are taking place, are especially effective arenas of persuasion. This is all the more true when one considers that music-listening is not only a leisure activity, but one where serious affective commitments are elaborated: the deep investment, for example, in the high cultural appreciations of art; or the playing out of various lifestyle politics through music. There is an amazingly developed literature of devotion to the art of popular U.S. music (blues, rock, jazz), often very technical and dedicated to the notion of innovative genius. From early blues through British punk, similarly, one of the major avocations of the music critic has been the use of secret codes known only to initiates, a professional dropping of names, and the bragging rights of the insider's anecdotes about the artist's troubled life.

In world music, however, these layers of meaning and traditions of codification undergo a disastrous transformation and traducement. What is, or was, on the mind of Marley in those slow, ganja-inspired, Jamaican plaints about Babylon and the march to an African Zion, is not on the minds of those who play him at parties in Chicago lofts. Again, this is no argument against the alternative uses to which music can be put, but it does add a note of clarity about the limits of hybridity in the still somewhat dubious emergence of a so-called world culture.

The complaint with world music, then, should not be confused with a misguided effort to preserve the purity of tradition. Reactions against this gesture have led to a kind of writing on the popular that extols cultures for making do while going without. These glorifications of the subaltern hero, though, usually ignore atmospheres that accompany musical shifts in taste in low-technology zones of economic disenfranchisement.[14] And yet, even here, it is easy to get confounded by prior expectations. World music is not always about folklorizing a non-transportable, domestic classicism (where "classical" means highly disciplined, codified, venerated, and possessing an archive or pantheon). In the act of reception, even the amateur knows that the categories are more complicated. A Gilberto Gil or a Youssou N'Dour, for example, cut their records in studios that early Seattle grunge bands could never dream of. Gil and N'Dour partake of a publicity apparatus whose layers of sophistication are mind-boggling. If there is an unspoken value system in which it is assumed that the raw material of third-world style is transformed in Western recording studios, the idea collapses in individual cases where the prestige or studio finish of the supposedly disenfranchised village artist undercuts the pretensions to stardom of rich kids from Westchester working out of their garages – even those who eventually make it big.

Beyond that, music as I have been using the term, recalls a larger issue of influence, one that is decisive in battles over the inclusion of new literatures or new cultural forms in the revised curriculums of universities seeking to expand into the postcolonial field. Where did, or do, the original ideas come from that are then taken up by others and used internationally in hybrid forms? While there is quite an emphasis on hybridity itself, or its counterparts – *mestizaje*, transculturation (emphases that seem to obliterate the emphasis on origins or the question of historical clout in colonial relations) – I do not think the issue of primacy is ever far from view. Who can or cannot claim cultural superiority always finds its place on the ledgers of comparative cultural value, and everyone wants to know who the inventor was.

As it turns out, with some exceptions, the greatest influences on Europe and the United States, culturally speaking, have been in the field of music. The flow and direction of North American and European society was much more profoundly affected by the polycultural blendings of *tango*, *mambo*, the Cuban *septetos*, American jazz, Jamaican reggae, Brazilian *samba*, and Hindi film music, than by works of literature. To judge from the Viva channel in Germany or from the specialized sections of the record stores, such flow and direction is also being affected by world music, although only in a containable form. It is not only that much of the music of the Western repertoire, in the classical as well as the popular cultural sphere, comes from other parts of the world, but that everyone knows that it does. Nevertheless, the use-values of the two types of foreignness are dissimilar. Unlike the passive listeners of movie scores, the audience of world music has otherness in mind. By contrast, the classical amateur hears Dvorak's Romany dances, Tchaikovsky's Arabic rhythms or Ravel's Cuban melodies as a whitewashed domesticity.

When I take world music critically or skeptically, I am not adopting a cultural imperialism model from the 1970s without alterations. This view typically points to the tyrannical export of mass cultural objects to the third world for the purpose of disarticulating native cultures, and I concede that the problem is more contradictory than that. But it is time to reject the over-reaction against that view from the 1980s and 1990s. Houston Baker is right when he observes that "a nation's emergence is always predicated on the construction of a field of meaningful sounds."[15] It follows that if those sounds are no longer identifiable as being from a nation or a specific people – if they are folded into a larger world music concept of "transborder" cultures – then the insinuation of powerful countries into the smaller ones is made much easier. However, what is at stake is also more than, and different from, cultural imperialism. Deborah James, for example, points out that a certain branch of ethnomusicology displays an interest in "'pure' traditional music, and a scorn for hybrid styles or those which have evolved out of the experience of proletarianized communities."[16] So Afro-pop, for example, elicits scorn from them because of its souped-up studio sound and its mimicry of English or American rock spliced onto more recognizably African communal forms.

Purist critics see this as dilution. But such a critique should not be confused with mine.[17] I am emphasizing the critical frame – one that obscures what the music is and is not doing. I am talking here about the problem of categories, which perhaps is a different way of posing the issue of cultural imperialism precisely in an era when the inclusion of non-Western cultures has become a strict Western doctrine.

The foreign at home

The problem of categories is striking when we consider hip-hop to be a *foreign* music. The lurid news coverage of hip-hop in the United States belongs in a study of the colonial encounter because it replays in many ways those reports by colonial officials in the nineteenth century on the primitive customs of unruly natives. The U.S. mainstream media's grasp of the genre known as "rap" is as distant from the source and often as hostile as much of the imperial travel narratives from earlier centuries. They view events within their own country with the confusion and distaste usually reserved for reporting on antique lands. Now with everywhere from Senegal to Cuba, from Sweden to Italy, spread out along the airwaves, certain dimensions of rap are all the more hidden.

One of the biggest rap stories in the popular press over a decade ago dealt with the wars between East and West Coast. New Yorkers contented themselves with knowing hip-hop was created in the Bronx about twenty years earlier (with many external influences, including Jamaican) by kids with access to home stereo equipment and their parents' R&B collections. Angelinos basked in the evidence of being the rappers most written about, the ones living in the neighborhoods where most of the big-distribution films about rap were set, and the only rappers who truly sold in the platinum range. It was a fight, one could say, with two different faces. But the mainstream reporting of the fight sounded in many of its particulars like the news coverage of intertribal warfare in Rwanda, the kind of association, in fact, that the writers of the articles tried to convey in not-so-subtle ways.

In the new urban geography of post-industrial America, this East Coast/West Coast feud pitted a decaying industrial, European and Caribbean immigrant New York of high rises and tenement halls against the sunny image-capitalism of decentered Los Angeles – a city with a large Asian and Latino immigrant base looking West toward the Pacific. East and West as the antipodes of America. The pairings that arose between them underlined a different and much larger conflict characterized in many ways by time itself: a conflict over modes of development and cultural definition that were occurring on a global scale.

Los Angeles vs. New York meant also celluloid vs. print, veranda vs. salon, microchip vs. finance; the celebrity or movie star vs. the author; the predominantly Asian vs. the predominantly black; the Central American Indian Latino vs. the Caribbean Island Afro-Latino; pastel stucco vs. the pseudo classicism of New York's famous steel-gray glass and steel; fun vs. seriousness; *the image vs. literacy*.[18] The deeply held American myth of the march West was invoked here, silently, as though the Westward direction of American history needed now, having reached the Pacific, to look still further to find its points of reference. Reminded that he or she lived on a globe, the Usonian found in the Orient paradoxically the next West to be discovered. Los Angeles in the rap sphere, as in other spheres, was for many, then, cutting edge. The present that would be future.

As the most celebrated instance of the East/West rapper feud, the death of Biggie Smalls (an East Coast rapper) suggested the complicated local specificity of even so widely known music as rap. This apparently very bald and easy-to-read sort of action – the murder of a popular songster – concealed stories that the reporters missed. The meaning of the murder turned out to be difficult to export outside its locality. Indeed, not only are the contexts of rap difficult to discern once exported to Nigeria or France, they barely leave the black community within North America without being transformed into a narrative with all the subtlety of melodrama. For Biggie was killed in, of all things, a drive-by shooting. Also, for this reason, the newspapers were able to portray the killing as part of a turf war among gangsters. The evidence for this news was drawn from the lyrics of the music the "gangsters" listened to, a remarkable illustration of the miserably ill-informed writing of otherwise intelligent American men and women on the subjects and styles of rap. It was like trying to solve a political scandal in the White House by reading a John Grisham novel.

For the better part of a decade, the press and public commentators had been equating rap as a whole with only a small branch of it: the form known as "gangsta." In a literalism they would never accept in an undergraduate essay on Shakespeare, these writers saw the murder as playing out the content of rap's songs, like a replay of a James Cagney movie or a scene from *The Untouchables* now for the age of crack cocaine.[19] Actually, the many genres of rap range from prankster and love lyrics to bootstrapping civic betterment songs and ganja-vegetarianism.[20] But what the media were calling "gangsta" was a given; it didn't have to be argued. And what the artists themselves were alluding to in their songs, without the media's being aware of it, was not so much a bad-ass form but a political aesthetic that bled into all of the rap genres, even the ones a neophyte would recognize were not "gangsta."

Unlike R&B or soul, rap would not fudge the language. It refused to speak the inviting creed of integration solemnified by the legacy of Martin Luther King, which had practically been the passport for black public utterance in the past. Nor was it that distilled heroin haze of bebop that could, along with Jackson Pollock, form a new classicism among the cigarette-smoking beat intellectuals of white America. Rap became popular in white suburbia as well as among American racial minorities that were not African American, and indeed throughout the world. In this, consumers displayed more savvy than the commentators.

Even with what is arguably one of the most globally disseminated forms of music since the European jazz craze that launched the new technology of radio in the 1920s, rap (unlike "world music") consists of a fairly untranslatable set of local meanings. Possibly more than other forms, it is dedicated to the in-joke, the group lingo, the neighborhood allusion, right down to a specific mass-cultural canon (kung fu films, for example), so that when it is wrenched out of place, it is capable of sounding desperately untalented. The real rap "war," like much of the gangsterism of its lyrics, has only a little to do with the killings of rappers like Biggie Smalls and Tupac Shakur. It is a trope carried on in a compendium of carefully constructed artistic debate by the Alexander Popes of the black community. On average, the East Coast rappers tended to be the ones asking (there were many exceptions): how much of the sacred can be pawned off in the quest for loot before something dies in the community?

The East/West split, although particularly charged as a matter internal to rap, and an issue that helps to clarify the bogus fixation on "gangsta," suggests something of that global stretching of boundaries that new technologies and deregulated corporations have produced, particularly in a place like California. New regional agglomerations of racially defined guest-workers, outsourcing, and color-blind capital investment cut across the boundaries boldly drawn on maps, making California more a part of Mexico and Japan than Kansas or Massachusetts. New York in that sense is more a Caribbean hub and European port than a sister city to L.A., and is also the artistic and intellectual gathering-place of the new Hapsburgs and Romanofs of the international bourgeoisie: Persian, French, Chinese, and English, with apartments on Sutton Place and memberships at the New York Athletic Club. The motifs of travel, migration, and transnationalism understandably dominate discussion in the humanities and social sciences today, but not when it comes to rap, which tends, for the most part, to be consigned to the African-American studies wing of popcult theory. In this sense, rap is no exception to that curious tradition of scholarship on the African diasporic music of North America (ragtime, swing, delta, bebop), which despite global dissemination is still seen as a confidently Usonian complex of musical forms. In other words, like blues and jazz before it, rap signifies as U.S. for most commentators even as the "transnational" is prophesied almost everywhere else. Rap's East/West split symbolizes a struggle over art and meaning that is central to the sorts of misunderstandings and violence of interpretation that accompany the physical violence of the United States in attempting to retain its role as world leader. This sort of interplay has existed for a very long time.

If multiculturalism is the non-Western at home, it has gradually given way to a multiculturalism based on the championing of American pluralism. So too has rap played a contradictory role both as domestic whipping boy and international brag – again, very much like jazz in this respect. A domestic minority is at the same time a key advertising feature of American vibrancy. By becoming the favored art of a transnational majority, rap is a North American form above all in the crucial role it plays as a mass cultural success story. Its marketability is instrumental in securing a transnationality that is basically Usonian, even as many blacks at home are consigned to a prison-labor system, frequently prevented from voting in presidential elections, profiled by the urban police, and in many places corralled into under-financed, dangerous neighborhoods which (not coincidentally) then become laboratories for creating new music: the sublimation of poverty as market share.

Usually cast as a turf war, the East/West split is actually a war over approaches to the market, and whether rap itself should be offering an analysis of crisis or a cynical revenge against it. Two aesthetic philosophies arise to be heard, and they are incompatible. As we have been arguing, there are regional and structural determinants to the war, based as it is in changing demographics, shifting sectors of investment, movements from industrial to communications-based industries and, above all, the image of the new economy as belonging to the froth of a California-southwest Florida axis of retirees, nouveau super-rich (in both its silicon valley and bling-bling versions), and the media masters of advertising.[21]

Greg Tate gets at still another dimension of this problem when he makes the following important point:

> The circumscribed avenues for recognition and reward available in the Black community for Black artists and intellectuals working in the avant-garde tradition of the West established the preconditions for a Black bohemia, or a Blackened bohemia, or a white bohemia dotted with Black question marks.[22]

The idea of the black core of all artistic rebellion itself can be found already at the beginning of the century. One finds it, of course, in the African shapes and forms of Cubism, the African nonsense poetry of early Dada, Rimbaud's African journeys, and the content of much of the self-styled primitivism and ritualized spirit-longing of surrealism. Even in classical music, with Gershwin in the United States, Kurt Weill in Germany and Darius Milhaud in France, the jazz popularized by early radio found its way into avant-garde expression and became, in a way, inseparable from it.

Although right to establish this important link between black popular culture and avant-garde Western practice, Tate implies other claims that are less persuasive. His reference, after all, is not only to a style of art but to a way of living. Bohemianism is about lifestyle. And it raises the issue of youth in particular, who are typically the ones filling the ranks of bohemia. What is more, he raises the question of the West where much of the black avant-garde lives, but which, in his account, are apparently not *of* the West, only in it. Finally, and perhaps most importantly, what allows him to write about this black bohemia with such confidence is that it has already become a public myth, accessible to everyone through the channels of mass culture, the gallery system, the music industry, television and popular film. And so the issue of avant-garde popularity – a contradiction in terms – is there at the heart of his quotation, although unresolved. We have to ask not only whether it is possible for a form of expression to remain avant-garde while being popular, but if so, what happens to the form in the arena of popular culture.

World music can only be understood by undoing the frameworks of dissemination and meaning of the forms that make it up. Afro-Cuban music, for example, as disseminated in the United States and in Europe throughout the twentieth century, finds itself (like rap) at the center of conflicts that modify our understanding of modernity. Much has been made in recent years of the role of neo-African music in the rise of "modernity," although not (as here) to remark how often these cultural forms are modern by giving voice to anti-modern sentiments. The ethos of the world music concept is drawn to a different message. What we typically find is a notion of cultural forms whose power is said to "derive from a doubleness, their unsteady location simultaneously inside and outside the conventions, assumptions, and aesthetic rules which distinguish and periodise modernity."[23]

The term "doubleness" (drawn in this case, with a certain amount of transgression, from the writings of W.E.B. du Bois) is similar here to the accompanying phrases "unsteady location" and "simultaneously inside and outside." They are not so much descriptions as celebrations of uncertainty and indefinability that the critic approves of ethically and politically. Without assessing for the moment the virtues of that position, this view ignores a good deal of Caribbean social and cultural theory over recent decades.[24] Underplayed in this emphasis on "uncertainty" are the defiant aspects of black expressive cultures which are not at all doubled. Many syncretisms, after all, are about mastering conventions as a revenge against the social processes endured. Black Atlantic cultures are filled with work dedicated to making location steadier and more clearly articulated – a feature very pronounced in du Bois himself, incidentally. Language suggesting ambivalence towards modernity is welcome for its ability to present ameliorative artistic strategies under the burden of racial antagonisms. But it cannot account for the many musicians, white and black, from the eighteenth to the twentieth centuries who felt themselves exiles within, and who set out to explode the market-logic of modernity.

World music before "world music"

At "Cheapos," a record store that used to exist on the bohemian west bank of the University of Minnesota campus, the world music section was cordoned off in a kind of security zone, sharing its privileged space with classical music. In this way the browsers behind enclosures did not have to endure the hard-driving sounds and brutally political lyrics of the store's normal clientele.[25] World music had become cultural capital.

What is now presented as a theory, and advertised as a campaign, is an idea superimposed upon an older practice. World music gives a new value to an earlier convention, privileging what before had been considered secret and guilty. Music from other parts of the world saturated American mass culture throughout the twentieth century. It was there in the background music of Hollywood films and the Muzak in department stores. Both now have a heavy repertoire of European techno music, British rock, and the always exportable Erik Satie, but they always had – less noticeably – popular Cuban hits, written by musicians whose names few Usonians knew. These included Osvaldo Farrés, Moises Simons, and above all, Ernesto Lecuona, who in the 1920s and 1930s wrote a number of songs for Hollywood films, and had more than his share in the hit parade.[26] A number of examples in the U.S. repertoire exist like that of Willem Grosz, Viennese composer of a cycle of "African Songs" (1929), who later wrote for Hollywood, his most famous tune being "Red Sails in the Sunset" for a film starring Ronald Reagan.[27]

There were also those times (much rarer) when the music of other places was actually featured in popular culture, and was highlighted for the very fact that it was foreign, and where one was meant to possess the foreignness on its own terms and to learn from it deferentially. The scene, for example, where James Bond watches a belly dance in the gypsy camp outside Istanbul in *To Russia with Love* (1963) is one of those moments in postwar film that goes beyond exoticism. It portrays a full musical performance that is intended to be admired as a dance, regardless of the part it is playing in establishing locale or reminding us of Bond's character as a ladies' man (evident in his admiring leer as he gazes at the dancer).

It is true that the usual Bond gimmicks – in this case the inevitable knife fight among jealous gypsy rivals for a woman's affections – seem to repeat that timeless practice in Western representation of exploiting jungle fever. But there is a vivid sense of life on the indeterminate borderlands of Europe where culture is similar enough to be known and strange enough to be compelling – a typical aspect of the film's Cold War premises. This would be a kind of proto-world music, one beginning to abandon the sort of dramatic allure that the foreign was given in hugely popular theatrical productions like *The King and I* (1951), itself the theatrical offspring of Orientalist nineteenth-century European operas such as *Lakmé*, *Aida*, *Il Guarini*, *Les Troyens*, and *Samson and Delilah*, where authenticity was completely unimportant, even as illusion.

In both the operas and in Rogers and Hammerstein, no attempt is made to capture the musical cultures (respectively) of Thailand, India, Egypt, or Brazil – not even in quotation. The settings are simply occasions for costumes, sonic filigree, and the plot devices possible in a setting where the fiction of the bizarrely different shelters a familiar domesticity. The tradition here descends from a similar fascination in

Europe with fake *Latinidad* (the music/dance exotic provided by the "Spanish" component in Europe and Europeanized America). Consider the case of Lola Montez, the subject of the Max Ophüls film, *Lola Montès* (1955).[28] She was a dancer, a lecturer, and a subject of scandal in mid-nineteenth century Europe, baptized Elizabeth Rosanna Gilbert in Liverpool in 1823, but born in County Sligo (Ireland). Educated in Scotland, Durham and Bath and bored by her first husband (who took her for a time to Calcutta), she re-invented herself as Donna Maria Dolores de Porris y Montez, a Spanish dancer. She arrived in Paris in 1844 at twenty-three years of age with a letter of introduction from Franz Liszt (one of her sexual conquests), and began dancing to very strong reviews which were written by critics who "fell for her fake Spanishness without a second thought."[29] She was a hugely successful *femme de scandale*, which was essentially her profession. In one review in the *Evening Chronicle*, she was admired for her authenticity:

> Her dancing is little more than a gesture and attitude, but every gesture and attitude seems to be the impulse of passion acting on the proud and haughty mind of a beautiful Spaniard; for she is exquisitely beautiful, in form and feature, realizing the images called up by a perusal of Spanish romance. Her dancing is what we have always understood Spanish dancing to be – a kind of monodrama.[30]

Her act was far more erotic than would have been tolerated by more respectable (in this case English) women. She had men all over Europe: in addition to Liszt, Robert Peel (son of the British prime minister), the Earl of Malmesbury, the Count of Schleissen, Lord Brougham, Savile Morton, and King Ludwig of Bavaria. We find here an example of a pattern which was beginning to make itself felt for the first time in just these years and would have enormous consequences later. The "Latin" element in music was proving itself exportable, ripe for appropriation, and unrecognizable as world music even while setting the stage for it.

It would not be enough to explain away Lola Montez by pointing to the predictable (and not really culturally specific) erotic component of her performance. In fact, in early world music before "world music," sex is often just a way to another message. In the Bond film, the protagonist's leer is a throw-away, and has very little to do with an exotic encounter. In fact, Bond's gawking is the formulaic given of his very being as a philanderer and has no other importance; it is there primarily as an excuse for the audience to witness the belly dance, which is the director's real interest. This half-nod in the direction of sex as a kind of appeasement of the expectations of the exotic had already been a feature of film from as early as Fred Astaire/Ginger Rogers in *Flying Down to Rio* (1933). A pure vehicle for song and dance, the film tells the story of a battle of the bands, with Astaire and his combo flying to Rio to compete in a nightclub contest with Brazil's local talent. Portrayed as cocky and indifferent at first, the band members sit idly in the nightclub's well-lit upper tier as the sleepy Brazilian musicians warm up. As soon as the first number properly starts, though, the North American musicians' jaws drop, and they look at each other quizzically knowing they have lost the competition without playing a note. The Latins are just too good.

The film might best be seen as a teaching-piece intended to introduce the American public to Latin music, and is as joyfully pluralist and open to difference as anything one finds today. The film's longest dance number after the more opulently choreographed "Flying Down to Rio" (around which most of the flimsy plot is built), "The Carioca" is an extravagant appeal to learn by broadening the range of reference, and became the film's unexpected showstopper, winning an academy award.[31] The singer who begins the number, does not hide her intentions:

> Oh, have you seen the Carioca
> It's not a fox trot or a polka
> It has a new rhythm, a blue rhythm aside
> It's got a meter that's tricky
> A bit of wicky-wacky-wicky
> But when you dance it with your *new* love
> There'll be *true* love in her eyes.

It hardly matters that the music is not really Brazilian but a sort of can-can Cuban mix, or that the dance has less to do with samba than *guaguancó,* or that "carioca" simply means people from the city of Rio de Janeiro and is not originally a dance at all. The lesson is about high professionalism and quality, about a U.S. reliance on cultural imports, and, of course, as a sop to Cerberus, about sex as well. During the film's longest dance number, the boys in the band, looking down on the dance floor from their second-tier perch, raise their eyebrows and giggle like frat boys who cannot believe the hip-thrust movements of the courtship section of the *vacunao* (one of the improvisational styles of rumba, whose name – literally "vaccinated" – refers to sexual intercourse).

Today's world music still finds its way to us under the guise of a dark erotica that has left the sexual arena to become, instead, a political aesthetics. One is drawn not so much to an imaginary place of license as to a foreign art savored for being political, dangerous, and above all, foreign, where "undomesticated" means "not domestic."

World music is still hungrily devoured by North Americans looking for a way out of that local pastime of making fun of foreign accents, ridiculing the customs of other countries in stand-up comedy routines and late-night shows. World music enthusiastically claims that art produced elsewhere in the world has value, but not just that. World music places North Americans in a position of aesthetic dependency on

Figure 1.2   *Flying Down to Rio* (1933), dir. Thornton Freeland.

other peoples of the world. This is, as far as it goes, a very welcome development, since it gives them a taste of life in the global periphery where, after all, most of the world lives, and jolts them out of this never-challenged sense that North Americans live at the center of things, and that everyone else in the world is on the outside looking in with envy.

Throughout the 1930s, 40s, and especially the 50s, music from the global periphery was often used in popular culture to give relief from cultural limitations. The last of these decades were the years when *mambo*, for instance, enjoyed its big U.S. success – one that found its way into *Guys and Dolls* (1955), a film about an overly modest New York Salvation Army volunteer played by Jean Simmons who goes on a date to

Havana with a local good-hearted hood played by Marlon Brando. There, under the spell of a less Protestant ethic, she liberates herself. In this sumptuous and smoky Havana, women dominate their men. The central dance scene features a Cuban femme fatale whose doting partner, permanently bent at the waist in an act of submission, is thrown around the dance floor like a rag doll. This voraciously sexual woman, dragging scandalously on a cigarette, preys on a willing Brando until the Simmons character (three piña coladas past the point of no return) steps in to punch her out. The music, then, as one would expect given the formulas of Latin exoticism, is about raw sex in forbidden zones outside Christian (Salvation Army) law. But there is more here than flipped gender roles – or sex. There is an undercurrent of violence and confrontation, as though the pleasure implicit in the sounds were actually dangerous and fearful.

This dimension of foreign music, at least in the form in which it actually invaded American ears before "world music," is not accidental. One finds it even more strongly emphasized in other films from the same period. In *Written on the Wind* (1956), the strategy is the precise negative of *Guys and Dolls,* although this very different film is equally under the sway of the U.S. *mambo* craze. In place of a joyful explosion overcoming repressed desire we find a somberness in which the release of Latin sensuality indicates only the impossibility of escape. The film is impossible to summarize briefly, but it is a long and painful study of the quiet, excruciating suffering experienced by the inarticulate rich dying to express themselves – a tale of friends divided by their love for the same woman and the machinations of another woman with her own designs who sows discord among them. Here it takes the inspirations of the *mambo* to express the true motives of this schemer (Marylee Hadley, played by Dorothy Malone, who won an Oscar for her performance). The *mambo* is shameful and satanic, which is why in this scene it has to be danced alone in a bedroom and kept out of public view. As Marylee cuts loose in the privacy of her room, the director (Douglas Sirk) cuts to scenes of her father suffering a fatal heart attack, and plunging down the grand staircase of his now superfluous mansion.

The sheer terror of liberation from social constraints is a constant motif of the genre of the desirably foreign, and much less commented on than sexuality or exoticism (which is anyway more modulated than it at first appears). This aspect of the Latin sound was not underlined only in the high-production, technically accomplished Hollywood film either, but can be found in middle- and low-brow genres as well, for example in the song "Jezebel" by Frankie Lane from the same decade. To a vaguely flamenco rhythm, and with a swirling brunette in a tight shift in the

Figure 1.3 Images from *Written on the Wind* (1956), dir. Douglas Sirk.

background (as performed on television), Lane sings: "If ever the devil was born/ without a pair of horns/ it was you/ Jezebel it was you// If ever an angel fell/ Jezebel/ it was you/ Jezebel, it was you."

After decades of living this underground existence, present everywhere and nowhere, Latin music was by far the largest sector of world music before the age of "world music." And it learned to play in two registers. Already an important presence on Broadway in the 1880s and 1890s, a pastime of Hollywood insiders from the era of Rudolph Valentino on, inspiration for Gershwin, Cole Porter, Dizzy Gillespie, and Doris Day, it still feeds the fires of that seemingly endless Usonian ritual of ridiculing the corny otherness of foreign cultures: those Latin dance send-ups one finds in a variety of U.S. media – most recently, since the genre never dies, Fred Armisen's "Ferecito," a wisecracking, gold-toothed, timbales-playing, Latin American bandleader who makes repeat appearances in order to deliver his catchphrase "I'm jus' keeeeding." This is a world in which it makes perfect sense that the theme music of the hit cable television show *Sex & the City* would be Latin jazz – an illustration of "background music" as I mean it here in the sense that the show itself is about white, upwardly mobile single women living on New York's Upper East Side. They wouldn't be caught dead in a Latin ballroom in Queens, or for that matter, the Lower East Side's more bohemian venue SOB's, where Latin jazz is often performed.

Doris Day's hit "Perhaps, Perhaps, Perhaps," appropriately enough in this context, is another example of a Latin song that does not, except subliminally, signify as Latin. The lyrics are artfully done, but pure Cole Porter-esque in her Anglicized version: "If you don't make your mind up, then how can we get started/ I don't want to wind up, departed, brokenhearted."[32] But the rhythms and harmonies are the sultry underside of the tropical unconscious, a traditional cover song from the same Latin repertoire that includes Moises Simons "El Manicero" ("The Peanut Vendor") from the 1920s and Ernesto Lecuona's "Siempre en my corazón" ("Always in my Heart") from 1942, from the U.S. film of the same title for which Lecuona was nominated for an Academy Award. Originally composed by the Cuban composer Osvaldo Farrés, the Doris Day song ("Quizás, quizás, quizás") continues to be played everywhere, from contemporary Mexican combos to the beggar balladeers of the New York subways.

In more intellectual pop fare, Latin music may well be treated with respect, but never without its square costumes and crippling gibes about accents, pencil-line moustaches, and macho poses. In one episode of *The Simpsons*, Tito Puente, performing at the "Chez Guevara," is interrogated by the police who are investigating the attempted murder of the hated industrialist, Monty Burns. In his defense, Puente asks why he would wound Burns with bullets, "when he can set his soul aflame with a slanderous mambo":

> I will settle my score on the salsa floor
> With this vengeful Latin rhythm
> Burns – con el corazón del perro
> Señor Burns – el diablo con dinero
> It may well surprise you, but all of us despise you.
> Please die, and fry, in hell
> You wretched mean old wretch
> Adios Viejo!

The knowing pitch, evident in the song's free use of Spanish while assuming its audience will get the point, suggests some of the associations of Latin music with danger and violence that we saw in the examples from *Written on the Wind* and *Guys and Dolls*. Exactly because this successful television show can have a jest with a big band Latin combo as its vehicle makes the accompanying threat of violence socially meaningful. That the song is tongue-in-cheek may add a layer to the symbolism, but does not change its character.

In complicated ways, the utility of foreignness seen as a release from limitation is here intermeshed with geopolitical associations and domestic attitudes towards a central, and growing, race and ethnicity. In all three senses, danger is at the same time compelling and unsettling – in the mind of a U.S. audience just like the politically explosive Latin countries that border the United States, supply its immigrants, and possess favored tourist destinations. These potent and mixed portrayals in film and television of Latin "background music" rely, in any case, on an aesthetic attraction based (unsurprisingly) on sex and violence. But to see that as the end of the story is mistaken. These should be taken also as a reflection of a domestic need for release from provinciality.

Sonority and structure in world music

The word "fusion" is usually understood as the grafting of one established style or genre onto another in which the formerly independent elements are transcended in a new unity. Examples would be, say, the blues/rock blendings of the Allman Brothers in the 1970s or the folk/punk fusions of contemporary "emo" bands like Hoover or (in its Midwest version) the Pixies, Hot Hot Heat, and Franz Ferdinand. But music from many parts of the world often exhibits what might be called a traveling fusion: a merging of styles and genres from different national-cultural milieux that retain their identities under assumed names. Not noticed for what they are, they are blended with familiar arrangements so that the foreign elements signify as the performer's innovation. Here, a well-known case would be rock's well-known appropriation of the blues and of Motown (in the early Rolling Stones, Eric Burdon and the Animals, the Righteous Brothers, and others). Sounds are mined without public acknowledgement, and without retaining the important myth of a primary cultural form – a myth that alone guarantees reverence for the traditions borrowed from. So in the rap piece "Addictive" by Truth Hurts, which fuses the music of Bollywood film with rap in its opening sample, we come upon another unexplored dimension of world music. Many of the elements of a music marked "American" are not only from other cultures but are, strictly speaking, *unchosen* by the artist.[33] They find their way into songs by overwhelming the artist, as it were, with their ubiquity, leaving him or her with little but an instrumental relationship to what they are forced to admire.

Music from abroad – which is described in popular music theory as signaling a new inclusiveness – might be seen from another angle as an invasion forcing a new order on the passive recipients of a now-dominant sound. The degree to which this is true depends on the arenas of listening and the logic of public reception, of course, but it is worth considering that the flow of sonic culture from one part of the world to another, and the humanizing contact and knowledge that comes with it, are all that can be said to be political in the music. It is not primarily a matter, again, of newly rebellious sub-communities or the sonic marking of rebel territory, but a small window into communities abroad whose artistic vitality is the result of its inadequately developed market.

Consider, for example, Arabic popular music. In the contemporary United States, signs of relief from the proscription against Arabic culture in the last few decades include the brief spurt of interest in Algerian *rai* music, for instance, about a decade ago, and the even more recent success of Sting's *Brand New Day* album (and accompanying tour) that found a new conduit for *rai* and related North African genres (*chaabi*). Arabic music finds its way into the North American sound machine because close European allies like France and England (which both have large Arabic and Muslim immigrant minority populations as well as a close and resonant colonial relationship) usher the music in, but also because the recent success of Hindi crossover cinema in the United States through directors like Mira Nair (*Kama Sutra, Mississippi Masala, Monsoon Wedding*) and Gurinder Chadha (*Bhaji on the Beach, Bend it Like Beckham, Bride and Prejudice, The Namesake*) pave the way. Traditional musical forms like the Urdu *ghazal* or recent pop fusions like *bhangra* find international audiences, if not uniquely then at least significantly, by way of these films. India also includes a massive Muslim minority community that happens to be disproportionately represented as well as cherished in classical Indian musical performance and among the pantheon of each new decade's Bollywood stars.

Afro-Latin music from the Caribbean has a special place in the world music invasion in the sense that it is more integrated and deeply rooted in the U.S. national scene than the styles of music that are more likely to be featured in world music anthologies: for example, *soukous* from West Africa, the township sound of South Africa, or *qawwali* music of the Punjab and Pakistan. It is not only that the United States is a bilingual country with a Spanish-speaking population, a steady inward flow of immigrants from Latin America (especially Mexico), but that the United States belongs to a common culture of the Americas. Latin music has an active, institutional presence in almost every America city in a growing network of salsa dance clubs and nightclub rituals that span several generations with no obvious race or gender divisions. It is both foreign and familiar, therefore: both obviously from here but not officially recognized as belonging here, and never given the props of being American or as being essential to the U.S. national self in the way that, say, Liberace, Tammy Wynette, or B. B. King have. Latin music forms a perfect counterpart to rap in that sense – which is also both foreign and familiar, as I have argued above – except that in rap's case the poles are reversed.

A corollary of arguing, as I did earlier, that European classical music and African-American popular music are truly world musics (although not "world music") is to point out how much their dissemination had to do with geopolitical strategies. They covered the rest of the world from the early years of the twentieth century through radio, traveling performers, and the vast publishing capacities of the United States. Almost every educated person knows them, even though they were broadcast to win the hearts of minds of others during real invasions of people's lands.

A clear illustration of the consequences of this argument about traveling fusion can be found in the recent world music success of Gigi. The translation of Gigi into market accessibility is not entirely predictable given that she comes from East rather than West Africa where most musical influences originated. In her promotional literature, Ethiopia is described as "civilization's cradle, birthplace of biblical consorts to the Hebrew kings and would-be messiahs."[34] She is said to summon the "fundamental truths" of that land, striking a biblical motif as though to purify the music by filtering it through a prominent Western literary and religious source. Gigi is said to have emerged with an effortlessly cosmopolitan voice, not in spite of, but because she is conversant in the "ancient language" of Amharic. The real living Gigi, hardly less interesting, grew up singing in the Ethiopian Church, later moving

Figure 1.4 Gigi (Ejigayehu Shibabaw).

around Africa – first Nairobi, Kenya where she worked as an actress in an expatriate theater group and later in a French theater production of the story of Solomon and the Queen of Sheba, which featured an all-Ethiopian ensemble. In her early twenties, she toured East and South Africa, and was eventually invited to perform at a Paris World Music Festival. There she was noticed, moving to San Francisco aged twenty-four, where she was recorded in a studio by "world music mastermind" Bill Laswell.

Her debut album was the product of a U.S. studio invaded by those unnamed (and forever anonymous) indigenous Ethiopian musical forms Gigi no doubt learned when honing her craft in the Ethiopian Church.[35] Although all of the instruments are played in the studio live and in ensemble (that is, the tracks were not laid down later by digital splicing), this music could not be played live in a concert hall. It is a studio performance. This aspect contributes to its wondrous artificiality, which involved Laswell's concept to wed Gigi's musical insights and phrasings from unnamed Ethiopian genres and singing styles with the American jazz old guard (artists like Herbie Hancock, Pharaoh Sanders, and Wayne Shorter perform on many of the album's cuts). This is not to say – although the intimation would be fatal to the pitch of her Web page – that the one and the other musical sphere have been forever separate. The large brassy jazz sound (heard right at the opening of the cut "Tew Ante Sew," for example) has been massively popular ever since Ethiopian troops fought alongside Americans in the Korean War; Duke Ellington's band played in Ethiopia in the 1950s. But the songs of the album are a complicated blend, mixing a funk undercurrent, sentimental love lyrics in Amharic, West (rather than East) African guitar influences, and a sound that cannot be confused with any of these touches – something nameless in terms of a technical vocabulary or a popular musical tradition to those unschooled in Ethiopian genres. The ad copy, and presumably most of her fans, settle for slotting these under the phrase "an organic flowering of ancient Nile rhythms." But surely a lot has happened since the pyramids.

Is it enough to say this is all just a happy gathering of difference? My view in this chapter has been to say no. As Gigi makes clear in interviews, her producer Laswell convinced her not to use the vibrato common in Ethiopian singing protocols. Under his advisory arm, she had to train herself to sing in an emotionless way and to depart from the rigid Ethiopian musical scales of her youth. Something more than hybridity is necessary to capture this complicated hit-or-miss negotiation. It may not be a crushing blow were one to destroy the premises of the Web page by pointing out that world music is typically hatched (as here) in well-funded studios in London, Paris, New York, or Los Angeles. And there is no reason to doubt that Laswell/Gigi are mold-breakers committed to the universal chorus, and themselves artists working without a roadmap. The problem is that the jazz accompanists have a story, and Gigi has a commercial. The problem is that an entire narrative of major actors, historical lineages of creativity, analyses of songs, anecdotes of lived relationships and so on accompany the story of jazz (and other Western genres) whereas Gigi's Ethiopia is found only in the shorthand of her own individual artistry, its generic and improvisatorial predecessors remaining nameless and condensed in the suggestive musical phrases of a single album's songs.

In Koffi Olomide, we confront a different kind of problem. From the Congo, and known as a performer of *soukous*, Olomide was the most popular musician in Africa, and the most popular African musician in Europe, throughout most of the 1990s and early 2000s. At the time, he was unique for having sold out Paris concert halls like Olympia and Bercy Stadium (20,000 seats) – the only African musician ever to do so. If Gigi filters indigenous traditions through a metropolitan studio screen,

Figure 1.5 Koffi Olomide.

Olomide built his career almost entirely *within* Africa, winning the coveted Kora award given in South Africa in 1998, and based on a popular vote. Although he began writing songs as a student of commercial science in Bordeaux, France, in the 1980s, those songs were performed entirely by musicians from Zaire, and his first concert tour in the United States in the early 1990s took place entirely outside so-called world beat circles, instead pitched to African – especially Congolese – immigrants in U.S. cities.

In interviews, he complains that getting noticed is a result of being "strategically managed" in such a way that a musician can "maintain good reputations with the foreign press" as a result of happening to know "Peter Gabriel, or people like that." Olomide speaks of two features of his music that might have something to do with his delayed entry into the world music hall of fame. In his own words, he wants to give the indigenous forms of the Congo a name: "There are many Congolese musics and styles. For example, Tshala Muana plays Mutuashi while we play modern Congolese music. You see, in Congo there are 200 to 300 different musical styles . . . There are even rhythms I do not know and cannot understand." These, I am suggesting, are not the words that the world music concept can contain. Olomide invents new terms as well, calling one of his albums "Tcha Tcho" in reference to a new style of music that he describes in the following way: "Tcha Tcho . . . is an attitude and a way of life . . . You see, I would not be able to sing for a bar of soap. I must feel what I am singing. That's Tcha Tcho. It means 'let's be true – authentic – every time.'" One can only guess whether his banishment from the world music bins is related to this uncompromising view on authenticity, but there is no doubt that the view chafes against the world music concept.

African music ("world" or not) like Gigi and Koffi Olomide is typically less traditionally African, in the religious sense, than the music of the New World. A conservative strain permeates Afro-Latin music but one that U.S. conservatives would not recognize. It is a pre-modern homily. The world music concept confidently states that music can effortlessly travel and make itself universally available. But this conviction is disorienting, for the only way to know "them" is to know "us" – which means already to have critically distanced ourselves from ourselves.

2

Surrealism and the *Son*

[I am referring to] a kind of revenge by oral languages over written ones, in the context of a global civilization of the nonwritten.

Edouard Glissant

If the neo-African elements in popular music resist Western religious and labor discipline (as I have been arguing), what role did they play alongside related movements in the arts of the early twentieth century? The European avant-gardes, for instance, defined themselves by attacking bourgeois complacency and hypocrisy. Is there a connection between the neo-African and the avant-garde in this respect? Although their literature and painting have been extensively treated, the musical preferences of the avant-garde have been much less explored. There is something to be learned from looking at the avant-garde milieu where neo-African musical forms entered Europe because of what it tells us about the disgruntled, forward-looking artist's attitudes toward the "modern" (with all of that term's civilizational associations).

There is controversy over whether or not neo-African popular culture has undergone a demythification. Many contend that most of the original African sacred elements have been purged. This is a common view, but I have been suggesting that this sacred world, even though it signifies as secular to its primarily monotheistic audiences, retains the ritual element of its myths to a degree that is striking given the arenas of entertainment in which it is produced and consumed. And in fact, this religious message (with an underlying ethical worldview) is posed against civilization in a manner unmistakable to its listeners who are drawn to it for precisely this reason. Samuel A. Floyd has persuasively shown that the primary *cinquillo* and *tresillo* rhythms of the circum-Caribbean (out of which the *son* and other genres emerged) are "symbols of African-diasporal musical unity" and vital "structures of feeling" for those who live in the region.[1] This is very true, but one can go further. They are also vital to those living outside the region (white and black), and the *son's* structure has a content that can be explained in narrative terms. The fact, for example, that the *son* is a "song that is danced" communicates a social value quite apart from the aesthetically compelling nature of that combination for its popularity. Below I would like to pursue this idea of the social symbolism of musical form by exploring what is communicated to audiences in the passage of *son* to salsa.[2]

The core of the music now widely known as "salsa" began to work its way into middle-class respectability in the Cuba of the 1920s under the sign of *son*.[3] As much a public event as a musical genre in that decade, *son* had until then a semi-clandestine existence, its performers being recent migrants from the rural regions of Cuba's Oriente province to the cities of Havana and Matanzas. There, hanging out on street corners or haunting the boardwalks, the early *soneros* eventually became too much a part of the urban scenery to be ignored, their music too much of the sonic landscape not to force its way into compositional imagination of the musicians with access to polite society. My point of departure in this chapter is the observation that the *son*'s entry into a broader kind of public acceptance coincided with two other events – the birth of surrealism and the rise of radio. All three did not just occur at the same time, but were talking to one another through global and regional circuits of migration and media.

The public acceptance of what would later be seen as Afro-Cuban roots music coincided, then, with its more or less simultaneous acceptance abroad, although in anything but a roots form. In France of the 1920s and 1930s, Cuban music took on a highly theatrical appearance – its performers wearing pleated sleeves, headdresses, and other pseudo-tropical paraphernalia – where they were given their imprimatur by the always decisive canons of French taste.[4] It is in the *son* that we see how apparently nostalgic cultural forms are most modern in their gestures of preserving a space where one can flee modernity's consequences – where one can declare one's unwillingness to accept modernity, which then stands exposed as an arrogant, reductive, fetish of the new.

The European avant-gardes played a key role in the public embrace of Afro-Cuban and other New World African music between the wars.[5] And yet, as a concept, the avant-garde indicates the desire for precisely that novelty I have just called into question. On the face of it, novelty is what the conservative religious legacies of Afro-Cuban music could never, it seems, deliver. But for a variety of reasons, this was not the case. To begin with, the interwar European avant-gardes (I am thinking here primarily of Dada and surrealism) were more aware of and dependent on non-European cultural practices and forms of political self-definition than is usually supposed. Although the story of their enlistment of the artistic "primitive" is well-known, the imaginative projection of the avant-garde artists of the early twentieth century and interwar period into a palpably anti-colonial (not only non-Western) space has been deeply underestimated. An often sardonic anti-colonial anger was the defining self-image of Louis Aragon, Rastko Petrovic, and Tristan Tzara, for instance. It was much more than a vague European disenchantment or a striving for subjective, spiritual unity that moved Tzara, Dada's founder, to state his preference for an art of "simple rich numinous naivety" rather than "this dark grinding whiteness" as he expresses it in a manifesto from 1924.

In effect, the avant-garde intellectuals understood their own revolt to be modeled on the colonies. As bohemians they were in their own minds metaphorically either "Black" or "Red" in the sense that they staked out positions of incompatibility with power by borrowing attitudes and tropes from the most profoundly marginalized social actors they knew: colonial intellectuals resident in Europe and interwar party Marxists or their fellow-travelers. This process which links marginal colonial constituencies and politically marginalized European revolutionaries has been largely ignored, and my brief look at a few of the major players in French and Cuban surrealism below is an attempt to open a debate about the extent of this intellectual commerce.[6]

The importance of such a linkage is all the more clear in the type represented by the bohemians of the avant-garde. It is commonplace for European philosophies of music to begin by marveling at its underworld, vaguely criminal origins among prostitutes, slaves, itinerant jongleurs, and paid functionaries of the court – an argument famously developed in Jacques Attali's *Noise*.[7] The 1920s in Cuba, for example, was the period when the *son* was migrating from the Cuban countryside to the cities, shifting from the black mutual aid societies (*cabildos*) and the small-town or rural guitar and *tres* combos to streetcorners and boardwalks.[8] Argeliers León has called what they produced "*fritas*" music. Writing of the legendary Parisian-trained Cuban classical composer, Amadeo Roldán, who frequented the avenue leading to La Concha beach in La Playa, León describes the kiosks selling fried foods (*fritas*), where popular musicians tapping boxes and striking sticks played for change as the leisured classes strolled by in the company of an occasional pimp and his attendant prostitutes.[9]

There is, then, already in music a ready-made analogy with the underpaid and ill-fed martyrs to art that bohemians are inevitably supposed to have been. The early history of surrealism suggests that the type was further complicated by the contradiction at its core in the era of early radio, whose success was largely the result of North American jazz, which in one form or another filled much of its programming.[10] Black music, political outreach, and advertising all jostled together in uncomfortable and confusing ways.[11] The long shadow of Bolshevism and the political rumblings from the world periphery (in these years, China, Abyssinia, Mexico, Haiti, and Morocco) supplied the image of an intellectual type confounding the bohemian for the very reason that it overlapped with it while departing from it. This black or red bohemian had baggy clothes, smoked cigarettes, and hung out in cafés, but not in the name either of a youthful aesthetic refuge from the past or the modernist invention of a new now – rather, a veneration of what age passed down, and the establishment of a local tradition in alien climes. Their revolution, to put this another way, was at least partly conservative.

The cutting edge, so to speak, cut both ways. The very same avant-garde that vamped on racial outlaws and leftist outcasts would in time create the imaginative repertoire of corporate mass culture, but only in a fashion that alienated it from itself.[12] How could the avant-garde find a way to prolong this resistance to the logic of industry and profit? How, it asked itself, could it remain unassimilable? Preceding television and the Internet, radio was the first testing-ground for a culture that could be both homogeneous and global at the same time. As it turns out, many of the strategies that proved most useful for reaching the commercial public in early radio were devised by the avant-gardes, including several of the key figures in surrealism.[13] We could say parenthetically that those who today observe that advertising takes its leads from MTV are addressing an older problem without knowing it. One is reminded here of the principle laid down by Alejo Carpentier in *La Música en Cuba,* elaborated by Gloria Antolítia and re-emphasized by Leonardo Acosta: namely, that in musical history "everything began a long time before you thought it did."[14]

With two very different kinds of musical programming, radio in those years posed symmetrical and inverted problems of reception. On the one hand, the mass dissemination of opera, symphonies and chamber music led to worried declarations of the vulgarization of the classics that dominated the mass-culture debates for at least two decades.[15] On the other hand, the mutual reliance of radio as a technology and jazz as a commodity made it impossible to miss the oddly symbiotic relationship between black music and modernity as technology and "modern life." To put this another way: jazz made radio popular while radio disseminated jazz. The technological device destined to create markets by creating a new kind of desire was borrowing, much as the avant-garde borrowed, from the formal repertoire of a colonial world it could not completely understand or exhaust – which is how it created the desire in the first place.

Afro-Cuban music, however, is not usually included under the rubric "jazz," although there are several scholars who have begun to question that premise (see Chapter 7). At any rate, there is no question that both influenced one another from the start. Afro-Cuban music was also popular globally from at least the beginning of the nineteenth century, and so was arguably as widely disseminated as the work of artists enlisted in the pantheons of North American jazz, even if less studied; and to complicate matters, some of what is called "jazz" by global audiences is Latin, African, or Asian. In the 1930s, Fernando Collazo and the Tres Hermanos Barretto, for example, were as much jazz to French audiences as were Jelly Roll Morton and Louis Armstrong. Whatever claim one wants to make about the North American provenance of the form, jazz is a Caribbean creation in the sense that like Miami, New Orleans was a Caribbean metropolis on the continental ridge of the Northern continent flooded by the architectural, culinary, musical, and linguistic influences of points further south. French- and Spanish-language newspapers in New Orleans kept steady pace with the English-language papers throughout the nineteenth century. The city was a true port town, an arena for casual visitors, immigrants, or ne'er-do-wells from throughout the Caribbean who considered it more characteristic of their own familiar selves than any other metropole on the southern edge of North America. Afro-Latin music was unlike jazz because its foreignness was less manageable, and because it was not the product of an emerging world power.

In the most sustained and vigorous study of salsa to date, Ángel Quintero Rivera develops a point that is relevant to this line of argument. He states more clearly than others a widespread observation that Latin (or as he puts it, "tropical") dance music stakes out an alternative modernity defined by the reorganization of Newtonian time.[16] Codified in the music's polyrhythms is, he argues, counter-rationality and controlled disorder. At the very least, what is created, he rightly maintains, is a new, syncopated order of circular movement that rejects the linear progression of crescendo, thematic variation, and coda. He convincingly elaborates on how ethnic reassertion in Latin music is achieved "in camouflage." The music's *mestizaje* (cultural mixing) is present not simply in the merging of European and African elements – guitars and pianos with *güiros* and *marímbulas* – but in the sense that Europeanized ears, trained to favor melodic development, are cleverly tricked by the music. The polyrhythmic lines are sold to the listener by the inclusion of a melody that is, strictly speaking, a matter of concealment.

A conservative strain of defiant preservation permeates Latin music, both as traditional homily to a venerated past (a sort of tic, or reflex action that has become conventional) and as an arch commentary on convention, modernizing the older gesture by insisting on its lived qualities. There is a shattering of the Judeo-Christian edifice with an African sensibility that predated it, and will (in the minds of the performers) outlive it. It may well be an act of camouflage, but it is also an act of civilizational impudence.

The study of Afro-Cuban music helps us appreciate the difference between bohemian revolt under stable governments where the public largely supports the prevailing power or at least can imagine no alternatives, and an art that under colonial conditions is dangerous to power because it points to a rejection of an order weakly established on the basis of exclusion. This paradoxical factor of art and revolt is what helps explain the avant-garde's interest in the arts of the other Americas in the 1920s and 1930s. What cultural forms like the Afro-Cuban *son* allow us to see is that the sort of resistance more likely to challenge power arises in colonial settings, in part because of the outrage that inclusion into polite society creates in that fragile political environment.

For decades, even after the repeal of slavery in 1888, New World African religious practices in Cuba were not simply denigrated by official opinion. They were illegal. After all, they gave cultural sanction to an African community that in the demographics of the Caribbean (unlike the United States) were far from a safely surrounded minority constituting only 13 percent of the population. The discourse of pluralism, moreover, invented in Latin America and later exported to the United States, was not yet generally accepted in the early twentieth century. There was no particular appeal, in other words, to include the African-based communities, even nominally, into a whole national body. The musico-religious practices were disturbing to the establishment because the African communities, not long out of slavery, remained too rooted in forms of expression that were strangely, and therefore dangerously, incomprehensible. Unlike in the heavily Protestant United States, their music had found a way to thrive in forms closer to their original instrumentation and collective performance, often in the original languages.

This is the pattern of musical revolt replicated in today's neo-African genres that are valued for being a "not-West." World music, as we saw in Chapter 1, has always signaled an open and systematic borrowing of foreignness in a context where the consumer already understands that this demonstration of a broad taste is a critique of earlier patterns of colonial cultural theft. In this way, television is actually less international than music since the technological levels, and financial capacities, necessary to create and disseminate televisual products belong only to very few countries, whereas music is, in principle, a low-technology art. Like much of the cultural theory found in Europe and the United States, world music relies on importations from colonial and postcolonial settings in which a borrowed resistance is defining.

But once these motivations are made clear, we can see from another angle why Afro-Cuban music fits so uncomfortably in a concept like world music. Of course, it positions itself internationally at the axis of a city like New York or Los Angeles, the Caribbean, and – I am somewhat contrarily arguing – interwar Europe. One can then begin to appreciate that studies of popular music are actually very crucial to theories of imperial history and geopolitical arrangements, especially when one is talking about African-based diasporic music, which is dominant in popular music in part because the great disseminator of mass culture on a global scale – the United States – is located in the Americas. Up until now, music has not really played this role, however. Even where Afro-Caribbean cultural achievement has been positioned as central to a new theory of modernity (in Edouard Glissant's theory of *la relation,* or cross-cultural poetics, for example), the treatment of music has been scanty. Since most critics find the names of Caribbean musical styles and traditions alien, and since educating themselves in them would take too long, they tend not to be discussed.[17]

On the other side of the problem, in some well-known theories of modernity that do, in fact, explore neo-African music, there is a constant falling back upon high cultural and literary tropes that do the work of clearing the ground for passing comments on the popular musical sphere.[18] In all of this, music is still not allowed to possess its own domain of expressivity. This is a problem for theory, since cultural practices from outside Europe and North America have penetrated metropolitan youth cultures through music more than through any of the other arts, and have done so without elaborate critical framing (which is one of their strengths). The issue of accessibility is in that way finessed: it is a ubiquitous force, but because so ubiquitous, it is unnoticed as a force. Music, furthermore, is what makes the African presence in the New World impossible to ignore. In the silent court of opinion that never stops operating, Caribbean music is the region's claim to global cultural influence and even leadership in a way that literature – despite the Nobel prizes of Derek Walcott and Miguel Angel Asturias – ever could.

But there are other and deeper reasons for placing African New World music in a theory of conflictual modernity. Music structures time. It gives meaning to time, and makes change audible. The free-play of signification beckons the critic to locate in the empowering contradictions of its immaterial presence both emotion and precision. As the art that fills space, the immanence of music obliges the critic to see through the object in order to create beyond its immateriality, where (as the music theorist and philosopher, Ernst Bloch, once put it) "the absence of meaning is in this case the presence of all meanings, absolute ambiguity, a construction outside meaning."[19] Much as Attali was to argue later, Bloch found that music foreshadows the future in form, "overshooting" (in Bloch's terms) the present possibility and overriding the conventions of modernity that are primarily literary.

In "The Philosophy of Music," Bloch speaks of the academicism of early medieval experiments with polyphony, which he insists "occurred only in European music."[20] The turn to the intellectualization of feelings, the transformation of the humanities into the "human sciences," are for him what characterize Western culture. The West, he suggests, develops technique, and hence his reservations against according musical genius on the basis of merely technical innovation, since this would be to search for solutions only in the mind – a mind that views, records, reorders, purifies, and misremembers. In Western modernity, the mental thrill of a mastery without goal or direction – or rather, in which goals have been venally specified – obscures a dubious undertaking. Losses accompanied gains where losses (environmental, spiritual, communal) were permanent, and gains (mostly technological) were temporary. The changes wrought were also material, of course, although their materiality could only be viewed as realizations of what had been previously framed and then interpreted, so that its meanings could either not be seen or, if seen, coercively denied as unthinkable or tasteless.[21]

Bloch had almost nothing directly to say about modern non-European musical forms – about which he seems to have known nothing – but he nevertheless alluded repeatedly in the interwar years to the hunger of the avant-gardes for a place outside and against the "West." His often very abstract attempts to describe musical desires flirt again and again with the intention of joining the idea of alien cultures with social transformations. Whereas for Bloch one loses oneself attempting to pierce the "opaque interior" of others, "sounding" brings them back again. "As a shaped longing and driving in itself ... [it] represents invisible human features ... The tone expresses what in man himself is still dumb." It is a "call to that which is missing."[22]

This sentiment resembles very closely the idea of "hearing a beat that is not there," which I referred to in the Introduction as one of the features of African music – evident also in neo-African forms from at least the time that ragtime, the Brazilian *maxixe*, and tango (*"les dances brunnes*)" invaded Paris at the turn of the century. They were performed by the French *canaille* almost two decades before jazz was a buzzword in the cafés of Montmartre.[23] And it is that feature of music, inflected as here with a colonial element that always moves the restless who resist the present in the name of the future – and who began to break out of their complacency toward Europe and its cultural centrality between the wars for a variety of reasons having to do with colonial uprisings abroad, highly publicized military scandals in Africa, a growing population of third-world immigrant intellectuals, and the Bolshevik revolution. These forces moved them to the order of a spell where music, against all the evidence, was thought to be revolt even though there, and under those conditions, it was only a form of containment in a better or worse dream of another life.

The American composer George Antheil captures extraordinarily well the way this bohemian homage to Africa plays itself out in the concrete conditions of the Americas in the 1920s and 1930s. In this passage, he points to the inadequately acknowledged reliance many had on the alternative classicism of New World African music:

> The first Negro jazz band arriving in Paris during the last year of the great war was as prophetic of the after-war period immediately to come as the *Sacre* [Stravinsky's] was prophetic of this selfsame war, declared only a year after the stormy scenes at the Champs Elysées Theatre in 1913 . . . It absorbed this period so naturally that in 1919 we find the greatest Slavic composer living writing "Piano-rag-music" and "Ragtime" almost without knowing it, and a whole school of young composers springing up in Paris deeply influenced by American Negro music . . . As for South America, Darius Milhaud, who spent a number of his years there connected with the French Embassy, brought back a collection of half Spanish-Portuguese and Negro music. These formed the basis of his well-known ballet, *Boeuf-sur-le-Toit* and his equally well-known collection of South American dances . . . For look where we may today beneath this classical music of Stravinsky, or beneath the cheap but infinitely touching "Berlinese" of Weill, or beneath the beery but interesting and strong (in a Breughel-like way) fabrications of Krenek, or for that matter the last creations of Shönberg, Milhaud, Auric, we find the note, the technic . . . the *aesthetic* of the Congo.[24]

My interest, among other things, is how musical forms can be influential without generally being recognized as such, and then how they intimate a rural past in specific local allusions that are, moreover, racially coded. How did they perform the role not only of a mode of leisure in an emergent world culture but of a pocket of unmodernity (mistaken for premodernity) within modernity itself?

What always needs to be explained in derisive comments about fake authenticity is why, in the face of the obviously artificial, people generally strive to have the "real" and the "original" anyway.[25] This is what perhaps characterizes modernity more than any other thing – this need to salvage what modernity has not yet destroyed by pretending not to notice that it is already gone while at the same time inventing its replacement. Afro-Cuban music does this, and this gesture is what makes its aesthetics a politics that is more than a simple outburst against intolerable but unchangeable conditions.

Son as social symbol

To the uninitiated, the idea that the *son* has anything to do with contemporary salsa seems unlikely. The former's sound is rural and, like so much of New World popular music, not obviously African in its inspirations – quite unlike, in other words, the brassy dance frenzy of salsa, which wears its syncopation on its sleeve. Compay Segundo's song "chan-chan" made famous by the Buena Vista Social Club seems hardly the kind of musical raw material out of which Tito Puente's *timbales* could later make their memorable debut. Nevertheless, as Acosta reminds us, this genealogy is no longer controversial: "All of the *salseros* admit that the basis of the music is the *son cubano* along with other important ingredients such as the *guaguancó* [of rumba], the mambo and the chachachá – all from Cuba."[26]

The passage from the *son* to salsa is, as we might expect, a history of gains and losses, but the palpable drama of the *son* as an indigenous (the Cubans would say "folkloric") form is rarely rehearsed outside scholarly archaeologies of Cuban national culture. By contrast, contemporary music criticism is impatient with such stories, which are usually footnoted before moving quickly on to recent developments. I am returning to it because I am concerned with the fissures that take place within the New World African musical complex. The significance of the *son* in later Cuban musical innovation, as well as in the acutely national-popular sense of tradition governing its creativity, is a crucial feature for understanding how North American jazz traveled a different road, and may even now have reached a kind of impasse. At any rate, my treating the music of the Americas as a unity with national differences also prompts this kind of juxtaposition. Because salsa (as such) was invented in New York, it represents a U.S. adaptation of a Caribbean musical innovation – one of the few, despite the late date of its rise, that at the same time publicly signifies as Caribbean (other innovations have not been so readily acknowledged).

The *son* is generally taken to be a form that emerged in the far eastern provinces of Cuba at the beginning of the nineteenth century, although some insist that it is as old as the (post-Columbus) island itself, and based heavily on rhythmic patterns and verse forms that circulated throughout the Spanish colonies.[27] More commonly, its origins are located in the influx of slaves and their masters from the French colony of San Domingo (present-day Haiti) following the slave revolt there in the 1790s. It was not only that the highly Africanized character of the French colony, much of whose population was first-generation African, added to the demographic shock of these encounters. Both the white and black French émigrés brought with them musical traditions unknown in Cuba at the time, and characterized by more disciplined performance protocols than were common in Cuba previously. It is in this way that the rhythmic phrase known as the *cinquillo*, clearly of African origin (and fundamental to many Caribbean genres) entered Cuba.

Figure 2.1 The *cinquillo* rhythmic phrase.
The lower phrase is the more modern form.

This phrasing has the rhythmic regularity and symmetry found in a number of neo-African-based dances performed throughout the Americas – a simplification of the African polymetric drumming out of which it came. As Carpentier puts it, "the modifications of European genres on the island by African-based rhythms functioned by modalities of interpretation – modalities not written down for a period of time, as happens with certain jazz pianists, but that soon created enduring habits."[28]

What is clear, though, are two aspects of *son* that are often downplayed in casual accounts of its history: (1) the basic outlines of the *son* are very old (much earlier than the early nineteenth century), and were already identified by Spanish writers of the Golden Age (late sixteenth and seventeenth centuries), who spoke with excitement about the newest New World dances; and (2) it went by many names over time – names of myriad dances that were essentially the same rhythm. These two observations are important for understanding the unifying role played by African rhythm in the cultural complexity of the Caribbean region (forming, one might say, a kind of unconscious), and for helping us recognize the pattern of flow and movement of cultural influences in which it is often difficult to tell whether a European or a non-European cultural influence is predominant. Among the dances alluded to by the Spanish Gold Age poets were the *paracumbés, retambos, cachubas, yeyés, zambapalos, zarambeques, gurrumbés, rumbas, bembés, sambas, batuques, macumbas, guaguancós, candombés, tumbas, chuchumbés, carrumbas*, and *yambús*. One of the most important of these was the *saraband*. Carpentier explains that, like the *chaconne*, it was "something from the Indies . . . similar in the case of the *retambo* or *retambico*, dances with vigorous movements, always sexual, in which the dancers 'look like they're in the throes of passion,' . . . 'kicking the apron,' exactly as would currently be done by a Cuban rumba dancer with the tail end of her dress."[29]

Percolating in the small towns and villages of Oriente for decades after 1800, and as a result of the new movements of peoples and political disruptions caused by the French colonial immigration, the African musical element began to mix with a tradition of creole ballads sung by white Cuban peasants that was based on the *punto* and *decima* verse forms inherited from Spain. After roughly a century of experimentation under these conditions, and existing in relative obscurity, the *son* emerged in the 1920s in the cities of Havana and Matanzas (further west and north) about a decade or two after the defeat of Spain and shortly after the start of the U.S. occupation.

Samuel Feijóo captures the essential features of the combination that makes the form when he speaks of its "insistent heated-up rhythm, its percussion section of neo-African instruments, and its extraordinary folkloric literary sense."[30] But Carpentier is more specific. The musical revolution that the *son* launched, apart from its supple blending of Spanish and African elements in a coherent genre, lay in the fact that it gave

> the sense of a polyrhythm subjected to a unity of time. Up until then, one spoke of *the* rhythm of the *contradanza, the* rhythm of the *guaracha, the* rhythms of the *danzón* (admitting to a plurality within that succession). The *son,* on the other hand, established new cate-

gories. Within a general tempo, each percussive element assumed an autonomous existence. If the function of the *botijuela* and the *diente de arado* was rhythmic regularity, that of the *timbales* was to enact rhythmic variation. If the *marímbula* worked on three or four notes, marking the harmonies with the insistence of a basso continuo, then the *tres,* furnished a cadence.[31]

The singing, he continues, was "sustained by the percussion . . . Furthermore, the *son*, in its maturity, came to us with a definite form: a *largo* and a *montuno* [the *montuno* being an instrumental solo, in faster tempo, after a "break"]. The *largo* was the initial recitative, the exposition of the ballad, anciently rooted and Santiago-based, in a deliberate time, sung by one voice." It is in this description, particularly its last point, that one can see clearly the later structure of salsa, which is characterized precisely by this slow opening followed by a sudden break and then a faster montuno/antiphonal section (see Plate 1: "*Son*").

The *son*, however, tends not to be the starting point of discussions of modern Caribbean music for chronological reasons alone, even if it is frequently treated in Cuban musical histories as the *ur*-form from which came all that was original in Cuba.[32] For this reason, it cannot play the role that Dixieland sometimes does in histories of jazz – the inventive but rough-hewn predecessor to the later sophistication of the bebop highbrows. On the contrary, the *son* is remarkable for its longevity and contemporaneity. It is a balance of contrary influences, bringing to aesthetic life the story of an historical event and a sociological process, embedded forever in the sediments of sound. The Haitian French (both upper and lower classes) meet the Spanish inflected by Arabic elements from Andalusia, and the white rural meet the black urban. Spanish ballads meet Arabic guitar and makeshift neo-African percussion (*botijuela, marímbula, maracas, cajón, bongó*).[33] A sound that grew out of the tense aftermath, physical dislocation and painful adjustments following the successful slave revolt in San Domingo, it also was a sound developed in an atmosphere of political defeat following the frustrated War of Independence against Spain in the early nineteenth century.[34] The *son* is remarkable for its perfectly equal, perfectly *non*-acculturated, off-kilter meeting of the European and the African – a meeting that produces a sound that is importantly not hybrid (a term that suggests fusion), and certainly not a union of the two elements, but rather a truce or mutually respectful homage. There is no precedence given to the elements, no overwhelming of one by the other to the point that only traces or hints of the one can surface in the playing of the other. Argeliers León calls it a "grand synthesis."[35]

Embedded within the *son,* then, is a condensed historical record that replays itself in each hearing: one that is symbolized in the separate parts of the contribution that are ethnically coded and that retain their identities. In the movement from religious to secular devotion – from the practices of *vodun* and *santería* to a Spanish/African dance ritual that was, at the same time, a song – the genre necessarily sublimated the supernatural aspects of a vibrant and material *nature* into the aesthetic ideas of a popular musical classicism, a discipline, governed by a musical pantheon. It is significant – a point Feijóo emphasizes – that in addition to being a dance, the *son* was a literary form with deep Spanish and colonial roots, a vehicle for social satire, political commentary, and creative punning and jesting. This all-in-one aspect of the *son* in musical history is decisive for understanding the differences between Afro-Latin music and North American black popular musical forms.

Consider that rap – as part of a single New World African musical complex – can be seen in this light as the necessary completion of jazz, one demanded by the need for satire and social commentary that had always remained central to the *son.* In the United States, this aspect had been exorcised from African-American popular classicism, although it continued, obviously, in a variety of vernacular African-American cultural practices that are habitually invoked as forerunners of rap (dozens, radio preaching, last poets, etc.). We tend to see rap as a miraculous invention responding to the social crises of the 1970s, whereas in the longer view it may be seen as rushing into a vacuum created by the cutting off of neo-African holism in the context of the music's mainstreaming. The literary strengths of *son* raise in a new light the victory of writing over orality in Western popular cultures as a whole, and the unbalanced emphasis on literary rather than musical trainings in the liberal arts. The rhythmic core of *son* based on the *clave* (itself derived from the *cinquillo*) may well be, as so many have argued, a discovery that found its way into many Caribbean musical forms, including jazz. But only the *son* is a still-developing song/dance ritual with a pronounced secular literary component (*calypso* too fits the same pattern, although with less rhythmic variation).

It is one thing, though, to set out to describe the rhythmic, melodic, or harmonic components of a genre, and another to capture what the audience of a genre experiences – what the protocols of listening actually are. The veneration of earlier masters accounts not only for the classicism of Latin music but its secular devotion. The gliding from one to another performer of *son* over generations will take the form, say, of repeating for the hundredth time a well-known couplet from the great Oriente-based master, Miguel Matamoros. To do so is something like a collective affirmation of an emotion fixed for all time in an expression of character. It is part of the repertoire not only of music but of a people-specific feeling. In this respect, León speaks of that aspect of *son* that I referred to as the "pantheon":

> The narrative of popular epic, a reflection of the old romances that sang of great deeds with no previous meaning to those in the Americas, resolved itself ultimately in the form of an allusion, often enigmatic, to local circumstances that, as it passed from one to another singer from one or another locality, from one or another generation, lost its concrete allusion and was converted into the symbol of a general fact.[36]

The key point, for those who have studied the genre, is that there remains in contemporary *son* a vivid ritual element of its first religious impulse, continually transformed into a collective affirmation. The twangy vibrations of the *tres* that accompany its traditional sound (this original instrumentation is, for many, essential to any *son* worthy of the name, despite the introduction of more modern forms of orchestration)[37] is less essential than "the manner in which the group of instruments are integrated, where the components of the orchestra respond to a synthesis of elements imposed by the black performers." The music of the African is characterized "by the superimposition of layers, or tissues of percussive timbre. The percussive individualization depends on the magical significance of the sonoric material, where the timbre is the sign of a ritual event."[38]

The work of the Cuban sociologist Fernando Ortiz has demonstrated that neo-African cultures were seeking in this musical arrangement "the representation or conjunctions of three elements: wood, leather, and metal, corresponding to 3 natural kingdoms: vegetal, animal, and mineral."[39] Acosta calls the Afro-Latin musicians of the Caribbean "alchemists" in the way that they added a small element to an existing form, proposed a new name, and thereby transformed the ordinary and accustomed into the magically altered. The *chachachá* was that kind of mixture of the *danzón cantado* and the *danzón de ritmo nuevo, mambo* and even incorporating into itself modalities as distinct as Cuban bolero and the Spanish *cuplé*.[40]

Notice here, then, the dimension in this musical universe that exists beyond sonority and lyrical content. One is talking about how the total form conveys a meaning that is collectively shared. It is, moreover, self-conscious and fully intended (in León's word, "el negro buscaba..." [the black performer was searching]) as part of its ritual function. What is "magical" in the African element here is precisely not transcendent or sublime, but hard, solid, earthly, human, and even plebeian – a move, to take a radically different context, deployed by Pablo Neruda in the early movements of *Canto General* dedicated to these same three realms (vegetal, animal, mineral) and covered in an epic poetry that encyclopedically praises rocks, plants, and rivers by naming them.

Compositionally, the *son* announces what will later be characteristic of "salsa": typically three rhythmic lines played off against one another, with a central 2-3 or 3-2 pulse known as the *clave*. The other formal features include an antiphonal (call and response) lyric structure common to most neo-African forms; and the overall two-part structure described by Carpentier above, consisting of a solo singer's story (the *motivo*) usually in slower tempo set against the collective affirmation of the chorus in the song's second movement (the *coro-pregón*), in which the tempo often explodes in a flurry of vocal improvisation and frenzied instrumental solos (*montuno*), or melodic repetitions by non-percussion instruments (horns, guitar, piano) performing a percussive role (*guajeo*). But the music later associated with rocking brass sections, lightning piano riffs, and extravagant costumes is a direct descendent of the *coros de guaguancó* played on wooden boxes, spoons, and a single large bass drum. The many distinctions within the Cuban sound-complex – the daunting number of Cuban musical genres, then – are ways of referring to which rhythm is prominent, what tempo is being used, what the orchestration happens to be, whether it is primarily a song or a dance, and often to something so vague as its "sound." *Mambo*, to take one example, although considered by some to be a separate rhythm, is a term that can also simply mean the bringing of Latin rhythms to the big band jazz sound of the 1940s and 1950s.

This bewildering list of terms gives a sense of how the global export of what later came to be known as "salsa" demanded of its devotees a kind of conversion. It is a history that cannot be read otherwise. However, as a syncretism already, and like other popular musics of African origin (rock and rap, for instance), its words are self-conscious. When not involved in social critique or expressions of love, the subject of the lyrics of salsa, as I am about to explore below, is usually salsa itself. The shift from religious ritual to secular pantheon witnesses the worship of "gods" who brought the sound that placed people and spirit in contact. The acknowledgement of performers who have performed in the past, or the tutoring of the

Figure 2.2 Music examples showing the rhythm for the *cinquillo* (top), the *tresillo* (middle) and the clave and pulse (bottom).

audience on the name of the rhythm employed, or the boast of the performer on his or her spin on tradition, becomes the topic of the lyrics as an adjunct to its message in sound.

As a formal and aural document, then, the *son* basis of salsa is not one but two, and my effort above to describe the basic elements of the *son*, musically speaking, was all in the name of a basic point. The *son*, I am suggesting, should be seen as a divided rather than a hybrid object – the latter being the political ethic of a world music aesthetics that I am saying is inadequate to Afro-Cuban music. The opening motifs of the *son,* as in later salsa, exist in a world that can bridge to its other only by way of a break – a radical departure, in which one identity is exchanged for another. Moreover the salsa dance step, struggling to mirror the 2-3 clave, experiences in each measure an unsettling lilt or caesura which approximates in microcosm the larger break of the *son* structure. And it does this over and over again, inducing a fear of loss and then again the pleasure of recovery. For the 2-3 (or 3-2) of the clave unit has two figures that are unequal; an element is called for, striven for, but missing, which then demands in its turn a momentary pause in the dancer's sway, a confinement of energy that drives one forward in the dance, and keeps one interested in the recycling of a future history of salsa's repetitions.

Attali has argued that the economy of music in the West sought in its representational mode (the rise of tonal music) "to replace the lost ritualization of the channelization of violence." In traditional societies, that ritualization had been, in his opinion, marked by the absence of a distinction between music and ritual itself. Music was originally, he argues, "an element in a whole, an element of sacrificial ritual . . . of the imaginary." But the *son* shows that this proposition is not exactly accurate. Salsa is the unfinished and unsettled confrontation in form of Arabic Spain and Africa, an anxious, desperate synthesis kept at the level of an exposed binary. And it is kept this way *as a matter of aesthetic conviction*. It develops a holism that is even now referenced in lyrical allusions to *abakuá* and *lucumí* ceremony, just as it did when it vied for inclusion in Cuban creole society and later clamored for renown in the commercial networks of radio, record, and nightclub act. Pop salsa musicians in Havana and New York routinely invoke Yoruba gods like Yemayá, Ochun, and Babalú (San Lazaro) in the lyrics even of studio songs and in furiously market settings.

The gateway to the *orishas* (deities) turns out to be a music that in a peculiar way transplants Cuba to metropolitan settings. Unlike the mass-cultural exports of the United States, though, the form is not accompanied by blanket access to the home country, which critically frames it and delivers it to audiences as "information" (that is, as knowledge that has already been digested through interpretation). The invocation of the *orishas* in studio dance music in commercial surroundings is not a memory of a practice, not a quaint nod in the direction of earlier beliefs that have become purely conventional, but the still-living practice itself.

This devotion survives because it is in calculated ways unassimilable – too difficult, too specialized, and too linguistically alien to copy without approaching veneration. It is an unmodernity gesturing towards a premodernity, whose forms are designed to signal the insufficiently merged, or rather, the happily unmerged living in a productive tension. The religious element in mass-cultural entertainment of the Afro-Latin type is designed to hold in stasis the elements of its perpetually delayed unity. As such, it is not a striving-backward but a contemporary response, marked as contemporary, in which ethnic longing allegorizes its own ends: an escape by immigrants or domestic laborers (no longer colorful urban griots) from the crudeness of the market into a new kind of local community based on face-to-face contacts, oral forms of communication, and collective art.

To illustrate this point, we might reconsider the *fritas* music described by León (see above, page 51). In his essay "The Origin of the Work of Art," the philosopher Martin Heidegger captures some of what is at stake as the *son* moved from the eastern rural regions of the island to western and northern cities like Havana and Matanzas:

> In fabricating equipment – for example, an axe – stone is used, and used up. It disappears into usefulness. The material is all the better and more suitable the less it resists vanishing in the equipmental being of the equipment. By contrast the temple-work, in setting up a world, does not cause the material to disappear, but rather causes it to come forth for the very first time and to come into the open region of the work's world. The rock comes to bear and rest and so first becomes rock; metals come to glitter and shimmer, colors to glow, tones to sing, the word to say. All this comes forth as the work sets itself back into the massiveness and heaviness of stone, into the firmness and pliancy of wood, into the hardness and luster of metal, into the brightening and darkening of color, into the clang of tone, and into the naming power of the word.[41]

The materiality of the world appears different, in other words, when it makes up an object of utility and when, by contrast, it constitutes itself as art. If we imagine ourselves on the boardwalk in the scene evoked earlier by Roldán, we would see men of the night stroll with women of the night past ensembles playing on wooden boxes and metal spoons. There is an incongruency in objects of use, or more accurately refuse. The play of noise demands that socially expendable performers be seen now as objects of social account; and this incongruency is symbolized by the music in the sense that it is evoked in the languid stroll of even tempo and the syncopation of a call to disorder. This call, while moving the instruments to speak, asks them not to be themselves. The objects do not serve so much as imply what they might otherwise be.

Bohemia and the *son* in New York

A great deal has already been written about the difficulties of excavating that history of enjoyment known as "salsa," which begin with the depressing inadequacy of the very word.[42] Many have pointed out that what one is actually studying cannot even be named. The belated coinage of New York record promoters in the 1970s, salsa prevailed only in the wake of other failures: *bembé, amor, sabor, fuego*. Although among these slogans only "salsa" survived, they were all attempts by Nuyorican musicians and white businessmen to recapture the successes of 1930s Latin jazz (the era of the Cuban-based Spanish entrepreneur, Xavier

Cugat) and 1950s mambo in the face of the rock-inspired decline of Latin appeal in the 1960s.

The older styles, ushered in by the Hollywood patronage of Rudolf Valentino and the novel tastes of the U.S.-Havana tourist trade had been primarily the work of transplanted Cuban musicians who turned the interrelated genres of the Cuban sound into big-band orchestrations, film scores, and ballroom dancing: part of that steady exchange between Cuba and North America that was already prominent at the time of José Martí's famous American sketches written during his exile in New York in the 1880s and 1890s.[43] Salsa, on the other hand, marked not only a period of more mixed influence in the 1960s and 1970s – with contributions from many Latin countries – but an attempt to compete with the recent successes of rock by giving the Afro-Caribbean sound a polished studio finish, and enabling it to compete with the fire and frenzy of rock as a dance music and a youth revolt. It was, in that sense, a popularization like the others, but more detached from its Cuban sources, a new music in exile whose structure was nevertheless primarily Cuban.

By rehearsing this story, I want to highlight the tension within the form between a naggingly persistent small-nation content and a global reach that made it both difficult to ignore and easy to misconstrue. "Salsa" is a very specific thing, and not at all reducible to the Cuban *son* (nor the *son* to the "salsa"). And yet so much of the Latin music from the Caribbean that is now listened to, because of the success of that marketing term, is called (or thought of as) "salsa." So "salsa" is both a specific genre and a catch-all term. That combination seems in some ways vital to its attractiveness and semantic richness in the eyes of metropolitan audiences who either are, or temporarily let themselves become, bohemian. Longtime performers and specialists like Mario Bauzá and Ray Barretto could only see the invention of salsa as a "publicity stunt" and a "marketing ploy."[44] For the music that salsa borrowed from was originally referred to only by way of more specific forms, many of them Cuban. There were names for rhythms (*guaguancó, mozambique, mambo*), for dance styles (*chachachá, vacunao, yambú*) or instrumental arrangements (*septeto, conjunto, charanga*), although it is important to note that some of these terms mean more than one thing at the same time.

The new attempt at publicity in the 1970s was not merely an act of condensing but of erasing a complexity that was integral to the music as a devotional form – where the word "devotional" refers not only to its African religious inspirations but to its constructed pantheon of innovators whose role in the music's development is often documented in the very lyrics of the songs that pay homage to them. Along with a humbling array of styles came a single interrelated sound-complex. In Cuban music as performed and enjoyed, legends surrounded legends. If you played the music or listened to it, you would know about Miguel Faílde, the creator of *danzón*; Enrique Jorrín, the creator of *chachachá*; the great *bolero* crooner, Benny Moré; the pioneers of big-band *mambo* like Dámaso Pérez Prado, Israel "Cachao" Lopez, and Bauzá himself.[45] For the amateur and the specialist alike, it was a point of pride to know about the special styles of *batá* drumming that distinguish the *santeros* of Matanzas and Havana; about the past masters of *bolero*, about the difference between the rhythmic patterns of son *montuno* and *pachanga*.

Central to *son* (and by extension, salsa) is, then, what I will call *self-reflexivity*. Its modernity in the clothing of African religion is modern because it is secularized, and yet it is secularized religion. The artist is immortalized in a musical pantheon whose spiritual role is prominent, since their musical contributions refined the instruments of access to the deities, even in commercial and public spaces. The music, quite plainly, is about itself. It obsessively refers to itself, manifesting itself in a devotional energy. This spiritual/mystical loop is an important aspect of the *son* aesthetic. The holism of an apparently ancient worldview localized in some of the world's most economically underdeveloped regions expresses itself in that quintessential gesture of modernism – self-referentiality – although not in a modernist way.

In fact, the *son* inaugurated this gesture internationally when "El Suavecito" was performed by the Sexteto Habanero at the Seville Exposition in Spain in 1929 – an extraordinary honor for a group from the provinces at the time. With an orchestration consisting of a lead vocalist, a contrabass, trumpet, *bongó*, guitar, and *tres,* "El Suavecito" (the mellow one) set the tone for Cuba's entrance into world music:

> Carola, you just love to dance alone
> the *son* from the hills,
> And you do it so lusciously.
> Everything fast gets slow and easy
> with your lover, and when you dance it
> you tell him, all pleasure:
> Take your time, make it gentle . . .
> . . . A beauty from Seville
> was telling her young husband
> honey, that Cuban music
> drives me wild.
> Easy, easy, take it slow.[46]

The whole song plays in a double register. The showmanship of alluding to Seville itself (an allusion easily changed when performing in another location) and the salacious undertone are both jokes shared with the audience. This looking at oneself and the audience simultaneously breaks down the national, racial, and aesthetic walls between them. The scandalizing frankness with which the singer draws attention to the guilty pleasures of tropical dance allows everyone to smile relieved, for now it is okay to enjoy since everyone is a co-conspirator. At the same time, though, the lyrics play a teaching role, telling the audience unfamiliar with this aesthetic that their movements should be neither regimented nor frenetic. This is a dance with a sensuous style in which, like the sexual act itself, holding back heightens pleasure.

This combination of elements arises repeatedly, for example in an entirely different context more than two decades later in Benny Moré's "Bonito y sabroso" (pretty and tasty) performed in Mexico City in 1952: "How beautiful and tasty Mexican women look when dancing mambo/ They move their waists and shoulders just like the Cuban women / With such a sure rhythmic sense of how to make dance an act of pleasure/ I can hardly believe my eyes: I must be in Havana."[47]

Moré manages an even shrewder boast than that of "El Suavecito": the best compliment he can pay his audience is to say they have become Cuban! Self-reflexivity is in this case a mechanism for broadcasting what is sought in international exchange. In what is arguably the most famous *son* of all, "Son de la Loma" by Trio Matamoros (1928), self-reflexivity has this same dimension, although with a twist. The emphasis is once again on the cultural underdog who commands attention and is desired, but the underdog is defined by class rather than nationality:

> Mama, I want to know
> where those singers I'm hearing come from?
> I find them quite sharp,
> and I want to be introduced to them
> so I can learn to play their fascinating songs.
> Where do you think they're from?
> They must be from Havana, or maybe from the magnificent Santiago.
> No, they're from the hills, and they sing in the plains . . .
> They're from the hills, but they sing in the plains.[48]

On the surface this *son* is deliberately naive, referring to nothing more than the attractiveness of the sound, although it is important that the attraction be presented as an irrepressible drive, a sort of reverie that leads people on a mission to learn. This aspect is pronounced, but there is another, and more subtle, one as well. What arises in the story is not only that this *son* is from the hills, but that all *soneros* are always from the hills, at least metaphorically. The boy imagines that anything so magical must have been made in Cuba's major cities, but he guesses wrong. The musicians come from the hills and they play in the plains (that is, they are salt of the earth) but also that their sound is sublime, exalted, from the "classical" heights while being rural, and yet performed on the plains, which is to say to ordinary people in humble surroundings.[49]

Again these features, with variations, continue throughout the history of the *son* into the era of modern salsa: for example, in Ismael Miranda and Orquesta Revelación's "Asi se compone un son" ("How to write a *son*"), which is a sort of musician's confession of what, technically speaking, inspires them in the form: "To compose a *son*, the first thing you need is a story [*motivo*]"; or Hector Lavoe's hugely popular autobiographical song, "El Cantante," about a *trovador* who is stopped by fans on the street who pour out their hearts to him (a stranger) because he has managed to capture their joy and suffering, the good and bad of their ordinary lives.[50]

It is the style of salsa that openly venerates its *son* origins (rather than pure party salsa or *salsa romántica*) which displays this self-reflexive character most – the salsa, in other words, by performers who refer to themselves as *soneros* or who highlight the term *"son"* in the titles of their CDs. It would be an overstatement to say that the *son* always referred to itself, but the trait is too frequent to be insignificant. Self-consciousness exists from the earliest period of the *son*'s development: for example, in the nineteenth-century *guaracha* "Mambrú" ("You are thick-lipped negro/ and I am better than you/ If I give you a slap upside the head/ maybe it'll make you dance the Mambrú ["Tú eres un negro bembón/ y yo soy mejor que tú;/ si te doy un bofetón/ te hago bailar el Mambrú"]) as well as in the Cuban dance *El Chuchumbé*, brought to Cuba from Europe in 1776, whose ribald, anti-clerical lyrics again counsel the listeners to "take it slow" while dancing.

Even a fairly random sampling of major modern and contemporary *soneros* reveals a similar pattern. From early traditional *sones* like "El Carretero" and Ignacio Piñeiro's "Échale salsita" to jazz *son* like Eddie Palmieri's "Azúcar" there is a persistent self-referentiality of the sort we have been describing.[51] But so too (to take a small sampling) in the modern salsa repertoire: "Ñaña Sere" by Los Soneros del Barrio;[52] "Quítate Tú" by Pete 'Condé' Rodríguez, Santos Colón, Ismael Miranda,

72 SECULAR DEVOTION

Johnny Pacheco, Adalberto Santiago, Hector Lavoe, Cheo Feliciano and the Fania All-Stars; "Químbara" by Celia Cruz with Johnny Pacheco; "El Que Se Fue" by Sammy Gonzalez; "Soy Boricua" by Marvin Santiago; "Pa' Bravo Yo" by Justo Betancourt;[53] "Agua de Clavelito" by Quinto Mayor;[54] "Los muchachos de Belén" by Rubén Blades, ("Venga America Latina, Vamonos a guarachear"); and in a flurry of Ray Barretto songs, among them "Guaguancó Bonito," "Aprieta El Pollo," "Guajira Y Tambó," "A Puerto Rico," "Ritmo Sabroso," "El Watusi," "Los Cueros," "Guaguancó Pueblo Nuevo," and so on.[55]

In "El Que se Fue" the twist on this tradition is especially ingenious. A tale of familiar romance dashed, the singer declares that he's taking the break-up philosophically. In life, people come and go; the minute your lover leaves, you discover another around the corner. You may be on the hunt for a *morena,* but you discover a *china* instead. But the chorus repeats: "You don't matter to me, just like I don't to you; I'm still having fun, and this rhythm [that is, of the song he's singing about the break-up], has none of you in it."[56] And it is, in fact, the most inappropriate rhythm and orchestration for the lyrics of loss – a driving, exhilarating, strong and controlled rhythm, unemotional, dispassionate, betraying neither joy nor sadness just sage expectation. The music forms in this way the *"ambiente mejor"* that he alludes to in the song – an entire world in fact, that is the arbiter of the good, and the sign of his happiness and his salvation.

This is the message as well of an entirely different kind of salsa from the traditional *son* variety, "Químbara." In the Celia Cruz version, it begins with a nod to traditional rumba with a slow, single conga drum opening against Cruz's chant in unrecognizable African onomatopoeia. It is almost immediately sentimentalized, however, in the style of the night-club quotation of neo-Africa for a sophisticated Latin audience – a turn that is announced by the song's first stylistic break in the start of the modern salsa horn section. Then the lyrics begin: "The rhythm of the rumba is beckoning./ Bongó, tell them I'm on my way/ tell them to wait just a little long/ and in the meantime, guaguancó/ Tell them it's no simple manner of speaking/ but a part of my very heart/ my life is nothing but that:/ a well-played rumba and guaguancó" ["La rumba me está llamando/ bongó, dile que yo voy/ que espere momentico/ mientrastanto guaguancó/ dile que no es un expresio/ pues di en mi corazon/ mi vida tan solo eso/ rumba buena y guaguancó"]. However stylized the sentiment in this case, it is a striking illustration of the meeting of religious veneration and nightclub relaxation at the crossroads of entertainment art. The logic of the self-allusion here is not a boast exactly (although demonstrating her trance-like servitude to the gods of the drum, in addition to being an allusion to the religious origins of the music, also serves as a certification of her authentic artistry), but a fusing of artistic excellence with possession. That her life is now only *guaguancó* is a way of saying that the thrill of the music as a form of aesthetic transport is a function of its devotion, a view that is assumed by many of her listeners to be only a convention (this is not *really* a religious act), but not entirely.

Another aspect of self-reflexivity is revealed in Quintero Rivera's work when he argues that the Caribbean is decisive in world history for having given the rest of the world an incalculable cultural gift. In his opinion this benefit is not, as one might expect, the politically influential concept of *mestizaje,* the commodities of tobacco and sugar, or even the world's only successful slave rebellion, but (in his terms) *happiness*. The jubilance of Latin music, resistant to self-pity, responds to difficult times with a resounding "yes." One could add that the vehicle of happiness and the content of its social commentary is frequently humor, which is abundantly present in all of the examples above. The lyrics of Latin music are frequently tongue in cheek – not *ironic*, which is a more literary attitude that mocks from a distance, wanting to maintain its separation. The humor of *son*, by contrast, is that of the shared joke, a formal feature of Cruz's preferred genre of Cuban music, the *guaracha*.

The history of salsa involves an initiation of mind-boggling intricacy, involving performance etiquette, religious observance, and the all-but-impossible demands of familiarity with instruments ranging from the *marímbula, clave,* and *güiro* to the *conga* and *tres*.[57] Every drum, and often the parts of each drum, had a different name. To begin to understand the Afro-Latin musical complex leading to salsa, then, is to internalize its reverential training, or at least to resist viewing it as a popular music that had no academy in the broader sense. Salsa always had the ability to confound the assumptions that popular music and European classicism, even if they were equally valuable in some cosmic ledger, were hierarchically distinct. Even those who admire the popular music of rock or jazz often insist upon their essential difference from elite musical culture in precisely this academic sense. Only European classical music is thought to have "a remarkable apparatus for producing and maintaining a discipline protected by rituals of learning, traditions of pedagogy, protocols of accreditations, performance, display, and so forth . . . an extremely specialized language."[58]

Although European classicism and the *son* complex of salsa are obviously not the same, the differences between them cannot be found in any of these features. It is true that European classicism has an incomparably large and detailed apparatus of aficionados, biographical and critical appreciations, networks of museums, professorships, and so on, which is matched perhaps only by Hindustani classical music. But it is unclear whether this difference has to do with aesthetic or intellectual refinement (as Max Weber would have it) as much as financial and technological capacity. We could at least go as far as to say that Cuban music has an internal life of great variety. Its apparatus and its protocols are bewilderingly intricate. Again, Antheil gives a glimpse of how this aspect of the matter appeared to a practicing classical composer on U.S. terrain:

> The African "sound" in music is usually a tightening-up of the musical force, an intensive concentration and compactness, and thinning-out of line, and brilliant and sudden rhythmical decisions more daring than those of any other people or race, a marked tendency towards the "black" on the pianoforte, and the inevitable eight-note on the strong beats throwing into an immediate quarter-note following, the latter with an accent (almost the Negro signature, for go where one will in Negro music, these two notes occur like the signature of Alexander the Great in the ancient world . . . The *Rumba* of Cuba and the *Biguine* of Martinique, although Spanish in dress, have Negro hearts and certainly nothing but Negro bodies. The peculiar rhythm of the present popular West Indian music still escapes everyone but the actual native orchestras; daily it becomes more and more astounding that a white orchestra cannot catch the exact click of the two wooden sticks or the momentum of the rattles, or, indeed, anything but the most simple outward characteristics of the rumba.[59]

But if *son* became more widely integrated into the Cuban middle classes in the 1920s, the same was not true of explicitly ritualized religious practices such as *santería*. Despite the euphoria of the early street bands and cafés, the period was still one of repression, and neo-African religious practices remained the work of outlaw cultures. There were regular police raids on lucumí *cabildos* to steal their religious artifacts and place them in museums for proper "scientific" research. In the early decades of twentieth-century Cuba, practicing the *reglas de ocha* was a crime punishable by prison. Partly because of this, Afro-Cuban music had blended into the classical and salon traditions before migrating to Mexico, New York, and Paris. As early as the period 1800–1840, black professional musicians like Juan Peña and Bartolo Avilés were in the majority among those performing the classical European repertory; and the most famous of the early crossover sounds was *danzón*, whose syncopation and sexuality pleased the creole elite in ballroom surroundings (see Plate 2). Once again, Antheil grasped the significance of this union while commenting on the U.S. musical scene just after the height of the Harlem Renaissance, taking Stravinsky as his point of comparison:

> In its original state in Africa, this music first impresses us as hard, wooden, incredibly complicated rhythmically, so that even the most involved Arabic music must seem tame in comparison . . . [The white musician] is invariably stunned by the machine-precision of the black choirs in rhythms and counter-rhythms even more difficult than the last cataclysm of the *Sacre* . . . One thing is certain, the Negro has a rhythmic sense second to none in the world; one can scarcely believe that one has not to do with a highly civilized race, masters of steel, mathematics, and engineering, in hearing these choruses from the Congo . . . so intricate in rhythmic pattern, so delicately balanced in contra-rhythms and proportions, and so breath-taking in unisons and choral *impact* are these extraordinary performances. One is reminded of a colossal *Noces* fabricated by a *single* people for ages . . . broader . . . wider . . . infinitely more intricate and at the same time more epic.[60]

Thus a pattern emerged of relocation and usurpation, as though the two were the same; and it is this type of confusion that I am focusing on here. Popping up abroad at the beckoning of money or being chased away by the guardians of white taste (like Sanchez de Fuentes in Cuba), the music could not make sense untranslated. What pioneers like the Septeto Habanero's Ignacio Piñeiro had done in the Cuban cities, who left his job as a tobacco worker and bricklayer to join a *septeto*, was to take a village improvisational music and submit it to classical discipline. If Piñeiro, in arranging songs like "El Suavecito," developed the work of nameless musicians from Oriente province, George Gershwin only returned the favor on an international scale, visiting Havana in 1932 and composing his own Cuban Overture on the basis of Piñeiro's *son*, "*Echale salsita*" ("put a little spice in it").

Until the age of bebop, the bid for a black vernacular music that was considered worthy of respect by the highly cultured did not exist in the United States outside a few pockets of non-conformists, ethno-musicologists, or (as I have been arguing) bohemians. In this shattering of the high-low distinction, Cuba and Latin America generally led the way, and pioneered attitudes that only began to take hold in the United States after the 1960s. Black classical composers existed in North America, of course, but the weight of white opinion and the now internalized strategy of bootstrapping dictated that they would keep images of plantation blues and rural church (much less gin mill and flophouse) far from view. They sought polite society and did not want to pollute themselves with associations of the living and breathing "folk" anymore than upper-middle-class African-American critics of rap do today. The scales of Cuban integration, in other words – not only of white and black performers, but classically trained orchestra members and weekend *soneros* – had no real counterpart north of the border between 1850 and 1940 (which is not at all to say that full-scale racial integration existed in Cuba then, or that there was no repertoire of abuse by Cuban reviewers for the "barbaric" sound of the African popular later, even after the revolution).

Edward G. Perry points out, for instance, that the challenges to the high-low distinction along Cuban lines did occur in North America, but that the composers seeking to bridge the two worlds remained obscure. They never were given a place in the classical tradition.[61] Among the accomplished composers and publicists between 1829 and 1880 in the United States, Perry mentions James Hemmenway, Edwin Hill, A. J. Conner, Justin Holland, Samuel Milady, James Bland (composer of "Carry Me Back to Old Virginia") and Septimus Winner (composer of "Listen to the Mockin' Bird"). The most distinguished was Samuel Coleridge-Taylor, an Englishman of African descent who, like most U.S. black musicians at the turn of the century (just at the dawn of jazz), were busy writing popular ballads. Perhaps the clearest example of the musical success of this merging can be found in Will Marion Cook, leader of the Clef Club Orchestra and the New York Syncopated Orchestra. These composers, though, never achieved the full cultural acceptance that Manuel Saumell, Ignacio Cervantes, or Alejandro García Caturla did in Cuba eventually, particularly after the revolution.

But more linked bohemia, New York, and the Caribbean than such encounters, and the early *son* was not simply latched onto as proof of national vitality but as an historical archive. If the social symbolism of the *son* is significant, it is because of the sheer impact the form had on the multiple sources of international popular music before the age of mass marketing. Its prehistory, as I have discussed above, lay in earlier forms that spread widely throughout the Caribbean by way of European and South American fashions (with many additions and refinements). The *contradanza,* for instance, is conventionally defined as a nineteenth-century ballroom dance that came originally from the English country dance and its French court variant (the *contredanse*), arriving in Cuba with the Haitian exiles. Its lilting rhythm has links to the Andalusian tango. And yet some have shown that songs like "La Guabina" sung in Havana before 1800 already contain this same tango rhythm and therefore the conventional chronology must be mistaken.[62] Similarly, the *habanera,* an early nineteenth-century Cuban song form is said to have derived from indigenous dances of the Caribbean and to have a close similarity to Argentinian tango, which when played at a swift enough tempo could serve perfectly "as the bass line of the *contradanza.*"[63] It gradually took on a European classical flavor "in the spirit of the minuet" and led to the Cuban *danzón* by way of the *danza*. As a well-established compositional form in the early nineteenth century, the *contradanza* clearly contained the habanera rhythm in the bass line (see Figure 2.3).[64]

Figure 2.3 Musical examples showing the notation of the habanera rhythm in the *contradanza*.

Carpentier (and many others after him) persuasively argues that there is reason to doubt the distinctiveness of these genres:

> What is known today as the rumba would be known under twenty different names in the American continent, dances with very slight variations. They were sexual dances, with a couple dancing apart, with identical gestures and intentions, their roots extending all the way back to certain African ritual dances They were known in Spain and Italy as

"sarabands." [It is] almost certain that the rhythm designated much later as tango rhythm or habanera rhythm was already known. With regard to the rumba, it was already in the air with all of its characteristics.[65]

By historical accident, as well as by virtue of Cuba's centuries-old maritime centrality as a stopping-off point for ships from throughout the Spanish empire, the island became a major production and transportation center for musical innovation.

This pattern of success, publicized by creole pianists in the United States like Louis Moreau Gottschalk and by Spanish publishers of sheet music, created the conditions for the triumph of the *son* in the early twentieth century. One even sees its effects much later on the orchestration and arrangement of Trinidadian Calypso and Nigerian "highlife." To anyone familiar with the early Cuban bands, it is impossible not to hear in the accompaniment of early calypsonians like Growling Tiger and Wilmot Houdini a distinctly Cuban orchestration, arrangement, and sonoric feel, although this significant point goes unmentioned (or underplayed) in major studies of calypso.[66] The 1970s breakout sound of Nigerian highlife music similarly laid the groundwork for such amazing musical personalities as Fela Anikulapo Kuti, whose jazz highlife and later Afro-beat drew heavily on Afro-Cuban jazz (according to the radio broadcaster Benson Idonje, the musicians Tunji Oyelana and Keziah Jones, and Fela Kuti himself).[67] The triumph of *son* and *son*-based offshoots went beyond the international consumption of a Caribbean musical product. The Cuban *son* and its offshoots, both before and after salsa proper, became a way of life, adopted by musicians in Japan, Senegal, Turkey, and elsewhere who formed combos, internalized the musical pantheon, and made it their own – exactly as is occurring today with rap, with which it is (in this respect) analogous.

Given the chaotic flow of influences in popular music, the issue of attribution is always open to question, however. Cristóbal Díaz Ayala, for example, points out that popular musical genres then as now went by many names without excessive internal distinctions.[68] But what is clear is that already in the nineteenth century, Cuba had succeeded in creating an international musical culture that was not a commercial market. There were obstacles to its development, however. After U.S. troops began their occupation of Cuba, the government they installed denounced Afro-Cuban culture with the eager assent of the cultivated classes.[69] It was the paradoxical outcome of the newly imposed North American market on Cuba that explained the next phase of the worldwide expansion of Cuban music, and its precociousness when set alongside jazz in the age of mechanical reproduction.

Looking to enter new markets and eager for middle and upper classes capable of buying their products, U.S. companies set out to learn about Cuban music. As Díaz Ayala points out, Enrico Caruso and other opera greats were not strong enough attractions to lure the public into buying phonographs. Something more emotional was called for: music associated with the individual countries themselves in which people had a passionate stake. Companies like Edison, Victor, and Columbia conducted a campaign to make recordings of authentic national musics in preparation for entering their markets.[70] For this reason, Latin music was actually recorded a full decade and a half *before* jazz. Since U.S. officials working for the recording studios did not know Spanish, there was no censorship of lyrics, which often happened to be critical or satirical of the U.S.-sponsored government.

Latin music, much of it Cuban, also exerted its influence from the early 1900s on the metropolis itself by way of Broadway, symphonic music, jazz, film, the novel, and (eventually) television.[71] The Afro-Latin influence is suggested by the names of such songs as Duke Ellington's "Moon Over Cuba," Max Morath's "Cubanola Glide," Charlie Parker's "Afro-Cuban Jazz Suite," and Oscar Peterson's "Cuban Chant." A number of less direct and ultimately more interesting stories grow out of this underplaying of influence. Emerging from the dull light of the 1950s, the New York of *West Side Story* was the product of a time when the U.S. avant-garde still had a left-leaning social conscience. But Latin music barely registered in this urban cultural memory despite the thematic hints of the barrio in the riffs of Leonard Bernstein's "America" and his "Dance in the Gym." The populist impulse and the hunger for new forms that marked that memorable era found the raw and unvarnished Latin sound as difficult to assimilate as others before them had.

The U.S. bohemias of the 1950s – one thinks particularly of Jack Kerouac and William Burroughs in Mexico – were staking out a realm of pleasure that drew its inspiration at least partly from Latin America even prior to the Cuban revolution in 1959. Resourceful, angry outcasts – the circles around, say, Margaret Randall, who would become one of the major proponents in English of the Cuban *testimonio* form after living in Mexico, and later Cuba – huddled in small mutual support groups at the Cedar Tavern dreaming of another life.

The history of the *son* suggests that the lines between literature and music are not as hardened as our disciplinary boundaries imply. In Cuba, the novels of Carpentier (a librettist in his own right) were musically based on the *son* and European classical music simultaneously. Feijóo's extensive research on *son* is conducted largely in the name of showing how the musical genre created the conditions for the rise of the black avant-garde poetry of Nicolás Guillén, Pichardo Moya and others.[72] Like the character of Columbus in his novel *The Harp and the Shadow*, Carpentier "demanded that Cuba be a continent."[73] Guillén's collection *Sóngoro Consóngo* deliberately brought Afro-Cuban syncopation and black popular themes to the printed lyric. In the United States, the Afro-Latin connection was explored among others by the novelist James Weldon Johnson in his *Autobiography of an Ex-Colored Man*. It also found a place in the bop poetry of Sonia Sanchez as well as in Amiri Baraka, whose famous early visit to Cuba and the essay it prompted made an impact on his poetry and politics alike.[74] Allen Ginsberg, Ishmael Reed, Paul Beatty, although from different generations, all took New York and its Caribbean musical sources as their point of departure.

It is good to recall, too, how completely the sorts of ironies associated with "magical realism" in the 1970s were an ordinary part of the musical development of the Caribbean, and how deeply they were internalized by Latin American artists before marvelous reality was ever theorized. Jacqueline Rosemain describes, for example, how French "bel airs" (light songs) arose from the raucous, pagan mouths of revelers at carnival in a period when "les sociétés de distraction" organized balls that did not neglect to feature lascivious dances like the *calenda, tarantella, fandango*, and *chica*. Down the street from the upper crust could be heard the music of the cabarets, which were meeting-places of "sailors, soldiers, blacks on the lam, free blacks, pirates, mercenaries, and women of small virtue launching their perpetual siege."[75] The inspirations for dancing and singing, writes Rosemain, came from a variety of sources:

> Tall tales of voyages, collisions, battles, everyday events, accounting rules, mockeries, angers, passing love affairs. The mobility of this cosmopolitan clientele and the bustle of the ports, especially those of Saint-Pierre, set the stage for the exchange of musics both traditional and insurgent, sea-chanteys that made unlikely improvisations burst forth from the singers. (74)

The audience for Cuban music in the 1920s has no necessary relationship to either the avant-garde or bohemianism (and many of the leaders of the *negrismo* movement were, in fact, either socialists or on their way to becoming one). And yet bohemian intellectuals in New York, as in interwar Paris, lived and worked in surroundings that best illustrate the uses of local cultural receptions as global ones. The bohemian senses, even without knowing it, the underworld history of music as a form, and finds his/her way to it in pursuit of a world where glory and disrepute are one and the same. But the two worlds that colonialism erects cancel out such symbolic slippages, and the bohemian revolt of the metropolis never quite reaches the cultural revolution of the colonial setting (or its anticolonial transplantation). Amiri Baraka in his Greenwich Village phase was an intellectual whose pioneering studies of blues and bebop appreciated the vicarious blackness of avant-garde practice and the indebted striving for "what is missing" among the early Village devotees of experimental 1950s jazz.

What makes Baraka helpful in an account of *son* – about which he had very little to say – are the lessons he drew about bohemian subcultures. He would later set up a contrast between, on the one hand, the Greenwich Village of the 1950s and, on the other, the Harlem or Newark where he fled in the 1960s; or better, the Latino Lower East Side that he frequented in the 1990s, staging original theatrical pieces at the Nuyorican Poets Café. It was what he saw while leaving bohemianism that brought into clarity his earlier uneasiness about a black music in settings of portable danger, safely confined to the Village Vanguard (whose name could not be more appropriate in this context). For Baraka the lessons of bebop's rise had to do with complaining about a white voyeurism that underplayed the devotional contexts and historical record-keeping that mattered to black audiences, but which tended to be rendered by the white critic simply as "high art" as though this was the greatest and final compliment.

Unlike jazz, the various Cuban genres never affixed themselves to an exclusive national stereotype (as the *tango* did in Argentina, for example). The music was very early on a global product, what Fernando Ortiz called "the cosmopolitan triumph of the Cuban drum" – which is perhaps only a different kind of nationalist boasting.[76] But this is not to say that the global success of Cuban music, noticed already by Eliseo Grenet in his introduction to *Música popular Cubana* in 1939, did not retain its national aspect. Performed today from Senegal to Japan, salsa had the paradoxical effect of forging a generic Latino identity in which the special contribution of Cuba was both ritualized and thematic (another way of seeing why the subject of salsa is salsa).

It was not only the so-called primitive art of Cubism or jazz that marked the interwar European intellectuals' obsession with the colonies. Pierre Mabille pointed out that Picasso's now legendary turn to primitive art in 1906 was only the beginning "of a revolution whose development will not stop and of which we are today still experiencing only the initial phases."[77] It was his view, in other words, that in spite of familiar history, the European avant-garde's inspirations were not limited to African sculpture nor were they limited to North American jazz. They were involved with an unacknowledged New World love affair that Breton's tour of Martinique and Haiti in the 1940s would belatedly affirm.

Interwar avant-garde musicians ended up producing the right access under the wrong conditions. Imagining a society that would have wielded the knowledge for different ends, they perfected outreach using the techniques of aesthetic modernity in the service of counter-modernity. The Italian futurist Luigi Russolo wanted to turn factories into "an intoxicating orchestra of noises." Like Dada's disgust with highbrow pretension, *Gebrauchsmusik* in Germany was devoted to erasing the distinction between art music and music for use. Paul Hindemith's *Spielmusik*, performed a similar function. In particular, it was Erik Satie whose manifesto of 1920 called for "furniture music" designed for law offices, banks, marriage ceremonies, and the home. As Joseph Lanza points out, creeping toward Muzak the avant-garde began by wanting to disrupt commercial culture, but ended up providing a blueprint for today's "sonic wallpaper" and "audioanalgesics" – a common aurality that would live to become "the music world's Esperanto" in Lanza's words.[78] Afro-Cuban music proved not to be assimilable in quite the same way as these forms. Salsa could be no Esperanto, which made it attractive to New York bohemians at a later date. The hidden power of global mass-culture is always that it continues to communicate its own locality.

As a descendent of *son*, salsa still grips urban middle-class audiences in part because it resists assimilation despite its many fusions, because it deifies the sensual body, exalts the intentional messiness of polyrhythm, and secularizes devotion. Only because of its colonial formation does its aesthetic amount to a meaningful politics, resisting modernity without falling back on the neo-traditionalist revivals of so many of today's monotheisms.

3

Face Down in the Mainstream[1]

In most contemporary writing on popular music, authenticity is considered nostalgic. The claim that a work is "authentic" seems to want to make a certain *time* of music, and styles conventionally associated with *place*, inviolable. To many commentators today, appeals to the genuine are suspicious, for it is always relatively easy for the critic to demonstrate that all genres of music are deeply unstable and that individual forms are rife with impromptu combinations taken from whatever is at hand. In every case, they are the product of a promiscuous borrowing.

In European art music, the notion of a faithful rendition of a composer's work (*Werktreue* – "work fidelity") quickly runs afoul of the fact that styles of "true" performance are highly variable historically. Performers project their own values onto the composer's intentions so that there is a built-in ambiguity about what one is really being faithful *to*. In popular music, a different kind of fidelity is at work – to a tradition, style, or school, or even to a people or race. But this ideal collapses at the first hint of prior exposure in those traditions to often very recent and disenchanted influences.[2] Invoking authenticity, then, is apparently guilty of a lust for purity, which is not only utopian in its attempt to recover the impossible but, much worse than that. It is a shallow response to what a little homework would show is aesthetically mixed and richly indeterminate.

In the prevailing story, advocates of authenticity are thought to be credulous, usually seduced by notions of a safe world before modernity. The task of the contemporary critic, then, is to demonstrate that the earmarks of modern life – usually figured as electronic media and fluidities of transport and communication – always lie behind these apparently rural, anonymous, or communal forms before the days of recording. The term "modernity," as I am using it, is a deliberate amalgam that refers to related ideas with indistinct associations. It is difficult to separate these historically from the experience of earlier colonial encounters, which gave the feel of truth to a series of polarizing dichotomies. Being from the city rather than the countryside, identified with the "West" and its civilization, of European descent, cosmopolitan rather than parochial, drawn to artistic or scientific experimentation, informed by mass media, and involved in the world of fashion and the latest commodities – all of these mean "modern" more or less interchangeably. So it is not surprising that those who want to debunk claims to authenticity appeal to technology – as Michael Ventura does, for example, in his brilliant essay "Hear that Long Snake Moan": "People who complain that amplified music is showbiz hype overlook the fact that the first musicians to start playing electrically amplified instruments regularly were backwoods, rural-blues players."[3] This rhetorical gesture of debunking the quest for purity is found everywhere in writing on popular music today, and is meant to establish the critic's scholarly good sense and rejection of romantic notions.

Accurate on its own terms, this consensus nevertheless overlooks important aspects of the problem of authenticity. Why, for example, do we take for granted that being outside or against the "modern" (in the above sense) means having backward-looking, conservative attitudes rather than forward-looking or transformative ones? Are all examples of the anti-modern to be understood only in this sense above, that is, as rural idylls manufactured by those who want to forestall the claims of the technologically and economically favored? Are there not challenges to the modern – understood again, as above, to be a sliding referent that includes the market and consumerism as much as cell phones, laptops, and fast food – that look to a future outside the logic of perpetual accumulation and the waste of natural resources? Once such factors are taken into account, it appears possible to defend authenticity by introducing a different criterion. The real question would then shift. It would no longer be a matter of this or that degree of modernity (where "modern" means less authentic) than the insistence that modern values are contingent. The issue would not be whether the music sullies itself by revealing its basis in (tacky, commercialized) modern life but whether it keeps contact (figurative or actual) with the social scene of its making.

Any blues aficionado gauges the quality of new music on a scale drawn from a relatively small group of canonical performers, among them, say, John Lee Hooker, Little Walter, Bessie Smith, Lightnin' Hopkins, Sonny Boy Williamson, and Howlin' Wolf. These artists (and a few others) form a standard against which the rest are measured. Whether or not there is an objective sonoric quality that these performers share and that would justify this canonical status is not the main issue for the moment. The point is that their individual sounds do not simply satisfy the taste of a few fans; they are rather, for reasons we are temporarily bracketing, the traditions that blues aficionados call "real." Is this simply an illusion? And if so, why is it a mass illusion of such consistency? To call authenticity mythical accomplishes only so much, and does little in the end to chip away at its supposedly absurd claims, for we are only left wondering why the need for it is still so central to the practices of listening.[4] The above blues artists do not, of course, all sound alike, but evidently there is an element found in all of them that unites them. What is this element we call the "authentic"?

The first answer would seem to be unambiguous: a music with no named predecessors or, to put it another way, a music impossible to duplicate without appearing to be a copy. But here the critics of authenticity have a point, for these are shaky grounds indeed. There is always a before that research discovers, and authenticity will then rightly appear as a concept that relies, above all, on a lack of documents. Artists who put enough years between themselves and the present will enjoy a situation where their gestures to authenticity are mistaken for a tradition they are really inventing (Bob Dylan emulating Woody Guthrie emulating legions of anonymous dustbowl balladeers). But this way of putting things is inaccurate as well, only now in the opposite direction. It forgets that this illusory mediation evokes a real and concrete illusion. What Guthrie did, after all, was articulate an image and a behavior for the dustbowl balladeer, one that was apparently widely shared. He created an approximation of that concept in sound, pitching it when the conditions of circulation allowed audiences to fill those sounds with a content derived from a shared projection. A style or attitude painstakingly imposed on the music gave form to a spirit already collectively produced. There was nothing unreal about that. But the footloose troubadour, moving from job to job in boxcars – at least one capable of making music they wanted to hear – could not actually be found or named. He did not exist until the Guthrie studio version, as it were, stepped forward to produce him. The real was not invented, then. It had only assumed its figure.

The dispatch of the concept of authenticity is in the end based on misreading and over-simplification – precisely what it pretends to address. It is unfortunate, too, that this line of criticism often dismisses the concept without actually engaging with it. The tone, more often than not, is condescending:[5]

> The zeal for authenticity is part of a specifically contemporary malaise which values detail above essence. Worse, by foisting dubious con-

temporary values on the past, its proponents threaten to diminish, not enlarge our musical horizons.[6]

The position sees itself as giving a more sophisticated rendering to a naive point of view.

> By the 1990s the term became discredited. Nowadays it is more customary to speak of "historically informed performances" and avoid any reference to authenticity. It is generally assumed that this development is the direct result of the enlightening and critical discussions of the meaning of authenticity during the 1980s.[7]

For decades one heard of "inflexible determinations" like "originality" and "authenticity." There were calls everywhere to "dislodge the manner in which these ideas inhabit everyday discourse" since they have "a flimsy conceptual foundation."[8] Frequently the negative evaluations of claims to authenticity were based, rather simple-mindedly, on the disparity between belief and fact – "origin myths of authenticity are convenient tools in this sense for legitimizing social claims, but may well have little to do with historical accuracy" – as though beliefs were not themselves facts crucial to the appreciation of forms of art.[9]

But these assertions that are still so prevalent are surprisingly hard to defend. If by authentic we mean original, it is admittedly a fictional term, for there are always those who came before, even if their names will never be known. If we mean untainted, we will have entered even more dangerous territory, for then we will have to posit notions of identity weakened by vigorous attacks over the last few decades from critics who have shown that identities like "black," "proletarian," "woman," "European," or even "Colombian" are deliberately constructed and so very difficult to define in any material sense. They are therefore labels whose unstable meanings are concealed in the attempt to give them unshakeable definitions. But if we mean by authentic honest or sincere in a setting of commercial jive; if we mean knowing one's own history and being able to map the traditions of sound that invented it rather than passing off shtick as a novelty of style, then it is hard to see why authenticity is not still valid.

Authenticity – to emphasize for a moment a different tension within the term "modern" – points to a certain relationship to a commercial setting. This is an aspect that tends to be either overlooked or cast in such a way that pure commerce appears simply environmental – which is to say natural, and so not worth questioning. The concept does not necessarily posit a lonely bucolic spirit, ethereal and unblemished, where art is a sublime abstraction, for there is room in it for advertising, commercial motives, and the mixing and matching of the bricoleur. But the authentic work, whatever else it does, always recreates an arc of influence, enveloping a lived situation. It stretches back from the individual to an anonymous group where a repertoire of associations is the common property of a people recognized from afar and identifiable within. The arc stretches as well from the innovation of the artist to the social scenes that gave the style its signature – the washtub backyards of the one-room shacks without basements that populate the roadsides of the Jim Crow South, the taverns underneath the zebra shadows of the Chicago loop, the Pullman cars on the St. Louis express.

This is just the kind of list, I realize, that invites charges of romanticism, and a number of critics would likely want to point out that the scenes of delta blues really had much more to do with far less idyllic sites: the meeting in the cigar-smoking mogul's offices at RCA, Chess, or Atlantic; the three-hundredth take at the studio where the producer whines into the headphones that the take was not "fresh" enough (by which he means, not black enough – or too black). But what makes this side of the equation more real? Why is the deflating anti-heroism of the cold facts of commerce or the technological tyranny of performance given priority in the realm of verisimilitude? Why suppose, in short, that even though some black musicians mug for provincial white audiences, performing a ritual recreation of self built out of stock images of cotton fields, prison yards, chain gangs, and rickety back porches, that authenticity is meaningless – particularly when that repertoire was not at all imagined, but made out of the distillation of a collective experience? The playacting and the memory of life are both true, if unequal. For the former would be moot without the latter and is parasitical of it.[10] The social environments of the birth of genre are, or at least should be, privileged. This arc is often explicit. Junior Wells's "Help Me (A Tribute to Sonny Boy Williamson)" and Bob Dylan's early "Song to Woody [Guthrie]" were composed before the assault on authenticity had gathered steam.[11] Looking back, it is impossible to think that the explosive excitement generated by Wells and Dylan had nothing to do with their rootedness in a sound from the past that they openly venerate. There are reasons for this that are unrelated to the present line of argument – for example, Williamson's talent for inventing stage-voice and Guthrie's prolific output and his genius for the popular lyric. But the rougher, harsher, less studio-polished sound of the elder statesmen – which Ventura would see, perhaps, as a kind of lure for the romantic critic who takes these surface features as airtight evidence that Williamson and Guthrie were somehow above business – is for all that deeply attractive and has amazing longevity.

This is not at all to say that these artists cut no deals to get a wider hearing, or inherited their sound naturally and without mediation straight from the American soil. But it is not enough when theorizing authenticity to rely, as so many contemporaries do, on the easy put-down that there are no true origins since there is no first time, or that art was never untainted by the quest for money, or that the codified dream of an ethnic or racial people is seldom like the messy thing itself. What draws the ambitious artist in the borrowing mode, or the appreciative audience in the reverential mode, to the rougher, earlier sound is something much greater than a matter of musical taste and not to be confused with a simple flight to some pre-technological fantasy. What draws them to this sound is its evidence of a time when the commercialization of music was less advanced, when the standardization of the personality was less obvious, when the metaphorical capture of ordinary people and their ways of life was an artistic strategy that one could use without a mocking, knowing, sophisticated irony. This sort of creation – or lie, if you will – is more honest. (Which is why Papi Oviedo insists that "The *son* without *tres* is not *son*."[12])

We can still learn from the uncompromising stance of the novelist Zora Neale Hurston in this regard. As a transcriber of folk tales and ethnographer, she has an authority to comment on these matters:

> There never has been a presentation of genuine Negro spirituals to any audience anywhere. What is being sung by the concert artists and glee clubs are the works of Negro composers or adapters *based* on the spirituals . . . To begin with, Negro spirituals are not solo or quartette material. The jagged harmony is what makes it, and it ceases to be what it was when this is absent. Neither can any group be trained to reproduce it. Its truth dies under training like flowers under hot water. The harmony of the true spiritual is not regular. The dissonances are important and not to be ironed out by the trained musician. The various parts break in at any old time. Falsetto often takes the place of regular voices for short periods. Keys change. Moreover, each singing of the piece is a new creation . . . *Negro songs to be heard truly must be sung by a group and a group bent on expression of feelings and not on sound effects* [Hurston's emphasis].[13]

Despite Hurston's injunctions, which are not at all confined to their time, most critics trained in the last two decades will consider these listeners gullible, believing that they are falling once again for a myth that the critic can easily explode. Most today learn to discount the following point made by Isabelle Leymarie: "At a time of increased mechanization and uniformity, Cuban music and its offshoots, with their extraordinary expressiveness, have generally managed to preserve their vigor and authenticity, a fact that once prompted *conguero* Ray Barretto to declare that *salsa* was 'the last bastion of honest music.'"[14]

Above all, what is never considered is the motive for this suspicion, which is usually expressed in such an extreme way that it should arouse suspicion all by itself. A market society forbids the concept of authenticity. This is the dogmatic law it imposes on its public. The whole logic of such a society is premised on the demolition of tradition and on infinite productivity and its necessary counterpart, obsolescence.

But let us make another distinction at this point. The movements of nineteenth-century literary realism and naturalism in Europe – in the work, say, of Jules Goncourt, Arnold Bennett, and Émile Zola – acted with the conviction that portraits of the lower depths, poverty, crime, drunkenness, and hovels were by definition more real on the grounds that these lurid aspects of society had been excised from literary texts because of their impropriety. They were that partial aspect of the real that came to symbolize the real itself by virtue of its previous neglect. Although the association between reality and disaster is understandable – we remember the bad more readily than the good because it hurts more, perhaps – it neglects to take life whole. For the facts of life include also the rich, the comfortable, the virtuous, the heroic, and above all, the uneventful, which even the most jaded students of human nature have to concede exist as strongly as the tragic or perverse. So the authentic in music should not be associated necessarily with the pastoral portrait of society's rejects: the unfinished, unschooled, gravelly sound played on borrowed instruments by vocalists in the last stages of tuberculosis. There is a necessary connection between nineteenth-century literary realism and the portrayal of a wretched underworld where lives end unhappily because the "real" in that nineteenth-century moment had a negative mission. It meant to face what others had ignored.

So in this sense authenticity has been given, in a comparable way, a partial and therefore untrue meaning. It is precisely the widespread revulsion against the commercialization of creativity and the tyranny of exchange that gives this restricted and damaged sense of authenticity its life. In the place of refuge known as music, a pre-capitalist or anti-capitalist pastoral is so compelling that any aesthetic means that conjure it (the hoarse tones of the singer, the basement recording style, the faded photographs, the songs that end mid-measure without fade-outs, the late interviews with the chain-smoking geezer whose teeth have fallen out, and so on) is a powerful and alluring exaggeration verging on myth. Fine, but there are inherent flaws to an outlook that suggests the Beatles and Britney Spears, George Jones and Toby Keith, Benny Moré and Desi Arnaz, or Chalino Sanchez and Trini Lopez are equally authentic. For in the first of each pairing there is a remainder having to do with degrees of faithfulness to the sites and times of experience where composition took place, with the clarity and integrity with which an artist adapted his or her material, and above all, with the artist's (real or imputed) desire for freedom from the anti-music standardization of mass marketing.

There have, in fact, been other challenges to the prevailing consensus on authenticity. In her study on the uses of food in the middle-class Indian diaspora, Keya Ganguly observes that authenticity in its strong sense is about "the primacy of the object over language" or, to put this somewhat differently, about insisting that represented reality has no priority over the truth of correspondence. She adds:

> It is the representation of truth that contributes to inauthenticity, not truth itself; moreover, there must be some way, beyond the mediation of the image, to actualize the authentic – not through any ascription of what [Theodor] Adorno calls a "positive vision of Utopia" but from within the experience of history and as its critical cancellation.[15]

In a persuasive account of the judgments about authentic and inauthentic food preparation in a community that is paradoxically defined by cuisine all the more because it is no longer living in its native country, she implies a strategy applicable to other forms of art. To invoke a situated group as arbiter is to place the artist in a position of dependency, and to recall the surroundings of the only place of creation that could have allowed the work in question. This awareness – this knowledge of social form – is part of what is meant (or at least should be meant) by authenticity.

The mention of Theodor Adorno above is a reminder that the line of reasoning adopted here differs in some respects from the work of that school of critics whose project was to show how popular culture had been harmed by a modernity defined by exchange and mass production. In the literary criticism of Leo Löwenthal, the art theory of Herbert Marcuse, the social and media criticism of Theodor Adorno and Max Horkheimer, and the music criticism of Adorno, the Frankfurt School put commercial mass culture firmly in its sights, diagnosing its organized system of damaged life. As a rule, these thinkers opposed the now mainstream view in cultural studies that mass culture is an explosive terrain of reappropriation, creative manipulation, and subversive consumption. The opposition was not absolute, however: Marcuse in "An Essay on Liberation" did praise blues and rock as harbingers of the counterculture (although he did not consider this particularly significant politically).[16] Trends in contemporary popular music theory dedicated to proving the resistance potential of rap or indie rock would have seemed, from the Frankfurt theorists' point of view, already in evidence in the 1940s and 1950s, and just as problematic then as now. They defended the viability of authenticity, but primarily in the form of the dissidence of the bourgeois artist, poet, or classical composer escaping the formulas of the market by an Olympian act of will.

The dismissal of authenticity by popular music theory and its antagonism toward the Frankfurt School are in fact related. This antagonism has often taken the form of attacks on Adorno for his dubious remarks on jazz, but my intention is not to rehearse that sort of argument here. In fact, I will not say anything about Adorno on jazz, which is a topic that has been extensively treated elsewhere. On the contrary, I would like to turn to one of the fullest and most detailed examinations of authenticity by the Frankfurt School in order to distinguish my argument from theirs and to show how effectively their analyses, with some important provisos, reinforce the point I have been trying to make.

Adorno's, Horkheimer's, and Marcuse's diagnoses of aesthetic form and social meaning in regard to modern production techniques, organizational business demands, and a blanketing market ideology are unequalled anywhere. Nothing written after them competes with the sheer intelligence and evidence of their claims. Nevertheless, certain features of their arguments have to be revised in light of the New World African traditions that by taste and training they often misinterpret, or, given their secular religious aspect, overlook altogether because they worked in social settings where the importance of such factors was not obvious. Marcuse's longer stay in the United States as well as his professional involvements there over several decades counter this tendency in him. But despite his range of interests and his prodigious intellect, his familiarity with the neo-African dimensions of American popularity was quite limited when considered alongside his knowledge of the Continental philosophical tradition. Given the knowledge all three had, it might seem flippant to say that their definition of the "popular" lacked an adequate theoretical foundation. But that is what I would like to argue.

Adorno's "On Popular Music" (written with the assistance of George Simpson in 1941) is an extraordinary piece of work and is indispensable to anyone interested in the classical/popular divide in music as well as in the ambiguity of the term "popular" in an environment where invention has to contend with the tyranny of sales figures and distribution networks.[17] The essay opens with a distinction between popular and "serious" music. It would be tempting at the outset to see Adorno's motives here as driven by a bias against simplicity and a built-in preference for refinement as against a chuckleheaded, "can-do" Americanism. But this would be inaccurate. Simpson and Adorno set out, in fact, to challenge common prejudices such as these, disputing (1) that all classical music is serious, (2) that popular music is less worthy because uneducated people listen to it, (3) that music is "serious" to the extent that it is complex, and (4) that their popular/serious contrast is another way of saying "highbrow/lowbrow" where the latter should be taken to mean "naïve" and the former "sophisticated." On the contrary, their goal is to translate these not-so-subtle judgments, which were completely taken for granted among journalists and academics of the time, into more precise terms based on a sociology of musical form.

Their first governing term and the principle for the rest of their argument is *standardization*, which they argue is the most fundamental characteristic of all popular music:

> Best known is the rule that the chorus consists of thirty-two bars and that the range is limited to one octave and one note. The general types of hits are also standardized: not only the dance types, the rigidity of whose pattern is understood, but also the "characters" such as mother songs, home songs, nonsense or "novelty" songs, pseudo-nursery rhymes, laments for a lost girl. Most important of all, the harmonic cornerstones of each hit – the beginning and the end of each part – must beat out the standard scheme. This scheme emphasizes the most primitive harmonic facts no matter what has harmonically intervened. (438)

These patterns always lead back, in their view, to "familiar experience" in which nothing fundamentally novel is ever introduced. Even the details are standardized, not just the overall form: the "breaks, blue chords, dirty notes" all these are hidden behind a "veneer of individual 'effects' " (438). If the quotation above suggests that the authors are thinking more of Bing Crosby and Judy Garland than Bola de Nieve and Blind Lemon Jefferson – that is, prime-time radio fare or RCA Victor studio products rather than the stars of low-life clubs for the initiates of the musical underground – they clearly mean to include blues and jazz as well ("dirty notes," "blue chords").

One could even argue that it is precisely black-inflected popular music that most preoccupies them, since they understand very well that this fabulously popular music associated with the authentic as low, gritty, poor, and vibrantly real, would make the strongest counter-case to their claims (so that defeating that potential counter-argument would clinch their point). They concede that European classicism has conventions that limit innovation – highly organized, strict art forms like the sonnet and fugue impose an unvarying set of rules on the artist and demand that he or she demonstrates individuality against the grain. But this superficial similarity fails to take account of the fact that only the popular song has "an externally superimposed, commercial character" of patterns that "canalize reactions" – a feature as pronounced for them in recognizably black urban or rural musical forms as in country, film-jazz, torch song, Broadway, or easy listening. For their target is not whatever intentions or practices might exist, and exist differently, among various artists, ethnic groups, or national traditions, but the dictates of being popular itself – of attempting to reach and be liked by broad numbers of people across races, ethnicities, and classes. In a market society, to try to reach people *as a mass* ensures a suffocating standardization that obliterates the revelatory possibilities of art. The production system as it is received, and within which one is forced to work, demands that there be a collision between the individual innovation of the artist (whose creativity belongs to an earlier craft-oriented or guild mentality) and the industrialized, conveyor-belt framework of record production, distribution, advertising, and broadcasting:

> The production of popular music can be called "industrial" only in its promotion and distribution, whereas the act of producing a song hit still remains in a handicraft stage. The production of popular music is highly centralized in its economic organization, but still "individualistic" in its social mode of production. (443)

On the terms in which they present their case, Adorno and Simpson seem to score a conclusive victory. The power of their thesis rests on the intimate ways they stitch together observations on musical form and structure with compelling sociological evidence. The culture industry creates in their view a depressing, victimized listener with which most fair readers of their essay can immediately relate. Because they promise relief from a domineering and unvarying framework, individual effects draw attention to details rather than the whole – something, anything, to break the conformity of the recycled hit or the blustery overture of the latest action film.

But the listener's "grasp of the whole does not lie in the living experience of this one concrete piece of music he has followed." Because publicity has already made it impossible for us not to perceive the music as fitting into a slot that previous success determined, "the whole is pre-given and pre-accepted, even before the actual experience of the music starts" (440). By contrast, in serious music "every detail derives its musical sense from the concrete totality of the piece which, in turn, consists of the life relationship of the details and never of a mere enforcement of a musical scheme" (441). Themes only gather their full meaning from the contexts in which they occur. Hence, the theme of the first movement of Beethoven's *Appassionata* "achieves the utmost dramatic momentum" only because it follows an outburst of sound that Beethoven has architecturally inserted just a moment before. Popular music cannot generate this kind of interest since the overall musical sense of a piece would not be damaged by the inclusion or elimination of any of the details, whose function is ornamental and coloristic.

At this point, any mildly combative rock critic would probably protest. Counter-examples to Adorno and Simpson's part/whole assertion are not hard to find. Especially in the 1970s (but also in holdover genres of the 1980s), rock (the Beatles' *White Album,* Jefferson Airplane's *Jefferson Starship*), R&B (Stevie Wonder's *Songs in the Key of Life*), and rap (Public Enemy's *Fear of a Black Planet*) all challenged the tyranny of pre-established market rigidities by creating total-concept albums. They quite deliberately meant in each case to outwit the demands of radio and record producers for short, singable cuts by composing albums where the cuts in ensemble (if not internally) were interdependent. Each piece moved in a determinate order of calculated, varying lengths in order to create momentum, lulls, unexpected detours, or elaborations. The pacing of the albums, and the patterns of dissimilar sounds and genres within them (the *White Album*'s dark, cacophonous shrieks from Lennon set alongside the '60s-spiritual sitar excursions by Harrison and the pure music-hall sentimentalities of McCartney) gave a punctuated rhythm to the experience of LP-listening that could only draw one's attention to the whole as a cryptic statement that Beatles' fans were intended then to decipher. The caesura of a Jorma Kaukonen guitar instrumental in the midst of Jefferson Starship's highly narrative performance about escaping the rotten life of earth – and the entire *Starship* album is a story of flight that unfolds song by song – was an important reprieve for listeners, a gesture to the established musical skill of an older craft type in the utopian surroundings of experimental fare, which depended in one instance on the use of vacuum cleaners to simulate the sounds of a space rocket during launch.

Similarly, the highly orchestrated scratching and sampling of Terminator X on *Fear of a Black Planet* introduced sound-passages that more resembled radio art than the coloristic interludes of the bass line "effect" working in counterpoint to the lyrics. On the contrary, each of the elements in the collage contributed to the whole and were inextricable from it. Clips from the speeches of John F. Kennedy and Malcolm X were spliced together with contemporary car commercials and the suggestive drawl of a southern cracker to suggest a series of stories from an African-American point of view – an aural glimpse, as it were, into the psychology of the slandered. The art of scratching and splicing throughout the album plays a similar role to the dragoman in theater, explaining to the audience the setting of the scenes that are about to unfold (like the narrator of Prokoviev's *Peter and the Wolf*.)

Even the individual cuts of the album were spliced together without pauses, bleeding into one another in a single multi-dimensional movement from loud to lyrical and from nightmare screech to the regenerative anger of protest and clarification. Although no one would confuse these works with symphony, there is little at the level of musical complexity that separates them from symphony. Apart from the obvious external matters of orchestration, what most separates them from the classical symphony is ideological intention, the audience adduced, and the historical and regional associations (of certain neighborhoods of New York, say, rather than the middle and upper-class life of France, Germany, or Hungary).

If Adorno and Simpson cannot be blamed for failing to take account of work that was not composed for over three decades after their essay first appeared in 1941, we have to recall that a similar riposte was already available in the Afro-Latin complex of music production rampant in the Americas which both had experienced by the 1940s. Furthermore, their case is based on popular music *as such* in a production setting that the passing of decades alone should not have been able to alter. They are not saying that popular music is manipulated by promoters to produce standardized responses but that standardization is inherent to the music itself. Whatever is complicated in popular music functions as "a disguise or embellishment behind which the scheme can always be perceived" (442). Whenever musical difficulty is heard, it arises only "as a parodistic distortion of the simple." Popular music is "predigested" in a way strongly resembling the fad of the literary "digest."

In the context of the mass culture debates, which had flourished for at least a decade by this point, this argument could not be more important.

The critique opened up an entirely new and welcome line of inquiry, moving the discussion about corporate control of resources and the standardizing of the emotions to much more critical terrain than existed in the populist and anti-populist strains of U.S. criticism – a criticism that sometimes seemed to offer little more than a shouting match over various guilty aesthetic pleasures between defenders of kitsch and stalwarts of the avant-garde. When it sinks in that Adorno and Simpson are writing in a sound landscape overrun by the likes of Kate Smith, Mel Tormé, and Rosemary Clooney – and before the particular twist given the mainstreaming of African music via rock and world music – the urge to accept Adorno and Simpson's critique without changes is very strong.

In taking exception to some of their conclusions, it is only fair to recall Adorno and Simpson's political traditions and the relationship they had to the idea of authenticity. The full flavor of Adorno's milieu is often lost in the many approving citations of his extensive musical theory. Music for Adorno was nothing less than a refuge from American trivia and political propaganda. As Rolf Wiggerhaus points out, "Schoenberg and Mahler together all at once meant for him: structured longing, a music of longing for vanished meaning, the longing to break out of a baneful and, at the same time, self-satisfied world."[18] Not unlike his nemesis Georg Lukács, Adorno wanted to make artists independent of the sale or non-sale of their works and so to overcome the commodity character of works of art. In fact, Lukács, working for the socialist government of Hungary after World War II, attempted to place control of art in the hands of artists.

A music directorate was established ... which consisted of Béla Bartók, Zoltán Kodály and Ernst von Dohnányi. Provided that art could be freed from its commodity character, provided that the economy could be put in the service of culture, and provided that the military defense of the Hungarian Soviet Republic succeeded, then – this may have been the thirty-four-year-old revolutionary's hope – an essential life would at last be possible again.[19]

Without taking anything away from these solid premises, the brilliance and, above all, the apparent thoroughness of Adorno and Simpson's argument is misleading. In fact, it is particularly the finer aspects of their case, the most unexpected and initially compelling, that one has to interrogate. In the spirit of the argument I have been presenting, there is support for their insight that standardization does not occur only because of its economic utility but because of a psychological response to the conditions of work. Music as a fractured unity of interchangeable parts is to them the result of imitation, itself the inevitable outcome of competition. The "hit" is copied so that another hit can be manufactured in turn. The centralized conditions of music production freeze standard hits, which are "taken over by centralized agencies, the final results of a competitive process, and rigidly enforced upon material to be promoted" (443).

> Popular music must simultaneously meet two demands. One is for stimuli that provoke the listener's attention. The other is for the material to fall within the category of what the musically untrained listener would call "natural" music: that is, the sum total of all the conventions and material formulas in music to which he is accustomed and which he regards as the inherent, simple language of music itself. (444)

The desire that popular music fulfills, then, is perceived by the one desiring it as being at once stimulatory and natural. Standardization has a dual character; to maintain interest, it must be stylized – that is, imbued with a pseudo-individuality that salvages the artwork while hiding the concentration of power that governs the culture as a whole. This illusion of individuality staves off a dissent that would be more general were centralization more obvious. A pantomime of taste and free choice is played out in a standardization that is not recognized for what it is because the unquestioned goal of novelty and individuality prevents it from appearing in its own clothing.

Serious students of sociology find it easy to concede that art functions in just this compensatory way in heavily consumer-driven societies like the United States. It was the Frankfurt theorists who first explained how this process works in a conceptually concise way. Their argument is not weakened by any political or intellectual limitations as much as it is by a partial range of cultural evidence. It is striking, for example, that Adorno and Simpson associate the routine aspects – the roteness – of popular music with dance. Despite the time they dedicate to other details, they give no space at all to defending the following assumptions: (1) that the composer is the inventive master of the whole work, (2) that composition is an act of intellectual reflection that alone makes folk material "serious," (3) that dance is inferior to instrumental harmony, and (ultimately) (4) that the body is inferior to the mind – that is, the body is more likely to produce standardization.

So, for example, in order to extricate European classicism from the charge that, like the popular song industry, it derived its leads from popular dance forms (the minuetto and scherzo of the Viennese School, for example), they argue that serious music deals with this problem by interconnecting the essential elements "in the manner of a dialogue" and the whole device is made "dynamic" by being subjected to "tension" (441). In other words, serious music relieves the simple and straightforward from being merely simple. But more than that, an equation is drawn between what is danceable and what is musically simple: tempos capable of accommodating the body, regularity of pulse, the triteness of phrasing that accompanies a social convention in moments of collective leisure, and so on. The idea here, then, is that musical dullness brought on by the peculiar demands of dance can be rescued in symphonic or chamber music only by placing its most conventional elements in quotation marks. They are made the subject of a strange encounter in order to distance them, giving them a deeper dimension by playing them off each other so that they can acquire an interest in combination like the subplots of a television drama.

Before considering how well these claims actually fit African New World dance, or how much they take note of its influence on European classicism, we need to raise a number of more general questions. In *Noise: The Political Economy of Music,* Jacques Attali takes a similar line to that of Adorno and Simpson on the matter of repetition, but like them, he never submits the concept to an analysis of its many conflicting components, seen not just in the macro-terms of the market or of music history but from the point of view of composition (which Attali consigns to a separate chapter).[20] In his view, repetition numbs and therefore arrests time by crippling thought. But one wants to ask, which repetition? Is there only one kind? There is repetition for emphasis, repetition for the purpose of memorizing, repetition for making bodily actions so automatic that they do not require thinking. There is repetition to fill time ("One Hundred Bottles of Beer on the Wall"), repetition because one has no imagination; there is repetition to pay homage (an aural allusion); and then there is the labor issue: repetition of oldies, of classic films or box-office smashes of the previous decade to avoid copyright fees or having to pay writers (the huge industry in today's Hollywood recycling).

Adorno and Simpson, in short, never explore strategies of art that *prefer* anonymity to signature and that appeal to repetition in the name not of mass production but incantation. For repetition is, apart from everything else, a declaration of what one shares with others, what others already know and recognize, what does not constitute a departure because one essentially is what others are to the degree that all belong to the same (national or ethnic) tradition. The authors are right to imply that the champions of democracy are fooling themselves when they see in the taste of the masses a bona fide expression of popular desire. And, in fact, it could be said that their entire argument is trained precisely on that prominent delusion in the postwar United States. But they do not have enough intercultural experience to entertain the idea that a challenge to mass culture is possible not from heroic individual artists at war with the "popular" or (by contrast) those easy democrats who subscribe to the idea that whatever is is right, but from an alien tradition embedded in the ruling culture. This alien element for historical reasons kept its identity, existed unrecognized in broad daylight, and was bent both on opposing the prevailing values and benefiting from the accumulated wisdom and weight of the crowd, seeing limitations in the strategy of individual non-compliance.

An illustration of what Adorno and Simpson leave out can be found vividly expressed in the work of the great Cuban sociologist Fernando Ortiz. A pioneer of the study of New World African religion and musical practices throughout the 1930s and 1940s, and in every respect Adorno's contemporary, he would have his reflections assembled in definitive form in *La Música afrocubana* (Afro-Cuban Music, 1975).[21] The majority of critics looking into the history of writing on mass culture will likely know figures like F. R. Leavis, Marshall McLuhan, Clement Greenberg, or Adorno, but very few of them, outside specialists in Latin America, will know Ortiz. This neglect, I am suggesting, is related to the weakness of the consensus on authenticity described above – including the otherwise inviting exposés of the corporatist aspects of popularity represented by the Frankfurt School. The specific conditions of Caribbean life made it possible for Ortiz to solve problems of theory that writers like Adorno could not find a way to formulate. It is revealing that there has been no systematic attempt to work through Ortiz's substantial contribution on popular neo-African musical forms (it plays almost no role in writing on African-American music or popular culture, for example); or to place him in counterpoint to Adorno, whose U.S. sojourn yielded so many of his insights on "cultural protest," damaged subjects, and the rise of the authoritarian personality.

Ortiz approaches authenticity not by interrogating the qualities of art but by focusing on its makers. All of his efforts are directed at determining whether the term "popular" actually refers to the *people,* and if so, whether the "people" can be defined and understood (is it more, in other words, than simply a politician's slogan?). His primary distinction, then, is not (as in Adorno and Simpson) between the popular and the serious, but between the "popular" – what is widely bought, circulated, known, and understood – and the popular – that which has been invented by the representative classes of a society, which is to say its majority, those who work for a living and are not themselves professional artists or intellectuals:[22] "The *people* does not just mean peasants, farmers, or the rural salt of the earth; they belong to the cities as well . . . [In fact] each one of us belongs in part, according to the occasion or place, to this basic social stratum" (13). If the lower or working classes, then, are sociologically distinct, they are also culturally, not just economically, *basic*.[23] Ortiz sees no fearful massification of the subject behind this fact, however, and insists on the survival of individuality. Popular music is not just some autonomous product of tradition. This is a "populist fantasy," he says. Even though they might be illiterate, individuals are constantly inventing popular songs that pass almost immediately into "tradition" (13–14), not on the basis of their immemorial origins or collective composition but their representative sense-making. They are representative.

Point by point, he sheers away the misconceptions surrounding the "folk." What is popular culture, he asks:

> It is not exclusively the art of illiterates, nor is it only transmitted orally. First of all, we can see that the most "cultivated" and refined music of the Far East is transmitted from one generation to another by word of mouth alone; but also, there is undeniably popular music that is right now preserved and disseminated by means of the printed word. Not all folkloric music is quotidian or vulgar either, for it can be remote and exceptional like certain hymns that are sung in temples only on assigned days as a ritual requirement, or in esoteric ceremonies. What is more, even though many are of the opinion that the popular is virtually defined by its existence in multiple, slightly altered versions, the spells and incantations of witchcraft (*brujería*) in all peoples of all times are characterized precisely by the unalterable fixity of its forms. (14)

This sort of popularity is distinct from another, official, kind: "The national anthem is popular, completely and utterly of the people; but it is not exactly *popular*" in the sense of representing the feelings of those on "the lowest level of the social pyramid" (14). What remains is the overwhelming evidence that large swaths of the general culture derive from its subterranean zones:

> Today popular music cannot be considered to be born and to live exclusively in the people, like some aquatic flower that has to germinate and bloom in a pond. Singing can come "from above," but ordinary people will alter it every time they sing it, like a humorous story or a satire changes its details when passing from one to another mouth

under the influences of different minds . . . But there is also the art born below that climbs from class to class, from the puddles to the mountain tops, adjusting itself to the atmosphere at every level, until it finally converts itself, thanks to its beauty, into an art whose gestation and early upbringing are utterly forgotten . . . [This was true] of the *zarabanda*, that sprang to life in a scandalous and diabolical impropriety among black conjurers and witchdoctors of the Congo, and then, with the passing of time, now made upright, pompous, and above all "white" (which is to say neutered . . .) was danced at the royal court to celebrate church councils. (14–16)

Ortiz goes on to develop a thesis about vertical and horizontal "transvaluation" of music as it paces through one or another plane on the social pyramid. Adorno's humane logic and command of classical form are almost unanswerable until one questions the discreteness of the creative blocs that form the basis of his distinction. The serious artist is in his rendering like a Homeric demigod, a freak of the system, who by the powers of intelligence and theory lives in, but not of, his society. A more unruly and convincing portrait of the clash between high art and low culture is captured in Alejo Carpentier's novel, *The Harp and the Shadow*, where the visit to South America of an Italian cleric, later to become pope, is described in some detail. "Mastai's first impressions of Buenos Aires was of black people . . . serving in lowly jobs," the "cult of steaks, filets . . . citizens . . . dancing in convents and stores and brothels to 'El Refalosa' and 'Cuándo, Mi Vida, Cuándo?' (When, my love, *when?*) – dances that were the rage."[24] By contrast, Ortiz's thesis on the fluidities of class contamination and the orgy of appropriation later forgotten or denied seems much more appropriate and, paradoxically, a more tactile account of the origins of that strain of the European Enlightenment that led to Adorno's humane logic in the first place. In Carpentier's novel, Mastai marvels at the

> clamorous assault of the "tango," the dazzling balls where the latest European dance music could be heard, Creole girls singing Pergolesi's *Stabat Mater* to please the young canon, and along with the overseas fashions in culture came the "dangerous passion of thinking." (18)

The rather messy intrusion into staged performances of an authentic outpouring of emotion, of inappropriate classes and races participating anonymously in the most sublime moments of the classical repertoire, and of the two-pronged assault on the absolutism of monarchy and church by musical feeling and Enlightenment thinking (which are linked here rather than counterposed) – all of this unforgettable atmosphere found in Carpentier and Ortiz is very much unlike the overly well-ordered approach found in Adorno and Simpson's framework of contrasts. Ortiz lived to see the official enshrinement of the "people" in post-1959 Cuba (he died in 1969). As a result of the embargo, the island since then has been in every sense an island: surrounded, at times invaded, and cordoned off until recently from the main currents of U.S. public opinion. Much of this setting of difference had begun to change as the special period wore on, and a certain similarity with other Caribbean tourist destinations began to be evident in Havana by the mid to late 1990s.

What is almost never recognized (and a similar point could be made about Haiti in an earlier century for the same reasons) is that Cuba's very pariah status and consequent isolation had for a long time helped preserve its African character as well as its Spanish colonial culture to a degree that struck foreign visitors deeply and surprised them. The indigenous – a concept closely related to authenticity in Ortiz's sense of coming from that sociologically specific stratum known as the folk – became in such sudden apprehensions palpable and intoxicating. The authenticity of Cuba was, in that context, closely related to the relative escape from advertising and consumerism experienced there. Are the isolation of Cuba and its promotion of an indigenousness that is primarily black related? Is it now anathema because it is so publicly and defiantly *popular* in Ortiz's sense (which does not necessarily mean "democratic" as a North American would use the word)? To what degree is the country's socialism based on its investment in the Afro-Cuban, and is this a part of the intoxication the foreign visitor feels? A partial answer to these questions is suggested by exploring another part of the Americas where popular and official art were for a time considered the same.

Nicaragua in the 1980s: a view from the metropolis[25]

Arguments over authenticity are often veiled debates over the pros and cons of capitalist exchange. This is what Adorno and Simpson, among others, force us to concede. In order to clarify those debates, one should take advantage of those rare cases when cultural movements found a way to develop outside the logic of a market. Although it was brought to a close by the combined forces (again) of invasion and embargo, the era of revolutionary Nicaragua (1979–87), should not be considered old news even if it no longer dominates the headlines as it did throughout the 1980s. It allowed us to see an alternative means of gauging what popularity might mean in art, and what claims to the serious such popularity might have.

One of the compelling reasons to explore Nicaraguan popular music is that as part of the larger Caribbean basin, and prominently involved in U.S. cultural and political affairs in an earlier decade, it does not fit easily within the New World African musical complex I have been addressing. Sumu, Rama, Garífono, Eastern European, and North American influences all intermixed there with the African, although the latter is a more minor presence than in either the United States or the Caribbean islands. I would like, for the moment, to suspend that emphasis and consider rather a widely and emotionally supported Christian revolution along socialist lines led by internationalist, foreign-educated intellectuals. My interest is in the effects this political mobilization had on the production of art, primarily music, in a market setting that was highly regulated by a socialist state.[26] It is evident now in retrospect how deeply the Nicaraguan experiment affected U.S. attitudes towards world events. The promise of its rise was as dizzying as the catastrophe of its defeat, and the sudden closing-off of the brief political openings it represented had a good deal to do with the conservatism that swept the United States during the 1990s – not only in government or media circles, but among U.S. youth.

Under the Sandinistas, the alternative to commercial art was not a classical tradition but a popular art that for complicated reasons had assumed the same prestige and authority of what was elsewhere considered "high." The particular audacity of character needed to resist police surveillance under the Somoza dictatorship gave vernacular work an epic character.[27] The Nicaraguan revolution produced a much more fluid relationship between its intellectuals and its ordinary people than was possible in larger countries with less traumatic histories. The term "metropolitan," then, posts a warning: very much of what is not culturally new there is going to be new for North Americans.

Popular culture in this case, then, might be taken not to mean a subset of artistic form but a willingness to consider a multitude of forms simultaneously in order to scrutinize them against the background of their vaunted popularity. The interest is not merely the topical one of the foreign policy conflicts of the early Reagan era. Since 1888, when the great Nicaraguan modernist poet Rubén Darío first entered the literary scene, Nicaragua was given a central place in Latin American poetry.[28] It was the half-*indio* Darío, a figure as towering in Latin American literature as Pablo Neruda, Jorge Luis Borges, and César Vallejo, who in 1888 launched *modernismo*, the movement that marked the final break with

Spanish literary dominance and allowed poets to thematize their lands in native forms for the first time.

The popular is inseparable in this context from the breaking of conventional rules and the shattering of aesthetic icons (not, in other words, a dilution of experimental effort but a challenging break from stale forms of sophistication). Even in the *tertullias* of Spain or France, Nicaragua had achieved a level of distinction. Cardenal, for example, had already a continental reputation for the documentary poem "Zero Hour" among his first published work in the early 1960s. The early Sandinista Vice-President Sergio Ramirez wrote his well-known experimental novel *Te dió miedo la sangre*? (Did the Blood Scare You?) in Germany in the early 1970s; and both treated and exalted the history of Augusto César Sandino, the Sandinistas' namesake, the *indio* father of the country, and the nemesis of the elder Somoza before the *Frente Sandinista* existed. Established writers of the three generations of Nicaraguan literature, all of whom were the recipients of prestigious scholarships, were from the outset participants and leaders in the new directions taken by Nicaraguan culture after 1979 – even Pablo Antonio Cuadra, who opposed the Sandinistas but who founded the Central American University and became (as he would later put it) "passionately involved in the recovery and incorporation of the Indian into our poetry."

Dissolving the hierarchy of skin – commonly perceived as resolving the enigma of the "Indian" in Central America except on the Atlantic coast where former maroon colonies brought the African element prominently into play – was a long-standing feature of the perpetually delayed struggle for democracy. The call of race rings all through the pamphlets and the slogans for more than a century, knitting together the cause of red, white, and black in the celebratory style of Mexican intellectual José Vasconcelos' memorable vision of a wholly desirable miscegenation: the *raza cósmica*. The Sandinistas adapted this same attitude of dissolving invidious distinctions, not only in regard to race but by bridging the gap between those privileged ones who studied abroad and who had been to Europe or the United States (the "been-to's"), on the one hand, and the street vendors, village soldiers, and subsistence farmers, on the other.

To devise a mood allowing for such a translation of the urbane and the erudite into the popular would have been impossible artificially. The general rejection of Somoza's rule by every sector of Nicaraguan society before 1979 made experiments like theirs possible. Not merely the student radicals of the Revolutionary Educational Front (FER), or the Christian base communities of the "Delegates of the Word," but a majority of the landholding and professional classes (whose best-known spokesman had been the assassinated editor of *La Prensa*, Pedro Joaquin Chamorro) plotted Somoza's demise after indignantly finding themselves reduced to the role of flunkies. Cardenal's early documentary poems depict Somoza speaking in a hackneyed English. Somoza's culture, inasmuch as he had any, was what Sergio Ramirez dubbed "the culture of Miami" – the marguerita by the swimming pool, the beauty pageant, Julio Iglesias played loudly on buses, and so on.

Long before anyone believed Somoza would be overthrown militarily, attempts were made to de-legitimize his rule. As a high school student, for example, the now middle-aged former director of Nicaragua's major artists union, Rosario Murillo, founded with Carlos Mejía and David Macfield the group known as "Gradas" whose stated goal was (in the words of Rosario) to "agitate with poems and songs in the streets" and to see the people not merely as recipients but as creators of culture. The much more bookish group around Ramirez and Fernando Gordillo, the "Frente Ventana," published its own clandestine magazine mercilessly exposing the insipid, borrowed culture of the Somoza clique.

When we think of revolution and culture in the same breath, we are conditioned to think in terms of government decrees about the proper and the improper in art. And yet, when I interviewed the Minister of Culture, Ernesto Cardenal or the head of the National Recording Studios, Luis Enrique Mejía Godoy, both were emphatic that cultural questions cannot be solved by decree. Their lament was only that more music like Stevie Wonder or Aretha Franklin was not available; too often they had to settle for Paula Abdul and Billy Joel. According to Cardenal, Nicaragua had no interest in curbing North American mass-culture broadcasts on radio and television, nor did the cultural ministry feel the need to curb what others might call cultural imperialism. Oscar Miranda, director of Sistema Sandinista (the national television network) explained that the problem of restricting content actually originated elsewhere. Since the U.S. embargo prevented them from importing Hollywood films, situation comedies, and soap operas, their greatest difficulty was filling air time. The crisis was not how to prevent U.S. cultural penetration, but how best to maximize the choice that existed before the embargo.

As in other parts of the economy, ownership and control were mixed. It was possible throughout the 1980s to receive as many as fifteen television and eighty radio stations, most of them non-Nicaraguan. This obviously included the Voice of America, and the radio stations of the U.S.-backed mercenaries known as the "contras," which operated from Tegucigalpa in neighboring Honduras as well as from the Costa Rican border regions along with the BBC and Radio Havana. Considered domestically, fifteen radio stations were administered by the Sandinista government while the private sector controlled between fifteen and twenty-five, some of these belonging to the Catholic Church hierarchy.

Metropolitan assumptions tended to distort the media reality. Nicaraguan television under the Sandinistas, for example, consisted of two channels, both of them owned by the government. But it broadcast for only part of the day, reaching only 60 percent of the country, and operated where less than half of the population has access to television sets. Until the embargo, 80 percent of the programming was imported. The system of Nicaraguan popular culture was, partly out of disorganization, partly out of philosophy, decentralized, rife with local disjunctions, made of semi-autonomous departments with different approaches and emphases. Nevertheless, its implicit value lay not only in what was created, but its attempt to create an art intellectually complex and publicly intelligible, affirmative and critical.

The intense press censorship of the Somoza years prior to 1979, for example, led the Union of Radio Journalists of Managua to create what they called "El Periodismo Catacumbas" (The Journalism of the Catacombs), a system of interpersonal communication enacted in secret church meetings and leaflets. It was with the help of stolen equipment and union expertise that the clandestine Radio Sandino began to broadcast by 1978 – a development that Humberto Ortega, the brother of the first president following the victory, considered to have been the precondition of the Sandinistas' coming to power.

Sandinista sympathizers communicated with the people for the most part through leaflets, flyers, *pintas* (graffiti), the seizure of radio stations, and through the broader counterculture itself, expressed brilliantly in the *muralista* movement, which has its own interesting history.[29] The birth of the national cinema, for example, can be found in the documentary war footage shot by FSLN regulars on the Southern Front. Its participants would later staff the Nicaraguan Film Institute. Other important countercultural projects were found in popular song. The best example of this is the now legendary album *Guitarra Armada* written by Carlos and Luis Enrique Mejía Godoy, broadcast over the airwaves of underground Radio Sandino in 1978. Its lyrics helped train urban youth in the use of weapons and explosives which were then needed for self-defense (this was a period in which Somoza's army was engaged in the aerial bombing of Nicaragua's cities using U.S. low-tech aircraft).[30]

Whether these ever actually reached enough combatants to be useful in training, or whether they were technical enough to be a bona fide military tool, is open to question. There is no doubt, though, that they communicated indirectly to well-wishers abroad, effectively arguing that armed resistance was justified and that military victory was possible (which very few supposed at the time, including Sandinista supporters). And later, in retrospect, after the Somoza regime had collapsed and there was no longer fighting in the streets, the songs of *Guitarra Armada* became the stuff of vernacular epic. They offered a peculiar blending of the jovial rhythms of carnival, the accordion laughter of a village fair, and a serious message about how to use and care for rifles and explosives. Nothing could be starker than the absence in *this* military of somber faces, hard boot clacks on the regimental pavement, or the barking antiphon of crew-cutted recruits in uniform. This was a new kind of military, not only very young but rebellious, playful, cheeky, and overwhelmingly Christian. Their rebellion was not about style or generational conflict. And there was no romancing of the gun either, the kind one finds in NRA rallies or high school shooting tragedies by the disaffected readers (and misreaders) of *Left Behind*. Rather, weapons were de-mythologized. In one of the songs, a narrator singing in a slow and sensitive voice conjures the image of a sniper who in looking down the barrel of his or her gun must learn to shoot "*sin amor, sin odio*" – that is, without a personal emotional investment in destroying another life, either out of love or hate.

The violation of these expectations frames the entire album, and should be contrasted to the apocalyptic gangsta stance of, for example, contemporary Mexican *narcocorrido*, with its affection for outlaws heroically avenging the crimes of the powerful by the acts of the brazen popular criminal.[31] This music, by contrast, like much of the culture produced during the Sandinista years, is a rare combination of Christian socialism and pragmatic acceptance of the often uninviting steps necessary for seizing power. The ethical outlook of the album is rare for adopting the role of warrior without glorifying violence or fetishizing resistance.

What kind of aesthetic is this? Luis Enrique Mejía Godoy wrote of the need "to organize the heart" (*organizar el corazón*). One can see what that means in practice when looking at the album's role playing and dialogue: its orchestration consists of a marimba, accordion, and guitar backing up a brash mariachi-like vocal style that gives way in other cuts to the softer tones of *música romántica*. The following lyrics from a typical *Guitarra Armada* son are sung quickly and lightheartedly, *allegro con brio*:

Its powerful bullet can hit a target five blocks away
Weighs only ten pounds and has an eight-cartridge clip
The Garand rifle is made up of three pieces:
The bolt action, the firing chamber, and the barrel itself
Before using it, you have to come to know its parts.
Let's lay them out now, left to right, which is the best way to get acquainted with them
First, let's take out the cartridge clip and give it a good inspection
Because when the bullets are flying, you don't want to put yourself in an even worse situation.
Chorus: Of all rifles, the Garand is the top dog
It fires a 36 caliber round
If you want to take it apart, you better follow these instructions to the letter
Knit that brow and concentrate, then prick up your ears and listen to this song.[32]

In lyrics that at first seem incapable of emotion or drama (just step-by-step instructions) the sheer understatement and insouciance of the protagonist giving the lesson underlines the urgency of the situation. As I learned from playing these songs to white middle-class Guatemalans in the mid-1980s under the Vinicio Cerezo presidency (a year after the dictatorship of Rios Montt and the worst massacres there by the Guatemalan army), they had the capacity of thrilling their listeners who could not believe their ears. The audacity of it forced the audience to smile as though experiencing a forbidden pleasure.

Carlos Mejía Godoy's *Missa Campesina* (Peasant Mass) had a profound effect on many Catholics still not swayed by the punishing rebukes delivered against the Sandinistas (particularly against the Jesuit, Ernesto Cardenal, then Minister of Culture) by Cardinal Miguel Obando y Bravo and, eventually, Pope John Paul II during his visit to the country. Its musical liturgy reinterpreted the Gospel by portraying Christ as a Nicaraguan *campesino* martyred by the National Guard. For youth, there was the rock group Pancasán with its agitational song *"Pueblo, Ejercito, Unidad"* (People, Army, Unity). All of this was combined with the cultural groups based in the universities. As one of the Sandinista leaders, Bayardo Arce, put it: their answer to disco was testimonial music, to Pope John Paul II, the Vatican Council.[33] The pop recording star, Francisco Seveño, tried to link the musical innovation to a broader social program when he referred to the ongoing Autonomy talks then taking place among the Indian and black minorities living on Nicaragua's Atlantic Coast:

[Our job is] to find the rhythm of each place. If we are national musicians, then we realize that there is more than one rhythm to Nicaragua. To be very Nicaraguan is to be universal. We don't stop music at our borders out of some chauvinistic urge.

The musician Luis Enrique Mejía Godoy had his own way of expressing the same inclusivity when he identified the point of his music as being the expression of a certain type: *Nicarafricanico*. Like many of the Latin American Left since the time of José Martí, he gave the distinctively American mixture of peoples a positive spin, and gave voice again to a "hybridity" that found its way into North American cultural theory in the 1980s and 1990s.

But it was Carlos Mejía Godoy who managed best to translate this sensibility to music, fusing the marimba and accordion of traditional Nicaraguan folk music (as Ortiz meant "folk") with themes and styles relevant to the new Sandinista political reality. Co-author (with his brother Luis Enrique) of the Sandinista National Hymn – an official marching song ritually performed at public ceremonies – he nevertheless was famous for a very different kind of song. His "La Tula Cuecho," for instance, is very far from protest art.[34] This outrageous song has much more in common with Chaucer's "Wife of Bath" tale or the characters of the Decameron than anything else in Latin music. It is the portrait of a village type, the gossip, a woman who (as he puts it) "unsheathes" her tongue to gab in public places, and give her listeners such a word-thrashing that her tongue can be seen dangling around her pendulous breasts in the city square. At one point in the song, the lead singer joins the chorus in a verbal tour de force, rattling off lines rapidly without pauses, and without taking a breath, to simulate the torrent of verbiage emanating from the loud mouth of La Tula Cuecho.

The brothers Mejía Godoy, who are almost completely ignored in studies of Latin American music, can be seen from this vantage point to be among the most innovative composers of the Americas in recent decades. But fitting no established categories, they suffer the fate Phillip Sweeney described when writing about African pop prior to the invention of "world music." The first reaction of most Western pop music critics to Carlos Mejía Godoy's song "El licenciado de la pobreza" (the degree-holder in poverty) for example, would likely be to discount it as a politically correct pose. But like "La Tula Cuecho," the song proceeds with a boisterous energy, employing a stage-laughter reminiscent of the signature howls of the Mexican mariachi star, Vicente Fernández. The song tells the story of those children of the rich who go abroad to study "en Britannia o Gringolandia," returning with fancy degrees and an attitude. Most of the kids on the street are silenced by the airs put on by the "been-to's," but Carlos gives them an answer. You too hold a degree, he points out. "How do you figure, man?" they ask. Just say this, he counsels: "It's true I'm not well read, and haven't had time to study/ any of the disciplines/ But I'm a graduate of experience /The courses I took/ Gave me PhD in poverty . . ."[35]

Although the Nicaraguan and Cuban revolutions were very different, including in their political goals, they arrived very quickly at a similar aesthetic attitude. It is striking how little theoretical attention is given to analyzing this attitude on its own terms by popular music criticism today. In the first years after the Cuban revolution, the nightclub mambos that had entertained tourists were quickly appropriated by artists eager to turn them to new ends. Quarteto D'Aida's "Yo, si!, tumbo caña" is just such a use of the mambo. A pure dance sound is wed to an enthusiastic embrace of the new order, including its actual policies: "I too am going to go cut sugar cane, damn straight." An inauthentic statement? There is no musical evidence (given the brilliance of the performance) to believe this, in part because there is no indication at all of those stagy or insincere sentiments one finds in national hymns or pious patriotic songs learned in grade-school civic classrooms. They seem to be, in fact, popular declarations, and the artistic integrity of the songs, as songs, suggests this is so. From Duo los Compadres' (pre-revolutionary) "Págame la caña bien" – a fast-paced, angry *guajira* about a sugarcane cutter whose foreman won't let him rest, and who threatens to leave for the capital if he's not paid better – to Carlos Puebla's (post-revolutionary) *trova* "El comité de defensa" we find an actual tradition of working-class populism whose genius is very rarely a topic for examination in popular music criticism.[36] We barely have a vocabulary for talking about it. What metropolitan audiences see as routine didacticism is a bona fide tradition with genuine popular sources.

Schmaltz as a category of popular art

If popular art in colonial contexts is often wrongly labeled "agitprop," it is also the case that agitprop itself is too easily dismissed as artistically impoverished or predictable. Why this would be requires an explanation. The aesthetic thrill of agitprop is evidently palpable, involving as it does the intellect, powers of decision-making, and outlets for aggressive emotional resistance. To be involved in consuming an art that offers these angry compensations is exhilarating and fully consonant with the purely formalist stricture that the aesthetic experience must always entail pleasure. But the metropolitan critic still lacks a vocabulary for appreciating the popular arts of developing countries when they attempt to sketch out clear political alternatives. Some of the reviews of David Kunzle's wonderful book, *The Revolutionary Murals of Nicaragua*, for example, show the problems with this peremptory attitude. After calling the author "shrill and partisan," one reviewer claimed to see nothing artistically valuable in the paintings themselves (even though they were awarded international prizes and attracted admiring visitors from around the world before being destroyed by Managua's mayor in the post-Sandinista period). The reviewer's judgment is absolute and unforgiving: "The Nicaraguan murals present a trite array of muscular peasants, workers, and martyrs familiar from a host of American post office walls and Soviet posters."[37]

The allusion to Soviet posters is especially interesting because their multicolored textures, sculpted bodies that appear to be made of stone, steep vanishing points and acute angles of vision, as well as their experiments with text/image layouts inspired the later poster art of Catalonia, Mozambique, Angola, Bengal and, for that matter, the United States during the popular front and World War II. To dismiss the Nicaraguan murals as "only a record of foreign and native agitprop" is to delay a reckoning with the aesthetic similarity of popular movements separated by culture and years – the scope of its differently configured sense of beauty that is remarkably unified by a political (rather than ethnic or regional) outlook on the world. How is it that so many people from so many different times and places found their way back to this aesthetic of the popular-organic with its celebration of community and heroizing of labor? What does it say about those who mock it for being "trite"?

The range of aesthetic options in Latin music, similarly, is subject to some of the same unsupported devaluations. Ismail Rivera's "Moliendo café" (grinding coffee), for example, is a fully developed social realism that one would never think of dispatching as socialist realism.[38] The title (possibly a sexual double entendre) is laid out in images of tedious, everyday toil. The pastoral of the Puerto Rican *cordillera* is the background for the singer who describes hearing a bitter song of sadness and love sung by an old woman grinding coffee: the song vibrates in the distance as night falls on a coffee plantation. In this, as in hundreds of typical songs from the salsa canon (Bobby Capo's "El

Negro bembón," Luigi Texidor's "La Pobreza y yo," El Gran Combo's "Y no Haga mas Na'," and Joe Arroyo's "Olores," to take only a few examples), a vast portrait of proletarian everyday life is presented without fake humility.[39] Proud in its own way, it is also unsentimental, philosophical, and self-aware. This evocation of labor, at any rate, has deep roots in salsa's relationship to the *son,* especially its literary form, where a repertoire of puns uniting the movements of performing and dancing with everyday work is large. In the *son* de la Má Teodora, the expression 'rajar la leña' [chop the wood] is taken to mean 'to be at a dance,' that is, working:

> It's interesting to note that this kind of idiomatic substitution – the idea of a noisy party, by means of an ironic allusion to work – is something that created a true tradition in the popular music of Cuba . . . "Cazar el verraco" [hunt the boar], "sacar la manteca" [remove the lard] were equivalents of "to dance."[40]

"La expresiva" – an early *timba* offering by the contemporary Cuban group N. G. La Banda – is one more typical example of a music steeped in the principles of situatedness in place, pride in a neighborhood, joy in plebeian creativity while being, at the same time, critical of government (the Cuban government, in this case) and aligned with the strategies of disgruntled, anti-authoritarian youth. The harsh dividing line between a song like "La expresiva" and, say, Madonna's "Express Yourself" is not, as one might think, between socialism and the liberatory wings of niche marketing, but between third and first worlds – between those for whom a sense of devised collectivity is a matter of survival and those for whom it is a matter of taste. As we have seen before, neglect and marginality have helped keep Latin music's plebeian ethos authentic, even against its own wishes perhaps.

Many salsa songs are a familiar twist on the proletarian folk-epic stream across the genres, and not limited to socialist societies. Tommy Olivencia's "*Santero,*" for example, is a loving portrait of the popular reliance on *santería* to heal wounded love, break the spell of infertility, or scare away premature death.[41] Crucial to stress, though, is the versatility of an ostensibly somber subject like communion with the gods. The song's spoken refrain – "*oraciones y novenas*" (prayers and novenas) – is uttered in an affectionate, almost mocking tone as it recites to an upbeat tempo the tools of the *santero's* trade (scapulas, rosaries, and votive candles) while wincing at the vulnerability of those who depend on such fragile instruments during a crisis. The Mighty

Sparrow's calypso, "Obeah Woman," is even more irreverent, winking at the audience about a community type they all know well.[42] The woman of the song's title practices the dark arts to win her man while the man himself – played by the singer – scoffs, protesting that her voodoo will not work. Try taking a shower and brushing your teeth first, he says. No need to threaten divine intervention when you're too ugly and ridiculous to get a man in any case.

The sincerity of neo-African religion in the popular music of the Americas is of a piece with its representations of everyday working-class life. For just this reason, both have been questioned. If the presence of neo-African cult belief was natural to the music performed in turn-of-the-century Cuban *cabildos* or in the ceremonies of the *reglas de ocha*; if it is unambiguously heroic in the forms it takes in modern *rumba* or the homiletic popularizations of the *cantos* to the *orishas* in a performer like Celina González; and if it plays a political role by alluding to the mystery of popular, indigenous power in the nationalist sentiments of 1960s and 1970s salsa, it is also an element considered dangerous and even unseemly for many Latin musicians from a different class position. In *Music in Cuba*, Carpentier gives a sense of the psychology lying behind this avoidance:

> The invocations to Erzili, the Assotor Drum, all maintained their traditional roles, principally in the slave workforce, where the magic rituals, the religion of Papá Legba and Ogun Ferraille were on the way to becoming a political weapon. For the concubine mulatto woman of the French settler who liked to be call Madame; for the musician who made a living playing at white parties; for the quadroon, the bold or simply dark-skinned person admitted to masqued balls as long as he did not abandon his box seat; for all those who could join in with the pleasant life of the city, voodoo was a sinister throwback to rural life, a carryover reminiscent of whips and stocks best left behind in the narrow street.[43]

The political significance, then, of injecting African religion into salsa's refashioning of Cuban mambo should not be underestimated. Willie Rosario's version of Machito's "Chango 'ta Beni" (Shango is coming) demonstrates the unexpected ways that religious figures are staged in contemporary salsa performance, and moves the question of authenticity again into the realm of African spirituality. Here, ordinary life is very far from irony and pastiche.[44] The mood is entirely different from Olivencia and Sparrow, carried on without jesting, and appealing less to the mundane glories of the everyday than to the wonders of nature – the world outside human control. We have in this arrangement a kind of exaltation. The large ensemble is heavy on brass played in a tight and disciplined unison, the lyrics punctuated with long, interspersed wails of joy. It is, when one first hears it, similar to straight party music without a hint of its more serious function. Its story not only alludes to the street-level practices of the folk religion of Latin neighborhoods (as above) but constructs a cinematic moment where the *santería* pantheon is translated for common use:

> Shango is coming, Shango is coming, Shango is coming./ With a machete in his hand, he comes to destroy the world/ The stomping of his feet through the valley, makes the earth tremble. [Chango 'ta beni, Chango 'ta beni, Chango 'ta beni/ Con el machete en la mano, mundo va acabar/, tierra va temblar . . .

One can almost see the small landholder on the *cordillera* north of Ponce looking to the sky as a thunderstorm enters the valley.

Could it be that the resistance of Latin music to assimilation, and its being turned into background music by its English-speaking audience, is related to its uncomfortable reminder of a popular culture (in the class-oriented sense developed by Ortiz)? This would be a layer of inaccessibility much greater than the idiomatic Spanish of its lyrics, or the degree of discipline needed to dance it properly (a discipline always terrifying to the uninitiated). More interesting is the way these complex factors are understood as simple matters of taste.

One of the strongest reasons that Latin music remains both outside the world music circuits and, until recently, slighted in accounts of popular music, is that it is judged by most U.S. and European audiences as schmaltz. The whole visual presentation of the salsa combo on CD covers and on club stages seems to most mainstream North Americans to be hokey. For prevailing tastes, there is a dated-ness to the hairdos and flouncy sleeves as though taken from a store window of a cheap beauty salon in the wrong part of town. The acrylic shirts buttoned halfway up the chest seem tacky. And the sound too, then, joins the general impression, having about it an old-fashioned feel that is vulgar, brash, and kitschy. In other words, there is a deep cultural disapproval – part ethnic, part having to do with status. There has always been, then, a disconnect between the long associations of Latin music with certain popular or traditional hits like "Guantanamera," "The Copacabana," "Lemon Tree," "The Girl from Ipanema," the "Mexican Hat Dance," and so on, and the inappropriate, alienating feel of these ostensible hits to anyone who knows anything about Latin musical traditions, or about how people consume music in various actual Latin American locations, what kind of music is attractive to what class of person, and so on.[45]

But the disapproval and distancing is very obvious in the way Latin music is often presented in popular television shows and films in the United States: Jim Carey's Carmen Miranda imitation in *The Mask*, the impromptu rumba danced by Leslie Nielsen and Priscilla Presley in *Naked Gun 2½* with that old routine of the index finger touched to alternate elbows, John Candy's Latin headdress gag on Second City television. In spite of sincere attempts by the now hopelessly old-fashioned crooners of another era to mainstream the Latin sound as more or less romantic (Perry Como's "Papa Loves Mambo," for instance), the associations with schmaltz are only reinforced today by being forced to think of Como himself when thinking of the mainstreaming of Latin music. This then would be another and related, aspect of Latin schmaltz.

A feel for this agonizing disconnect is central to Ruben Blades's compelling film *Crossover Dreams*, as well as in other attempts in commercial film to bridge this gap (in *La Bamba*, *Selena*, and more recently in Marc Anthony's biopic on Hector Lavoe, *El Cantante*). The careers of musicians and impresarios like the Spanish-born, Cuban-based Xaviar Cugat; the Cuban-born, American-based Desi Arnaz, or (less well known, but more salient here) the Scotsman Roberto Inglez (né Bob Inglis) are more complicated. As a bandleader between 1946 and 1954, "Roberto Inglez" sold millions of arrangements by Ernesto Lecuona, Osvaldo Farrés, Zeguinha Abreu, and Ary Barroso in a style molded to the sensibilities of the schmaltzy stringed orchestras of easy listening, usually in combination with arrangements of Chopin, Schubert, and Cole Porter. In his rendering, in fact, all were equally Latinized (Chopin included) and indistinguishable from the others: a uniform, furiously tame and mellowed music for the middle-aged and elderly at the Savoy Hotel ballroom, where he frequently performed.[46]

Every American's or European's view of Latin music is affected by this collection of pop vehicles that serve to disfigure and demote the seriousness of the culture for metropolitan listeners. Although many resist seeing the matter this way, the aesthetic impasses here – too often written off with terms like "schmaltz" and "kitsch" or (somewhat differently) "agitprop" – are completely bound up with issues that are not always ethnic, racial, or even linguistic. They have to do with social status, colonial condescensions, assumptions about proper political norms, and, in a word, *class*. Understanding what is "classical" about Latin music means getting past these prejudices, which also means getting past the prejudice that authenticity is an empty concept. On the contrary, it is completely valid, and is the only way to make sense of the ongoing war over musical taste.

4

Rap and American Business

> I like opera 'cause it has rape, gangs, drugs . . . it's the most realistic art form.
>
> *Geto Boys*

Hip-hop and salsa grew up in the same New York, only blocks apart, both products of the late 1960s and 1970s. Loud and audacious, both actually were symptoms of a cooling down – an era of retreat from a critical decade in which Hollywood was still capable of making films that portrayed everyday people (wage earners, housewives) in a tragic and heroic way (*Norma Rae*, *Blue Collar*, and *The Deer Hunter*).

Reeling from the new rise of the heroin trade in U.S. inner cities, edgily watching the first waves of gentry into New York's poor but available communities, and out-maneuvered by the British rock invasion, hip-hop as a lifestyle came to reign only after the destruction of the civil rights movement – a destruction that some rap enthusiasts have lately applauded with all the fanfare of a counter-movement.[1] Others saw it as a desperate preservation of small essentials by a community of strategically unemployed and hounded teenagers with their backs against the wall or (just as common), black and white college kids from the suburbs who found strength in a certain image of blackness in order to send a message to the coming "me" decades. They decided to trade in their claim to national and civic attention for a lifestyle that pissed people off while giving financial power to those lucky few among them who could buy a mansion on a southern California hill.

As Raquel Rivera points out – and as early hip-hop films like *Wild Style* testify – New York Latinos were deeply involved in the creation of hip hop from the start.[2] Steven Hager's *Beat Street* bears witness to the central role of Puerto Ricans in the New York graffiti movement, for example, which is to say that rap (not *Latin* rap, but rap) was made in black and Latin communities with all kinds of people taking part. This would seem unusual only to those unfamiliar with the Bronx and its many criss-crossing communities. The joint efforts are even less surprising when one considers the Caribbean musical contributions to rap itself: the borrowings from Jamaican dancehall, Count Matchukie's "versatility at the microphone," the early rap beats' taken from Puerto Rican *plena* and *aguinaldos*, the similarity between the drum breaks and scratching of rap and Caribbean percussion techniques, the whole competition aspect of the boast with its roots (among other places) in the physical showdowns of the *calinda* (stick fighting) dance as well as the social satiric heart of the lyrics of *calypso* (the form that governs the dance competitions of Trinidad carnival).[3]

Hip-hop in its formative phase did not embrace Latin music consciously, however. It remained (as I have been arguing) "background music" – always present, usually noticed, sometimes loved, but rarely acknowledged. Afrika Bambaataa grooved the crowds at his DJ-ing sessions in 1973 with "Latin-tinged funk," which he claimed got the crowd moving more than reggae. His audience insisted they did not like the Latin sound, but he would throw out a break while concealing its source, and the dancers would go "crazy."[4] Juan Flores writing about Puerto Rican music in New York tells a similar story about Charlie Chase, born in El Barrio in the 1950s, who recalls at a hip-hop house party "sneaking in the beat from the number 'Tú Coqueta,' right 'in the middle of a jam. I'm jamming, I throw that sucker in, just the beat alone, and they'd go off. They never knew it was a Spanish record.'"[5] These were the crowds, it should be remembered: who defined rap taste in the all-important early days.

My own questions, though, have less to do with Latino contributions to rap or rap's Caribbean influences than the different musical responses offered by rap and salsa in the 1970s. The sense of an impending social storm was evident in both, and later borne out in the Reagan years, which saw the beginnings of the dismantling of welfare, the rise of the religious right, a new Cold War chill, vast media centralization, the launching of the war on "terrorism," and a bolder "cooler" racism, expressed without apologies by an increasing number of public figures and media celebrities.[6] Rap and salsa, although both art forms based on embattled self-assertion, represented a cultural fork in the road. They moved in decisively different directions even though they were created in the same (by U.S. standards, highly integrated) barrios of a single city in almost exactly the same years.

The salsa musician and teacher Marco Katz has written of returning to his old haunts in New York where he had played throughout the 1970s.

Looking back, he paints a picture of the South Bronx during the rise of salsa:

> Driving along in silent disbelief, bassist Goodwin Benjamin and I contemplated the burned-out streets of what had once been the South Bronx neighborhoods where we used to make our livings playing salsa. There was no more Hunts Point Palace, nor was there a Cerromar Casino. In fact, there was nothing but the unvaried sight of vacant lots along quiet streets that, several years earlier, had hummed with activity day and night. The eighties had begun and salsa was only a small part of the vast culture being swept away by the razing of buildings and a rising tide of gentrification.[7]

For two decades the music saturated the barrios where rap would see its rise. This music, he recalls, was everywhere "on the streets of our neighborhoods, through the walls of our apartments, and in the stores and restaurants we frequented the steady background for our work, love, and dreams."[8]

The rise of salsa in New York was the work of Caribbean bridge communities, everyday people of modest means who had kept their attachments to *bohio* culture, and who played with open emotions and a sincerity that seemed out of touch with the alert cynicism that governed most U.S. commentary.[9] Its images were drawn from a small-town culture of the old fashioned, the formal, and the wryly humorous, and it met the challenges of "becoming American" with a deliberate nostalgia, reluctantly accepting new habits of consumption and more distracted kind of human interaction. This is not to say that market pressures had no effect on the styles and contents of salsa, or that there were no forces working against this general outlook.[10] As an aesthetic, the music operated in two registers, conversant with mass culture but surrounded by the strangeness both of the language of English and of a society of fast-paced impersonal competition. Thoroughly cosmopolitan and modern, salsa nevertheless sought an image that appealed to the rural by paying homage, first of all, to a classical popular canon. It set out to re-interpret for new generations already established Latin masterpieces – the principle employed, for example, by La Sonora Ponceña, Los Soneros del Barrio, Eddie Palmieri, El Gran Combo, or in the *rumbero* gestures of the polished, old-style *charangas* of Ray Barretto. This Latin classicism involved an explicit enlistment of the trappings of the *son*, the open use of neo-African religion, and the idealization of the countryside, evident, among other places, in Ismael Rivera con Los Cachimbos'

"Soy Boricua" and "Mi Negrita me Espera" or in Justo Betancourt's "Pa' Bravo Yo." They were alluding also to the colonial past, as in Cheo Feliciano's "Anacaona." Not all of these artists were New York–based, but the airline routes between New York and San Juan made the experiences of both places a shared one in many ways.

Rap could not be more different. Its audience took media saturation for granted, and its lyrics were packed with allusions to the likes of Oprah Winfrey, bad 1950s sci-fi, and clips from the evening news. The world it invented was not, in fact, always cacophonous, nervous, angry, or apocalyptic. It could be moody and sentimental as well. But it always teetered on the sharp edge of present and future, seeing everything (above all itself) as disposable, on the move, assaulted by a crazed dynamic of power and official lying. So what is its place in a study of Afro-Latin music? If the neo-African, as we have been showing, is often consumed by audiences that sense in it an escape from modernity, the theme and reality of rap is just the opposite: a merging of protest and big business, or rather, the big business of protest. According to key producers, rap is driving the entire music industry today, accounting not only for most of its sales, but for the sales of other genres as well. Between 1984 and 1989 alone – that is, well before its peak – it grossed over $300 million.[11]

There were always counter-trends, then and now. The works that opted out of the business pitch were among the most interesting currents of rap and, some would say, its only true form. The content, styles, and even the modes of distribution of early KRS-One, Poor Righteous Teachers, and Gang Starr's Guru all militated against the bling-bling common sense of MTV and the Grammys, and this commitment is still very lively – in fact, unquenchable as an essential component of rap philosophy – as seen in today's indie scene by performers like Aesop Rock, El-P, Cannibal Ox, Sage Francis, and Immortal Technique, among others.

By seeing rap from a New World perspective – that is, as part of a larger New World complex of musics – we can begin to see one of its crucial aesthetic and social functions. Rap was called forth by a need within the traditions of secular devotion to provide a word-centered, oral-literary component to beat: the component missing from African-American holism but found in a number of Latin American genres that combine and hold in tension those essential neo-African components of ecstasy and challenge, leisure and social commentary. It had to arise, even if belatedly, in order to provide the essential satirical content that in other corners of the Americas was available in musical dance genres like *guaracha* and calypso, and that was so deeply a part of the sensibility of neo-African spirituality in its popular cultural guise.[12] The politics of rap is divided, not only in the above senses but in another sense as well: it is torn between its mission of critique and its role in creating a pure dance form lacking in the pop R&B that prevailed during the years when it was entering the mainstream (the late 1980s and early 1990s). Neither the dance element nor the satirical element was available in jazz after it became "America's music" and a massively popular form, and after its later flight from the mainstream to bebop and "cool" took the form of an experimentalism reserved for connoisseurs and spectators sitting on chairs.

This diffusion, I am suggesting, is exactly mirrored in the rise of *timba* music in Cuba, which I discuss in Chapter 5. *Timba* is the *música bailable* (dance music) designed to offer alternatives for Cuba's black communities to established folkloric neo-African forms like the *cantos* to the *orishas* and traditional rumba along with the intellectual folk and protest music known as *nueva trova*. It does this in the name of appealing, among other things, to a certain positive vision of the wily entrepreneur in a savage market. Like a good deal of rap, it invented a stage persona who, as the hero of the song, displays an eagerness to make as much money as possible no matter who it hurts or how. That *timba* in Cuba has been promoted under the banner of a new black identity politics is all the more reason to see parallels not only between it and rap but between commercial salsa and the Cuban music exported to the United States in the 1940s and 1960s. This is an approach that has not been pursued, but that offers a number of informative parallels among different sites of a common New World African music.

Rap took a romanticized image of a specific black social type – insolent and unemployed – and made it mainstream. The class fraction it latched onto, and chose as a fictional stand-in for blackness itself, was not at all the one idealized in blues, jazz, gospel, or Motown. Although a great deal has been said about rap's borrowing from earlier African-American "baadman" narratives like Stagolee, there is a problem with this thesis. The well-known blues ballad actually portrays Stagolee as a monster, not as a resourceful and irreverent outlaw. It is good to remember that the story of Stagolee is told in sympathy with his victim, Billy DeLisle. Even "Superfly" – who is much closer to the type found in rap – possesses the '60s mentality of an urban guerrilla battling the corrupt police; his vision is more Robin Hood than Meyer Lansky. And so rap, in some ways, does not easily fit these traditions even though it is frequently considered to have done so.

A number of media commentators in the early 1990s dwelled on the apparent contradiction in rap between its narrative logic of making the lumpen a defiant hero and its warm commercial welcome. To a point, the observation was true enough since rap's supposed alternative to the postmodern age of Reaganism was, at least in its mack-daddy variant, little more than a twist on the "me" generation it was supposedly rejecting. Although rap was dependent on samples from earlier African-American music, it was essentially abolishing the ethics and politics that inspired it. But this sort of debate takes a different turn in African-American expressive forms because of the historical exclusion of blacks from the U.S. economy where commercial acceptance, even though poised to undermine the music's danger, remains a major goal of the project from the start. The protest of rap is less in the lyrics than on the charts; the intended goal of this sort of protest is to be included in the money-making ventures typically denied the black unemployed (whether or not the rap performers really belonged to this sector is not the key issue).

Lumpen bourgeoisie

My argument in this section is based on an essay I published in 1994 on rap aesthetics – especially its encyclopedic character and its glorification of the business world it sought to enter.[13] When the essay appeared, little had been written about the art of rap, and practically nothing about the paradoxes of its first signs of entering the pop charts. What dominated people's attentions at the time was its links to the outlaw legends of African-American oral myth – an approach that almost always led in a sociological rather than sonoric direction.[14]

The cultural commentary that focused on Madonna, romance novels, computer hackers, and rock in the years of pomo ascendancy (the 1980s) dwarfed that on rap, although one could still argue that only Madonna came close to matching hip-hop's shaping of an emergent international style (and it is rap rather than Madonna, I think, that realized it).[15] What was generally not done in those years was to claim that the pleasures of rap, like the colors of da Vinci or the polyphonies of Bach, had to be learned deliberately as a matter of art appreciation. Or that those who could not, at least by projection, understand such pleasures were in some basic sense uneducated. The obstacles to this training deserve study. For even supposed allies in the multicultural crusade had a zero threshold of tolerance when it came to hip-hop, even after its later runaway acceptance. It is not difficult to find intellectuals who value dub, country western, acid, or reggae but still find rap repetitive, childish, and ugly. Like the novel, rap is perpetually announced to have already seen its day, as being defunct and over the hill, when it continues to march on and gather strength.

Throughout the 1980s and 1990s, rap tended to be fenced in, not liberated, by the familiar frames of Los Angeles (after the riots), the censorship debate prompted by the 2 Live Crew and Tupac episodes, and meditations on the "crisis of the black family." This containment was not the work only of doughty assaults on black youth in the mainstream media. The counter-assault by liberal thinkers and tuned-in journalists led to a similar diminishing critical range. Although gangsta rap is by no means an exclusively West Coast form, most rap criticism of any kind originally centered overwhelmingly on West Coast artists. East Coast rap – which accounts for the majority of artists in the brilliant indie rap camp (mostly from New York and Philadelphia) – joins the strong scene of American cities like Houston, Chicago, Atlanta, and Minneapolis in carving out a space for rap left over from Nike commercials and the awards shows.

The work of Cheryl L. Keyes is crucial here. Her approach to rap is primarily verbal, and she explores less hip-hop culture as a whole than rap, which she defines as "a musical form that makes use of rhyme, rhythmic speech, and street vernacular, which is recited or loosely changed over a musical soundtrack."[16] It is this focus on the cut which leads her to make a distinction between West Coast and East Coast that manages to avoid the hyped gang war imagery that I alluded to in Chapter 1. She has found the right emphasis, I think, when she points out that West Coast rap is associated with funk and gangsta whereas East Coast depends on "verbosity and rapid execution over musical soundtracks that vary from sparsely textured mixes to hard bop, soul, jazz and Jamaican dancehall . . . Verbal dexterity is one of the distinguishing features of New York or East Coast MCs."[17]

The early gangsta successes of Ice-T, Ice Cube, and NWA were catapulted into a national issue by the L.A. riots. This paved the way for a second wave copping the formula of the first, and hungrily greeted by a record industry largely based in Los Angeles; a movie industry close at hand to help mythify the gangsta leads in first-run, mass-distribution films; and studios where L.A. television shows could further perpetuate those well-known images associated with California life: laid-back surfers, sexily dressed women hangin' by the beach, and above all, driving nice cars. When that second wave took shape as Dre and Snoop Doggy Dogg, the California easy life got grafted onto the earlier motifs of L.A. gangsta rap: run-ins with the police, climbing out of poverty by any means necessary, and so on. That formula of mixing black desperation with Hollywood, perfected by Dre and Snoop Dogg, spawned hundreds of rap videos that still fill some rap showcases as gangsta's third and fourth waves. The move was symbolized best by the physical move from the inner city of Compton to the suburb of Long Beach under Snoop Dogg's influence, which led to the big success of Warren G.'s West Coast Funk, a sound that can only be called "Jeep Music."[18]

But in sketching out this history, there is a talking at cross purposes. What "rap music" actually refers to is uncertain. The whole musical sense, the message, and the audience of, say, Kanye West or El-P, on the one hand, and Too Short or Eve, on the other, are bound to lead to confusion. From the start, there has been a sharp division between underground (or independent) rap production and commercial rap, and there are dozens of gradations within. One has to go out of one's way to find the rap that isn't blaring from the networks and major radio stations, but only doing so will make the point that radio-rap and indie-rap are entirely different branches of the genre of music defined by Keyes above. Throughout the 1990s, and in many circles today, the entire discussion has centered on rap as a sociological problem rather than an art form, let alone one with links to other non-U.S. African diasporic genres.[19]

It is good to remember how far, and low, the abuse against rappers had gone by the mid-1990s, for it helps explain why so much of the rap commentary stuck to the basic task of defending an angry music from the rage of the moral panic. Conservative columnist Mona Charen in the *Chicago Tribune* sneered, for example, about 2 Live Crew's ungrammatical speech ("people does") and labeled the lyrics not obscene nor pornographic, which are technical terms, but with a wink in the direction of Chicago's then-new white mayor, "barbarous."[20] Apparently she had not gotten around to reading the linguistic scholarship on African-American vernacular English, which shows it to be "a product of free African slave labor, having evolved from a seventeenth-century pidgin English that was a lingua franca in linguistically diverse enslavement communities throughout Britain's North American colonies, and based on the Niger-Congo family of African languages (for example, Yoruba, Wolof, Efik, Twi)."[21] This language includes features that have been well marked by linguists: multiple negation, the aspectual "be" to indicate iterativity, the zero copula, and semantic inversion (a.k.a. "flippin the script").[22] Paul Delaney in the *New York Times* had more the air of the ingratiating shrink. Explaining the behavior of "crotch-holding rap artists," he averred that "as more teen-age girls became mothers, their sons grew up hating what in their minds their mothers represented –

'bitches' and 'ho's' This left the boys with serious problems in dealing with women." Delaney quickly abandoned psychoanalysis, though, to talk in a franker and more revealing register about rappers as "scheming, bumbling buffoons."[23]

A decade and half later in 2006, Erik Eckholm in the *New York Times* focused on one Byron Hurt, a former fan of hip-hop who now, as a thirty-six-year-old filmmaker with dreadlocks, tries to wean kids off the music.[24] The article offers an interesting twist on the older line about "violent and sexually demeaning songs and videos" by suggesting that this familiar trend was exacerbated by "the growth of the white audience for rap and the growing role of large corporations in marketing the music" – a statement that is never followed up in the article, which instead quickly moves on to Hurt lamenting that black kids "try to conform to the script."

This conjuncture of scandal and militant retort shows what the rap crisis has notoriously been about all along. Take Joseph Sobran's ingenuous phrasing in a syndicated piece from *The Milwaukee Journal*:

> Rap is art for those who lack artistic taste and talent, music for those who can't carry a tune, poetry for those who lack basic linguistic skills ... It is roughly to freedom of expression what S&M is to romance ... It consists of monotonous patter in irregular prosody set to a thumping background rhythm ... A lot of rap is frankly pitched to what the Victorians called the criminal classes ... The mission of shocking the bourgeoisie has passed from the avant-garde to common thugs.[25]

Hating rap had achieved its own scale. In Sobran's reliance on the social vision of Victorian Britain, lower classes can be referred to simply as criminals without blushing. And then, in an equally revealing shift to the later era of European modernism, he can reserve the ability to shock for an avant-garde youth he permits to be alienated on the grounds that they possess an aesthetic vision in keeping with the approved tastes of the college seminar room. Rap is, a priori, not permitted to have such a vision. In this mood, a writer can play to known responses with the assurance of an automatic public assent, as Bruce Willis did in the film *The Last Boy Scout* when, taunted by his torturer ("Just once I would like to hear you scream in pain") Willis quips, "Play some rap music."

The fight over rap, in part because it was already associated in many people's minds with black youth in a declining economy during an age of supposed globalization, had to be fought allegorically in a debate over art and artlessness: a position that (interestingly) does not prevent the critics from exclaiming proudly that this U.S. music had been taken up by youth across the world. The hysteria was not coming only from the great white way. The well-known African-American jazz critic Stanley Crouch instructed readers of the *New Yorker* that:

> Rock and Roll and rap are about adolescent sentiments, which are completely foreign to jazz. In jazz, the focus is on adult experiences, and the skills required to express them are far more sophisticated than in rock, because they are of greater emotional complexity. It's good for young people to test themselves in the arena of jazz, because it forces them to confront the fact that there are some things out there which are more profound than what they're dealing with.[26]

He is developing a theory of music, the article goes on to say, "in which the forces of barbarism and the forces of civilization compete in a battle that is at once aesthetic and ethical."

Unlike the examples in earlier chapters, rap obviously is long on radical lyrical content. But the political implications of rap lie as much with its claims to high art and literariness as with its urge to convey messages. Rap is central to any discussion of "imperial jazz" since it bears on the empty space in Western liberal education represented by the gap between the required study of literature and the elective study of music. In New York, rap drew on neo-African sources to blur the distinction between text and music, re-injecting poetry with the drum and reclaiming the right to write for the formally untrained. In college classrooms, courses on rap are not necessarily a way for aging professors to "get down," but a way of discussing what is arguably the most consequential poetry being written today.

In the song "Ebonics" (2000), Big L has fun running down a word list to explain, in a mocking tone, what terms like "lifted" (high), "chips" (money), "bones" (cigarettes) and "okey-doke" (con) mean in his lingo. The song's "flip" is to say what it doesn't mean, appearing to cop to the charge of speaking the ill-educated slang of a low-life ("criminal slang, that's just the way that I talk, y'all – vocabulary spills, I'm ill") when he is really boasting about the productivity of his and others' verbal invention. As a defining component of rap structure and outlook, the *boast*, in other words, is not always, or even mostly, carried out in the metaphoric terms of an assault (the metaphoric terms typically mistaken by commentators who misunderstand the music, taking these boasts for the glorification of killing). A song like "Ebonics" indicates, among other things, that despite its apparent call for initiation into a broader hip-hop culture with its own rules of dress and movement, rap's primary impulse is pedagogical.

Masta Ace's "enuff" (2001), for example, apart from being a clever sliding among different registers of the title's meaning (at once self-mocking and bitterly critical of those around him) is a critique of the never-satisfied, and the ethos that drives everyone in this kind of society to possess more, buy more, do more – all to uncertain ends. It is not the sort of message one associates with the rollin' in the benzo, puffin' on a blunt sort of rap that dominates the prime-time video shows. The pedagogical urge of rap, though, although present throughout from Grandmaster Flash's "The Message" (1982) through KRS-One's teaching-pieces (for example, "Free Mumia" on *KRS-One,* [1995]) to Kanye West's "We Don't Care" (2004), reaches only those who have already made the leap to seeing rap as a worthy art. That, in turn, requires examining the technical resources that dictate the music's productive form, a task usually accomplished in the by now familiar gesture of rehearsing rap's prehistory:

> Whatever the disagreements over lineage in the rap hall of fame or the history of hip hop, there is one thing on which all are agreed. "Rap is nothing new," says Paul Winley. Rap's forebears stretch back through disco, street funk, radio DJs, Bo Diddley, the bebop singers, Cab Calloway, Pigmeat Markham, the tap dancers and comics, The Last Poets, Gil Scott-Heron, Muhammad Ali, acappella, and doo-wop groups, ring games, skip-rope rhymes, prison and army songs, toasts, signifying and the dozens, all the way to the griots of Nigeria and the Gambia. No matter how far it penetrates into the twilight maze of Japanese video games and cool European electronics, its roots are still the deepest in all contemporary Afro-American music.[27]

This helpful commentary, though, weights the case a little too strongly in favor of U.S. precursors. The toasts of Jamaican DJs, for example, have much more to do with hip hop aesthetics than Cab Calloway does. The two are not comparable sources since only the former has the essential quality of an improvised voice-over covering a pre-existing track.

Many have worried that focusing on rap aesthetics in the name of supporting it also petrifies it, just as jazz has become in some quarters almost a museum piece. Amiri Baraka's essays on jazz describe with precision that tension between a bebop of "nonconformity, musically as well as socially . . . a music of rebellion," and a music centered crucially in the Village world of "artists and writers, intellectuals and bohemians, the struggling and the poseurs."[28] But jazz never had rap's air of the criminal. Although underground, bebop's struggles were over "the primacy of improvisation" as pitched against European classical music, a digging down into the "heavy rhythmic flesh and blood" of the black majority to articulate not a mere technique but a whole (black) attitude that the critical amateurs rarely fathomed.[29] Its rise was inseparable for Baraka from the upward mobility of blacks brought on by the relative prosperity of the war years. Again the class fraction evoked by rap, very different from jazz, is crucial here, and for that reason rap is much harder to kill in the act of extolling it as art. Its commercial gutting poses a more likely danger.[30]

The philosophy

What, then, is the rap aesthetic, and how do we place it in a broader context of the neo-African music of the Americas? There are three neglected aspects of rap's ideological constitution, its noise: (1) excess; (2) regenerative chaos; and (3) the form of all African-American forms.

The central aesthetic of rap in its prime (the late 1980s and early 1990s) was excess, saturation, disposable productivity. What was new two months ago is no longer, which is the exact opposite of pop R&B in which the same twelve cuts are played endlessly over the course of an entire year. In rap, every cut has an album, every album its group, every group its posse and its extended family of groupies, hangers-on, journeymen rappers, savants, intellectual apologizers and promoters – all of them tomorrow's rappers or elements in the interchangeable components of another group or posse (like the relationship today between Ali G and Atmosphere in the Minneapolis rap scene, or between Aesop Rock and Company Flow in New York).

Thus the best DJs of that era (Kid Capri, DJ Red Alert, Funkmaster Flex, and others) could not, like the white jazz aficionados or the erudite scholars of delta blues with their mastery of the performance history, be outside of hip-hop production looking in as amateurs. The publicizers in this world are often rappers themselves, or part of the rappers' crew. What at first appeared a problem of commodification (rapping as planned obsolescence) was often an attempt to outwit the style of the "new" by making the new serve as a defense against appropriation. The accelerated aging process of the rap classic led to greater sales and more star slots but also to a frenetic informational overload that kept the poseurs at bay.

Unable to escape what David James in an essay on punk has called "the evaporation of presence" (the displacement of the work from its "intrinsic pleasure" and its original "telos"), rap's transgressiveness managed to evade in most cases "the rapidity with which [punk's] negativity was drained." This is so even though there are significant trends going the other way: for example, the featuring of P. Diddy or Lil' Kim in the Style section of the *New York Times*, or the fact that Eve is the star of a major sitcom.[31] Appropriation, nevertheless, was already well underway even by the mid-1990s: Ice Cube appeared on St. Ides malt liquor commercials; Kriss Kross pushed soft drinks; Digital Underground's Humpty played straight man to Charles Barkley in Nike commercials. All were renegades on tap. Many, though, were eager to defend rap against commercialism.[32] This strain, which in the early 1990s included Gang Starr, A Tribe Called Quest, Brand Nubian, Main Source, Poor Righteous Teachers, Black Sheep, EPMD, and KRS-One, helped create a major subgenre dedicated to talking about the rap sellout. But unlike punk, rap is less about rejecting the culture industry than demanding a place within it on its own terms.

Rap "excess" radically departs from punk's neo-modernist strategy of opting out of commercialism per se. Passively, excess marks out the vitality and intensity of the message as though there were so many previously mute now speaking that the CDs and television could not contain them. But excess also requires being in, rather than about, the culture. There is no sense, in other words, of lingering over the great work of even last year, of admiring its art (although naturally, rappers are constantly learning from this past, and copping it, often brazenly). The combination of a disposable canon and a flagrant theft of riffs from last year's classic is so obvious that wild productivity should be thought a conscious strategy rather than a by-product of a commercially viable music created in a competitive atmosphere.

And it is more than simply style – rather, protection from the taming by an overpowering commercial acceptance. Early rap songs that talked about the scandal of R&B stations refusing to play them (Yomo and Maulkie's "Mockingbird," Public Enemy's "Don't Believe the Hype") are already part of a bygone era.[33] In New York, all of the major commercial black stations have *featured* rap since the mid-1990s. Some of rap's most innovative, experimental, and traditionally non-commercial artists then began two-tiered careers. Gang Starr's Guru, for example, cut hardcore for one audience but duets with the R&B artist Mary J. Blige for the audience of KISS-FM. The art lives on in part because rap keeps flooding the market, and the image of infinite productivity is enhanced by the shifting names of posses and performances. Like calypso, rap's theatricality is also an alias; its stage names play with pseudonyms. They conjure images of those on the wrong side of the law or, alternatively, point to larger imaginary worlds, as in all-star wrestling: Grand Puba, 50 Cent, MC Pooh, Floetry, Hurricane, Big Pun, Flavor Flav, and Dead Prez.

Like excess, tonal clash (the second element of rap's ideology) promotes non-inclusion. Tonal clash is the dissonant rampage of sound, the starting and stopping of the scratch and the punch phrase that tumbles and trips forward, keeping the listener jerky and on edge. There is no aural stream to guide the listener through. Those who despise rap's fraying of the nerves are not hearing different sounds, just missing the point. The techno-screech and thud-thudding of the bass line unsettle the ears in the name of simulating pain; they please by being unpleasant. These technical details amount to regenerative chaos, which is homeopathic. It does its job best in inappropriate places: the bedroom in the early morning; the car on a cruise; a mixed party with older friends. And because it helps purge the social chaos taken in from outside, blanking it out like radio jamming, it offers its audiences a way to endure. In that sense, rap is often not social realism but thrill – a decade ago, Cypress Hill's "Puffin' on a Blunt"[34] and more recently, the "horror core" of groups like Necro, Jedi Mind Tricks, and Cage.

More importantly (and third), rap is the form of all black forms. There are limits to how closely one can hitch rap to Bo Diddley (although the immediate Bronx precursors of post–Public Enemy production, for example, Afrika Bambaataa and DJ Kool Herc, are another matter). But rap is not simply an innovation, not what Motown was to the 1960s or bebop to the 1940s and 1950s. It does not simply assume its place in the lineage. Rap is more like an encyclopedia or commentary on African cultural production. It is not postmodern because it is not trying to blur the distinctions between period, genre and style in a new, ahistorical collage of sound. It is better thought of as an aural museum and display case, or perhaps (as I have been saying in regard to salsa) a religious veneration not unlike a fetish which gives the listener power. Quotations from Dick Gregory or Louis Farrakhan, documentary testimony from penitentiary prisoners, samplings from the Jackson Five or Little Richard: these are not innocent fragments jumbled non-hierarchically next to rap's many allusions to popular culture as a whole (Keebler cookie commercials, *Sally Jessy Raphael*, the film *Ghost*). Although alluding at every turn in the lingua franca of mass cult imagery, rap in its message-oriented mind-set wants especially to protect and exalt black traditions.

Rap is, then, to its creators, a culmination. It is, in that explicitly African sense, a holism.

It is tempting to write about rap "fusions" of various sorts, but rap is all fusion and nothing else. Neo-African styles are not so much quoted in localized allusions but projected as subgenres of earlier styles: rap in the funk tradition (Brand Nubian, Digital Underground, Del the Funkée Homosapien); reggae roots (Poor Righteous Teachers, KRS-One, Jungle Brothers); jazz/blues tradition (A Tribe Called Quest, Pete Rock and C. L. Smooth, the Guru); R&B smooth (MC Lyte, Big Daddy Kane); Latin flavor (Cypress Hill, the Beatnuts, Kid Frost); and the pop sound, and friendly outreach, of the rap meant to strike a lighter, less threatening, note (Positive K, Will Smith, Arrested Development, Digable Planets, Heavy D, Kriss Kross). Rap is not a single style to be used up and passed over in the face of tastes challenged by media burnout. It is rather a mode of commentary on African-American achievement and struggle. It is not a thing, but a medium. So it lives on.

The verbal rather than rhythmic primacy of rap is borne by this line of approach. The aesthetic of rap sampling tends to push critics to study studio technologies as well as the media literacy that inspires these sound collages. But the sample, actually, has a verbal and largely poetic logic. These are basically speeches constructed from the fragments of many peoples' verbal statements (like the famous 1980s LP *Malcolm X, No Sellout* which was literally a juxtaposition of fragments of Malcolm X's speeches). Terminator X's mixing on side A of Public Enemy's *Fear of a Black Planet* represents a kind of beauty that is very different from the equally stylish, but much less baroque and more understated phrasing of DJ Premier's mixing on Gang Starr's "Who's Gonna Take the Weight?"[35] But despite their varied ears, the "mix" is the art of syntactic regularity, and the intelligibility of the flow of the whole.

The same could be said of "voice," which in any deliberately oral-literary art, has a semantic not only sonoric function. Any popular musical history of the West would surely linger over the tonalities of Frank Sinatra's or Sara Vaughan's voice, deliberating over accents, timbres, and pauses. And yet this exercise has been extraordinarily rare in rap appreciations, except by the performers themselves, who often comment on their own and others' voices within the lyrics of their songs in a meta-critical gesture. Tone is not only varied and inventive but exposed even more than in more explicitly sung musical forms. A number of writers on rap have begun to think less of the recorded drum tracks (which move the dancers, or provide the sonic wall that is so important in public displays of rap insouciance) and emphasize instead, say, Yo Yo's delivery (especially her playacting); the headstrong new jack energies of Nas; the almost avuncular ease of Lupe Fiasco; the playful, silly speech of Brand Nubian's Derek X (later Sadat X); or the bass-low mellow swiftness of DARC Mind?

A perfect example of the literary and craft-oriented verbal emphasis in rap, and its anti-postmodern side, can be found in Rahzel's "All I Know" (1999). His showmanship here is to mimic with the sound of his own voice the reverb and scratching techniques accomplished by others with the use of studio technologies. His mimicry (extraordinarily like the real thing) is also a mockery. A lot can be learned by studying the technical equipment used in rap production, but what gets lost in such studies is rap's insistence on the art of the performer – a point often obscured by the idea that sampling and drum-beat machines are basically parasitic, and involve little input from the artist apart from some lame poetry superimposed after the fact.

The rap experience is, above all, about rhyme and voice. Rhyming is not just obligatory (which is true of most popular music), but the site of signature. The point is not to show that one can rhyme but that one can rhyme differently. In general, the prosody depends on stretching it. The lines are not written of equal length, for the most part, but with a mind to message and idiom. It therefore becomes a display of MC finesse to fit the verses to the unyielding arithmetic of the drum track, which is accomplished in two opposite ways: piling up words delivered with lightning quickness in a speed dub or, conversely, stretching them with absences. If the great ally of the country-western lyric is the pun, the ally of the rap lyric is the caesura.

In a more figurative sense, stretching it can mean the intentional preposterousness of the rhyme itself. Here we are in a world of the tour de force where, in the malleable accents of the oral, near-rhyming is taken to an extreme. In this world, *hardcore* rhymes with *proper*; *had this* rhymes with *madness*; *answer* rhymes with *chance ta*; *defeat us when* with *Peterson*; and so on.[36] A list of virtues would be needed to catalogue the tonalities of the MC voice. Tension (Sage Francis), low sonority (DARC Mind), tease (Rhymefest), speed (Necro), articulation (Louis Logic). All have an exaggerated intonation, a sort of stage personality,

The importance of an adopted stage persona to oral-literary meaning is illustrated in the duet between Eminem and Royce Da 5'9" in "Nuttin to Do" based on an actual freestyle competition in concert in Detroit in 1998. Royce ("bad") goes after Eminem ("evil"), and gets his own in turn.

> [Royce] Yo if it wasn't for your whip, I'd have nothin to strip
> [Em] If it wasn't for your wrist, I'd have nothin to slit
>   If it wasn't for the shrooms, I'd have nothin to chew

[Royce] Yo.
[both] I'm just fuckin with you, cause I got nothin to do
[Eminem] I am bored!!!!!
    I came in the diner with skateboarders, and placed orders
    Ate hors d'oeuvres, and hit the waiter with plate warmers (crash sound)
    Let you inhale the glock smell, while I'm rippin your wallet off
    and slippin a Molotov in your Cocktail (take that!)
    Burnin your contracts, punch your A&R in the face (punch sound)
    Smash his glasses and turn em to contacts
    I'm on some shook shit, if it's missin I took it (whoops!)
    Nurse look at this straightjacket, it's crooked!
    I go to jail and murder you from a cell
    Put a knife in an envelope and have you stabbed in the mail (FedEx)
    So how do you describe someone, with a decapitated head when the rest of his body's still alive RUNNIN?
[Royce] Comin with five gunmen, waitin to do a drive-by
    So when you see the black 500 (what?) hide from it
    For every hundred MC's rhymin about birds
    only about two-thirds'd really said it without words
    Yo ain't a thug, I can make you bitch up
    Pick the fifth up, cock, spit, you would swear it's rainin slugs (what?)
    . . . Spit a round, lift your chin up, you get hit, ten down and ten up (what?)
    I take it if you run your mouth, then you wanna get sent up
    Heat it up, you be leakin' blood and spittin' phlegm up
    Now we rivals, cause of a small name or title
    You stepped, got devoured and left with a flower and bible

Eminem's voice here is intentionally squeaky, and delivered in long streams eliminating all the usual accents of English, and giving the whole a stumbling flatness. Each line ends with a level pitch, as though there could be no end to the insults pouring out of him. Something about the dissonance between the bratty high-pitched whine of the voice and the cold-blooded threats gives his side of the rivalry an infuriating aspect, as though the insults cut even deeper given how obnoxious they sounded in the telling. But the extravagance of the metaphors in Eminem's case (which one could argue is his calling card), the funny extremes of the hyperbole (killing his rival from prison by sending a knife in the mail) are harmonious, and not dissonant at all, with the real objective: namely, out-competing his freestyle partner at the mic by showing greater skill. The crazy flow of the language, and the claims of the rapper to be actually crazed (this straitjacket is crooked!) allows the violation of meaning to do something positive. And so even though "Molotov" is not the dangerous ingredient of a normal cocktail, we get the idea of the threat just fine – a brilliant stroke that makes us laugh, and wouldn't if it were expressed accurately.

The whole logic of the boast is, as here, to compete verbally in order to gauge your social worth by the approval of onlookers, and the classical nature of the art can be found in nothing so clear as its organization in couplets. If the structure rests on a literary conceit (Royce's imagery of a boxing title bout – "spit a round, lift your chin up"), Royce's choice is, for this kind of competition, a little too obvious, and he loses points. What Eminem is doing here, though, is condensing the usual extended conceit pattern (the kind found, say, in the old freestyle between Ice T and Donald D, "Lost in the Freestyle," which carries on a ten-line conceit based on a soccer match) into little stories that are embedded in tight two-line units, which quickly shift from one to the next with admirable brevity.

From the restaurant antics (lines 1–2) he moves to the comfort of Royce's home (cocktail) where he's killed his crew with an automatic weapon, stolen his money at gunpoint, and spiked his drink (lines 3–4). Then suddenly he's at his rap rival's lawyer's offices, destroying his recording career by burning Royce's hard-won contracts and breaking the glasses of his paid bean counters (lines 5–6). The next two lines boast of his scary unpredictability, jumpy on drugs, a master thief, but defiant and in command, even in the asylum. Then on to the next two lines about his long reach from captivity (neither jail nor distance can stop him), and then the final two, which unlike the rationale of the imagery thus far – which telegraphs the full detail of narrative in abbreviated images – now takes too long to say: you're a chicken, and I'm about to cut your head off. Irony in language is mobilized here not in the name of subtlety but accusation. The poet uses words that will evoke racist caricature only to spin it into a brag about being wily entrepreneurs and refined exhibitionists of craft. He shocks because life is shocking. No respect for middle-class hypocrisy when it won't respect him.

The female mack

If rap is no longer (as Chuck D put it so long ago) a "Black CNN" simply because it is now played on CNN, and if it has lost some of its flavor because it has lost its need to rebel, then rap has achieved its ends. Now start others, not only in the independent and alternative rap scenes, but in Cuba, the German Turkish communities, Senegal, and South Africa.[37]

It is true that rap's mainstream life is a very peculiar one, a vilified and embattled centrality that is not at all like what is meant by "mainstream" when referring to Bill Cosby or *Everyone Loves Raymond*. So it is important not to overstate its welcome. As we have seen, there are still articles attacking gangsta rap as though that is all rap ever was, and as though the many other subgenres of rap did not exist (art rap, emo rap, political, prankster, love duet, Afrocentric, horror core, and so on). The old attempts to criminalize black culture by creating fear are stronger than ever. As though time had stopped, the Christian Right finds it can still score points by picking up where Bill Clinton and Bob Dole left off when using rap to score points during their presidential campaigning in the 1990s. But even gangsta as such is misunderstood because there are many ways of telling the same story, and rap does not work like a simple wish-fulfillment or a two-dimensional report.

Notice how different the feel is in the boasts of traditional salsa, a form (like calypso) that is full of them. Something of the laid-back life of the front porch remains; the tenor is less mean than on the mean streets of the city, and the underlying emotional atmosphere is funny and even self-mocking. Take this example from Marvin Santiago's "Estaca de Guayacán" ("Beating Stick"):

> *Chorus:* They call me a hard man,
> The hardwood "beating stick"
> They call me a tough guy
> The hardwood "beating stick"
> *Marvin:* I put the green back in ripe fruit
> Deal out punishment to everyone around
> I make the future return to the present
> I could go toe-to-toe with Superman.[38]

Santiago delivers these lines with bravado, and listeners smile hearing claims more absurd than they are brave. He's as strong as a wall, and can see in complete darkness with the sight of an eagle, and so on. We have here, in other words, a succinct example of the multi-dimensionality of the "gangsta" theme as boast in New World African music.

The disarming humor of Santiago's boast, the insistent playfulness and tongue-in-cheek quality of his worldview beyond tragedy or mean-spirited contempt – this deeply *humane* sensibility so out of sorts with the austere Protestantism of the north – is literally everywhere in Latin music, a distinctive twist given to a common cultural phenomenon. And there are mutations and gradations as well. On the face of it, the popular Cuban pianist and singer Bola de Nieve in the song "Chivo que Rompe Tambo" (The Goat who Breaks the Drum) expresses anger, and promises revenge against the mischievous goat who has broken his instrument. But he pounds out a song with all the vocal theatrics and lightning solo piano riffs of Ray Charles (although with much more pianistic skill and an even more guttural vocal showmanship). His outlandish lyrics are more like a shaggy-dog story than a confrontation.[39] It soon becomes clear that the real point of the song lies elsewhere, as the chorus says: "El negro no es nada sin tambo" (blacks are nothing without their drum). The playfulness, although based on an act of violence, finds its way back to pastoral and the kind of self-referentiality that makes the performance itself a topic of the song, as does much African-inflected Latin popular music.

If the central figure of most gangsta rap, by contrast, is ugly in the moral sense, it is an ugliness that cuts both ways. The persona of gangsta is the mack daddy, a well-dressed, sometimes garishly dressed, figure with cane and bowler hat and obscene looking jewelry – traditionally a pimp. The mack daddy is a positive image, the artful conniver who carves out a business life in an environment of exclusion. He is one who may have lost his morals but who has won a kind of dignity, and whose justification is success. The songs of the most prominent rap commercially (the kind featured on television and in the magazines) is about raking in loot (Kanye West's lines about "dealin' drugs just to get by/ stack your money 'till it get sky high/ we're supposed to be dead by twenty-five/ jokes on you that we're still alive.") Primitive accumulation is always carried out by the brigand who wants to be made a nobleman. The process by which rap became mainstream during the 1990s suggests that the "gangsta" figure was actually *encouraged* by commercialization; the companies pushed rap in that direction. It was not, in other words, that the gangsta message was the result of African-American single-mindedness or lack of originality preventing otherwise decent rap from being heard.

In the space of less than five years in the early 1990s, the commercial R&B radio stations shifted from a stance of refusing to play rap to a stance of featuring it all day long from coast to coast. The hardcore lyrics of yesterday's rap are filled with stories of that exclusion in which sugary-voiced DJs complained of rap being too harsh, too political, too boring. When it was played at all, rap was given a special slot at night, smothered by five or six easier new-jack or slow-jam tunes as though to ward off the pain. All of that changed by the time the Rottin Razcals in "Hey, Alright" could recall "when the radio didn't play/ what we had to say/ but now it's a new day." Take, for example, what happened on New York's 97.1 FM, "Hot '97."

In the mid-1990s, New York had four major R&B stations, three on FM and one on AM. In addition to featuring the likes of R. Kelly, Jodeci, Ce Ce Penniston, and Mary J. Blige, these stations were clearing houses for information of special interest to the black and (marginally) Latin communities, with one of the stations specializing in the Caribbean and also in roundtables or call-in shows featuring local political issues like police brutality or upcoming mayoral elections. The most commercial and best funded of these stations at the time was KISS-FM, showcasing standard R&B fare. Wendy Williams, the DJ in the prime time slot, though, very clearly liked rap, and predicted there was no way, in fact, to contain it.

She started working more rap into her spin charts, slowly, and not without having to field hostile comments from listeners during the "shout-outs" section of the broadcast. It all worked up to a crescendo in which she was bringing artists like the Wu-Tang Clan and Gang Starr into the station for long interviews. After about a year and half of this preparation, the owners of KISS-FM changed their format entirely, deciding to go retro by shifting to a so-called classic soul and R&B station. Wendy Williams moved to KISS-FM's sister station Hot '97 which overnight became a center of hip-hop conceived as a marriage of contemporary R&B with rap. At KISS, she had been the one jokingly referred to as the "Valley Girl from the Hood," and some of that hint of the suburbs allied with the intercity was evident in the new station which took as its slogan: "Bringing you ALL the flavors of hip hop . . . the Station that's rockin' the Hip Hop nation." In other words, one of those hip-hop "flavors" was (in their conveniently expanded sense) R&B, which would have been an impossible association when rap was too criminal to grace the airwaves.

Hot '97 was hugely successful, and began the long trajectory of rap from house party to Emmy showcase. Its footprints are everywhere – from the supporters' lists of spin-off video television shows to the sponsors' credits of concerts and parties in the New York tri-state area. This mainstreaming of rap could be seen by the rise of other venues as well: rap video programs on prime time cable for the after-school crowd: *Rap City* on Black Entertainment Television; the *Video Music Box* on Channel 3, and the *Hip Hop Body Shop* on ESPN2, which crossed exercise videos with a how-to program teaching viewers the latest hip-hop dance steps.

So much of early rap had been set against this sort of commercialism and so deep in a communal ethos of embattled survival that it would be surprising if there had not been attempts to counter those trends. There soon were. One was a show called *Tomorrow's Flavas Today* on Saturday afternoons on New York's Channel 16, a very low-production community-access outlet. Its goal was to preserve the hardcore, and its constant slogan was "keep it real." There was continual interplay between audience and performers in the sense that viewers could call in for free and have their "Bigg Ups" (their shout-outs) aired on television against a blank screen. The program even played videos that are made by unknowns who have never cut a record. Even on Hot '97 itself, there were gradations of real. Evil D's *Monday Nite Flavor Mix* was much more hardcore than Funkmaster Flex or Dr. Dre and Ed Lover, DJs who dominated the rest of the week. Most traditional of all, in the good sense, was Flavor Flav's *Sunday Night Home Jams* which specialized in airing work only by those who had no record contracts.

It is against this backdrop that one can appreciate the rise of the female mack. Heather B's "All Glocks Down" from this era is a good place to start. The flavor of the video has partly to do with its homemade feel, made with an inexpensive video camera, without professional actors or lighting technicians and a lightly garbled sound. This basement-production look was actually a pose in this case, even if approximately half of the videos aired on the show did come from homemade productions (according to the show's producer). Such structured authenticity is itself the point, however, and whether artificially created or not, the low-life aesthetic was a significant departure from other fare on the commercial airwaves before the age of reality television. Heather B with this video joined the ranks of the female mack in its New York mode.

A video like this was, first of all, a refreshing antidote to the techno-polish of *Yo! MTV Raps*, which represented an acceptable middle ground for rap's public defenders during the tail end of the first anti-rap craze of the 1980s (which I described briefly above). Heather B, by contrast, virtually begs to be misunderstood. Her video's noir shadows, frightening stills of graffiti skulls, and frenetic arm-waving seems to be saying to those unfamiliar with this scene that this is a music about violence and hostility. And yet, the shadows and the skulls join scenes of unmistakable intimacy. In the ethos of the ladies luncheon or the pontificating editorial, these images must appear as a kind of ethnographic documentary of terrifying tribal customs. But, of course, to anyone who knows the music, this is a video about a woman defusing hostilities among men. It is not about gang violence at all, but about rejecting gang violence, as the refrain clearly states: "All Glocks Down" (Put Your Weapons Down). The woman takes charge. She has a real camaraderie with her male friends rather than a simple sexual relationship as is the case in most pop music video of any type (whether rap or not). There is a deep moralism in this kind of artistic production that is almost impossible to find in most commercial fare.

In a way, I have already misstated the problem. The offbeat shows are known in many cases by big-money performers or the big radio stations that are sure to give their names and money in support. For their part, the offbeat shows mix together home-jam tapes with bootleg versions of the high-production quality found on MTV. Naturally, all of this scene has changed now with YouTube and napster, which allow for an entirely different dimension of niche marketing, and make an independent, "underground" art financially viable (although, at the same time, subject to inundation by the sheer amount of music now available on the Internet). It is all one mash. The radical changes to these venues or sites of listening and performing as a result of wholesale acceptance have profoundly affected the music produced. So the rap/R&B fusion already by the mid-1990s was often structured as a duet in which a famous rapper was given half the song and a famous R&B artist the other half. Complementary, they then complimented each other in interviews following the playing of the tape. One has to understand that such a set-up violates the central aesthetic of excess. Radio rap, at any rate, was now frozen in the old R&B strategy of playing the same cuts continuously for placement on a chart.

In response to the ongoing assault from the press, rap had its artists who turned nostalgic for the old days when rapping was out of the limelight, and kids signified in parking lots and on rooftops – like Paris's "The Days of Old" or A Tribe Called Quest's "Check the Rhime." Seeing that hardcore and fluff are both part of a continuum, there's a way of saying that this difficulty in distinguishing the two was the result of packaging. The sense of the distinction not only remained strong among the partakers, but was the very thing that made the composing of rap possible under hostile conditions. So while strongly felt by the amateurs, the distinction got blurred by the industry that picked up the hardcore clips from the cutting room floor, so to speak, and packaged them as a seamless hip hop with a lot of junk and jive.

Everyone was caught in that process and could not get out. The war on rap never ended in other words; it was simply carried on by the music industry in the form of promotion, although unsuccessfully, since it did not understand the peculiar feature of rap as wanting to storm the gate of big business. At all costs what had to be destroyed was hip-hop in its old sense. East Coast hardcore, for the most part, did not sell as much as West Coast; the audience had spoken. But this would not explain why Interscope records released both Dre's *Chronic* album and Akinyele's *Vagina Diner* in the fall of 1993, but gave all of its promotional money to Dre, dooming Akinyele to sales below 100,000 albums in spite of its fabulous popularity on the college underground radio networks. That pattern of backing can be seen across the board.

One specific and formal casualty in this process has been the total-concept album, now replaced by the single cut. In one sense, the single cut in LP form had almost been central to rap, of course, as used by the DJs for scratching. But in that case one is not talking about a technology that allows for scratching, but a tag for selling albums. In certain more architectural works of rap, playing a single cut obliterated the meaning of the whole in which it was found. The listening experience was crafted song by song, often with musical interludes or transitions between the individual cuts that brought a person into another world, an extended world like the novel. There was a need to build mood, and this was done usually by picking sinister or dissonant samples, very much like the Kung Fu and horror movies that are so important to the way a certain hip-hop culture understands itself.

In this atmosphere, the rise of the female mack had aspects of both continuity and opposition with these trends. Some women artists responded to the bitch-and-ho talk in gangsta by basically taking over the image of the mack daddy, out toughing the toughs, by creating characters who, as women, dominated their men and used them for their own pleasure. This was a fascinating change, with many earlier forerunners and, today, a legion of inheritors from Lil' Kim to Missy Elliott. But it was in the mid-1990s that the paths were forged by Adina Howard, Smooth, Heather B and Lin Que, not at all the first strong women in rap (following Yo Yo, Queen Latifah, and MC Lyte by a decade). But in very different ways, they were the first to create intentionally a style of music meant to offset gangsta and explode it from within. They were responding to that male mind-set, even among socially conscious rebels like Public Enemy, described so well by Greg Tate:

> Flav goes on and on insinuating that women are garbage for watching garbage. In light of Chuck's plea for crack dealers to be good to the

neighborhood on "Night of the Living Baseheads," it appears PE believe the dealers more capable of penance than the sistuhs. Remember *The Mack*? Where THE pimp figures it cool to make crazy dollar off his skeezes but uncool for the white man to sell scag to the little brothers? This is from that same mentality.[40]

But there was a rather odd bid for female domination at work in the first-wave response. Seeming to counter misogyny and more blatant kinds of sexist boasting, the female mack often seemed to be offering up further images of male sexual desire, now signifying as wanted by, even demanded by, women themselves.

Smooth's "Mind Blowin' " is a stark example of this confusion. This was, one could say, the female mack motif in its L.A. studio mode, a very clear example of the strategy of countering gangsta's sexism by reversing the poles of sexual command. Men here are meant to be reduced to servicing female desire. But given predominant male sexual attitudes of being only too willing to service, male desire remained the center. The video is also and separately a clear example of the R&B/rap hybrid with its heavy jazz nightclub colorings. Keyes has remarked on this mack shift as well, making distinctions within the trend. There are, for the "queens" (Latifah, Souljah), the Fly Girls dedicated to "erotic as power" who wear "clothes that accent their full breasts, rounded buttocks, and ample thighs" (Salt-N-Pepa, TLC, Yo-Yo, Missy Elliott), and the "Sistas with Attitude," meaning aggressive women who challenge male authority (Roxanne Shanté, Lil' Kim, and Foxy Brown).[41]

· The phenomenon of the female mack says less about African-American culture or the bad taste of rappers than the music markets themselves. The individual woman artist was, after all, being told by the sales figures and record contracts that gangsta was in demand. What would make more sense than to devise a women's gangsta, but one that plays to the desires of the largely male audience that consumes rap?

This female mack is also a good way, though, to separate those parts of the gangsta style that go to the heart of rap from those parts that constitute what might be called a post-Snoop Dogg pose. In its more hardcore variants, say, in the neo-beat poetry of Lin Que or Heather B, there were important lessons, if only because the brash, the loud, the dissonant, and the crazed were thought to *be* gangsta whereas they were really the formal constants of all rap, non-gangsta as well. Both Lin Que and Heather B snuff out gratuitous gangsta by being communal; they are just as hard, but not abusive. They take away the exploitative gender war and leave the beauty of the brittle, jarring sounds. Take Lin Que's "Let It Fall," for example, which exemplifies this move:

> Now we got clowns, I'll slow 'em down in instant replay
> When I'm heated up, I speed it up like a freeway
> Your D-Day is comin', so summon your creator
> The life-fader, no place to meet like alpha-beta
> Collect the data, you're going to need it to defeat me
> They tried to sweep me off my feet, they must be sleepy
> They're going to have to bring it stronger than that
> I'm onto your rap, and, damn!, not a part of your crap, uh
> So chill before blood spills and you're the victim,
> My words a pit bull, and then they kill when I say "sick 'em"
> See I can pick 'em out of a crowd of a million, the villain
> Illin' not only here to make a killin'
> You're under pressure, off the hardcore text of the wrecker
> You hear my steps comin' to get ya,
> Stunts who talk that junk, I never front
> If it's hardcore that you hunt, then I'll give you what you want
>
> *Chorus:* One, Two/ One, Two
> "I let it fall on 'em, I let it fall on 'em"
> "Drop it all on 'em, drop it all on 'em"

The stage personality she adopts is both tough and defensive at the same time. Its subject-matter is, of course, textual. That is, it is about MC skill. She is surrounded by friends and supporters, her chorus, especially the well-known rapper, MC Lyte, who as an actor in the video steps in to complete Lin's refrain in the second half of the chorus. The feel of this sort of art is social, even familial. Its bleak black-and-white settings of subway tunnels and alleyways are regenerated and recovered by creativity. In lines like "Illin' not only here to make a killin'" she makes it clear that rap, although a business, is about much more than cash, and is finally nothing if it loses a sense of roots purity, or if it fails to see the difference between (in her words) "junk" and "hardcore." The surprise of the campaigns against gangsta rap (Time/Warner's contemporaneous disassociation with Interscope Records, for example) lies in the fact that they never fathom the morality of this art, never suspect it is even there.

The Chicago-based group Common spoke of being "children of a greater god," and by doing so appealed to a practice of art described by Robert Farris Thompson as the "profoundly moral" concept of art that prevailed in neo-African forms.[42] The artistic gesture of keeping it real is in this case, as in earlier examples in this chapter, a socially ethical one as well.

Nothing alien to them

How could it be that a truly international form – a global, world form – like rap would be uniform in respect to its politics? As Melissa Rivière explains, even though the global cult status of films like *Wild Style*, *Style Wars*, and *Beat Street* have made New York the Mecca of hip-hop, it tended to enter a country like Cuba by way of countries like Panama, Mexico, Jamaica, and Colombia because of the U.S. embargo. As a result, the evolution of hip-hop there displays more influences from New Orleans than directly from New York:

> I believe this is due to Cuba's historical role as a refuge for the Black Panther Movement and Black Nationalists more than influences from the commercialized style of U.S. mainstream Hip Hop from New York City. The Cuban Hip Hop movement with leaders such as Asata Shakur (Black Panther leader exiled in Havana) and a communist socio-economic framework has developed a lyrically political charged movement in comparison to the mainstream commodified American designer Hip Hop with leaders such as Russell Simmons (founder of the Def Jam label and Phat Farm Clothing Co.).[43]

In the United States, by contrast, what most rappers propose about themselves is more modest. Hip-hop's philosophy is not about revolution, in spite of political rap like Immortal Technique's "Military Minds" or "Bin Laden" or (in the Afro-centric genre) Rass Kass's "Nature of the Threat" with its message that everything official religion and school tells you is a conspiratorial lie.[44]

In the quest for alternatives, rappers have turned to Islam, vegetarianism, community self-defense schemes, blunt-smoking, or visions of an emergent black bourgeoisie. Paris, Tupac, and The Coup (all Oakland based) used to voice an implicit left agenda that sounded very much like the Panthers. In other variants, Sister Souljah, Chuck D. and X Clan came out of the orbit of black Islam (although to very different degrees) and Souljah was an ardent segregationist. Some of the variables of rap politics – the hedonistic, the religious, or the entrepreneurial – are unstable markers, shifting from performer to performer and from CD to CD in pursuit of two much more stable principles. One is surely cultural uplift. But again, the call is found not only at the level of the cajoling lyric beckoning listeners to stay in school.

The opposite claim would also be untrue – the argument, that is, of Todd Boyd and others that rap is a new rapturous politics of refusing to play the integration game, opting out of the legal strategies of civic betterment enshrined by the civil rights tradition: that rap, in short, is a reinvention of politics as such.[45] Calling the civil rights movement "outdated and passé" (51), his analysis of three transitional phases around identity in the black community might be seen, rather, as evidence for the thesis I am presenting here:

> I talked about the Race Man, I talked about the New Black Aesthetic, and then I talked about the emergence of the nigga . . . N-I-G-G-A is an individual who fits comfortably in hip hop and who is not interested in necessarily appeasing the masses or fitting into anybody's category, but instead is interested in doing things their own way in spite of the consequences.[46]

This might be seen as incipient entrepreneurialism that wants to allow black men and women to share the national dream of enrichment in the war of one against all: "I never thought of myself before as an American because to me American was another way of saying white. And I certainly wasn't white so I didn't think I was an American – What am I? Well, I'm a nigga. And I don't have no problems with that. But I think something clicked in me. Well, I was born in America, I was raised in America, so to that extent I guess I am technically an American" (53). He puts the matter even more clearly when he turns to class: "To me there has always been something that emerged from the Lumpen that a lot of more middle-class or bourgeois-minded African Americans don't really want to deal with . . . to me that's real" (58).

One can argue about the authenticity of rap's vision or about the class origins of its stars, but not about the social character of its desire. The lures of business success, with rage as one of its principal commodities, had an organizing effect in this structurally abandoned and targeted sector of the U.S. economy. Even a massive failure of a generation of would-be rappers, even ploy and counter-ploy to keep rap off the airwaves, had the effect of a shock to the system. If the paradoxical strategy of choice for a political genre is to bring it into the category of art, the paradoxical strategy for the dispossessed is to bring it into the category of business.

But this option, although it succeeded in getting rap heard and inspired a savagely honest social commentary, could not offer anything like the sense that an alternative society with a different way of being was possible. Its role of performing the social satire that neo-African philosophy demanded was therefore a limited one – either widely heard and ambiguous, or underground and unambiguously direct. In that sense, it experienced only that old repressive desublimation that marks the limit of social protest in the United States generally. Apart from complete obscurity (where everything is allowed because it doesn't matter), the country seemed to offer its iconoclasts only two choices: either the satirical hopelessness of the *Colbert Report* or the "I'm a get mine" demands of a minority whose radical claims could go no further than the right to be what those it hated already were.

5

Global Youth and Local Pleasure

> The emergence of the independent African states . . . was destined to produce young intellectuals [who wanted] an art that would reach the people . . . as popular as the Impressions or the Miracles or Marvin Gaye.
>
> *Amiri Baraka*[1]

According to a joke long circulating in Miami, in one of Fidel's famously long speeches in the Plaza de la Revolución, he implores the assembled to affirm their serious social tasks. Reaching a crescendo at one point, he thunders: "*Compañeros, no somos pachangueros*" (Comrades, we Cubans are no silly party-animals). And in a great swell of approbation, the followers timidly repeat in unison: "*No, Fidel, no somos pachangueros*" (No, you're right, we're no silly party-animals). And then again, to drive the point home, Fidel repeats, "*Compañeros, no somos pachangueros*"; and they once more prove equal to the task: "*No, no somos pachangueros.*"

And so the teller of the joke gradually begins to prolong the syllables, now syncopating them so that the people's antiphon becomes the call-and-response of salsa. Soon, the back-and-forth of the words "*no, no somos pachangueros*" takes the form of the tapping of a conga. Before long, in the joke-teller's rendition, one can see the crowd rocking to the words' rhythms, riffing on their sound, unable to resist the beat of syllables that only a moment before were condemning the pleasures of the dance. The gag here serves the purpose of trying to get us to see that Cubans, try as they might, want only to break free of revolutionary puritanism. They are at heart no more than *pachangueros*.

From a certain point of view – one widely held in the United States and in the more well-heeled circles of Latin America – this is an effective barb, and there is no question that what the joke is communicating about sacrifice in socialist societies is more or less assumed from the start by the audiences that hear it. Cuba can in this way be neatly dispatched as a country standing for a kind of militarized altruism and the demand for public displays of conformity. But even satirical jabs have to have a logic if their critique is going to hit its mark. In this case the humor falls flat because it describes something not simply caricatured (which goes with the territory) but the opposite of the truth – not only false but false in a neatly symmetrical way.

Although the funding of dance venues and the support for publications naturally changed drastically with the post-market conditions instituted in Cuba after 1961, an argument can be made that Cuban popular music was never promoted so vigorously as after the 26 July Movement came to power in 1959. For one thing, in two decades, more serious scholarship on Afro-Cuban musical forms and religious expression found its way into print than had appeared in all of Cuban history up to that point. Afro-Cuban culture enjoyed a massive respectability in official circles for the first time – indeed it became part of the national patrimony – a situation that no other country in the Americas, including the United States, can claim.

On the other hand, there is a reputable literature that documents cases of governmental restrictions on the arts in Cuba, incidents of harassment, even periods of hostility toward entire dance genres, and so I am not seeking to mitigate the criticism of a certain dogmatism or overreaction to what the Cuban state has, at various times, perceived as *peligrosidad social* (social danger).[2] My point is only that the sea change in perspective toward Afro-Cuba and the popular arts initiated by the revolution is not destroyed by these examples of faltering, and that it remains hugely consequential to a degree not generally granted in the mood of ideological conflict that governs the censorship narrative. An adequate perspective is impossible, moreover, in a mere listing. What is required, by contrast, is an effort to characterize the logic of opposed social systems, which is rarely undertaken in the telling of this particular story.

Cuban socialism has an Afro-Cuban center, not because its leaders have always appreciated or understood Afro-Cuban religion or the popular music that emerged from it, but because the dynamic of the liberation movement extending from the nineteenth to the mid-twentieth century demanded it. The complexity and variety of Cuban music is not directly the fruit of the 1959 revolution, of course, although it certainly is the fruit of revolutions of earlier eras. And yet, the revolution did come about because those who created it had the emotional and aesthetic make-up, cultural training, and ideological conviction capable of producing a form like the *son*. The Cuban revolution was and is a revolution through race. Both its opponents and supporters understood this to be so from the outset. What is more, the scholars who turned to the study of Afro-Cuba after 1959 saw this connection very clearly, and left detailed renderings of how and why this had to be. There is, after all, always a lag between the intellectuals of a movement and its political functionaries. Perhaps the most extraordinary, but certainly not the only, evidence of the Castro government's invaluable support for Cuban popular music can be found in the scholarly renaissance that followed its accession to power. Cuba's Ministerio de Cultura issues an annual bimonthly bibliography of acquisitions at the Biblioteca Nacional José Martí titled *Bibliografía Cubana*. If one consults the volume dedicated to the years 1921–1936 and compares it to the volumes dedicated (respectively) to 1962–1978 and 1982–1989, one gets a very clear sense of the explosion of research on Afro-Latin music that took place after 1959.[3]

Although almost completely untranslated, this rich collection of scholarly projects is extraordinarily varied. It encompasses studies of early Cuban classical music from the colonial era; the Spanish popular theater of the nineteenth century; individual dance genres and their histories; the panoply of Afro-Cuban instruments; rock and carnival music; Afro-Cuban religious, nightclub, or classical performers; the impact of jazz; and the musical landscape of Oriente province.[4] After reading critics of the stature of Argeliers León, Samuel Feijóo, Gloria Antolítia, Alejo Carpentier, Leonardo Acosta, or María Teresa Linares, one begins to appreciate that a developed understanding of the political significance of neo-African popular music was substantially worked out in Cuba before it was in other countries – at least as a body of work with a critical mass and momentum.[5] And yet this body of work is largely ignored by contemporary critics of popular music, including critics of African-American and Latin music. It is not going too far to say that entire books and research projects that have won positive attention in the United States and Britain have more or less repeated Cuban predecessors or work by Latin American scholars familiar with Cuban scholarship.

This body of work illustrates from the start an intense interest in the Afro-Cuban contribution to culture during the very period that the Cuban government is blamed for showing hostility toward Afro-Cuban culture. This work, moreover, displays a rare appreciation for the goal of obliterating the high/low distinction between the popular and classical arts and reaches a theoretical level unattained in most popular music criticism available in English in at least one respect: it contemplates fully the interplay of music and literature, of movement and word, dance and text. This is fabulously evident, for instance, in the work of Feijóo, León, Germán Bode Hernández and of course, Alejo Carpentier.[6] What must be understood is that the revolutionary government grew out of the *negrismo* movement of the 1920s and 1930s that provided this research with its first leads and its basis. The revolution was, in fact, the logical extension of that movement.

One finds evidence again and again in Cuban scholarship of a structured pride for what was culturally unleashed in Oriente province in the early nineteenth century. There have been attempts to dismiss this work as an official appropriation of black culture for nationalist ends; but this view is belied by the commentary of the researchers themselves, and appears tendentious. No doubt, there are nationalist feelings unleashed by encomiums to the genius of the *son*, but their distance from the patriotic sublime of U.S. jazz criticism, for example, is very marked. The Cuban scholars do not seek to hide from their readers the multiple contributions from the Americas, from Moorish Spain, and from French and English planter societies in the making of this concoction called the *son*, and indeed, their entire point is that the Antilles are a laboratory for the re-emergence under many names of the same musical logic and achievement (a zonal, rather than patriarchal, etiology).

Dances with different names continually arose as new and excited discoveries, although upon scrutiny, they proved to be very similar. Variations on the *fandango*, for example, would be *malagueña, rondeña, granadina*, and *murciana*. There was also an intense variety that pointed to far-flung contributions from numerous sources, regional, chronological, and ethnic: the *areíto, contradanza, zapateo, congó, bolero, guaracha, la resbalosa* (a black dance performed in Argentina and Chile), *fandango* (a dance introduced into Spain from the Indies – basically known as the *calenda* in the Windward Islands, *congó* in Cayenne), *batuque, saraband*; songs like *guantanamera* (an old peasant song), *tiranas* (old Spanish folk songs), *seguidillas* (flamenco songs and dances), and *chuchumbé*. We know about many of these songs and dances and their mutual connections from Cuban scholars although they are far from being uniquely Cuban forms. They are just attuned to the creative life of the plebeian sectors of society: in the words of León: "the life of the alleys, backroads, fields and street . . . the slums and huts" of this and earlier centuries ("la vida del los callejones, atajos, trillos y calles . . . bayeyes y barracones.").

What one always finds in Cuban musical scholarship is the long view. We are given a detailed grasp of broad regional histories, economies, and population shifts – the panoply of movements, peoples, and oddities that sprang to life in era after era in the complexities of Caribbean experience. The individual musical examples are studied with an acute understanding of the historical accents inflecting them. Such criticism had reached a high level of technical expertise already in the 1920s in the early work of Ortiz, and had achieved its popular theoretical form already by the mid-1940s with Carpentier – neither of whom has in essential respects been surpassed. Although jazz criticism certainly extends back that far, and although work of equal sophistication in classical music criticism can be found in Europe during the same period, in general it must be said that Cuban popular music criticism matured in advance of Anglophone criticism and is still superior to it.

There were also direct inspirations on musical performance itself. In the early years of the revolution, artists wrote jubilant *guarachas*, *mambos*, and *son boleros* filled with revolutionary content, which aired on the radio and were cause for celebration at public gatherings[7] Skeptics have seen these as bad-faith adaptations designed to persuade the gullible, but the creativity was too extensive and durable to think of them as anything but genuine artistic enthusiasm. With official encouragement – such as the First National Art Festival held in 1959 – popular movements set out to redefine Cuban identity as black, white, young, and mixed. In their own minds this was logical as a way of realizing a sovereignty that was also an act of internal racial and ethnic unification: what the nineteenth- and twentieth-century independence movements had always chiefly been about.

Is it simply accidental that one of the most productive sites of African New World music had suddenly become a place of political controversy and international tension? It is inviting to see these two factors as intertwined, and much of what I have been arguing in this book suggests they are not coincidental. We must consider from another angle the kinds of issues that remain difficult to face, both in popular music theory and in public discourse as a whole. What is the relationship of Cuban socialism to popular music? My interest in Cuban music, I would like to insist, does not stem from the country's socialism, since its innovations in sound would have existed regardless of who had come to power after 1959. But given that this historically central island with its peculiar colonial history happens to be socialist, how does that fact affect the reception of Afro-Latin music and further clarify the meaning of secular devotion? Let us begin by looking at the transition from the old to the new regime.[8]

Cuban socialism certainly did not launch Afro-Cuban popular music, but the intellectual movement of Afro-Cubanism in the 1920s and 1930s (mirrored later in the networks of aficionados, chroniclers, and publicists who continue to make the music thrive) were central to the independence movements whose leaders directly inspired Castro's 26 July Movement.[9] Indeed, those who lived long enough to bridge the two eras saw more continuities than departures. From their perspective at least, the revolution of 1959 was the consummation of the great exponents of Afro-Cubanism in the 1920s and 1930s (Ortiz, Carpentier, Nicolás Guillén) along with the important work of Lydia Cabrera on the *Reglas de Congo* and on Afro-Cuban folktales in the 1950s and after (Cabrera lived in exile).

The sentiments of the early movements against Spanish, and later North American, occupation, which were most closely allied with the work of Martí – who very early on advocated a racially inclusive national identity – were finally coming to realization. It made sense for Castro and others in the government to invoke the Afro-Cuban elements of their society as being at the very heart of the Cuban self.[10] Curricular changes in the art and music schools, still run with an attention to formal discipline and classical training, reflected a valorization of creation from below combined with folkloric recovery work and the African influences on the classical repertoire. The schools and institutes themselves, it is true, often moved in the direction of discouraging the popular arts in favor of European classical training, but they also imparted a performative and compositional expertise that proved decisive to the musicians who, under the influence of other sectors of the revolution, threw in their lot with popular genres. Specifically, the rise of *timba* music (see below) was aided greatly by the classical training of its best performers, and this was a very old pattern, evident as well before the revolution in the rise of the *danzón* and in the virtuosity of black performers from the nineteenth century like Claudio Brindís de Salas who straddled the two camps of the popular and the classical. It would not be putting it too strongly to say that the new government identified itself with a national musical (including Afro-Cuban) patrimony, helping to drive home the already disintegrating division between high and low culture that had been a part of Cuba's cultural past. For example, in the early years of the revolution, labor unions sponsored tours by folkloric ensembles, a number of new dance genres emerged in the early 1960s (the *dengue*, the *pacá*, the *guarapachanga*), the jazz scene thrived as never before, and creativity flourished with the return to Cuba of former exiles wishing to participate on new cultural terrain.[11]

This kind of work, apart from its importance to the Cuban national project itself, was also conducted in the spirit of a protest against prevalent misconceptions regarding Latin music in general in Europe and North America. We have to remind ourselves of the level of ignorance abroad. In his memorable book of sketches, *A Puerto Rican in New York*, for example, Jesus Colón recounts how the widely trusted U.S. broadcaster Edward R. Murrow once proclaimed that the jilty hip-movements of the Dominican *merengue* were the result of the dance having been invented by an Irish captain with a peg leg, and that the tango came about as the result of the Argentinians not being able to dance the waltz properly.[12]

Socialist Cuba's promotion of popular music, however, was inconsistent. Between the early 1960s and 1970s, the combination of financial crisis and the ideological rigidity of policies reacting to external political pressures led to a severe weakening of the Cuban dance scene. The "Bay of Pigs" invasion of the country at Playa Girón set a radical new tone. Many active venues were closed down with the abolition of the *sociedades de recreo* in 1962, and forms of support dried up for musical performers specializing in some of Cuba's most popular styles. As several commentators have noted, the negative pressures were not all ideological. Popular uprisings against the casinos (which many associated with pre-revolutionary period's elitism, tourist excesses, or flagrant immorality) led to looting and vandalism that the government sought to curb, and many of the dance schools were closed because of their links with prostitution. It was a period of darkness and disorientation that reached its nadir in 1969 with the wholesale closing down of dance clubs in order to keep people's attentions focused on the sugar harvest. By the 1980s, the emphasis within the art schools and conservatories was decidedly Euro-classical, and focus on the popular arts had declined drastically.

A number of observers have reported a different kind of problem as well. For some members of the government, the rhetorical commitment to the Afro-Cuban population regarding equality before the law or the dismantling of an earlier discriminatory system based on race did not extend to a genuine enthusiasm for Afro-Cuban religion or the music that emerged from it. *Rumba* and *mambo*, for this brand of socialist, was a lamentable vestige of peoples deprived of "real" culture, and therefore a sign of embarrassment. In this dogmatic perspective, the uneducated (black and white) needed to be raised to a higher cultural level, and given the opportunity to be more. At certain times and places, these attitudes – this fissure, that is, between official policy and practice – created obstacles for the free expression of Afro-Cuban music.

These counter-trends cannot be simply explained away, and they have been dealt with judiciously by scholars like Yvonne Daniel, Peter Manuel, and more recently Robin Moore (not to mention a number of Cuban critics, especially Leonardo Acosta).[13] But even accounting for them, one is left with a remarkable record of official encouragement that needs to be acknowledged more openly. Almost always, the decisive piece of evidence preventing such acknowledgement is the exodus of musicians after 1959. But the framing of that discussion distorts our understanding of the forces at work.

The point is rarely made, for instance, that Cuban musicians had been fleeing for financial reasons to the United States and Mexico long before the revolution. It is at least arguable that primarily commercial reasons are the ones still in play today, despite efforts to make it seem a matter of democratic "freedom." Many of the artists cited as fleeing revolutionary Cuba actually lived in exile in New York *before* the revolution, among them Frank Grillo ("Machito"), Graciela, Mario Bauzá, Miguelito Valdés, Arsenio Rodríguez, Chano Pozo, Chico O'Farrill, Anselmo Sacasas, René Harnández, Cándido Camero, Vincentico Valdés, Armando Peraza, Gilberto Valdés, Chocolate Armenteros, Mongo Santamaría, and Marcelino Guerra y Chombo Silva.[14] Nor is it the case that artists who left were necessarily driven by ideology, any more than that those who remained in revolutionary Cuba were, for that reason, in full support of the new society. Family ties, identifications with place and country, fear of the unknown, antipathy to U.S. culture, racist attitudes, and any number of related reasons were at least as responsible as pro- or anti-market ideologies. The array and numbers of artists who remained – the kinds of artists showcased in *Buena Vista Social Club* gives a sense of their authority – were in the majority.[15] They included, for example, Sindo Garay, Niño Rivera, Ignacio Piñeiro, Carmelina Barbaris, Elio Revé, Celeste Mendoza, Celina Gonzalez, Miguelito Cuní, Félix Chappottín, José Antonio Méndez, Paulina Álvarez, Ester Borja, Compay Segundo, and such groups as Orquesta Aragón, Los Papines, Muñequitos de Matanzas, Sonora Matancera, and Septeto Nacional. The better-known artists who arose within the revolution and stayed (sometimes critically), include Los Van Van, Irakere, Son 14, La Original de Manzanillo, Grupo Sierra Maestra, Anacaona, Azúcar Negra, Bamboleo, La Charanga Habanera, Manolin "El Medico de la Salsa", and NG La Banda.

Given Cuba's role in inventing internationally successful leisure products for over a century, there is a certain irony in the claims that the country has crippled the pursuit of pleasure. As recent film and concert tours have reminded the U.S. public, Cuba's cultural influence is found in a number of places in U.S. popular music, theater, and film for a century and a half, from the penetration of the *habanera son* into the U.S.

heartland to the *mambo* craze of New York in the 1940s and 1950s (captured in recent years in the film adaptation of Oscar Hijuelos's novel, *The Mambo Kings Play Songs of Love*). These only repeated the impact on U.S. popular culture by Latin hits like "La Paloma" in the 1870s, and "Cuban Song" from the Broadway play *The Idol's Eye* in 1897, or (as I mentioned earlier) in the academy award-nominated film music of Ernesto Lecuona, whose work was widely heard in Hollywood and on the radio from the late 1930s to the 1950s.

But think, too, of Cuba's efforts in other realms of popular culture. The island nation was home to the golden age of 1970s poster art, and was where Julio García Espinoza developed his theory of "imperfect cinema"; it was where the *filin* songs of the 1960s were launched, and the place where two of the best-known *nueva canción* composers in Latin America wrote (Pablo Milanés and Silvio Rodríguez), creating a form of troubadour modernity influential throughout Europe and Latin America for almost two decades. It is important to recall Ulf Hannerz's helpful revision of the center/periphery construct when he observes that there are actually many regional centers in the global arrangement of states.[16] Qom is a major religious hub, for example; Mumbai (formerly Bombay) is a distribution source for a style of musical film that touches most of Asia and Africa; Cairo a center for Arabic publishing, and Mexico the favored exporter of the *telenovela*. For Latin America and the Caribbean, Cuba has acted as this sort of center. The Havana Film Festival and the Casa de las Americas awards in literature have prompted a regional creativity in explicitly Latin American literary and cinematic forms outside the direct influence of North American audiences or U.S. advertising. Among these forms was the *testimonio*, whose early practitioners and theorists included Miguel Barnet and Margaret Randall, then resident in Cuba (the genre of *testimonio* itself being, arguably, a Cuban export).

More recently, one finds examples in the international *rumba* festivals in Matanzas, the Havana '94 *encuentro* (meeting) bringing musicians and aficionados from around the world to celebrate Afro-Cuban music, and in one of many examples of openness to the outside world, the IX Habana Hip Hop 2003 conference.[17] Nor does this begin to appreciate Cuba's visible role as spokesman for the Non-Aligned Nations, a role filled dramatically at the Rio Summit less than a decade ago in a widely publicized confrontation with the United States over the environment – not an issue typically recognized as being among Cuba's priorities, but which has become one given the low-tech innovation forced on the country by the U.S. embargo.[18]

Only a peculiar kind of insensitivity could pass over these contributions without comment, or fail to observe that Cuba has also excelled in another popular form of cultural expression – sport, the activity claiming hours of popular free time, and a stage for the enactment of dreams and desires.[19] As the victor in the Pan American games of the early 1990s, Cuba was, among other things, exporting a cultural message about the style and modes of funding possible under socialism itself. It offered, along with athletic excellence, an advertisement for teamwork, state sponsorship, and the broad accessibility that alone could allow a country with a relatively small population to out-compete rivals from much larger and wealthier nations.

In Cuba, socialist culture certainly is implicated in the system of government (how could it not be?) that helps name its heroes, devise its myths and so on. But it is astonishing how little our criticism mentions these kinds of examples, or how often it tends to fall into the trap of inherited modes of discussing Cuba. One has no trouble understanding the pressures that produce this outcome, but it has nevertheless silenced a number of promising lines of inquiry. Since socialist style or ethics are discussed in a serious or neutral way in the West only rarely, my attempt to do so here will probably be thought a declaration of partisanship rather than an effort to *open* inquiry by entering an understudied space. The fact is all the more lamentable because most U.S. popular music critics do not support the *cordon sanitaire* set up around the island. Still, even among the highly informed critics of rock magazines and academic publishing houses, the view is still very common that Cuba is an enemy of freedom, and that Cuban youth live in a straitjacket woven from the idealist dreams of their now-aging '50s and '60s parents. Because this mainstream outlook is coming from the resistance cultures of music theory, they carry a special weight, and are much more likely in some circles to be taken at face value.[20]

In some quarters, this has expressed itself as an effort to demote the cultural role of Cuba in Latin music, particularly after the revolution.[21] "Salsa" in particular has come to be understood as an entirely non-Cuban, pan-Latino form of U.S. vintage whose virtues are tightly bound up with its dedication to a kind of party music that is also aesthetically accomplished. In one recent anthology, in fact, a Venezuelan percussionist is quoted as saying that "Cubans cannot play salsa. There is not a Cuban salsa group, it does not exist."[22] If one defines the term "salsa" narrowly enough, this is no doubt true, but the real meaning of the statement lies elsewhere. The understandable resentment many Latin American musicians feel because of the enormous attention paid to

Cuban music in the press and in scholarship is one of the points of the statement, and so a motive for singling out an immensely popular genre as a non-Cuban preserve. But there is also something more subtle happening – the deployment of political belief in the guise of a form of identity. In this sense, "salsa" is meant to symbolize a set of social values that a socialist country like Cuba can never have. The same strategy reappears in another of the anthology's chapters on women salsa performers. Here the author looks exclusively at U.S.-based singers either transplanted or native, implying that women musicians only flourished once they left their native countries, and that feminist concerns were an exclusively metropolitan affair.[23]

On freedom: the cases of salsa and timba

In fact, the relationship of salsa to Cuba is more complicated. If the form in general can be said to combine the song structure of Cuban *son*, the hybrid European/African, high/low orchestration of *mambo*, and the sexualized dance rituals of *guaguancó*, it is also the case that musicians like Tito Puente, Machito, and Cachao (who lived to witness the rise of salsa) all denied that the music was anything but the Cuban music they had been playing in the 1940s. In an interview for the documentary film, *Roots of Rhythm* (1994), Celia Cruz expressed exactly the same sentiment: "I don't like communism, so I learned that what I sing has another name: it's called 'salsa.' But it's not a new rhythm. It's Cuban music by another name."[24] This sense in Cuba itself that salsa was only a belated repetition of their sound was made worse by the isolation of the country in the 1960s, which abruptly stopped the steady stream of musical influence from Cuba to New York. Post-revolutionary Cuban innovations like *pachanga* and *songo* had little influence abroad, although Pedro Izquierdo's *mozambique* did filter through the blockade, finding its way into the work of Eddie Palmieri, Ritchie Ray, and El Gran Combo. With the explosion of salsa talent in New York in the 1970s, with its own stars and look, and with the triumph of British rock, Cuba for a time fell from view.

As the salsa craze began to wane, the struggle of its performers to create a new market for the music led them to experiment with more listener-friendly forms like Hispanic pop and *salsa romántica*. This watering down of the original sound further alienated Cuban artists. The indignation felt in Havana made salsa for a time anathema there, and it was dismissed in Cuba as a point of "national honor."[25] In time, salsa was accepted in Cuba as its own thing, and underwent further changes there (as elsewhere). Some of the forces that propelled salsa back to popularity in the

United States and Europe in the 1980s and 1990s were, once again, not unrelated to Cuba. These forces included the contra war in Central America, the growing U.S. Latino immigration, and heightened aggression against Cuba. In different ways all three introduced middle-class youth and acculturating Latinos into a new appreciation of Latin music and a devotion to its past, and is the principal social setting that accounts for the rise of salsa schools and Latin dance undergrounds that today exist throughout Europe and North America.

If this history explains why Cuba might feel vexed in its relationship to salsa, it does not capture the other side – the objective musical conditions that justify some writers in invoking salsa as a symbol of freedom from Cuban influence and an embrace of metropolitan youth (with all the political overtones of such a move). It is important to insist, in other words, that salsa is much more than a refashioning of Cuban components. Its manner of performance and the way it combines percussion instruments, for example, depart from its Cuban predecessors. So too its penchant for piano *montunos* (rhythmic improvisational solos), the use (after rock) of electric bass guitar and electric piano, the use of trombones, the arrangements and orchestration, its vocal inflections and improvisations, its scenic movements, and above all, the kinds of texts that are sung, with their treatment of the everyday life of minority communities and, more specifically, a rural imagination surrounded by a metropolitan world.[26]

It is *timba*, though – one of those post-revolutionary dance innovations in Cuba that is sometimes called *salsa cubana* – that has played an important role recently in the arguments of those who question Cuban socialism by claiming that it "fails to understand the specificity of Afro-Cuban culture" and even that it "hide[s] the fact that the great majority of dance music made in Cuba after the revolution ... incorporates influences from Afro-Cuban folklore."[27] This statement interests me a great deal, since it is seems to be contradicted by the evidence I have been presenting both in this and other chapters. From what perspective is it made, and what are its theoretical assumptions?

Timba has been called, variously, an eclectic fusion mixing *son* with Afro-Cuban rumba, U.S. black music and other Afro-Latin popular styles. and an "aggressive, intensely rhythmic, extremely danceable" music based on "foreign genres such as jazz, funk, and rap."[28] The significance of *timba,* according to some researchers, lies in its combination. It was, until recently, hugely popular in Cuba; it flaunted an irreverent black, lower-class identity; it mixed the technical expertise of the Cuban conservatory with officially embarrassing references to the problems of contemporary Cuban life; and it experienced, from time to time, run-ins with the authorities. Although *timba* is now played publicly throughout Cuba without incident, and although its performers travel abroad and command large performance fees, there have been cases where performers were arrested for lyrics that appeared to mock members of the government, and a general sense that its identity politics were fomenting (with the help of imported U.S. ideology) a black separatism based on a "gangsta" mentality similar to that found in rap.

Indeed, although *timba* is often called a "music of the barrios," it is more accurately seen as a particular take on the barrios (or the solution to living in them). Some of its songs display an eagerness to merge with U.S. styles in a symbolic act of non-cooperation. The problem, though, is more complex than that. For there is in fact some merit to the charge that the official hostility to *timba* is based in part on the kind of aesthetic revulsion the intellectual left in the United States sometimes has for rap. Acosta, for instance, likens the stern criticism of *timba* by newspaper journalists and critics in Cuba to the angry dismissal of earlier dance styles (*danzón, son, mambo, chachachá*) by conservative circles interested in the 'aesthetic education of the masses.'"[29]

Timba often replaces the call-and-response structure with an extended rap section. But unlike rap, it is about creating a trance (some songs last over a half hour). In groups like Azúcar Negro and Charanga Habana, one finds a single, linear, drive with only minor syncopation, a frenzy of loud percussion with indistinct melodies. The dancing tends to be less articulated and intentionally jumpy. In practice, however, the genre is as mixed as any other Cuban form. At the end of Charanga Habana's "Como Cambian los Tiempos" ("How the Times are Changing") for example, one finds a slow, passionate, sincerity. The "break" at the end of the very long song, a kind of coda, is romantic, sentimental, and wholly unthinkable in a U.S. rap concert – and to that degree is very Cuban in the full revolutionary sense of the word.

Finding in *timba* signs of the "Cuban crisis" – that is, seeing in it a register of an emergent popular demand to be freed of the constraints of socialism – is a view that draws very heavily on the rhetorical concepts of metropolitan cultural theory. Vincenzo Perna speaks of the music's uneasy relationship to the Cuban political establishment:

> As a type of black dance music it resists cultural elitism, empowering Afro-Cuban culture and contesting visions of ethnic pacification and social harmony. Through its appropriation of foreign styles, timba challenges discourses that seek to construct a demonized image of

capitalism, and evades notions of narrowly-defined cultural nationalism. Popular support and economic relevance, therefore, have not saved timba from a head-to-head collision with the Cuban authorities, who, in the late 1990s, attacked its perceived excesses and banned the activity of the most popular timba band.[30]

The implication that the "Cuban political establishment" looks with disfavor on dance forms that are not elitist is odd to anyone who has visited Cuba or knows its musical history. From the *tresero* performances on every Havana street corner to the impromptu *rumba* gatherings in city squares to the organized tours to Matanzas *santería* altars, there is evidence everywhere that the popular is, on the contrary, what the country boasts of having, and at both the official and unofficial levels.[31]

Although the charge is untrue, it does point to a more sensitive question, and one that requires more care in answering. It lurks in the reference to "ethnic pacification and social harmony." This is an allusion to Cuba's discouragement of sectoralist organizing and its resistance to the political rhetoric of racial difference. The issue is confusing for many in the officially multicultural United States who are not accustomed to imagining themselves in a foreign political reality, but who have instead acquired the habit of projecting what they consider natural onto the rest of the world. As I argued in Chapter 3, to mobilize a different conception of the popular than is used in Cuba is not to establish elitism. From the Cuban point of view, foreclosing gross economic disparities and generalizing social access; eliminating the legal or de facto segregation governing attendance at schools, clubs, and access to housing that prevailed before 1959 – from this point of view, identity-based politics is divisive, particularly the mercenary kind promoted by some *timba* performers.[32]

The hostility towards Afro-Cuban sectoralism has been exacerbated by the special economic period. One gets a hint of what is at work in the reference above to *timba*'s challenge to "demonized images of capitalism." A less circuitous way of putting the matter is that some *timba* performers see the disaffection of blacks and youth as possible to overcome so long as one introduces a consumerism that is identified by the performers, not so subtly, with the United States itself. The values of self-enrichment are made equivalent to a liberatory challenge to black disenfranchisement – captured in the exaltation over *timba*'s "anthemic, street-wise, ambiguous, and hedonistic" capacities. Not really explored in the passage above is the dark side of this underground that sets itself against "revolutionary ideals." What values is this underground counterposing to the institutions of the Cuban state, and what exactly are we being asked to endorse? The discourse of heroic subalternity found in U.S. cultural studies provides a clue of what is really at work in this kind of analysis. There cultural expressions of "peoples and communities," on the one hand, are set against "the master narratives of the nation state" on the other.[33]

Leaving alone the fact that the (still fragile) ideals of the Cuban state are the result of the work of several generations of "peoples and communities" who have sacrificed a great deal for independence from the very country from which many of the theorists of subalternity come, it is hard to call the beleaguered nations of Latin America the beneficiaries of "master narratives." The truth is that their narrative can barely be heard above the din of debt coercion, military threats, and hostile U.S. radio and television programming. Are states everywhere the same, presiding over populations of servants? Or should the phrase "master narrative" be reserved for states that govern actual empires? The "code switching, syncretism, and hybridity" that this sort of metropolitan criticism locates in people of color everywhere enshrines the political ideal of in-betweenness – which is to say, living outside of the "political lexicon of the nation state."[34] Historically, though, the truth is very different. Cuban sovereignty has quite rightly been seen by Cubans themselves as a pre-requisite to the partial reprieve from the U.S. color-bar.[35] To seek to propose a "new" theory of race relations in Cuba based on "cultural mix, a stylistic and ideological bricolage" is perhaps not the move forward that it wants to be.[36] On the contrary, it leaves the country open to the U.S. penetration that has proved so fatal to equality (including racial equality) in the country's past.

The idea of freedom itself must also be interrogated in this discourse. Every constraint on freedom – and life is filled with them, after all – is cast in discussions of Cuba as the work of an oppressive state. In the books on salsa and *timba* above, as well as in a good deal of the writing on popular music available in English, we are told, for instance, that the system of musical production in Cuba marginalizes aspiring artists who are unable to receive official recognition and that these pressures influence the types of music they perform. What is remarkable here is not that such a statement is untrue – it probably is not – only that it implies more than it says. Are we supposed to believe, for example, that in the United States official recognition is not denied aspiring artists, or that musicians are immune to the directives of a not-so-subtle road-map to stardom provided by agents, ad-men, and the corporate boardroom? It is fairly easy to demonstrate the closed networks of producers, lawyers, and distributors who make life difficult for younger artists and kill their dreams. Lyrics are censored, albums labeled for content, careers foreclosed. Allergic to ideas, many large U.S. and European record producers manufacture scandals while insuring that music is kept antiseptically cool, or powered by the fake rebellions of Grammy rap and its counterparts in other genres. A market-driven music industry is at least as peremptory as anything one finds in the comparatively lavish system of rewards given to artists in Cuba, although, of course, some artists who remain edgy and inventive break through the U.S. filtering devices from time to time, just as bad music that is politically safe is at times promoted in Cuba.

Yvonne Daniel, Hernando Calvo Ospina, and Tony Évora have all written valuable studies that although rightly critical of various aspects of socialist policy in certain periods avoid the anti-Castro reflex.[37] Above all, such work has come from Cuba's own music critics, who are not only highly accomplished but relatively ignored in English.[38]

Globalism and youth

The discourses of pleasure are political.[39] On the one hand, peripheral countries are popularly depicted not only in the media but in many scholarly studies, in either the drab tones of destitute barrios or in the carnivalesque colors of mayhem, starvation, and war. On the other, the entertainment industries of the major industrial nations imagine that the pleasures of travel must, like an MTV special, be either about tourism or distanced spectatorship rather than learning about a different cultural logic. Weaker countries are kept weak not only by assaults on their resources or by debt interest, but by a barrage of images of enticement, which together form a powerful claim that technological prowess yoked to a leisure economy gives the metropolis a monopoly on pleasure itself. By way of well-equipped recording studios, the special-effects of film, and satellite transmissions, musical forms of entertainment are so mobile and ubiquitous that their political subtexts are a formidable act of persuasion all by themselves. Conventional wisdom, like the joke with which I began this chapter, casts alternatives to the market in the role of a hopeless oddity.

"Socialism," needless to say, in the universe of commercial culture, is genetically humorless. The grim gray apartment complexes of Poland come to mind; the tawdry, ill-made shoes of the Czech factory worker; the Moscow apartment-dweller's diet of potatoes and cabbage. In each image there is only colorlessness and tedium, no hint that some less fortunate countries fending for themselves without the wealth of past imperial enterprises actually take the trouble to provide housing, clothing, and food for people who would not otherwise have them, thereby "spreading the poverty" as much as spreading the wealth. Today's Cuba may not correspond to an image of the suburbs, or Times Square on a Saturday night, but neither is it the unbroken rural destitution found in many parts of Central America, areas of Bangladesh, or parts of Africa (or, for that matter, inner-city Detroit). In North America, socialist pleasure is not just elusive but forbidden from public discussion. The term "socialism" does not even have to be defined.

When we consider global popular culture, it is good to remember that "globalization" attained its widespread use only after the fall of the Soviet Union and the Eastern bloc. The rise of the one accompanied the fall of the other. Along with the fall of a coherent, geopolitical space outside the market came the collapse of a set of international alliances that once appeared as a viable rival to a widely exported U.S. way of life. In Mozambique, West Bengal, the Indian state of Kerala, China, and Cuba, for instance, socialism tended throughout the 1970s to mean little more than an official resistance toward unchecked capital penetration. Although a highly charged, even tainted, word in U.S media renditions, "socialism" for these countries meant primarily local autonomy, political sovereignty, literacy, and development, all seen as the minimum basis upon which the invisible classes of those countries might approximate the quality of life outlined in the United Nations Universal Declaration of Human Rights (1948). On the global periphery until 1989, freedom from an unrestrained market was typically considered a precondition for sovereignty. It hardly needs to be said today, after a series of externally dictated and disastrous structural adjustment programs in the Ukraine, Argentina, and Poland, or after the invasions in Iraq, Afghanistan, and Colombia, that the perspective adopted by these countries had merit.

Globalization, taken in some circles to signify the inexorable emergence of an exciting world culture, can also be seen less invitingly as a mass global conversion. Particularly at this kind of juncture Cuba arises as a decisive case for testing the claims of globalization as a whole, not least because the trope of exile in globalization discussions seems so obviously in conflict with the quarantining of Cuba by U.S. opinion-makers. Exiles are the proper adjunct, one could say, of global culture, a world of supposedly diasporic peoples venturing into new territory. But it does not take long for this sense of the term to seem overly jubilant when exploring Cuban art. One recalls, for instance, the scene at the airport in one of the early moments in Tomás Guttiérez Alea's famous film *Memories of Underdevelopment*, when the protagonist Sergio surveys with bemusement the departing bourgeois minions in bouffant hairdos and nervous smiles.[40] This image of class awareness only finds it way into North America with difficulty. The critic always errs on the side of wanting to stake out a position of neutral expertise, eager to demonstrate awareness of any issue's "many sides." The self-critical intellectual protagonist of the film is, in fact, the very definition of ambivalence, which is one of the reasons why this product of the early revolutionary Cuban film industry – based on a novel by Edmund Desnoës, a New York-based Cuban author who returned to Castro's Cuba to work in the offices of Casa de las Americas – was such an international triumph. Its painful abandonment of unruffled middle-class points of departure is equally unmistakable, however, and accounts for the major turmoil of the central character.[41]

The history of Cuba and its music is conditioned by a tropical Cold War discourse. Unlike the Latin economic refugees of recent decades, those in the first wave were overwhelmingly white, highly educated, and to the plantation born. Caught in the vice of the U.S. encirclement of Cuba on the one hand, and intimidation of Cuba's potential allies and trading partners on the other, another round of economic flight has emerged over the last two decades. The first generation of exiles, however, was one in which the connection between exile and foreign travel had been blurred for generations. They were fleeing a country, it should be remembered, not only about to regulate their profit-making and restrict their inherited privileges but whose image of itself was about to become officially Afro-Cuban, not just Spanish and creole. Associating Cuban exiles with a "boat people" driven by the quest for political asylum does not in every case fit the history of movement to and from the island. The flow of Cuban exiles for over a century before the revolution included people who later found themselves in Tampa cigar-rolling centers, New Orleans music halls, and the New York and New Jersey metropolitan areas.

The haze of the multiculturalism debates in the United States has in this sense clouded the contribution of Cuban socialism to racial diversity, a connection that is rarely made in celebrations of American pluralism in the United States. Even before the ousting of Battista, the long-brewing revolt of color against Cuban high society stamped itself on the character of the revolution throughout the decades of de facto U.S. rule. It was marked both by a colonial servility and a country-club snobbery captured beautifully in Nicolás Guillén's poem, "No me dan pena los burgueses vencidos" ("I don't spend time worrying about the rich after they've lost power") and later set to song by Pablo Milanés. The revolution, in short, was always largely about race. A prominent, if not universal, aspect of Miami Cuban culture was disgust at Cuba's "vulgar" promotion of black culture after 1959, and the new prominence that Afro-Cubans came relatively to enjoy, even though racial discrimination certainly still exits in Cuba, as it does throughout the Americas. At the same time, as in the United States itself, Afro-based expression in painting, sport, dance, and music were the most culturally attractive products disseminated abroad.

As an instrument of globalization, popular culture is almost by definition about marketing, whereas the demands of marketing dictate a certain structure of playfulness that affects pleasure. Questions are seldom raised, though, about the degree to which a market can be pleasurable. Since we are discussing *global* popular culture, one might be driven to explore those places where the popular is inimical to the market, but where, at the same time, popular culture is still produced before being consumed globally. This kind of consideration brings one inevitably to Cuba.

At the outset one would suppose that a meditation on desire and pleasure would immediately raise the issue of entertainment. But how much is this really so? Much of the criticism on the day-to-day life of the entertainment industry in the United States suggests that pleasure is not always wrung from the arduous task of being entertained. Think only of the title of Neil Postman's memorable book, *Amusing Ourselves to Death*, or Andrew Goodwin's study of MTV, *Dancing in the Distraction Factory*, to take just two more or less recent studies of the "entertainment state."[42] The economy, and by extension, private fortunes, peripheral poverties, and a number of seemingly unrelated government policies, are built on a foundation whose supposed product is distraction, release, relaxation, enjoyment. But, as any executive will tell you, it is very hard to find joyful release with one eye on the clock. Or to put it another way, with so many serious things riding on the game of pleasure; or with so many business interests wanting a cut of the action of our "carefree" moments away from work, pleasure itself is being harnessed for someone else's game. The U.S. economy is increasingly built on the fortunes of an ephemeral product whose function is release, relaxation, and enjoyment. While appearing to be a service for us, the product of this industry might be said to be, by contrast, simply *us*. That is, *we* are the product they are creating, a certain "us" that consumes.

The consumption of desire, moreover, prompts an elaborate network of image-makers for outreach. When reading the research of managerial specialists and advertising experts, one quickly learns that one of their principal targets is youth. The very concept of market research, and also this practice of identifying youth as its special target, is the invention of the United States, and dates from the 1920s.[43] Youth is key to the concept of a global popular culture for a number of reasons. Youth is considered by market researchers to comprise a standardized group. Advertisers are statistically confident that their responses to stimuli are predictable in whatever culture they appear, regardless of significant differences in the way that predictability is expressed. In the blunt mode of address that managerial theorists adopt when talking to one another, two aspects of youth above all are considered crucial: (1) youth carry their patterns of preference far into adulthood; so if their behavior is modified early, it remains throughout their lifetimes; and (2) if one can reach youth, one has in effect reached the rest of the family as well, since parents and siblings are forced to conform to the drive and urgency of the young who determine the "now-ness" of all trends. Youth, in short, is not simply the young; it is the ideology of youth.

Youth, then, is perceived in these circles as the wedge, arbiter, and force of revolutionary dislodgement. There is no globalization without the idea of youth, which is the group whose friendliness toward the new gives it the power to issue calling-cards to foreign capital, or provide openings for next year's documentaries on the next wave of twenty-something entrepreneurs. Their experimentalism and novelty, which supposedly comes from having thought less along the rutted paths of their elders, can be moved by inches to the concept of entrepreneurship (as it is in today's quintessentially postmodern images of the computer hacker, the New Age environmentalist clothing designers, the Silicon Valley nerds). The well-known colonial contest between civilizations where capitalist technologies and dynamism, on the one side, are pitted against traditional religious or rural life, on the other, is here recast in a macro-contest between youth and age. As the managerial specialists would have it, at any rate, capitalism is for youth. Capitalism *is* youth.[44]

For that reason, resistance to designer radicalism can often take the form of *preservation* (a point in concert with the general concerns of this book). The accepted idea that kids all listen to rap, recycled punk, or emo does not bear up very well under scrutiny. Sniffing the corporate winds, a lot of youth rebel (paradoxically) by adopting their parents' tastes – or rather, by taking the unexpected view that music from the 1960s and 1970s is more worth listening to. It is very little commented on how many young people immerse themselves in standbys from the '70s – Led Zeppelin, Neil Young, and the most obvious case, the Rolling Stones. It is in this spirit that Thomas Frank in *Commodify Your Dissent* issued a declaration to corporate advertisers refusing to play his assigned role.

> You snicker that our identities are little more than a patchwork of lines remember[ed] from episodes of the TV programs we watched as children . . . We refuse to accept your central historical/televisual myth . . . To us the idiocy, depravity, and soul-crushing cruelty of

your human machine is so obvious, so plain and undisguised, that we set ourselves in opposition to it as a matter of course . . . The business of business is our minds.[45]

Apparently, *National Geographic* understood this formula perfectly in its special issue on "Global Culture" some years ago (Figure 5.1).

Figure 5.1 *National Geographic* cover (August 1999).

On the magazine's cover an upper-class Indian mother dressed in a sari sits beside her Anglicized daughter, dressed in shiny patent leather. There, starkly featured, sit two poles: the traditional (age) vs. the modern (youth). The mother's admiring maternal glance stands in counterpoint to the daughter's steely, unsentimental, and ambitious stare. As if parodying Gandhi's *swadeshi* movement against British imperialism (in which Gandhi counseled his countrymen to make "homespun" cloth in order to boycott British manufacture), the insouciant daughter wears a tight black jumpsuit "of her own design." Even as the mother projects quiet professional dignity, the daughter intimates a subtle, and therefore acceptable, sexual availability by her slightly parted legs. Youth, sexuality, and entrepreneurship are inextricable. Beneath the make-up, and the created desire (which depending on the viewer might involve sex, fashion, or the exoticism of India, now whittled down to size), the shibboleths of globalization are sold: hybridity, opportunity, diversity, untrammeled contact, brave new creative forms, and technological wonders. These are the values that operate uncritically within most writing on popular music and the politics of cultural protest.

The systems of desire and pleasure

If there is a specific pleasure to socialism, it would amount to more presumably than altruism or the solemn comforts of justice. In a system outside the zero-sum contest of competitive individualism with its perpetual wrangling over spoils, there would be, say, the pleasures of a slower pace. In a society not calculated to push its citizens anxiously on the road to mindless acquisition, a person wouldn't have to hurry up to die. Sharing would extend not only to resources but to enjoyments. That is, spectatorship would more often take place live, jointly, and in public places: in squares, plazas, parks, and the street.[46] Criticism of art and politics would be both a personal matter and one that took place in the presence of others rather than in the form of a lonely gazer on the televisual gift delivered from on high.

More of life would take place face-to-face. If the mass ownership of cars was no longer a requirement of economic health (mass ownership of cars would be, on the contrary, too expensive and irrational given available mass transportation), city life would thrive by way of a series of personal encounters that were no longer dependent on the Internet or text-messaging. The relative lack of commodities – at first glance an anti-pleasure – would actually allow for a less extreme division of labor, freeing one from illusory "choices" and the mental overload of advertising, as well as a greater (if not absolute) freedom from the tyranny of things. The body would become more than an identity-corkboard, resuming its status once more as a "person"; and the person would, in turn, assume his or her political identity as a citizen, leaving behind its preferred late capitalist designator, the "subject," with all the intentional ambiguity of that term (vassal or lord?).

What, by contrast, can one say then about capitalist desire? Given the need to sell products, the most compelling desires that capitalism offers are strangely compelled: owning a car in Los Angeles, for example, employing Qwest as one's phone service in a market where only Qwest offers phone service, switching from vinyl records to compact discs, from cash to credit cards, or from slower to faster Internet access. Desire amounts to a constantly delayed satisfaction. It is present as either a set of demands to seek what cannot be found or as addiction (video game, cigarette, valium, sitcom). Desire, moreover, in its capitalist forms often involves what might be called a kind of libidinal terrorism – the conquest of the libido by incessant repetition, the splicing of sexuality and hunger onto the attractions of purchases. It involves the making of all value quantifiable where the question "how much" replaces "how good"? Q: which film was the most creative, the most offbeat? A: *The Blair Witch Project* only cost $100,000 and made over $40 million; Q: Will it be fun? A: Yes, it will not take much time. Q: How old is this fashion model? A: She is the youngest ever to be on the cover of *Talk* magazine.

Figure 5.2 Image from Pedro Coll,
El Tiempo Detenido: La Habana.

Subcultures, instead of being sites where a symbolic "no" can be uttered against the system, turn out too often to be the containment itself. As it did in the advertising manuals of the 1940s, youth at times has figured as the dodge of elderly establishment power. Let's examine two cases of youth, pleasure, and global culture.

Marketing youth: *Las Jineteras* and the Plaza

In Cuba they say "We are exporting mothers," which means we are exporting even mothers to get cash. But it also explains two other things: 1) why there are so many mother-fuckers and 2) why so many Cubans are sons of bitches.
Sonia Baez (official with Cultural Ministry)[47]

Throughout the 1990s on Havana's meandering seaside boulevard, the *Malecon*, with windswept hair the women known locally simply as *"las chicas"* lured tourists on warm nights to cruise slowly in taxis driven by panders. Exceedingly young – between sixteen and twenty years old – the women were not professionals in the usual sense. The "new" prostitution in Cuba is no longer news, and has been analyzed by a number of journalists and scholars, all of whom have pointed out the paradox that the government cleaned up the gambling and prostitution of the 1950s only to see it revive unofficially under the edicts of tourism in the "special period," the local term for the time after 1989 when trade with the Soviet Union and Eastern Europe collapsed.

As of January 1993, food rationing had not plummeted to the degree where Cuban teenagers would be driven by hunger to "date" foreign visitors for payment. The economic indicators were nevertheless severe. In addition to the decline in production brought by drastically curtailed oil imports, Cuba suffered three devastating tropical storms in March, May, and November of 1993. The one in March of that year – the so-called storm of the century – might have been the worst Cuba ever experienced, although it has been heavily battered since. Asked by prospective clients, the women themselves would simply bear out what much of the 1993 American press had been reporting: namely, that prior to the new currency laws allowing citizens to hold U.S. dollars, teens were unlikely to be able to get things like makeup, pumps, dance dresses, and cosmetics without the "gifts" of visitors.

The new Cuban prostitution, flagrantly illegal but also officially tolerated, was therefore not about survival or the creation of a class of professional prostitutes. The motive in this case, only slightly less depressing, was about style, nightlife, frills, the taste of liquor, being bad, being on the town. For some time in the bootstrap mode, Cuba confronted a three-fourths decline in its standard of living over a four-year period; malnutrition began to set itself upon the poorer barrios of the larger cities with the appearance of a mysterious eye disease as one of its probable effects. The Torricelli Bill, passed in this period by the

170   SECULAR DEVOTION

U.S. Congress, promised to deliver more of the same.[48] Under George W. Bush, the once rarely observed formal policy of the U.S. Treasury proscribing travel to Cuba became a harsh and punitive law, and Cuba itself – more economically surrounded than at any other time in its history – pushed itself to levels of self-sufficiency (particularly in agriculture and bio-technology) that have prompted interesting observations by foreign scientists about the benefits of isolation from the "free world."[49]

Figure 5.3 Image from René Burri, *Cuba y Cuba*.

But these statistics of misery overlook other sorts of deprivations. With no other way to enjoy the clubs, women might spend one night every week or two with a tourist drinking, dancing, and coasting the dance floors. The not always implicit promise would be to sleep with him at the evening's end, although the difference between this and dating could always be rationalized in the end. From the point of view of the government this was the logic of the market on full display, and an assault on the type of improvement it thought it had always stood for. The dictator on the island had become foreign currency, which did not stop the U.S. media from reporting it as another Cuban failure and a result of the government's hypocrisy.[50]

Some of the drama on display on the Malecón arose in Cristina Garcia's novel *Dreaming in Cuban*, which characterized Cuba as suffering a rift between the generation of Playa Girón (the Bay of Pigs) and the generation of Michael Jackson: "'We're dying of security!' [Felicia] moans when [her mother] Celia tries to point out the revolution's merits. No one is starving or denied medical care, no one sleeps in the streets, everyone works who wants to work. But her daughter prefers the luxury of uncertainty, of time unplanned, of waste."[51] Youth in this narrative seems to undermine the socialist project of satisfying needs by standing for the superfluous consumption that attracts people of any class for its hint of small-scale luxury. To be rich, after all, is to be able to throw things away, to pass time idly, to buy clothes for looks rather than protection from the elements.

Historically, the socialist movement knew and knows all about this, from Paul Lafargue's late nineteenth-century tract, *The Right to be Lazy*, to Henri Lefebvre's remarkable study "Renewal, Youth, Repetition" from his *Introduction to Modernity*.[52] Antonio Gramsci observed in 1918 that socialism itself depended on selfishness – a selfishness that, as it were, could only be selfish collectively.[53] One did not join political groups because it was more moral to share, but because one could not get one's own any other way. As everyone who has lived through adolescence knows, among people's many needs is the need to be bad, to be lazy, to be useless – a sentiment expressed eloquently in the socialist tradition by Bertolt Brecht's early play *Baal* and by Vladamir Mayakovsky's poem "A Cloud in Trousers." As critics of Cuba's phases of dogmatism know, the Cuban government has not always understood this, or at least lived by its lessons.

As is now commonly known, the *chicas* of the Malecón are among those referred to by a term that uncomfortably summons associations with an oppressive past overthrown by the revolution. They are called "*jineteras*" – a word derived from an image of a plantation foreman on a horse, and popularly used for con-men and cheats who prey on naive strangers. Expensively produced advertising by companies in the United States is unnecessary for tempting the libidos of the Cuban consumer. In the special period at least, something as simple as shampoo was a luxury, and plastic slippers were finagled only in a complex protocol of (usually sexual) give-and-take.

If streetwalking on the Malecón gives a vivid picture of the market as it enters Cuba in full splendor, official gatherings in the Plaza de la Revolución may be taken as one, but only one, of the more traditionally socialist refusals of the market. On New Year's Day, tens of thousands of Havana residents – most of them teenagers – gather to watch a well-organized open-air concert featuring the country's most popular musicians. With a comparable billing in local terms to that of Britain's Band Aid/Live Aid concerts, the events are free. They demand payment only in the listening to a speech.

The ponderous address on one evening in 1993 was given by the leader of the Communist Youth in the presence of Fidel, who stood patiently to the side of the podium in full view of the crowd. A mass of nattily dressed teenagers, uncannily sober, leaned casually on bikes, small-talked, or bought soup from the event's only hawker of wares. But with the exception of the thousand or so waving banners at the base of the stage, they were not paying attention to the Youth Leader's speech, and the crowd's hum was reaching the audible registers of a distraction. Most in attendance were there for the smooth rock-pop teen idol Carlos Varela. Others had come to see the all-women's group Anacaona (now in its third generation), or to watch the tightly engineered light show, moving the audience's gaze from one stage to the next to allow abrupt shifts between acts without causing a tiresome delay – from the acoustic lyricism of Silvio Rodríguez on one stage, to the big-band electric brass of Los Van Van, on the other. Already an hour into the preliminaries, Fidel's turn at the mike prompted a speech of unexpected brevity. Cocking his head, he spoke simply about the need to have fun.

Later that evening on television, he chatted with two Cuban journalists (a man and a woman) who were dressed informally in open shirts and who sat on an outdoor patio overlooking Havana's city lights, prodding him with candor about the shuffles and murmurs of the crowd during the Youth Leader's protracted oratory. As striking as this patter was between reporters and a head of state (a White House press secretary would likely have filtered out any embarrassing comments, for instance, and served as a screen between the president and the public), even more striking was the concessionary response. People, especially young people, he answered, are sick of speeches about sacrifice during a period of sacrifices. "I cut my comments short because I did not want to burden the crowd. It is a difficult time."[54]

Somewhere beyond this acknowledgment of the need for a space in leisure outside of politics lies the nightlife of the *jinetera*, which is also a fixture of Cuban life but much more fatal to its spirit of the future. The point that arises in this juxtaposition, then, concerns a cross-wiring of two cases of socialism and the popular. One of them is found in tolerance as a principle, which the above suggests was operating in Cuba in this instance;[55] the other points to a tolerance toward social forms (like prostitution) that are allowed because of economic exigency even when they violate the principles of the society one is trying to build. Meanwhile, the Cuban government, cast repeatedly in U.S. accounts as a police state, continues to be ridiculed for, of all things, its excessive *permissiveness*.

As Sujatha Fernandes has argued, the rap scene in Cuba, which began in the late 1980s, bears witness to some of these same contradictions. The financial pressures of the special period are forcing an equation of popularity with profit-making that (Fernandes points out) is undermining the goals of socialism. As the Cuban government adopts policies of austerity in order to compete in the global economy, individual families become more dependent on remittances of hard currency from family members living abroad. But since "the majority of Cubans in the diaspora tend to be white, it is white Cuban families who benefit most from remittances." As a result, "liberalization" (rather than the socialism that seeks to limit liberalization) is what is creating an *increase* in racial prejudice in Cuba.[56] In an age of tourism, rap (like *timba*) has not only talked about, but at times promoted "hustling and consumerism . . . [as] alternative options for black youth" which is one of the reasons the government has been so hostile to the form.[57]

What we see, in fact, is not a neat picture of restless black youth chafing at the hypocrisy of the socialist government and demanding recognition for black identity but a deep divide between "commercial" and "underground" Cuban rap that parallels, in many respects, the East Coast/West Coast divide in the United States. The commercial rappers have been given vast leeway under the special period because of their ability to generate cash, and have done so by deploying the "bling-bling" formula. The "underground," on the other hand, acts as a kind of cultural intermediary:

> They continue to promote the ideals of the revolution, they are critical of the emergence of consumerist values and practices among the more commercial rappers, and they identify with the official characterization of Cuba as a "rebel nation." . . . Hip-hop movements work in critical alliance with official institutions.[58]

Sovereignty and pop

What then of the other half of the equation – not the youth in Cuba who (we are told) want desperately to become "free" like their U.S. counterparts, but the youth to whom the global market has successfully reached out? Here one sees a largely unacknowledged confluence of two extremes as it concerns the image of Cuba. Youth frequently arises as a category in U.S. cultural theory, and when it does is portrayed as a reprimand to older, now outmoded kinds of protest. The focus in such writing is usually on subcultural style. Youth is made into the very image of a revision of older forms of political thinking at the same time that it is associated with the innovation, novelty, and experimentation of the mass culture it supposedly employs as a weapon. At the same time (somewhat contradictorily), it gestures towards the anti-authoritarian breaking with tradition of the historical avant-gardes whose members were overwhelmingly young.

In the 1990s, some U.S. cultural critics started speaking of this kind of youth as "a new, deterritorialized, organic intellectual of the subaltern, capable of acting effectively in global circuits of power and representation," a fitting match of what one critic took to be Latin America's new "desiring subject . . . whose sense of inner lack can never be compensated." This new Latin American youth is "a Caliban . . . interpellated culturally . . . by the mass media."[59] Given the terms of our argument, it is not surprising that this subject is depicted as having left traditional Latin music (including salsa) behind as part of an imaginary "authentic" past.

To make his point, one critic turned to Victor Gaviria's highly acclaimed Colombian film, *Rodrigo D.: No Futuro*. Like the many reviewers of this unusually successful small-market film, the critic found it significant that the film was "about punk rockers" in Colombia – a message (it was said) that made it hard to talk about rock as a form of cultural imperialism. *Rodrigo D.* interested its admirers because it suggests the emergence of a new kind of subject based on an inner lack and desire – ideas drawn, in these critical circles, from the writing of the French psychoanalyst, Jacques Lacan. This restless desiring is said to unite the experiences of young Colombians and unemployed British working-class youth (the ones who first invented punk). It that way, the film is said to capture the transnational language of rock among a global "subproletariat in formation." Created neither by nor for the elites, so the argument goes, it is an insurrectionary articulation that is not only plebeian but market-identified (6–8). I have spent time repeating the terms of this argument to suggest the uses by metropolitan theory of peripheral situations. For, as we will see, neither the film nor the Colombian scene depicted in the film bears much resemblance to the comments outlined by this postmodern critic.

Set in the slums of Medellín, Gaviria's *Rodrigo D.* is indeed about "punk rockers," although this is a very partial way to describe the film. It belongs, first of all, to a now-familiar genre in Latin American cinema: that of the roving street urchins or bands of scavenging, sociopathic youth – the refuse of already "superfluous" populations. As a lyrical anatomy of Medellín's *pisto-locos*, the film fits into a well-known Latin American subgenre about abandoned, criminal youth, joining such films as Luis Buñuel's *Los Olvidados* (1950), Hector Babenco's *Pixote* (1981), and Fernando Meirelles and Kátia Lund's *City of God* (2002). In one of the film's two subplots, Rodrigo wanders the streets refusing to work, smoking dope with friends while engaged in an odyssey to buy a drum set to play in a punk rock band. But the major screen time is spent elsewhere, zeroing in on aimless teenagers with no direct relation to Rodrigo's quest. For these kids, punk has little meaning (although it does for Rodrigo), even though their activities as *pisto-locos* is set against a background score of punk and heavy metal, where they joke with each other at storefronts, make love at cousins' houses, steal cars, and hold up people at gunpoint on motorcycles. In the closing moments of the film, these separate plots (which never meet) reach their respective climaxes. The street kids shoot a member of their group for no apparent reason while Rodrigo enters an abandoned high-rise office building and, staring out of its broad windows, jumps to his death.

It is dangerous to draw conclusions about the truth of contemporary Colombia from a film, of course, even when that film has a semi-documentary edge, and even when the point about that truth has to do with the social effects of images. However, this is only one aspect of the problem confronting the critical position of the U.S. cultural theorist. Here, at any rate, one is moved to foreground Gaviria's particular vision within the formal constraints of the subproletarian genre, and then set it against what others, in different contexts, have written about Medellín youth. The following account is crucial, I would argue, to understanding the context of *Rodrigo D.* although it plays no part in the critic's comments above, and it is the *type* of information passed over in cultural theory generally.

Gaviria, first of all, was twenty-nine years old when *Rodrigo D.* first appeared, although he had begun work on the project several years before. He had published three volumes of poetry, had shot eight-millimeter films, and had directed a mini-series for television. But for a long time he had "been obsessed to make a film about real life: a 35 millimeter, feature-length film documenting an incident that had occurred in Medellín."[60] He had found that incident paging through a newspaper in which a feature article told the story of a sad boy whose mother had just died, and who wanted to kill himself by throwing himself off a high-rise building in order to paralyze traffic on one of the central avenues. An older woman and a fireman, however, succeeded in preventing him. "We placed an ad in the Medellín newspapers," Gaviria recounts, and "within a week, the offices of Modern Times were filled. More than three hundred people had shown up. All were young and down and out. Many of them were rockers and punks. I hadn't known that punk really existed in Medellín" (37). As he began to interview the applicants, he eventually fixed on two kids. "One was the quiet type. I really didn't think that he would turn out to be the protagonist. He was a drummer . . . I heard his music because, apart from being a drummer, he was a composer. What I was finding were some really scandalous lyrics. I thought it was rock, but it was punk music" (38).

Given the slight differences in age and status between Gaviria and these *pelados* (kids), it is not necessarily significant that Gaviria was unaware that punk music existed in Medellín, although it hints at the fact that novelty and the unexpected were what drew him to it, rather than its being a representative social norm, even among the *pelados* themselves. This fact is underlined by the account of Angela María Pérez, the woman who wrote the article on which *Rodrigo D.* was based, and who collaborated on the film's original script. Posed originally as a cautionary tale in the mode of a feature story on fearful developments among Colombian youth, the article's point of departure had in fact been the very question the older woman had asked "Rodrigo" as he stood poised to throw himself from the window: "How did you get so disenchanted?"[61] That question had kindled much public interest at the time, since Rodrigo Lara Bonilla, the Justice Minister, had only a short time before been murdered by a sixteen-year-old *pisto-loco* in a drive-by shooting. In the first script, Gaviria had basically assumed the point of view of the older woman in a closed conversation with a "Rodrigo" who had now become a stand-in for Medellín's disenchanted, and now criminal, youth.

What one first notices, then, is how little from the point of view of its makers the film was interested in cultural importations, much less a specific reference to American or British mass culture. Upon seeing the finished product, Rodrigo Alonso (the real-life double of "Rodrigo") was even angry that his character would commit suicide against a background of punk rock, since he thought it more logical that a kid in that state would listen to the mournful melodies of *vallenato*, a rural Colombian dance music roughly analogous to country-western music. Neither in his native barrio of "Las Communas" nor in the poorer barrio of "Marrique" alluded to in the film itself was punk very popular. Tango was.

While Pink Floyd and the Sex Pistols both appear briefly on the sound track, most of the score is punk's Colombian variant, locally produced and performed in Spanish. But even if that sort of hybridity is partly the point of the postmodern critic's view, it is important to recognize that the music was superimposed afterward by Gaviria in a gesture of artistic license rather than quasi-documentary accuracy.

More telling perhaps is what Pérez herself points out: that hard rock is about a more or less familiar generational conflict. "Every sixteen-year-old in the world is singing hard rock," she says. "It doesn't say anything particular about Colombia." The problem with the reading of the cultural critic is its emphasis on cultural importations, and in the reading that punk has become both an aesthetic refuge and a form of symbolic resistance to the forces that victimize third-world youth. "No Future" is a subtitle with much more literal, and romantically humanist, overtones. Walking the barrio streets with her son at 3:00 a.m., one mother in the film asks "why don't you care anymore?" "I am going to be dead before I am twenty," he answers. Although the only execution Gaviria has time to explore takes place among the *pelados* themselves, the meaning of that answer alludes to reports that have emerged in the early 1990s that homeless children in Medellín and Bogotá were being swept up and murdered by plainclothes police. There has been, in effect, "an increasingly vicious crusade aimed at vagrants, criminals, prostitutes, street children and drug addicts, all known as 'disposables.'" According to one researcher "almost 2000 people were killed from 1988 to 1993 as a result of Colombia's *limpieza social* (social cleansing) . . . children are a main target for the vigilante groups."[62] But while the outlines of this tragedy are fairly well known, the reports have often inexplicably referred to an aspect of the killing that is relevant to the topic of cultural resistance inasmuch as the latter often plays the role of quiet substitute for organized political revolt or military insurgency: "In July, a group calling itself Colombia Without Guerrillas issued a statement saying it was forming to attack anyone connected with left-wing rebel groups."[63] The existence of these paramilitary squads, created by the government as an extra-legal means of combating its political opponents, has now (in the late 2000s) become general knowledge. Congressional opponents of a controversial trade pact with Colombia backed by the Bush Administration in 2008 have brought these abuses to light and widely publicized the scope of paramilitary terror in the country. But even more interesting for our purposes is this connection in the mind of the vigilantes between guerrillas and "disposables" – the confusion, in other words, between a cultural and a military resistance.

In a series of interviews, Alonzo Salazar has documented how the *pisto-locos* are a form of guerrilla insurgency gone haywire, many of them having been trained, originally by the M-19 guerrillas in the popular barrios during a brief ceasefire in 1984 under the government of Belisario Betancur.[64] Others have variously drawn on the popular legends surrounding guerrilla priest Camilo Torres, and others still, on "Desquite" – a liberal bandit leader during the era of repression between 1946 and 1966 known as *La Violencia*. Demobilized former guerrillas seeking to join the political process suffered various campaigns of extermination (including the now-famous massacre at Bellavista prison) until a "kamikaze culture" eventually developed under the impact of the drug cartels. Most interesting in Salazar's account is the radically different reading he has of the effect of U.S. popular culture on the *pelados* of Medellín: "a consumer society constantly bombards [the poor] with ever greater offers, thereby debasing the idea of a modern society into a tragic contributory factor of the violence [by highlighting] the gap between this pressure to consume and available income" (112). How then could cultural imperialism be passé? Somewhat later, he gets even more explicit: "contract killers are consumer society to its extreme: they turn life (their own and that of their victims) into a commodity to deal in, into a disposable object . . . Brand names, fashion, the means to consume are all important to the hired killers . . . This is one of the aspects which differentiates them from the punks, a counter-culture which rejects the consumer society" (120).

That last comment sounds at first like part of the cultural critic's point: emergent punk as the emblem of resistance to a GATT culture, and a departure from the culturally specific and local musical forms that (as Salazar points out) became popular in the dangerous neighborhoods by way of the old-style gangsters. But the actual musical fabric of the culture, when looked at closely rather than as it appears in the slogans of cultural theory, reveals a very different reality. It turns out that it is *salsa*, not punk, that permeates the *pisto-loco* culture: "Salsa and rumba now constitute part of the philosophy, the bible of the *pelados* from Medellín's hillside neighborhoods. They identify with the music because it talks of . . . death as something to celebrate . . . Salsa tells them of Pedro Navaja, of Juanito Alimaña, of tough guys and their neighborhoods" (121, 123). For just these reasons, then, *Rodrigo D.* appears a more idiosyncratic, less representative film, and therefore less easy to generalize about in assessments of the effects of U.S. mass culture on semi-occupied, highly dependent countries like Colombia.

The story related in *Rodrigo D.* is less an obscene anomaly than a general cycle repeated throughout Latin America. At least some of the political confusion surrounding the musical identity of the *pisto-locos* resolves itself in a related example – the Mara Salvatrucha, an international border gang from southern California and northern Mexico, which sprang to life in the tough neighborhoods of Los Angeles in the late 1970s and 1980s, its membership fed by targeted youth fleeing the political carnage in El Salvador.[65] Beset upon arrival by the already existing youth gangs like "M" ("Mexican Mafia") and "N" ("Norteños" or "Nuestra Familia"), the Salvadorans organized themselves into an effective fighting force defined by heavy metal music and hard drugs (especially speed). As John Ross explains:

> The etymology of the gang's name is open to question. Presumably, the "Salva" prefix refers to the members' country of origin, but it could also mean "save yourself" in Spanish. The "trucha" is a trout, the slippery fish whose agility in navigating troubled waters is a characteristic of these hardened youths' lives. "Mara" is Salvadoran slang for a group of friends but may borrow attitude from the "Mara Bunta," a particularly virulent Central American army ant. In the Salvatrucha lexicon, the "mara" is a tattoo, mandatory ID for the gangbangers.

A steady stream of Salvatruchas enters Mexico every day, a different kind of invasion from those of the past. About five thousand of them in seven cliques, spread out over eight states of the Federal Republic, have their capital in the squatter colonies around Tapachula where, according to Ross, "stolen cars, kilos of cocaine, pounds of human flesh – seems to be for sale on its teeming streets."

But the major point here is, again, the displacement of civic revolt by pathological violence, and the substitution of one kind of indiscriminate preying by another. The product of a stymied guerrilla project, desperate kids learned the ropes of dog-eat-dog in the laboratories of the U.S. inner cities only to find their way home in the form of a social catastrophe. When the war in El Salvador was winding down in the 1990s, the Salvatruchas drifted home, some of them forcibly sent there as deportees from the California prison system. In the chaos of postwar Salvadoran politics, where rules were being made anew, the "jomies" ("homeboys") bullied their way into the street rackets, sold dope, and may have been involved in the sharp spike of kidnappings for ransom. In Ross's account, half the murders in El Salvador have been attributed to them by the World Health Organization.

The context for reception of *Rodrigo D.* made it difficult for those in the United States to understand its meaning to Colombians. With a North American release in 1988, it was prominently reviewed in the United States only in 1991, the beginning of a two-year stretch of blanket publicity surrounding the *limpieza social* and Medellín drug cartel.[66] Although its friendly reception was, of course, related to its visual and textual brilliance, its immediate social relevance was also a contributing factor. If the film is not primarily about punk, and if punk is not even a dominant reality among the social types fictionally represented there, its idiosyncratic flirtation with the rare *pisto-loco* culture involved in punk conjures troublesome images for any assessment of a welcome counter-cultural rebellion. The rockers Gaviria interviewed (and eventually employed in the film) were not likely material for "a new, deterritorialized, organic intellectual of the subaltern, capable of acting effectively in global circuits of power and representation," as cultural theory would have it. Deterritorialized perhaps (Gaviria calls them "pure nomads"), what did this deterritorialization bring? "The most important thing for [them] was to get a revolver," writes Gaviria, "they didn't believe in love, they didn't believe in anything. A person for them was dandruff, a kind of blemish."[67] The bid to view the present dispassionately, shorn of its romantic poses, seems to have led in some cultural theory to a romanticism of its own.[68] Like Salazar, Gaviria observes that the punkers despised the ballads of salsa and *vallenato* which made them sad, and "reminded them of everything they didn't have." It is not that they didn't read. "They read all right: Vargas Vila, Nietzsche. And they hated blacks. They're misogynists, totally . . . the sons of wardens and policemen even as the policemen hunted them down. They're demoniacs" (40).

Instead of a picture of escape into a mass culture that has been appropriated and altered, the film in unexpected ways is about tradition. Because stray youth implies a crisis in the family, the film goes out of its way to portray the family as a necessary support group. There are all sorts of solidarities in the film between the generations, since both the old and the young have been displaced and marginalized. The punk lyricism finally depresses the viewer for being so manifestly ineffective a way of dealing with the sickness the film portrays. That is its intention. In that sense, the humanist lament that fuels the film's imagery casts the punk score itself in the role of a NAFTA foil, as though the film's subjects – robbed from, assaulted, and cast out, with nowhere to turn, by agents from afar – are given in return a clash of second-hand sounds that, as fake rebellion, echoes the very forces dispossessing them. Before he dies,

Rodrigo's only gift is to be able to live inside its songs, to find comfort in the prison of its outraged shrieks.

This vivid contrast between the inconveniences of *timba* musicians, on the one hand, and the devastation of the *pisto-locos*, on the other, is deeply significant. It should certainly make one pause before making easy evaluations of the comparative effects of different social systems on the welfare and opportunities of youth.

6

The War of Writing on Music: *Mumbo Jumbo*

In the spring of 2004, partisans of the then decade-old Haitian mercenary group FRAPH were jogging up the streets of Cap Haitien in American-issue army boots. Benjamin Constant, taking a vacation from his insurance business in Brooklyn, donned his old fatigues and returned to Haiti to play the part of a popular rebel on behalf of U.S. outsourcers and enterprise zones. The rotund Gerard Latortue (the "tortoise"), a New York-based economist, hand-picked by a U.S. council, later arrived to legitimate the occupation by U.S. marines brought in to "keep the peace."[1] Out goes the only democratically elected president of Haiti in recent memory (Jean-Bertrand Aristide) while the *New York Times* portrays the affair in the carnival colors of a popular insurrection.

This latest coup in Haiti, if it did not crush Ishmael Reed's spirit, could only have made him laugh. For he predicted all of it more than three decades ago in his novel *Mumbo Jumbo*.[2] Although set in New York, the novel takes as its point of departure a brutal but little-considered historical fact: that Haiti endured a U.S. military occupation from 1915 to 1934, beginning with the invasion of Port-au-Prince by U.S. marines to quell a popular uprising that had overthrown the dictator Guillaume Sam. In other words, from World War I to the end of the flapper era – the period that comes down to us as the "roaring 20s," Prohibition, the Harlem Renaissance, and the Great Migration – U.S. forces occupied Haiti, an occupation that even became a sensitive election issue on the eve of the presidency of Warren Harding (who was later assassinated). The premise of Reed's *Mumbo Jumbo* is that these two developments, flapper era and occupation, were not coincidental. The history of Western civilization, he further suggests, is built almost entirely out of the rivalries of secret societies, all of which trace their origins to pre-dynastic Egypt, and to the later events spawned by Egypt throughout the Eastern Mediterranean in Greece, Turkey, and the Levant. These secret societies have a common source but relative levels of authenticity.

Some are the real thing, others only spinoffs, and authenticity is itself race-based though not race-exclusive. Civilization, in short, is a race war in which the recent coup in Haiti, like that of 1915, is not only predictable but viciously logical.

My interest in this chapter is to explore the collision of music and writing against the backdrop of New World secular devotion. In this light, or indeed in any light, Reed's *Mumbo Jumbo* is among the most important American novels of the postwar period. Usually taken to be postmodern farce, it strikes many readers to be merely playful at first, zeroing in on the fleeting nature of meaning as displayed in an omnivorous array of prose styles drawn from popular cultural genres like the gangster film, the sci-fi monster flick, and the Walter Winchell gab of early commercial radio. The text indulges freely in typographical jokes, the juxtaposition of suggestive photos, drawings, diagrams, news-clippings, and leaflets, and the narrative is interlarded with impromptu poems, headlines, journal scribblings, and quotations drawn promiscuously from obscure primary sources. If it is also an over-the-top satire of race relations in the era of the Harlem Renaissance, there is no contradiction among these apparently conflicting propositions. Since the novel's barbs are delivered from the vantage point of the unkempt 1960s, readers find it tempting to see this overkill as part of the era's Dionysian excesses, which would allow for this kind of combination.

Written off as a 1960s period piece, the novel has been seriously misread and certainly under-read. Its ribald gestures conceal a deadly serious intent. This counter-history of Western civilization draws on two contrary sources: black oral history and the secret societies of the white establishment. Reed adds to the well-established if not popularly known facts of Christianity's African origins a glaring conjecture: namely, that the source of humanity – the way, the truth, and the life – has been forced by European conspirators to live on mutely in obscurity and disparagement. In fact, the level of viciousness toward the true people of the Book is directly proportional to the venom and insecurity felt by those who have stolen their secrets, and who must go to great lengths to abolish their priority. With the help of a weighty bibliography, Reed contends (and he means this to be a revelation) that New World African music is the only remnant of mankind's first culture. The Bible, the birth of Christianity, the rise of Islam, the age of European conquest, the triumph of the white race, all of these are cast as a prolonged act of theft whose true nature is cloaked by a conspiracy to flip meaning.

Hiding in the light, the truth is everywhere evident but misunderstood. History is a kind of pun. The subservient appear strong and the inventors and keepers of the spirit appear as hollow imitators. The extraordinary importance of Reed's novel exceeds any of its specific references to Egyptian rites, masonry, the Knight's Templar, black Islam, voodoo, the Harlem Renaissance, or U.S. foreign policy of the 1920s. For here, better than anywhere, is the elaboration of the idea that civilization depends on prioritizing letters over sounds, and literature over music. Here is repeated, in a different context, the motive behind an official schooling that requires the study of literature in the liberal arts but not oral history, dance, or song. This directive that comes not, as is often argued, from the book-centeredness of an English national culture inherited from the British Empire, but from a much more ancient conflict.

It is remarkable that no definitive study has yet been written on the body of literature inspired by New World African music – a tradition not simply *about* music in many cases but written in sonoric mimicry of it, or dedicated to reproducing its theory. This is particularly so given that it has been a major subgenre of literature in the Americas. *Mumbo Jumbo*'s proper literary company is found, for example, in the syncopated wordplay of Sonia Sanchez; James Weldon Johnson's honky-tonk classicism; Amiri Baraka's bebop prosody and scat vocalizing; the counterpoint of sociology and song, European and African vernaculars in W. E. B. du Bois's *Souls of Black Folk*; Allen Ginsberg's saxophone smack haze; the Lower East Side siren wails and Madonna chatter of Paul Beatty; the conga jumps and sharp palm beats of the phantasmagoric world of prose rhythms and hallucinations in Luis Rafael Sanchez's *La Guaracha de Macho Camacho*; the mellifluous inventions – as on a Spanish church organ – of Alejo Carpentier; and the jerky off-beat stresses and polysyllabic neo-African coinages of the poetry of Nicolás Guillén and Luis Palos Matos.[3]

To invoke this tradition is to enter a more elaborate and densely forested territory than one first expects. If *Mumbo Jumbo* portrays European secret societies like the Rosicrucians and Masons, and describes the ways in which each appropriates African creation by reproducing the outward form of what they fail to understand, these societies too were the target of mainstream European resentments as well as attempts to de-authenticate unapproved *texts*. The world that *Mumbo Jumbo* opens up to the curious reader, then, far exceeds what the novel itself is able to cover or Reed himself finds time to mention. Let us turn first to the novel, and then step back to place it in its proper framework.

A counter-history of civilization

The story of *Mumbo Jumbo* opens in 1920s New Orleans where the mayor, in a panic, has just heard that the city is in the throes of a dance epidemic by the name of "Jes Grew." The term comes from James Weldon Johnson who, writing about the songs of the South, said that the earliest ragtime songs were not composed by anyone in particular; they "'jes' grew." They were, in Reed's words, a "creeping thing," a "psychic epidemic" that knew "no class no race no consciousness," self-propagating, an "anti-plague" characterized by "ebullience and ecstasy." In the novel's opening pages, the writers of newspapers, politicians, and the makers of official opinion are all mortified by a craze that affects people of all ages, black and white. Much more than fads, dances like the Eagle Rock, the Sassy Bump, and the Mooche, the Turkey Trot, the Funky Butt, and the Black Bottom possess their hosts like friendly gods, enslaving them in glorious rites of frenzy. Powerful public forces set out to contain the enjoyment and stop the spread of the music, putting an end to bumping and grinding, calling a halt to spooning. An actual Warren G. Harding platform slogan (related by Reed in such a way that we assume it is fiction) was "let's be done with Wiggle and Wobble."

An underground group of highly placed movers and shakers known as the Wallflower Order is brought in to lead the charge. It is made up of the sort of people whose kids go to Yale, who listen to John Phillip Souza, and thank Stephen Foster for purifying the music of the slave shanties and the honky-tonks. One could characterize the book, first of all then, as being about a struggle between this Order and the much less organized forces of those Reed has the habit of calling the J.G.C.s (the Jes Grew Carriers – in the sense that one "carries" a disease). The latter's figurehead, who significantly does not know he plays the role of figurehead, is one PaPa LaBas who, Reed tells us, "carries Jes Grew in him like most other folk carry genes." The son of an owner of a mail-order root business in New Orleans, LaBas runs the Mumbo Jumbo Kathedral out of his apartment in Harlem – a Hoodoo joint that publishes a small newsletter prophesying the conspiratorial hypothesis that a secret society is molding the consciousness of the West. He keeps a *santeria* altar in his living room, offers counsel from his apartment office, and organizes "Chitterling Switches" – rent parties to raise money for campaigns against the lynching that plagued the South during the 1920s.[4]

Over the course of the novel, LaBas slowly comes to consciousness. (LaBas, or Legba as he is sometimes called, is the Yoruba gateway or messenger god, the one who opens the lines of communication between the spirits and the living). As Alfred Métraux puts it:

> In any catalogue of Voodoo divinities first place must certainly be give to Legba – the god who "removes the barrier" and who is saluted first of all *loas* . . . In Dahomey, Legba acts as interpreter to the gods . . . Master of the mystic "barrier" which divides men from spirits, Legba is also the guardian of the gates and the fences which surround houses and, by extension, he is the protector of the home. In this latter role he is invoked under the name of Mait'bitasyon (Master of the habitation). He is also the god of roads and paths.[5]

The novel is primarily the story of LaBas's coming to see that his "Knockings" (his premonitions) are divine – that they are not what is normally meant by intuition but are quite literally a communication with the gods. They are, however (and this is important) no less vernacular and everyday for all that, since the divine in this world is vulgar, corporeal, and utterly normal. Against the backdrop of LaBas's slow-motion revelation there arises a significant subtheme. We learn that history is not the creation of circumstance or unplanned behavior but a conspiracy perpetrated by the forces of the "Left Hand." LaBas is therefore involved, meekly at first, in a momentous struggle for the future that involves a necessary reckoning with the past. The history of the origins of civilization has to be completely retold because the version we live with in the West is a tragic and offensive lie.[6] This lie is repeatedly mobilized to quash the forces of Jes Grew which periodically spring to life only to die once more because they had not found their Text. The last time (prior to the 1920s) in fact, was in the 1890s when revelers were dancing the Bamboula, the Counjaille and the Juba in the Place Congo of New Orleans. But the Wallflower Order snuffed them out.

The bewildering subplots of the novel are too numerous to recount. One of them deals with the *Mu'tafikah* – a multicultural cadre of revolutionaries who break into art museums in order to liberate the treasures of the "aesthetically victimized civilizations" whose finest work is kept locked within the museum walls, effaced by curators' impudent framing, or worse, consigned to a basement locker.[7] Reed calls museums "centers of art detention."[8] There is the gang war between Buddy Jackson and Schlitz, the Sarge of Yorktown, over control of the Harlem gin-running and dope-selling rackets. There is the rise to power of Warren G. Harding, who, according to Reed's sources, was one of the United States' eight black presidents, and who out of blood-loyalty wanted to relieve Haiti of its military occupation but was forced by the Wallflower Order (Mayflower, uptight, prudish, East Coast financier types) to abandon his quest. The Order invites him to a closed room after his inauguration to inform him who really runs the country. And there is the story of Hinkle Von Vampton, the 700-year-old member of the Knights Templar, who has arrived in the Americas to ensure that Jes Grew is extinguished at its root, and who does not believe that the crude, impromptu means employed by the U.S. business elite and its various henchmen are up to the task. They do not fully appreciate what is at stake or how long the struggle has been going on. Von Vampton's strategy throughout the novel is to find and groom a "Talking Android" – that is, a fake leader of the people, who will work "within the Negro, who seems to be its classical host" but who is really there to "drive it out, categorize it analyze it expel it slay it, blot Jes Grew."

The Wallflower Order is, then, part of a game it does not understand, just as LaBas, working for the other team, is the hero of a drama whose author he does not know. The Order keeps bumping up against Von Vampton, unable to discern his authority, and its members are perplexed by his interference in the mutual desire to crush Jes Grew. What they do not appreciate is that Von Vampton is the source of their heritage, the link to the Europe of the Crusades at the time of the founding of the Knights Templar (the organization that, after many internal changes and years of hiding, came to be known in Enlightenment England as the Masons). His name, then, is a cross between that white impresario of black culture during the Harlem Renaissance, Carl Van Vechten (author of *Nigger Heaven*) whom Reed despises, "vamp" (as in imitator), and of course, "vampire." He has been at his work for centuries and knows what he is doing. Much of what happens in the novel, then, are the intrigues, the debates within cigar-smoke-filled meeting rooms, the abductions, assassinations, and takeovers of New York newspapers by two uneasy allies working toward the same goal. Both jockey for position as the most potent enemy of the black community, struggling to recruit pliant blacks to embrace a version of the jazz virus that renders it limp and ineffectual (the dancing of Irene and Vernon Castle, for instance; or the garden parties for the black literati of the Harlem Renaissance). If one suspects Reed of indulging in caricature in the novel, the sources on which he amply relies prove that the reality of the era is itself a caricature. If one bothers to consult Vernon and Irene Castle's *Modern Dancing*, for example, one finds the following advice:

> Do not wriggle the shoulders.
> Do not shake the hips.
> Do not twist the body
> Do not flounce the elbows.
> Do not pump the arms.
> Do not hop-glide instead.
> Drop the Turkey Trot, the Grizzly Bear,
> The Bunny Hug, etc. These dances are ugly,
> Ungraceful and out of fashion.[9]

At the same time, although not exactly in a parallel way, LaBas is busy finding his way to the Work. Even as his daughter Earline is possessed by Isis (the Egyptian goddess known in the Americas by a variety of names – in Brazil as Yemanja, in Cuba as Yemayá, in W. C. Handy as St. Louis Woman, or the Girl with the Red Dress On),[10] and even as his daughter's lover, Berbelang, is murdered while working for the *Mu'tafikah*, LaBas embarks on a series of discussions and debates with representative *types* from the black community. These conversations become a way to knowledge, a slow and difficult journey to the correct path. They allow him to reject the other roads to salvation found in these various representatives of possible black selves: for example, that of Hank Rollings, the snobby super-English Oxford-educated Guianese art critic; Woodrow Wilson Jefferson, the Marxist from Re-mote Mississippi who credulously arrives in New York at the offices of the *New York Tribune* wanting to talk to Marx and Engels personally, and who is determined to leave behind all talk of haints, spirits and witches like the backward folks that surrounded him during his upbringing; or Abdul Hamid, a.k.a. Johnny James from Chicago's South side, the black Muslim bent on ridiculing Hoo Doo psychiatry, in part by impressing his Christian critics with his knowledge of the Bible and agreeing with them on the ultimate wickedness of women. LaBas fields these debates, which take up a good deal of the novel, first by soberly assessing them, later by working his way around them while following his instincts on behalf of Hoodoo. Eventually help arrives from the outside. A ship from Haiti called *The Black Plume* pulls into New York harbor carrying Benoit Battraville (Von Vampton's "white magic" counterpart working for the forces of Jes Grew).

At one of the New York parties for the Harlem Renaissance poets, held on one of those estates north of the city, Von Vampton announces that he has found the Talking Android (which turns out only to be his partner in crime, Hubert "Safecracker" Gould, dressed in blackface). But the party is raided by Battraville and his men, who take Von Vampton and Gould into custody. At that point, the novel turns. Sensing that LaBas has apprenticed long enough and is at last ripe to learn the secrets of the "closed book" of history, he sits the man down in the presence of the party guests and recounts the conspiracy that is the rise of Western civilization.

Long ago, Osiris – "a young prince who was allergic to thrones" – went off to university in Nysa in what is now Yemen. He would commute from time to time across the Red Sea into Ethiopia and the Sudan where the agriculturalists there had perfected a new rhythm for dancing and singing called the "Black Mud Sound." He came back to Egypt where he is known as the "man who did dances that caught on." His brother Set, a dilettante, hated agriculture, and was jealous of his brother's popularity. It riled him that people laughed at his lame dancing, he couldn't "shake it till he break it," and it pissed him off that Egyptians were enjoying themselves when there were "countries to invade, populations to subjugate." Things continued that way with Egypt at peace until the people started grumbling because all the dancing was out of control and no planting was getting done. A wise old artist came to Osiris and explained this was because the mysteries had "no text to turn to. No litany to feed the spirits that were seizing the people," so the artist, Thoth, induced Osiris to do his dances in his presence so that Thoth could write them down – a Book of Litanies, the first anthology by the first choreographer.[11]

Set finally found his chance to trick Osiris, and managed to murder him, scattering his body parts all over the land. But Isis kept the faith, and a number of Osirian alter-egos sprang up – Mithras, Adonis, Bacchus, Attis and, most famously in his Greek incarnation, Dionysus, who "traveled to Greece where the Dance 'spread like wildfire' even though Homer doesn't mention it." Osiris was what Voodoo calls a *houngan*, a priest who knows the real thing. But after his death there arose a number of people drawn to the Black Mud Sound's power, but who did not understand the Text. They tapped some of its energies, but used it for the wrong purposes, cheaply, like a sideshow barker who does magic tricks for "15 bucks and change." This is what voodoo calls a *bokor*, or a priest who practices black magic: one who does not know how to "get down," who is "frontin'" (which is also known as "practicing the Left Hand"). Set went about trying to destroy the wonderfully pluralist polytheism of Egypt by setting up *Aton*, the sun god, as the only deity. This was the atmosphere in which the novel's chief *bokor*, an Egyptian named Moses, comes on the scene. He steals the Book of Thoth, cops the Atonist idea of a single god (giving it the name Jehovah) and then runs off to the upper Middle East where he sells his wares to a credulous tribe of penniless wanderers known as the Israelites. Jesus is a minor deflection, a little blip on the screen of a larger story. Only after the Osirian and Dionysian mysteries have been definitively suppressed in the late Hellenistic period does Christianity amount to anything at all, and only then as a copy of the Dionysian cults whose energies live on there in a distorted form. And for this reason it is forced to rediscover itself in the mid-twelfth century during the Crusades when the heart of Christendom is put back in touch with its eastern Mediterranean origins.

Von Vampton, we learn, was the librarian for the Knights Templar (a.k.a. the Knights of the Temple of Solomon in Jerusalem), an organization formed during the Crusades. Originally a purely military group founded by Hugh de Payens in 1118, it was officially recognized ten years later by the Pope, who liberally received from these mercenaries' gifts of estates and money. The group took its orders only from the Pope not from the local nobility, and its headquarters were in Jerusalem. It is they who popularized the insignia of the red cross on a white ground, and it is they who became the leading money-handlers of Europe free from secular control until as late as the fourteenth century when they ran afoul of kings who wanted to borrow money on easier terms. They ended up perishing at the stake.

As Battraville nears the end of his account, he instructs his guards to bring from the back of their limousine the large silver-and-gold-lined box with the Egyptian designs carved on its exterior that they had earlier recovered from the basement of the Cotton Club. With great fanfare they open the box before the assembled guests. But it is empty! Von Vampton, it appears, had sequestered the Text in its corrupt form (the one found among the Masons) and paid fourteen members of the Jes Grew Crew a monthly salary to keep it moving in a chain of disembodied parts so the authorities would not get suspicious (what separates him, again, from other members of the anti-black establishment is his awareness of the book's power). But Abdul Hamid, one of the fourteen, broke the chain, keeping the Text. He was killed before he could describe its fate, but he left a letter to LaBas that hinted at an explanation. He had translated its hieroglyphics into the language of "the brothers on the street," and sent it off to a publisher. But a sacred black book was not considered marketable and Hamid was sent a curt rejection slip. The copy, it appears, was lost in the mail, and he believed it still might turn up one day. As for the original copy of the Book of Thoth – the one Battraville expected to reveal to the guests – Hamid in a fit of puritanical Islamic ardor burned it. He decided that black people could never have been involved in such "a lewd, decadent thing" and that what the black community really needed was "somebody to whip these coons into shape."

Egyptomania, Europe, and the Black Mud Sound

Mumbo Jumbo is not simply an attractive novel to use when teaching popular music. It is more like an indispensable text book for understanding the very meaning and reception of popular music, and should arguably accompany the teaching of African New World music as a matter of course. It is the only novel of the Americas that clearly lays out the stakes of doing so, the only one to pose musical enjoyment as a clash of civilizations, and the only one to cast the entire New World musical complex in terms of a subversive religious unity. It did so, moreover, at the dawn of a new fundamentalism among the world's three muscular monotheisms.

Mumbo Jumbo's extraordinary role in African-American literature rests, above all, on Reed's systematic mutual translation and merging of an entire array of New World African belief systems, and then, in turn, his translation of these into the bookish wisdom of classicist, philologists, and religious historians about the relationship of Egypt to the rise of Europe. The scholars who, for instance, know the latter with clarity rarely have any feel whatsoever for the vernacular practices of African Americans in the diaspora, and it would be far from their minds to consider a connection between the two. Similarly, as I have been remarking throughout this book, most specialists on African-American culture have scant awareness of the ways that U.S. black tropes and styles find their independent counterparts in the Caribbean and Latin America: that the "Y" that appears there (Erzulie, Maria de la O) is a rough equivalent of the "Y" that occurs here (St. Louis woman), which in turn has its Egyptian analogue (Isis). This is so, moreover, because all derive from a common African source that is *not* the West Africa of the slave trade but the East Africa of the origins of all humanity and, importantly from this point of view, the origins also of civilization and the book, both credited officially with having begun in Mesopotamia and the Levant. But even more, Reed's novel is profound for theorizing rather than just thematizing (as in most other New World African fiction) the war of writing on music: the deep civilizational origins of the prejudice against the vernacular religion of the body, sex, and physical pleasure in the name of the hard-edged reason and control of the text. The latter stands in here not simply for the advanced, literate, technologically superior and modern West, but for a mode of thought and affect where text is permanent record, unalterable history, official dogma, and mastery of the magic of thought and ideas rendered palpable by writing.

The novel, then, is several things at once: a recasting of the familiar outlines of a well-known era of American history in the contours of Voodoo – that is, an extended rendering of these events as proof for the cosmology of Voodoo, which is severed finally from its mystique and fear to become the "word on the street" of those who are "with it." A Christian fundamentalist with a talent for sabotage and an unholy obsession with the devil (Von Vampton) is, at the same time, a shady secret service man in the employ of wealthy politicians who use hired thugs to do their bidding (Gould).[12] This is a familiar-enough pattern in the twentieth- and early twenty-first centuries, and is arguably their very paradigm. But when one adds to this pattern the project of dissembling power or of recruiting clueless collaborators from among the ranks of the oppressed, one has precisely that relationship described in Voodoo where the good partake of a mystical marriage with the *loa*. The cult of the dead that seems so morbid in its Western rendering here takes the form of white magic – expressed in secular and colloquial fashion as a respect for tradition with a healthy caution for the uses of spiritual power (the exact opposite, in other words, of American capitalism's brave new world).

The counter-image of the same practices is found, as Métraux explains, in the expeditions of black magic. The dead are sent out as *zombis* in the employ of *bokors*, "in a state of idiocy" to distribute wanga (poisons). If in Reed's universe it is difficult to see this description as referring to anything more than American television spectators or mall-goers, he has actually worked into his novel a more explicit reference to this aspect of Voodoo. For it is precisely this process of zombification that Reed successfully secularizes and de-mystifies in his pop-detective film-like rendering of the Talking Android.

But the novel is also after more intellectual game. It turns necessarily to the sort of thing we would expect from an artist whose métier is language, and who plights his troth to a tradition located smack in the middle of the oral world of drum and chant. *Mumbo Jumbo* is one long conceit on the material, sensuous embodiment of spirit that is not *word* – as in "the word made flesh" of the Gospel according to St. John. In the beginning is not the Word, but rather sound, tone, rhythm – what he calls "*Text*."[13] Grappling with these two antagonistic visions, history is not surprisingly a chronicle of misunderstanding, essentially the failure to grasp a pun between Book and book. A genuine people has been kidnapped by another who knew a profitable scheme when it saw one, capitalizing on the other's genius. The real people of the Book, it turns out, are written out of the Book's authorship, and demoted within it – if by "Book" we mean Bible. It is the ultimate case of missing the joke, literalizing the Text by making it exclusively *word*. True to its demand to return to the demotic and the polytheistic, *Mumbo Jumbo* is inclusive. It is a "both-and" rather than an "either-or" version of the past which does not exclude language, but places it in a complementary role in the progress of Spirit.

The five-page bibliography at the novel's end will, for these very reasons, be taken by many as an ironic gesture. In fact, they are Reed's way of saying that the themes he takes as central are found only rarely in books, and among these, only the most heterodox and marginal. If we look up E. A. Budge's *Osiris: The Egyptian Religion of Resurrection*, for example, we find confirmed that Osiris, far from being only the god of the underworld, was the legendary ruler of pre-dynastic Egypt who launched civilization by creating agriculture.[14] It is driven home that Osiris was worshiped by cults throughout ancient Egypt and throughout the Mediterranean world, still active and resilient as late as the fifth century A.D. Madame Blavatsky is there to tell us that Isis was equally popular and widespread, remaining one of the chief religions of the Roman empire. The worship of Osiris, Isis and Horus was resistant to the influence of early Christian teachings. Aleister Crowley's *The Book of Thoth: An Interpretation of the Tarot* tells us, similarly, that Thoth was the Egyptian god of magic, wisdom, and the arts; by convention, he was said to have invented writing, geometry, and astronomy.[15] He was a messenger god (like Legba in the Yoruban religion), and was known by the Greeks as Hermes Trismegistus, to whom was attributed an actual, but no-longer-extant text: the "Book of Thoth."

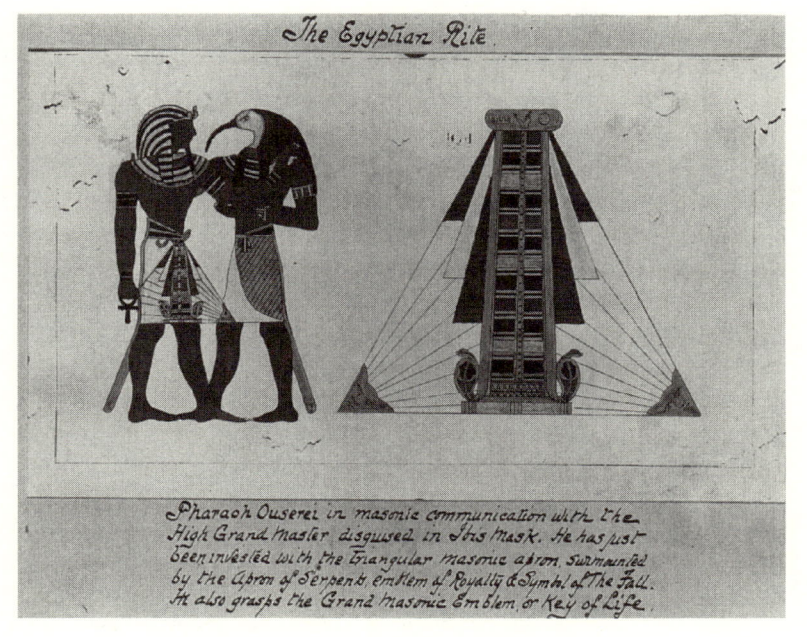

Figure 6.1 The Masonic "Egyptian Rite."

In Samuel Kramer's *Mythologies of the Ancient World*, we discover that Aton was the solar god given prominence under the Pharaoh Iknahton, who denied recognition to all but this one god until he died, when Egypt's customary polytheism was restored.[16] In Calvin Kephart's *Concise History of Freemasonry,* we learn that freemasonry descended indirectly from the Knights Templar, resurfacing after a hiatus of several centuries in the mason's guilds of medieval Europe, which adopted and transformed many of the former's symbols.[17] Like masonry, these locate their source in Solomon's temple, the sun god, and in Egyptian hieroglyphics, seeing the human body itself as the "Temple of God" and perceiving death not physically but as "an individual psychological process" in which the "subject is introduced by re-enacting the murder of the Principal Architect."[18] These clear echoes from Egyptian myth were domesticated in the version of masonry best known today, which derives from eighteenth-century England. In masonic ideology sacred buildings symbolize the universe. In the anachronistic vision of Heliopolis conjured by masonry, Moses, Christ, and Mahomet are revered as magi even if the city is ruled by Hermes Trismegistos "as sun priest, philosopher, king, and lawgiver."[19]

Donn A. Cass's intriguing *Negro Freemasonry and Segregation* reminds us of the black masons, the Boyer Grand Lodge #1 inaugurated 18 March 1845 by the Prince Hall Grand Lodge or African Lodge #1 chartered in 1776 by the Duke of Cumberland.[20] The masonic imagery of parallel lines (the "Law of Duality" usually figured in architectural columns) is averred to allude to the echo-worlds of Christianized, rationalized Africanism found in masonry alongside their precursors (and companions) in the rituals of Voodoo. To put this more plainly: the iconography of masonry and voodoo overlap (Figures 6.2 and 6.3).

As Reed's research-focus gradually sinks in, one understands that it is not a general but a very specific hidden history that Reed has in mind. The European Renaissance, which we tend to think of as inspired by humanism, was equally characterized by a fulsome return to mysticism. In 1460 Cosimo di Medici purchased a manuscript

> which had been recovered from the library in Constantinople before it was captured by the Turks in 1453. The documents in the manuscript form a literature of mystical experience in an Egyptian/astrological idiom. They are known today as the *Hermetica*, and are recognized as having been written in the second or third century A.D, probably in Alexandria. However, Marsilio Ficino, the Italian scholar and monk who translated them for Cosimo conceived that they were the work of

Figure 6.2 "The elements of Western metaphysics as represented by Masonic symbols."

an Egyptian named Hermes Trismegistus who he regarded as a contemporary of Moses.[21]

But one has to go beyond Reed's bibliographic sources to appreciate how resonant and explosive his revelations and conjectures are. After all, nothing in his sources offers anything like the synthesis of ideas and movements he provides in his novel. These, on the contrary, were his own

Figure 6.3 "*Vévés* (images) of Haitian Voodoo."

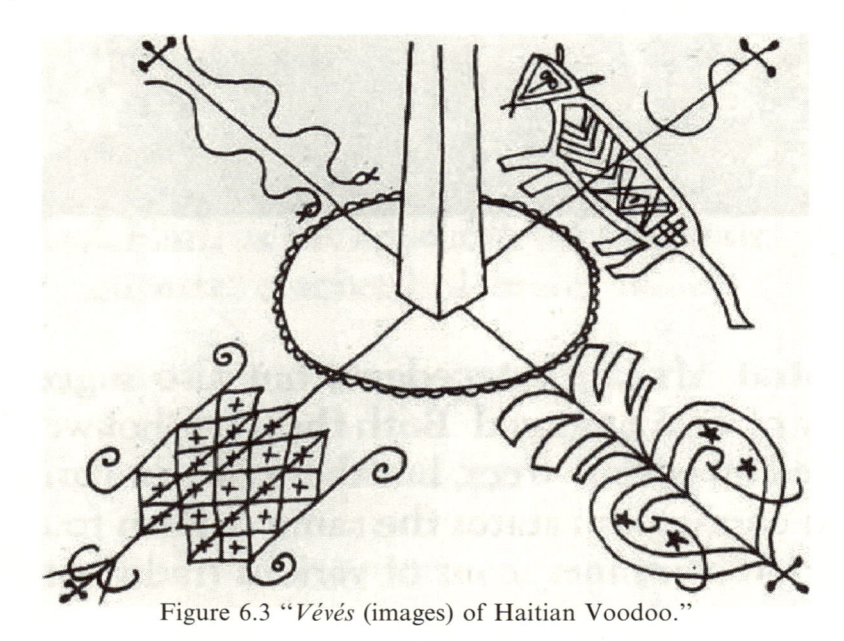

inspired creation – or rather, his original setting-down of a past already known and taken for granted "on the streets" of the black community.

Throughout the middle ages, the Church sought to expunge Egypt from the European script by crushing two intellectual lineages that were conduits for Egyptian knowledge: neo-Platonism, the direct Hellenic pagan inheritor of Egyptian religion; and Gnosticism, its Judeo-Christian counterpart. However co-optation was at least as serious an obstacle as repression. Christian thinkers turned Egyptian religion into philosophy. Hermes Trismegistus was, then, a rationalized version of Thoth, the Egyptian god of wisdom, who was taken by thinkers throughout the medieval period to be the actual author of the texts written during the last centuries of Egyptian religion before Christianity wiped these heresies out.[22] Sir Isaac Newton, for example, after being drawn to the Neo-Platonism of the Hellenistic world that was defined by its own rediscovery of Egypt, had a late change of heart. Appalled by the threat of pantheism inherent in Egyptian religion – its vivid embrace of an animate universe without need of a single regulating divinity – he set out in the latter part of his career to carry on the erasure work of the scholar Isaac Casaubon (1617) whose discredited work is still cited today as definitive proof of antiquity's over-estimation of the cultural influence of Egypt on the Greeks and of the fraudulence of the Hermetic tradition.[23] Casaubon had infamously tried to prove that the Hermetic texts did not date back to the fifth century B.C., as the ancient Greeks attested, but were recent, post-Christian inventions. Newton too "employed his critical scholarship to undermine Greek sources on the antiquity and wisdom of the Egyptians."[24] Thus, throughout the eighteenth and nineteenth centuries we find a de facto association of all textual criticism with Hellenism and the forms of Christianity that grew out of it. In this particular vector, "Aegypto-Masonry" was considered a great threat by Eurocentric scholars like Casaubon.

Casaubon and Newton were only carrying on what had been a centuries-long campaign extending back to the time of classical Greece. Plato and Aeschylus, although well aware of the Egyptian influence, were ambivalent about it since they were keen to emphasize the original contributions of a Greece then emergent and newly self-confident. Plato had nevertheless studied in Egypt, and one of his most celebrated dialogues, *Timaeus*, was drawn from Egyptian sources. The tendency of both to play down the extent to which Greek science, religion, and philosophy were based on Semitic and Egyptian sources provided a de facto opening for modern scholars with different agendas to discount the connection altogether. They did so to a degree that Plato and Aeschylus themselves would have found nonsensical. This is all the more true given the fact that Greeks from the classical era, most famously Herodotus, had no qualms about acknowledging the immense cultural debt to Egypt.

All of this ancient way of viewing the world, at any rate, had to pass through the censoring filter of the one oriental cult that displaced Egyptian religion in the second century A.D. – namely, Christianity. Only by way of a process of extermination, imprisonment, and doctrinal fiat was the early Church able to obscure the ancient common sense about Egypt. According to the scholar Martin Bernal (and he is very persuasive on this point), it was only when scholars of the romantic era, drawn for complex reasons to empire and nation-building, began to devise the "Aryan model" – which denied the influence of Egypt on Greece as well as the blackness of Egypt itself – did the current understanding of Western origins take hold. This myth stipulated that Greece was the *fons et origo* of European rationality, and it took as its creed that "the two purest essences of a 'race' [are] language and folksong."[25] The Aryan interpretation of Greece stipulated the following:

> Although racism was always a major source of hostility to the Ancient Model and became a mainstay of the Aryan one, it was matched in the 18th and 19th centuries by an attack on the significance of Egypt from Christians alarmed at the threat of the religion or 'wisdom' of Egypt...

[1815–1830] were years of intense reaction against the Masonic rationalism seen to be behind the French Revolution . . . In the 1820s, the Göttingen professor Karl Otfried Müller used the new techniques of source criticism to discredit all the ancient references to the Egyptian colonizations, and weaken those concerning the Phoenicians. These techniques had also begun to be used to attack the reports of Greeks having studied in Egypt. The Ancient Model had placed a barrier in the way of the new faiths that Greek culture was essentially European and that philosophy and civilization had originated in Greece.[26]

Music, then, presents theory with a disparity of means. Its ability to permeate and surround, to affect without argument, involves a deficit: the curse of being without signification, of being non- or anti-literal. Reed's novel, in fact, apart from being a sober, literal history is also an allegory in that it goes beyond an attempt to expose the obliteration of African influence on an ashamed and dependent America. Taken from Egypt, Greek myth is by definition archetypal. To take a well known example, Demeter's trip to Hades to reclaim abducted Persephone is about the cycle of the seasons; less well-known is that the tale arrived with the cults of Demeter and Dionysos (that is, Osiris) from Egypt into Attica about 1450 B.C.

In the Egyptian *Book of the Dead*, some of whose passages were inscribed on bodies prepared for burial by the devotees of Orpheus (whose name is "Geb" in Egypt), there are intriguing allusions to "the books of Geb and Osiris" – a discovery that no doubt has some archaeologists busy examining earthenware jars at archaeological digs. In the record of Egyptomania, in other words, there is a recurring pattern of discovery and conjecture. A book widely talked about and sought is never held in the hand. Was it destroyed by the envious or fearful? Was it too ancient to have survived the ravages of time? Or most interesting of all: is it still here and around us in a form we do not recognize? Demeter is not historical, of course, even though spring arrives each year. But as we shall see, Reed is ambiguous about the status of the book of Geb, either because his text is not literal (that is, it is the kind of "text" one reads only in bodily acts of secular devotion) or because it is an oral text that would benefit from being written down, a text whose Moses or Homer or Valmiki is still waiting in the historical wings. Or, finally, to take Reed at his most unmetaphorical, it is a text that exists in hiding, buried in the crevices of an Egyptian cave like the Gnostic gospels had been, or in the basement of a Bolognese library, spirited away by jealous monks who appreciated but never understood its threatening power.

The oldest extant version of *The Book of the Dead* dates from the early fifteenth century B.C., the period of the "Heliopolitan Recension" according to classicists. The older versions (not extant) are from significantly earlier than that, by as much as a millennium. The former detail is important given Reed's elaborate attention in *Mumbo Jumbo* to the "Atonists" – that is, the worshippers of the sun in that brief hiatus of dynastic Egyptian history when the capital was moved to Heliopolis, and Ikhnaton transformed Egypt into a monotheistic society. That the hunt for the lost text of African religious expression in dance would actually have such compellingly suggestive support from scholars who establish a chronological connection between Egyptian Text and Aton, exceeds Reeds own sources but not his expectations. This evidence, although not cited by him, would not surprise him either, and is fully a part of his inspired leap into historical theory. But *The Book of the Dead* cannot be the same sort of book that Battraville describes as a "choreography" when explaining the origins of the Black Mud Sound. Here the textual, understood with colorless literalness, is about death insofar as it is about monotheism and the blind observance of ritual.

The recent success of Dan Brown's *The Da Vinci Code*, to take one kind of example very close to home, clearly derives from its tapping of sources that Reed had assembled and surpassed thirty years before him. Brown's novel is also a striking confirmation of the story of appropriation and bowdlerization of black wisdom that Reed is so eager to tell. So much of what Brown unleashes as startling discovery is calmly and sardonically delivered by Reed as everyday wisdom in those parts of society relegated to official darkness. The plagiarism case against *The Da Vinci Code*, which contended Brown had stolen from Michael Baigent, Richard Leigh, and Henry Lincoln's *Holy Blood, Holy Grail: The Secret History of Christ, the Shocking Legacy of the Grail* (1980), never mentions Reed – the one U.S. novelist who clearly scooped him.

And yet, there are important differences as well. Like Reed's, Brown's novel is a collage of conspiracy theories, but unlike Reed the drama takes place entirely within the obscure and (by world historical standards) tangential confines of early Christianity in a then-peripheral Europe. As Reed would be quick to observe, Brown's flirtations with heresy are consonant with the spirit of Christianity, whose reveling in mystery and miracles obscures a deep psychological need for establishing truth as transcendent, sublime confusion. As Reed would have it, it is the view of the ambitious know-nothing who often lags behind or is buffeted by higher classes or superior intellects and so associates deep meaning with anything that resists understanding. For Reed, this sleight-of-hand is one feature of occult wisdom, and in this case it merges neatly with American hucksterism and the sort of self-serving popular history concocted for the gullible.

But Brown's book is also the latest in a long, even ancient, effort to save Christianity from its ascetic dead ends by reintroducing the sensual, the feminine, and the sexual (accomplished in the novel by repeating the old legend from the Gnostic gospels that Jesus was married to Mary Magdalene). All of these elements harmonize perfectly with the turn, which is also ancient, away from frigid doctrine, pontifical rulings, and (by contrast) Protestant "good sense" – to *knowledge*. This latter search for the truth requires effort and interpretation rather than revelation, which is unsurprisingly welcomed by generations weaned on catechism classes and whose only reprieve from such tutoring is the burgher sensibilities of Reinhold Niebuhr. Brown's Gnostic heterodoxies, although intriguing to that degree, are in the end only bemused Christianity, disappointed Christianity, and so never outside its orbit. From the perspective of the history of the various faiths in play, Brown's is a very timid radicalism which is why (unlike Reed) it has so effortlessly entered the mainstream. To a large degree, the pleasurable scandal offered by the book is part of a distant reckoning with the Eastern cult origins of Christianity itself, not merely its belatedness or hidden histories, but its rather decentered and unremarkable place within a constellation of fertility cults traveling north from Egypt and West from the Levant.

Reed, by contrast, does not simply offer a plausible mystery story on the basis of European Catholic secret societies which were themselves based on earlier Oriental mysteries (naturally, that part of Reed's story is left out by Brown and his redactors). Reed goes significantly beyond such a project in at least three respects: (1) his emphasis is not alternative Christianities, but African origins; (2) his emphasis is not the survival of secret societies in obscure corners of institutions like the Vatican, but their full, conscious, and conspiratorial play in the everyday secular world of U.S. power politics; and (3) his emphasis is not arcane codes, insignias, and secret handshakes but the fundamental plainness, openness, and demotic vibrancy of what is rendered mysterious by those who fear it. Instead of treating this history with somber majesty (which only gives it more power), he brings it crashing back to earth by translating its message into everyday terms of popular entertainment.

These connections are important not simply because philology is always tantalized by the ur-version, or beginning text, that continually recedes from sight in the presence of the later emendations. Heliopolis is the city built to worship the sun (Amon-Ra) – a departure from Egyptian polytheistic religious practices instituted by a fanatical king. So the birth of writing is in this way associated with monotheism, its founding texts based on a no-longer-extant wisdom that has been appropriated and changed. This chronology reconstructed by Egyptologists reinforces Reed's conjuring of a theme usually absent in the historians: black music, the force that casts writing under suspicion.

Again, Reed is not merely being transgressive when he appears to mix Northeast Africa, of uncertain racial composition, with sub-Saharan or Nubian Africa in an effort – or so it would seem – to fudge the distinctions between Saudi Arabia, Ethiopia, and Lower Egypt.[27] Early Christian portrayals of Egyptians usually depicted Egyptians as black, and certain European tradition of the fifteenth century associated blackness with wisdom on these grounds. If William Mitford in his *History of Greece* averred that Greece was the first country in Europe to emerge from barbarism, he did not forget to add the logical observation that "this advantage it seems to have owed intirely [sic] to its readier communication with the civilized nations of the East."[28] The privileging of reason, which becomes the form taken by "soul" in the West where the mind is overlord of body, is related to the privileging of writing. For, as Bernal puts it: "With the possible exception of writing, all the elements of which [civilization] was composed – cities, agricultural irrigation, metalworking, stone architecture and wheels for both vehicles and pot-making – had existed before [Greece] and elsewhere."[29] A particular relationship to writing, if not writing itself – which certainly predated Greece as well in cuneiform and hieroglyphic – is therefore paramount in Western definitions of cultural superiority in part because it is often cast as its unique contribution. The main point is that this uniqueness was established from the start as a contrast to body, to movement, and to sensuality, which arose fearfully (from the later European point of view) from the East and South.

The thoroughness of Reed's critique is evident in his exploration of the business and criminal aspects (often indistinguishable) of the era of transition in medieval Europe, when the continent moved from the status of occidental outpost to trading rival using the Middle East as its literal and ideological battlefield. As Norman Mackenzie points out in *Secret Societies* (a point buried in *The Da Vinci Code* as well as that novel's sources), the Knights Templar was itself based on "the Assassins," a secret society that begin in eleventh-century Persia as a religious order.[30] Although uproarious, the novel serves as a wedge to pry open neglected scholarship. The novel's contents appear absurd only because the bizarre facts have been so successfully glossed by later redactors. The Assassins' secrets are known only by way of the Templars' mediation, since their books of doctrine and ritual were burned in 1256 with their library at Alamut. In the judgment of Mackenzie, "The Assassins, rather like the

Mafia of later times, operated from their strongholds a protection racket under threat of death" (112). Not unlike the collusion depicted in Reed's novel between Von Vampton and the police, they were domestic allies of the Crusaders by helping to divide the native peoples of the Holy Land making conquest easier. This de facto relationship was later concretized in joint business ventures, which in turn led to their being memorialized by European chroniclers in the later romances. These influence of these romances in some cases rivaled that of the Bible. Hugh de Payens, the Burgundian knight who founded the Order of the Temple, modeled his organization on the Assassins right to the point of adopting the colors of their *rafiqs,* who wore red caps and belts and white tunics. This was slightly modified to become the Templar's red crosses on a white ground.

Figure 6.4 "St. James, the Warrior Spirit (Ogu)."

As a commercial operation, the Templars purposely avoided converting the Assassins to Christianity because their laws allowed them to collect a ransom from non-believers. Like early European colonists in the New World, the personnel that made up the Templars were among the most unscrupulous ruffians to be found anywhere. According to St. Bernard, they were mostly "excommunicated knights, who had nothing to lose . . . never combed . . . rarely washed, their beards bushy, sweaty and dusty, stained by their harness and the heat . . . [T]heir mantles remained on their backs until they rotted off or were slashed apart by enemy swords."[31]

They, however, became fabulously rich from donations of land and estates made by grateful Crusaders who had recently returned. This wealth allowed them to become Europe's major moneylenders. In a foreshadowing of later masonic ritual, they devised a complex set of ceremonies of initiation called "The Rule of the Temple." They began to fall out of favor when part of their crew conspired with Saladin during the disastrous Second Crusade. It did not help their reputations that they spoke Arabic and wore long beards in the Muslim fashion, or that their first residence was a mosque built on the site of Solomon's Temple in Jerusalem. When the Pope sought to steal their money and estates, and to remove the power they had over him as moneylenders, he did so in part by launching the rumor that they secretly worshipped the phallic idol and black god *Baphomet* (probably a corruption of the name "Mohammed").

Lost texts

As the story of a hunt for a lost text, *Mumbo Jumbo* is nevertheless open to misconceptions. Part of the containment of 1960s culture generally – and Reed's novel is solidly, if idiosyncratically, a part of that decade – is to call it "avant." It goes almost without saying that *Mumbo Jumbo* will be taken by many contemporary readers to herald the ludic verbal experimentalism of late modernism, an effort to raise the African-American novel out of its autobiographical, historicist obsessions. There are huge typographic excesses – for example, interlarded photos, drawings, and secret symbols, apparent quirks such as writing the impersonal pronoun "one" with the numeral "1." Reed discards quotation marks, and uses a literary style that oscillates wildly between the dialogue of film noir, gangster films, Damon Runyan, and a mishmash of black street lingo, sometimes marked as being from the speakeasies of the 1920s, at other times (and playfully anachronistic) from the 1960s Black Power Movement. The merging of traditions, hidden but obvious, leads to the merging of body and text itself, as in the depiction of the letter "X" found in the novel's pages (Figure 6.5).

Although very much about race, Reed's is no racialist theory of civilization. The Egyptians are divided among Atonists and Osirians, between "been-to's" and autochthonous celebrants. Like Freud, Reed understands Moses to be an Egyptian. The Israelites play the role not of villains but second-order opportunists and latecomers. Reed's theory is

Figure 6.5 Image from Ishmael Reed, *Mumbo Jumbo*.

not that Set, Moses, and Thermutis were inexplicably evil, just lazy, stealing a tradition but stealing it badly, mocking it by mimicking it without "getting down." There is no great war of civilizations, one white one black conjured here, at least as a matter of initiation or bona fide membership based on race or inheritance. This is not the proclamation of a chosen people, but of the unheralded contributors to a commonly

Figure 6.6 A Dionysian celebrant depicted on a Greek vase.

shared knowledge. Even the powers of the Left Hand (the black magic of Voodoo's "bokor") emanate from an Osirian source, thrown out of balance by the class nerds, snobs, con-artists of the ancient world who never got the "hang of it."

As a word, "jazz" is almost completely unmentioned. Instead, Reed speaks of "gutbucket music," the descendent of the "Black Mud Sound," and then later of "heathen sounds" so described by Moses after descending from the mountain in the Book of Exodus to find his people worshipping the Bull god Apis, the animal that carries the living spirit of Osiris (Exodus 32:15–21).

Music does not supplant writing in this counter-history, however, for there is the Book of Thoth. Von Vampton, after all, is a librarian. Pages can be torn from Thoth's book. Africa knows the art of word (viz. Reed) without enslaving one to its fetish. Reed's point is rather that Text cannot find release except when joined with its music. And the malevolence of the civilization based on Set's reduction of many gods to one, and of Moses' theft, resides in the brutal separation of dance from the demotic rituals of celebration in a collective divinity at one with funk. The forces of assassination, conspiracy, and nuclear war are the work of a limitation. Rationality and classical balance, evident in the calipers and Doric columns of the altars of a Masonic Lodge, are inextricable from a kind of nervous tension borne by the inharmonious and therefore clueless apprehension of the mystery of life as well as a lingering guilt for having been the bastard offspring of another's power. Like the potentate who tortures dissidents using the same punishments he believes his own crimes deserve, the West lashes out at the innocent Source as if trying to obliterate the phantom that is their own shadow. Western civilization suffers from an inferiority complex draped in the crinolines and jewels of an uneasy brag. The actual books (Mayan, Aztec, Muslim, Alexandrian) have been incinerated by the conquistadors, ancient and modern, forcing the Book to live on orally, a semi-conscious "being-in-feeling" which is, at the same time, a reading between the lines of the fragments that remain of actual writing: the Book of Thoth (Hermes Trismegistus).

These are not analogies but anagoges. Von Vampton is the copy whereas LaBas (Legba, Eshu-Elegba) is the legitimate heir; Guede, the first dead man raised by Legba is the authentic re-emergence of Osiris's severed penis whereas the raising of Lazarus is the parlor-trick of a *bokor* whose later ascension only serves to render the body ethereal. Gnosticism and masonry were both rational options for European dissidents, but Reed sides with the very different world of secular devotion. The novel translates Christian mumbo jumbo into the vernacular while avoiding the hypocrisy of the radio preacher. The conventional Gnostic dictum that self-knowledge is knowledge of God, that the self and the divine are identical, can be seen as an intellectualist version of LaBas's process of self-recognition.

As a theory of cyclical recurrence, Jes Grew in Reed's terms is hardly a glorious declaration of return. Although ultimately indomitable, Jes Grew the anti-plague often fails to hit its mark, subsiding into obscurity and failure, as so many dance crazes have had their day only to fall out of fashion before re-emerging at a later date transformed. The point, then, is not to calm the faithful with articles of proof that all is under control but only to assure the Atonist-influenced congregation that the apparent causes of history are not what they seem, that they have a source in an ancient conflict arising from Egypt: that civilization is the work of others. The most notable absent cause, in this sense, is the inspiration for the great black awakening known as the Harlem Renaissance (about which Reed is mercilessly disparaging). Its era, the 1920s, is important for precisely what the glitterati found everywhere around it but which it mistook or were oblivious to: the invasion and occupation of Haiti, Harding's black and compromised presidency, Mumbo Jumbo Kathedral. The Harlem Renaissance that has been passed down to us today was all about whites in blackface, or the hiring of black entertainers as hired help (an image unforgettably registered in the novel by the fact that the Book of Thoth was kept secretly in the basement of the Cotton Club).

Mumbo Jumbo is not just multiply conceived by an author with a massive repertoire writing at the height of his youthful and associative powers, and it is not fabricated only on the basis of significant research using a small library of disparate, learned, often simply weird books (among them, Black Herman's *Secrets of Magic, Mystery and Legerdemain*, John Huston Craige's *Cannibal Cousins*, Albert Munsell's *A Grammar of Color*, and the works of Julian the Apostate). Although appearing to be a hugely willful, flat-out satire on first reading, the book is not, for all that, idiosyncratic. Reed's book exemplifies, although does not allude to, discreet belief-systems in African-American culture that are very seldom talked about or, when they are talked about (as in James Baldwin's essay, "Negroes are Anti-Semitic Because They're Anti-White") are defensive.[32]

Many African Americans believe that Africans explored, and in many cases settled in, the New World long before Europeans arrived in the late fifteenth century – a view laid out in some detail by writers such as Ivan Van Sertima, Jan Carew, John Henrick Clarke, and Lerone Bennett, Jr. Others, that the Jews of the Old Testament were black people from

Africa, that their story of bondage referred to black African enslavement, and that the story of Moses is a latter-day appropriation by a different and lighter tribe. These are both views that cannot be spoken of easily. Reed sees himself not simply as cooking up self-contained outrage in order to give a veneer of dignity to the affectionate prejudices of his people. He defiantly belongs to them, and takes them seriously, which is not to say that he has not discovered in *Mumbo Jumbo* a way of making the view palatable.

The story is told cinematically or in a pulp fiction mode, using all of the typographic techniques of 1960s experimental black poetry. But part of the genius of the presentation is its ability to upset credos by appealing to the paranoias of the dominant culture that inherited Europe and that, in the case of Freud, preserved its self-aggrandizements. The conspiracies it documents are much more central than those surrounding the Kennedy assassination or Roswell. Although the masonic convictions of the founding fathers are well known, masonry also weaves its way through American letters. Egypt and hieroglyphics were central to the foundation of Mormonism in the 1820s and were a major influence on mid- and late-nineteenth-century American writers like Melville (*Moby-Dick* often displays Egyptian symbols and hieroglyphs as does Hawthorne in *The Scarlet Letter*). The occultist Aleister Crowley, an Englishman writing at the beginning of the twentieth century and the founder of the Ordo Templi Orientis, is less well known, but may be more representative of the paranoid mysticism and elative symbolism of this strain of literary thought. His poems, plays, and essays rave as they dwell on raving itself, seeing in it a religious impulse. In poems such as "Rosa Mundi," "Orpheus," "Gargoyles," and "Eleusis" he expresses his love of paganism, his opposition to secular society, and his faith that the state is the murderer of all true faith.[33]

Despite these classically conservative positions, Egyptomania usually had its roots in protest. An opponent of the established church, English Hermeticism was typically allied with political radicalism. One of Europe's most celebrated heretics and revolutionaries, Giordano Bruno, is widely known as a fiercely popular heretic; less well known is his actual offense. He did not merely cross the papacy with a heterodox interpretation of scripture or by challenging the scope of Church authority. He attacked the Judeo-Christian tradition itself, calling for a return to Egyptian religion. In modern black movements of protest, a variant pattern can be found in Rastafarianism with its roots in Ethiopia. KRS-One's "Why is That?" is only one of many sources in contemporary popular music with the view that the original Hebrews of the Old

Testament were African. Many of the secular traditions of English radicalism, although they avoid the excesses of Egyptomania, tend to fall into a different trap by underestimating the vitality of these secret histories. The great historian of colonialism, V. G. Kiernan, for example, laments the cultural destruction of Africans in the diaspora who are forced to live "out of any real contact with their own people." As a result, "unlike Hindus or Muslims they had no religious anchor strong enough to hold against the tides of the new age."[34] His conclusions, though, are quite inaccurate.

No literary Egyptophile, however, could be more relevant to *Mumbo Jumbo* than the author he never mentions. Vachel Lindsay drew his own illustrations for the volume of his collected poems published in 1925 – word-image collages (following the practice of another mystic of English letters, William Blake), which Lindsay called "hieroglyphs."[35]

Figure 6.7   Image from Vachel Lindsay, *Collected Poems.*

The miasmic intellectual space that produced the likes of Lindsay or Crowley was so pervasive and reached so deeply within the Euro-American psyche that Reed may not have been ignoring him, only uninterested in this one version of a garden-variety American obsession. Whether or not Reed had Lindsay's poem "Congo" in mind when writing his novel, the poem illustrates negatively much of what Reed is trying to say.

The Congo

A Study of the Negro Race

(Being a memorial to Ray Eldred, A Disciple missionary
of the Congo River)

I. Their Basic Savagery

    Fat black bucks in a wine-barrel room,
    Barrel-house kings, with feet unstable,
    Sagged and reeled and pounded on the
        Table,
    Pounded on the table,
    Beat an empty barrel with the handle of
        A broom,
    Hard as they were able,
    Boom, boom, Boom,
    With a silk umbrella and the handle of a
        Broom,
    Boomlay, boomlay, boomlay, Boom.
    Then I had religion, then I had a vision.
    I could not turn from their revel in derision.
    Than I saw the Congo, Creeping through
        The Black,
    Cutting through the Forest with a
        Golden Track.
    Then along that riverbank
    A thousand miles
    Tattooed cannibals danced in files;
    Then I heard the boom of the blood-lust
        Song
    And a thigh-bone beating on a tin-pan gong.
    And Blood screamed the whistles and
        Fifes of the warriors,
    Blood screamed the skull-faced, lean with
        Doctors,
    Whirl ye the deadly voodoo rattle,
    Harry the uplands,

> Steal all the cattle,
> Rattle-rattle, rattle-rattle,
> Bing.
> Boomlay, boomlay, boomlay, Boom,
> A roaring, epic, rag-time tune
> From the mouth of the Congo
> To the Mountains of the Moon.
> Death is an Elephant.
> Torch-eyed and horrible,
> Foam-flanked and terrible,
> Boom, steal the pygmies,
> Boom, kill the Arabs,
> Boom, kill the white men,
> Hoo, Hoo, Hoo.
> Listen to the yell of Leopold's ghost
> Burning in Hell for his hand-maimed host.
> Hear how the demons chuckle and yell
> Cutting his hands off, down in Hell.
> Listen to the creepy proclamation,
> Blown through the lairs of the forest-nation,
> Blown past the white-ants' hill of clay,
> Blown past the marsh where the butterflies
>   Play: –
> "Be careful what you do,
> Or Mumbo-Jumbo, God of the Congo,
> And of the other
> Gods of the Congo,
> Mumbo-Jumbo will hoo-doo you,
> Mumbo-Jumbo will hoo-doo you,
> Mumbo-Jumbo will hoo-doo you . . .[36]

Reed understands what many in the United States do not. Lindsay is a potent type, a norm, rather than a crank at the turn of the last century. *Mumbo Jumbo* delights in picking over the manias of its symptoms to reveal, like an ethnographer, its savage customs. The poem moves from repulsion to embarrassment to unseemly glorification. To what he mocks and fears Lindsay gives power, projecting that mockery and fear onto the opinions of the racists he means to expose. He suspects, rightly as it turns out, that this hate and fear derive from a darker conspiracy than human emotion. As he portrays them, blacks drink, whore, preach; all of them grin and stomp in speakeasies, flophouses, and in the present euphemism, the "inner city." But the coon stereotypes that thickly populate this poem are, as Lindsay intended them, ironic. They are meant to reveal the prejudices of his early-century audience and publicly revile the crimes of colonialism in Africa ("Leopold's ghost" punished in hell). But in the pages of Reed's novel there are verbal landmines to kill the unwary. Lindsay's thinking embraces the African divine but only from a distance. In the poet's rendering, the inhuman has passed from animal to god without pausing for breath, never lingering in the human itself. Egypt's dog-faced gods are gone but not forgotten. Reed spends much of his time in the novel brushing off such attempts at understanding.

Mumbo Jumbo both unravels a history of conspiracy, and diagnoses what he takes to be the credulity of Americans. If U.S. civics classrooms intone the nation-defining slogans of "liberty or death" or "I cannot tell a lie," Reed insists their actual motto is "there's a sucker born every minute." His is both the re-telling of a past and a critique of the conspiratorial frame of mind responsible for the parade of moral panics on alien abduction and fluoride in drinking water. In literature, this frame of mind reveals itself in books like Tim LaHaye and Jerry B. Jenkins's *Left Behind* or *The Turner Diaries*. Reed, by contrast, is part of a left American literary tradition of conspiracy based on historical research into the dirty secrets of U.S. power – a tradition in which novelists like Thomas Pynchon and Don DeLillo (among others) would also fit.

If no Battraville ever arrives from the wings to carry away the transgressors; and if no ship from Haiti ever shows up to counsel the New World African brethren about their true heritage, the wish-fulfillment is something Reed's great villain, Freud, would have understood perfectly.[37] Above all – and this is why I have included this chapter in this book – Reed's novel is Egyptomania with a difference: an explanation of why the Black Mud Sound continues to attract and why it is continually suppressed.

7

Imperial Jazz

> "'... It's a Wonderful World ...'
> [sung in the style of Louis Armstrong]
> What was so wonderful about picking cotton?"
> *The Fugées, "Nappy Head" (remix)*

According to convention, ragtime paved the way for jazz, inspiring early performers like Jelly Roll Morton, the later stride piano style of New York's James P. Johnson, and the second true American dance craze, the Charleston. Some even argue that the word "jazz" was never used in New Orleans before 1920. People from that city called their distinctive sound simply "ragtime" – which is to say music in "ragged time" (syncopated).[1] Whatever its name, ragtime became famous for the startling new way it combined classical harmonies and melodic imagination with a funky mood expressed in cascading melodies played in octaves (or sometimes fifths or tenths), transformed by off-the-beat phrasing in the right hand and by a regular, staggered rhythm in the bass. Ragtime's most famous composer, Scott Joplin, was born in Texarkana, apprenticed in Chicago, and cut his teeth in St. Louis, where ragtime enjoyed its golden age.

One of Joplin's best-known rags is "Solace: (A Mexican Serenade)" from 1909 (see Plate 3). Biographies of Joplin are strangely silent about this curious title, which may reveal more than it intended to. He, or his publicists, probably meant little more than that the song to him (or them) had a vaguely "Spanish" feel, following the convention of dubbing "Spanish" anything from Latin America. In a similar way, "Mexican" was a word used for anything generically Latin, just as it is today in much of the American heartland.[2] But what musical features exactly were Joplin or his publishers calling Latin? Does the term fit only this one piece or is there a Latin and Caribbean element to ragtime in general?

After listening to the work of Ignacio Cervantes, the Cuban composer who died in 1905 and whose career in Cuba preceded Joplin's by twenty years, it is hard not to say "ragtime in general." One genre in which Cervantes excelled, the *danza*, resembles ragtime to a fault. Comparing the scores of the *danza* "La Celosa" (the jealous one) (Plate 4) and Joplin's "Solace" one can see at a glance that both possess the same rhythmic figure in the bass line that we have already seen in the *habanera* (see p. 77 above): the dotted eighth, sixteenth, and two eighth notes phrase that was the essential rhythmic feature as well of Louis Moreau Gottschalk's *contradanza* "Ojos Criollos," written in Martinique in 1859 and published in New Orleans the following year.

To the ear of the non-professional musician, the *danza* (at least as Cervantes popularized it) has exactly the same lilt and sway on the upbeat as ragtime does, combining high piano technique with a frolicky, risqué feeling mobilizing classical harmonies on behalf of illicit, lowdown pleasures. There are differences as well. Ragtime has about it the chirpiness of the broad-brimmed straw hat and gazebo-in-the-park overtones of mainstream America at the turn of the century, whereas the *danza* brings to mind a book-lined study with velvet curtains. Nevertheless, to hear the *danza* is to suspect immediately that "Solace" is from the same musical family, and the close connection is altogether obvious on the pages of the musical scores.

In the hands of Cervantes, the *danza* was primarily a short, stylized piano piece based on the *habanera*.[3] Both the one and the other were forms of dance music whose singable element pervaded the whole, constructed with a repeatable bass line (usually of 8-beat phrases in 2/4 time) that "accompanies the melody but that represents a divergent rhythmic design."[4] How could it be otherwise, one might ask, than that the swaying syncopations and phrasings of Joplin's bass line (as well as the technical piano vocabulary that here involves repeating the same rhythmic pattern in the right hand on a different beat of the measure) were inspired by the *habanera*, if not directly from Cervantes where many of the same elements are found?

Upon this framework, Joplin certainly added his own brilliant coloration – the rapidly ascending and descending thirds, fifths, or octaves in the melodic line, and the signature coda of his song-phrases typically punctuating a major key with a closing minor chord as a way of announcing the approaching bridge. But how is it possible to think that so widely known a musician and pianist as Gottschalk, who performed at concerts repeatedly and very publicly in Cuba, the French Caribbean, New Orleans, and other American cities in the mid-nineteenth century, would not have put his stamp on North American ragtime?[5]

It is almost demanded, in this spirit, to give a more literal understanding to "Mexican" in Joplin's title. Mexican octets, which were military bands, were famous in the United States in the 1880s for their superb technical facility and they played up and down the Mississippi on the river's sternwheelers throughout that decade.[6] The conquest of Mexican territory in neighboring Texas and the Southwest, and then later, the first rumblings of the Mexican revolution at the beginning of the century, put the United States in military contact with Mexico. According to John Storm Roberts, these sorts of encounters were already explicit in 1884–85 when New Orleans hosted the World Industrial and Cotton Centennial Exposition which brought people from throughout the Caribbean to witness inter-cultural fare at various national pavilions. One of the successes of the Exhibition was the band of the Eighth Regiment of the Mexican Cavalry, glowingly reviewed in an 1885 article for *Century* Magazine.

It is not only that Buddy Bolden, often considered the first true jazz trumpeter, soaked up such fare as a young man in New Orleans but many of the members of what is widely reputed to be the first jazz combo (which he assembled) were veterans of the Spanish-American War. Like the band's trombonist, Willie Cornish, they had spent months in Cuba at the turn of the century playing in a U.S. military band. W. C. Handy, who is thought to be the "father of the blues" traveled to Cuba in 1910 with the U.S. Army on the tails of the annexation of Cuba by the United States, later talking excitedly about the small bands he had discovered playing in Havana's back streets: " 'More than thirty years later I heard that rhythm again. By then it had gained respectability in New York and acquired a name: *rumba*.' He brought a few Latin rhythms back to Louisiana and incorporated a *habanera* in his St. Louis Blues, written four years later."[7]

In this chapter, I would like to begin by laying out what we know and do not know about the provenance of jazz since it seems to me crucial to an understanding of neo-African musical forms as well as to my argument that these forms are, in fact, a unity: a single New World complex of musics not only a distinct set of nationally defined musical genres. In part, that unity can be explained by the common cultural origins of the people transported from Africa who populated the entire Caribbean basin, a vast region extending (south to north) from Brazil to Tennessee, where in many cases they were the majority. Their beliefs, practices, and languages – extremely varied at first – were condensed and simplified under the harsh conditions of New World slavery. It is the historical experience of conquest, enslavement, and repression, in other words, and not just the original West African place of origin, that accounts for the coherence of neo-African modes of expression, and this is the first sense in which I mean the term "imperial jazz."

As the major musical form to emerge in the United States, jazz is unthinkable, obviously, without the imperial forces that called forth slave labor. The "historical experience," however, was different in parts of the Caribbean basin, and so the unity I speak of is qualified by varying modes of treatment. These had profound effects on music. For one thing, a different order prevailed in the Caribbean Catholic New World as opposed to the U.S. Protestant New World. The former allowed much greater degrees of African worship among its slaves, and professed a religion whose own pagan survivals made it much more receptive to neo-African syncretisms.[8] These differences led, predictably enough, to different relations to ritual, to the drum, to public gatherings of dance and celebration, and to contact with the deities. The secularity of devotion was in many ways dissimilar in these different parts of the Americas – on the one hand more camouflaged, on the other less. And so, musically speaking, jazz – although it belongs to the New World – is also the specific product of a place with a unique combination of qualities.

Part of the story of jazz, and probably the most pressing one, is the features it has in common with New World African music. But equally important is how it differs from the *son*. Below, I would like to suggest that: (1) in jazz, the popular became classical only by becoming individual – or better, individualist. To be considered "serious" music, its performers were forced to abandon dance, moving instead to establish technical expertise with instruments (including the instrument of the voice); (2) unlike the *son*, authenticity in jazz was expressed as a staged primitive; it fell out of contact with the blues, and its lyric content was restricted to the emotional key of a lament over personal misfortune rather than, as in *son*, a modulated literary performance of social character; (3) the sophisticated lyrical content of *son* and its rhythmic complexities are inter-connected. Lacking the first, jazz found it difficult to continue developing. In losing its holism, it had lost some of its ritual function.

I will take up these issues as the chapter progresses, but let me be more specific about what I mean by "imperial jazz." Most commentators, either left or right, concede today that the United States is also an empire, and that it has in fact been building that empire since the turn of the last century when jazz was first recognized as a musical form. "Imperial jazz," though, does not refer to a kind of music that happens to be heralded in, or taken to be the symbol for, a nation that is imperial. I am not saying, in other words, that since jazz is from the United States and the United States runs an empire, that jazz is "imperial." I am talking rather about the ideological outlook that comes naturally to an imperial power. There are demands made on researchers and the public in advance that this politically and symbolically potent music be considered officially (and only) the possession of one nation. It is as though the United States would seem less strong or influential to many critics if its most representative music had been created jointly with others, when those others live outside its territories or (worse) in its dominions. This view is, not surprisingly, as strong among many African-American scholars as in the white establishment, since there is huge cultural capital at stake. Jazz is broadcast across the globe by the U.S. cultural elite as quintessentially *American* – a rare moment when the black American is welcomed as a full and unqualified member of the national self.

Let me mention one final way to understand the term "imperial jazz." As it turns out, the phrase can also be interpreted literally. The music that most North Americans are referring to when they say "jazz" sprang to life in part as a result of U.S. military operations abroad – as an accidental by-product of foreign occupation. It was always heavily marked by military influences of various sorts. Even more dramatically, and precisely because of its national symbolism, the music was deployed from the start for the purpose of pacification abroad. This takes nothing away from the brilliance of the music or the artists who created it. On the other hand, it was no coincidence that it was used this way given the careful manner in which its early chroniclers cut it off from its sources, drawing a boundary line through its very middle.

America's art form

My position is not that jazz was invented outside the United States necessarily, only that it is a neo-African, New World form whose origins were the result of non-U.S. influences as well. Obviously there were contributions from a number of sides, and eventually a style was consolidated (or rather many styles corresponding to jazz's different phases) that took on a distinct national character. What was disseminated to the world as big band jazz, for instance, was clearly Usonian. This does not mean that the conventional accounts of jazz's origins are coherent or that they give evidence of having paid attention to Latin and Caribbean music (or colonial history) when making their claims. On the contrary, they seem insistent about not doing so. Let's look at the actual wording of such accounts.

- "It must have been about 1891 when a Negro barber in New Orleans named Buddy Bolden, picked up his cornet and blew the first stammering notes of jazz, thereby unconsciously breaking with several centuries of musical tradition."[9]
- "Jazz arose from its surroundings, then, as any primitive art does – spontaneously."[10]
- "[Jazz arose] in the Southern states of the U.S.A – *and there alone.*"[11]
- "It is true that New Orleans was the most important city in the genesis of jazz. It is false that it was the only one . . . Similar ways of playing evolved in Memphis or St. Louis, Dallas and Kansas City, in many other cities of the South and Mid-west."[12]
- "As any history of the music will tell us, jazz started in New Orleans."[13]
- "Jazz occupies a unique place in American cultural history. Although it has been influenced by many countries, it remains purely an American phenomenon."[14]
- "Jazz was developed in the eighteenth and nineteenth centuries by black Americans, who were the first to combine the heritages of African and European music."[15]
- "Jazz happened in America, and it could have happened only there . . . Jazz is part of the social history of the United States, and must be seen in that context."[16]
- "Jazz did not exist until the twentieth century. It has elements which were not present either in Europe or in Africa before this century. And at any of its stages it represents, unarguably it seems to me, a relationship among rhythm, harmony, and melody that did not exist before."[17]
- "Jazz is not classical music, or folk music, or black music, but, rather, *American* music."[18]
- "[Jelly Roll] Morton was in fact among the first to play jazz, its first theorist and composer and master of form, the first to write it down."[19]
- "It appears that jazz came into being around 1900, by the coalescence of a number of existing popular musical styles, primarily ragtime and the blues."[20]

I have taken the time to quote so many authors in order to give a sense of how pervasive this view is in U.S. and European writing that jazz is uniquely North American, that it began at the turn of the last century, and that its essential features (combining "the heritages of African and European music") were completely unheard of before it came on the scene. Some of the quotations above date from the 1940s, others are only a few years old. In other words, the essential view has not changed. It is not that all jazz criticism is comfortable in eliminating the Caribbean contribution, and one can find occasional mention of "Afro-Caribbean culture," usually in passing.[21] But even in these gestures, nothing is said (or, one suspects, is known) about the history of the *habanera*, the *danza*, the *son*, the career of Gottschalk, and other issues that have been richly documented and discussed in Spanish-speaking circles for decades. Even more problematic, New Orleans itself is neglected.[22]

One of the great exceptions in jazz criticism in this respect is Marshale Stearns, who in 1956 began his *Story of Jazz* with a short history of the city that points vividly to some of the weaknesses of the "big bang" theory of jazz (the theory that it arose "spontaneously" and could only have done so "in America" – meaning, in this case, the United States). New Orleans was a Latin-Catholic possession of France for eighty-two years before being thrust into the British-Protestant sphere after the Louisiana Purchase (1803). For thirty-six years during the eighteenth century, moreover, it was a Spanish possession. At the time of the Louisiana Purchase, the population was half white, half black, and within a decade, the population had doubled, many of them coming from the West Indies (primarily French possessions like Guadeloupe, Martinique, and San Domingo [Haiti]): "The slaves were mainly Yorubas and Dahomeans, worshippers of *vodun*. From 1809 to 1810, more than 3,000 arrived from San Domingo, by way of Cuba, their French masters having fled the Haitian revolution."[23] The diasporic patterns continued this way throughout the century: "Africans from the French West Indies, who had already absorbed something of European music, continued to arrive and a further blending was under way."[24]

We are already familiar with this pattern of exile and musical influence from the history of Cuba (a story that, from another angle, is enshrined in Reed's *Mumbo Jumbo*, which also focuses on the centrality of San Domingo as the launching point for African culture in the Americas – an argument endorsed by Zora Neale Hurston as well, whose most famous novel, *Their Eyes Were Watching God*, was at least partly composed in Haiti). In assessing the flows of jazz (or we might say "ur-jazz" or "pre-jazz"), it is necessary to question the divisions that might account for a separate development. Both the United States and Cuba were colonial societies, both were riven by destructive civil wars in exactly the same period, both experienced a rejection by the white establishment of the black character of their societies, and their proximity meant a constant movement of peoples and ideas between them.

The *habanera*'s basic rhythm was described by J. B. Roseñord de Beauvallon in 1844 as "composed of sighs, of lively movements, sad refrains, of chants that are suddenly arrested . . . bristling with syncopation and counter-time measures that for performers present an almost inaudible difficulty."[25] A common culture of the Caribbean filtered through Cuban and Haitian expatriates and travelers to New Orleans, and found its way up the Mississippi into the entertainment circuits of rural and small-town America. New Orleans itself was a stomping ground of French opera, Cuban popular melodies, Haitian drumming, American spirituals, and Andalusian ballads, with sizeable representation of the groups associated with these forms resident there.[26]

The French culture exported to Cuba from San Domingo would, therefore, have been part of a milieu that fit this scene nicely and allowed for easy cultural commerce. As Isabelle Leymarie notes, Gottschalk's work in New Orleans "gave rise to the so-called 'tango-bass' or 'Spanish bass' which crept in around the start of the twentieth century."[27] While exploring the frequent travel of free blacks from Cuba to New Orleans during the nineteenth century, for example, Helio Orovio points out that even though Buddy Bolden is considered the legendary cornetist from Storyville, "no less an authority than Sidney Bechet insisted that Cuba's Manuel Pérez, a cigar maker turned jazz cornetist, was the better musician."[28]

It was Pérez, he insists, who established the first real vocabulary for the trumpet – a vocabulary that quickly found its way to New York City. Again, there is an actual documentary trail behind such statements. The confluences do not all arise at the point of origin, either, but express themselves also as the stamp put on jazz in its early decades of development. In New York, "violinist Alberto Iznaga played in big bands and composed pieces that introduced Cuban rhythms – especially *rumba* – to American jazz (we are talking here of the 1930s).[29] A Cuban flutist, Alberto Socarrás, not only played in New York City big bands but also founded his own orchestra."[30] Most attempts to argue for the neglected role of Latin musicians in jazz, even by the devotés of Latin music, begin with Dizzy Gillespie's conversion in the late 1940s through the invention of so-called Cubop (a fusion of bebop and Latin jazz). The actual connections were, in fact, much more persistent and much earlier. Duke Ellington was already using *rumba* in his recordings in the 1930s, the same period that Don Justo Aspiazu took his Cuban orchestra to New York.

The issue of jazz's origins, then, is related to the influence of Cuba (not only Haiti) on the United States. Leonardo Acosta has provided a succinct outline of the case for this influence, and its conduit was not only New Orleans. White and black Cubans lived in what is now Florida throughout the second half of the eighteenth century, and the "Batallions of Pardos and Morenos," out of which came the first typical orchestras of *danzones*, took part in the American War of Independence.[31] There was a

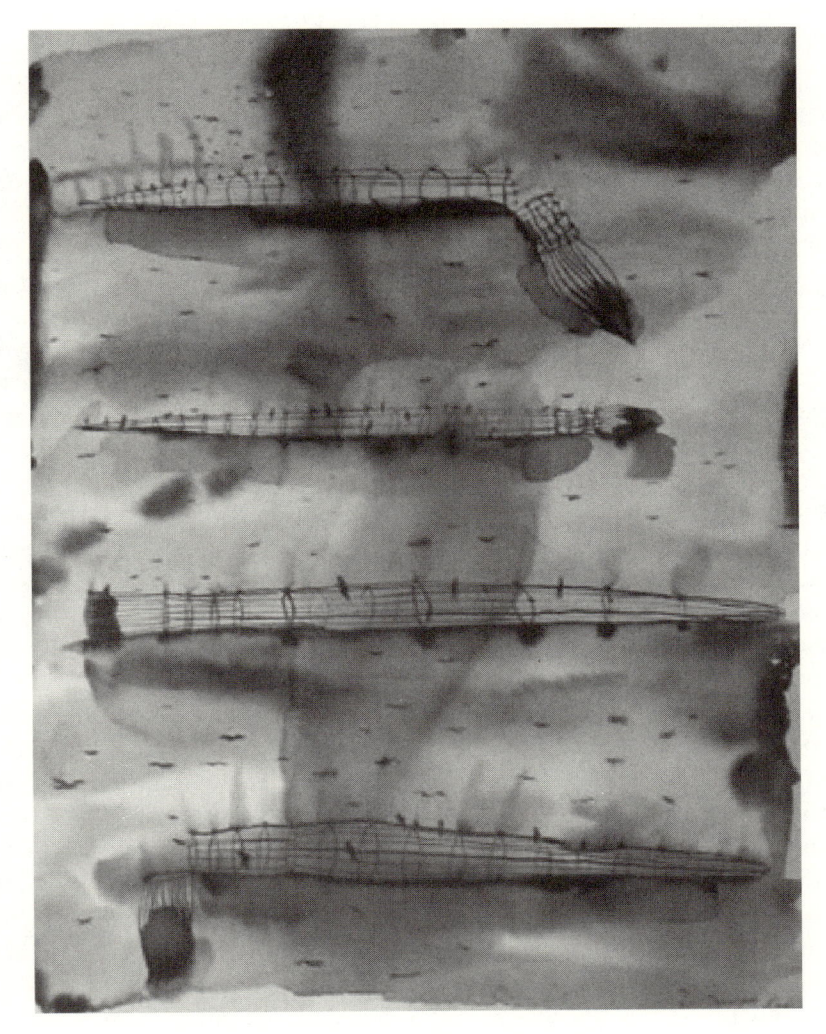

Figure 7.1 Painting by Kdir (Kadir Lopez).

continuing Cuban emigration into the United States for political reasons during the nineteenth century, which brought Ignacio Cervantes, who lived for a time in New York (the exodus of Cuban musicians also went in the direction of Mexico, South America and Europe). "As early as 1850, Cuban music was being published in New York."[32] The abolition of slavery in Cuba in 1886 impelled ex-slaves to move to the countryside and cities of Cuba, but the lack of work obliged them to undertake a new exodus. Their primary destination was New Orleans, which from the beginning of the nineteenth century was the principal enclave for Cubans in the United States.

There was, then, a "direct relation between those new immigrants and those rhythms and Afro-Cuban rhythmical patterns that arise in the formation of jazz."[33] At the end of the Spanish-American War, several African-American soldiers stayed in Cuba. One of them, Santiago Smood, made a name for himself as an interpreter of the banjo and a singer of the blues in Cuba, and he went on to become a *tresero* and *trovador*. In the opposite direction, a Cuban musician named Pedro Stacholy moved to New York, founding the first Cuban jazz band. The rise of well-defined styles like *habanera*, *danzon*, *son*, and *rumba* in places as far apart as Buenos Aires, Paris, Tokyo, and Mexico eventually attracted North American recording companies who saw their sales potential. Along with the success of Lecuona and Simons in the U.S. market, there were performers and arrangers like Vicente Sigler and Nilo Menendez. The critical economic situation in Cuba and, later, the political situation there as well were also factors explaining the new flow of Cuban musicians to New York. Socarrás, Iznaga, Mario Bauzá; later, Desi Arnaz, Anselmo Sacasas, Miguelito Valdés, José Curbelo, Machito, Chano Pozo and finally, Arsenio Rodríguez were some of the better known musicians playing throughout the five boroughs right through the end of the 1950s.

These chronologies are even more suggestive when one considers the imperial lines of cultural flow that mark musical reception, which is the relatively underplayed part of the matter of influence and one that has not been explored sufficiently in some of the attempts to chronicle the Latin influence on American popular music. No black jazz band was recorded in the United States until 1920 and none extensively until 1923.[34] It would most likely surprise most jazz critics to realize that Latin music was being recorded by U.S. companies as early as 1898, both in New York and in Havana.[35] Companies understood that opening new markets abroad required mastering the indigenous sounds of the cultures they meant to woo. These early recordings of Cuban and Puerto Rican artists, although deployed instrumentally, helped determine later patterns of global reception, even if they did so in contradictory ways.

Traditional histories of jazz had their most luxuriant example, perhaps, in Ken Burns's PBS Series *Jazz*. In episode one, *Village Voice* music critic

Gary Giddins strikes a theme that runs throughout the series and (as we have seen) in American jazz criticism as a whole:

> Jazz is the quintessential American music. And the important thing that you have to begin with is that it can only happen in America. It's not an African music obviously; it's not a European music obviously. It's something that comes right out of this soil, out of influences that come from all different kinds of cultures. And all of these come together in jazz. But in jazz unlike in all of the other folk musics of the world it blossoms into an authentic art.[36]

Whose soil can he be referring to? Are the "different kinds of cultures" that he concedes came together to make jazz all found in the United States? It may well be that jazz is not African (rather neo-African), but why is it "obviously" so? From the perspective we have been developing in this book, it seems particularly absurd to argue – although it is very common all the same – that jazz is the only folk music in the world that blossomed "into an authentic art." In episode three, on the jazz age (the 1920s), we find an earlier version of this same attitude, a sign of its entrenchment in the national psyche. There no less than F. Scott Fitzgerald alludes to jazz's breaking of the mold of "proper" musical taste, declaring: "We are the most powerful nation, who can tell us any longer what was fashionable or fun?" Later, the documentary considers the Depression era, when we hear that jazz was:

> called upon to lift the spirits and raise the morale of a frightened people . . . Jazz epitomized the American spirit, the spirit of freedom and swing . . . We are a young vibrant nation. The way we dance represents the way we listen to music – this was purely and uniquely American . . . Swing's tunes became the anthem of war time America.

This chorus, still largely unchallenged by the inclusion of discordant voices (although many are available), has been praised over time from unexpected quarters.[37] A national agenda, fed not only by generals but artists and authors (both black and white), severed jazz from the rest of the New World. Apart from Jelly Roll Morton in the early days of jazz (the son of a creole from Haiti) or, later, Dizzy Gillespie (who collaborated with Chano Pozo), jazz men and women were for the most part unaware of the larger musical orbit of the Americas. They were, perhaps understandably, above all "Americans" and so just as likely as their white counterparts to see the country's cultural and actual borders in indelible black ink.

In 1941, no less of an iconoclast than Richard Wright, for example, made the music an allegory of liberation from racism: "We live on, and our music makes the feet of the whole world dance, even the feet of the children of the poor white workers who live beyond the line that marks the boundary of our lives. Where we cannot go, our tunes, songs, slang, and jokes go."[38] In an eloquent outburst, Wright mints a theme that no one since has put better, yet gives energy to the contours of a national creation:

> Why is our music so contagious? Why is it that those who deny us are willing to sing our song? Perhaps it is because so many of those who live in cities feel deep down just as we feel. Our big brass horns, our huge noisy drums and whirring violins make a flood of melodies whose poignancy is heightened by our latent fear and uneasiness, by our love of the sensual, and by our feverish hunger for life. On the plantation our songs carried a strain of other-worldly yearning which people called "spiritual"; but now our blues, jazz, swing, and boogie-woogie and our "spirituals" of the city pavements, our longing for freedom and opportunity, an expression of our bewilderment and despair in a world whose meaning eludes us. The ridiculousness and sublimity of love are captured in our blues, those sad-happy songs that laugh and weep all in one breath, those mockingly tender utterances of a folk imprisoned in steel and stone. Our thirst for the sensual is poured out in jazz; the tension of our brittle lives is given forth in swing; and our nervousness and exhaustion are pounded out in the swift tempo of boogie-woogie.[39]

Neither James Weldon Johnson nor Ralph Ellison was an exception to this pattern. Those who emphasized the Caribbean connection were minorities within the minority: Claude McKay, a transplanted Jamaican; Langston Hughes, whose personal connection (and frequent travel) to Mexico and Cuba were self-defining; but above all W. E. B. du Bois, whose organizational ties to the Pan-African movement gave him an internationalist outlook that rendered such sentimentality impossible.

African-American culture was and is "contagious" in exactly Wright's terms, but apart from its genius, it was also exported and promoted by a government only too eager to have the music created by its own oppressed peoples symbolize a virtue taken to be inherent in the national patrimony. Under this rubric, U.S. foreign conquest itself yields mixed emotions when so redemptive an aesthetic form lies within the very soul of the intruder. In fact, black music has played this role in U.S. foreign policy from the inception of the country's ambitions abroad.

Is it enough, though, in establishing the pan-American character of jazz to rely on circumstantial evidence – massive though it might be? Anyone who makes an effort to imagine the culture of New Orleans in the nineteenth century, the likely kinds of interactions among its French and Spanish Caribbean occupants, the well-documented publishing history of musical scores, the state of musical invention among the peoples moving there, and so on, will find it very hard to give any credence at all to the conventional view about jazz's origins. And yet, the early recordings of Handy's "Memphis Blues" (1919) for instance, or Fletcher Henderson's "Sugar Foot Stomp" (1925), do not seem, especially to the amateur, to have much to do with Latin music. What, then, musically speaking, does the one have to do with the other, and how far can we take the argument that jazz is part of a common New World African music?

A number of musicologists have begun to adopt the position of Thomas Fiehrer that "the roots of jazz are actually Afro-Latin American."[40] But perhaps more to the point, many contemporary jazz musicians have begun to express the same point of view based on their experience of actually playing the music. Citing extensive interviews with these musicians, the performer and critic Christopher Washburne has presented a persuasive case that "certain rhythmic cells in the jazz repertoire ... are most typically associated with Cuban music styles: the *son clave, cinquillo*, and *tresillo*."[41] He begins his argument by framing the inquiry in the way we have here, by observing that New Orleans "was already a century-old 'Latin-American' city" by 1803, that among its immigrants (a crucial fact here) was "the prominent family of Mexican-American music teachers, the Tíos, who taught many of the great jazz clarinetists."[42] As the largest island of the Caribbean, Cuba was responsible for most of the migration to the southern United States and Europe during this period. But even more telling, in the first quarter of the eighteenth century, "about half the residents of New Orleans had spent at least a decade in Cuba, having previously lived or been born in Saint-Domingue, now known as Haiti."[43] The Cuban *habanera* and *rumba* were already very popular rhythms that were tied to the brass band ensembles used in public celebrations – the kinds of bands inseparable from the New Orleans brand of jazz at its inception.

In earlier chapters, I discussed the *cinquillo, tresillo*, and *clave* (so I will not reproduce them here), but here it is important to emphasize that "clave" (literally key, clef, or keystone) refers as much to a procedure or principle of doing music as it does to a set rhythmic pattern – what Carpentier and others had stressed about the bewildering variations of Caribbean dance names when he observed that the essence of the neo-

African musical revolution was above all "a way of doing things."[44] The jazz aesthetic is like the Latin to the degree that both are about constant variation and patterns set up to be broken (although below I will argue that there are fundamental ways in which they differ as well). Washburne's important research extends to musical transcriptions of the most common syncopated rhythms found in jazz.[45] In compiling them, what he discovered was that fifteen of the twenty-six most common patterns in jazz correspond to the *clave* strokes and "could easily have been performed in a Cuban setting." The significance of the finding is clear:

> The frequency of these rhythms in early jazz suggests that the Caribbean influence was so tied to its developmental stages that the rhythms became part of the rhythmic foundation of jazz ... Their absence in other African-American styles not as closely associated with New Orleans as jazz – such as work songs, field hollers, spirituals, gospel, and some blues traditions – attests to the unique nature of New Orleans.[46]

The reason Mario Bauzá was assimilated so quickly into the Cab Calloway orchestra, the reason that the Puerto Rican Juan Tizol was taken on so eagerly by Duke Ellington, and Manuel Pérez could play so seamlessly with the Onward Brass Band lay in the pre-existing structural similarities of their musical styles and logic.

There has been a certain politics of emotion that governs the reception of jazz in the United States, and the PBS jazz series exemplified it perfectly. With all the promise of an insurgent knowledge – and there is no doubt that the series' appeal had to do with its grave and exalted celebrations of the creativity of the underclasses – it is really a parochial "American spirit" kind of discourse that too often emerged from the program.[47] Intellectuals who herald the study of regions rather than narrow nationalist enclaves, who speak of a common "black Atlantic" culture and fertile "contact zones" have not always been capable of giving the right emphasis in jazz to the "Latin tinge" (as Jelly Roll Morton famously described the "Spanish" element in jazz). The deep roots of this thinking, its necessity even, are revealed in some attempts to force jazz history out of a linear narrative of emergence while being, at the same time, hesitant to violate national borders. For example, in *America's Music: The Pilgrims to the Present* (1955), Gilbert Chase wrote:

> The music that came to be called "jazz" was rooted in the cultural, social, and racial conditions of the South. No single city – not even New

Orleans – can legitimately claim to have been its exclusive birthplace. African survivals in American folk music, the hot rhythm of the camp-meeting spirituals and gospel songs, the form and inflection of the blues, the improvised "washboard" bands, the marching brass bands that played for funerals, parades, and picnics, were common to wide sections of the South. The early ragtime musicians who had such a strong influence on the beginnings of jazz came from various parts of the Midwest and the Southwest.[48]

With limiting inclusiveness, so sweeping and democratic, Chase finds it perfectly natural to exclude all non-U.S. areas from his search despite an opening gambit ("not even New Orleans") that almost begs for an extra-national focus. He later provides one of a sort, but without solving the fundamental problem raised by the Usonian bias of the overall attitude: "Everyone's valorizing jazz," he complains, "as a popular expression that is simply and purely North American. It's worth giving a little attention to jazz in its involvement with the high-art music of our century. A study based on the global influence of jazz has still to be written" (166). Here we have finally broken out of U.S. confines, but only to explore our influence on others, not theirs on us. That jazz be taken more seriously in classical circles relies for him, paradoxically, on its ability to conquer foreign tastes. Because she is not proud and defensive on behalf of "America," French critic Isabelle Leymarie finds it easier to tell a more plausible story:

> In places like the old Congo Square [in New Orleans], blacks rattled jawbones and plucked the same rumba boxes as their brothers in Santiago or Matanzas, and names like Augusto Centeño, the three Tíos (Lorenzo Sr., his son Lorenzo Jr., and his brother 'Papa' (Luis) Tio, of Cuban origin), Alcide 'Yellow' Nuñez, the cornettists Ray López or Manuel Pérez (born in Havana in 1863) . . . cropped up in the first jazz bands.[49]

In an era filled with declarations of migrancy and border-crossing, it is still difficult for many to accept the thesis of multiple causes of creation when it comes to the all-important art form of jazz. In addition to the Spanish-American War, U.S. soldiers and their camp followers had fought long campaigns in Mexico under Pershing and in Haiti for a six-year stretch in the early 1920s at the height of the Jazz Age. Also forgotten is that flood of joy-seekers and night-lifers who rushed to Cuba during Prohibition because drinking there was legal. The national-cultural categories imposed on jazz make even the attempts at inclusivity sound provincial: "How . . . would modern American music (jazz's direct offsprings such as rhythm and blues as well as other twentieth-century forms) sound had there been no Louis Armstrong, no Duke Ellington, no Bessie Smith, no Charlie Parker, no John Coltrane?"[50] Good point. But how would Armstrong have sounded without Cervantes, Manuel Saumell, or Gottschalk?

The redemptive ideology of jazz has a distinguished history, and is expressed in its classical form by Ralph Ellison as a strident individualism:

> True jazz is an art of individual assertion within and against the group. Each true jazz moment (as distinct from the uninspired commercial performance) springs from a contest in which each artist challenges all the rest; each solo flight, or improvisation, represents (like the successive canvases of a painter) a definition of his identity: as individual, as member of the collectivity and as a link in the chain of tradition.

This has become very much the standard view. Phil Schapp, for example, whose jazz program on WKCR FM, 89.9 New York is known throughout the tri-state area, frequently emphasizes the "solo." Typical of this genre of criticism was his program on a summer evening in 2004 when he declared that although the brilliance of Louis Armstrong is already known, it is Clarence Williams of the "Blue Five" in the fall of 1923 who "truly launches, for the first time, the trumpet solo proper."[51] What strikes one here is not so much the judgment (since attributions in popular music are always debatable and what "solo proper" means is open to interpretation), but the utter lack of pressure to know or say anything at all about the Afro-Latin presence. No one – not scholars, amateurs, or the general public – finds anything amiss in this confident claim, or expects a more exacting treatment. Leymarie suggests with a good deal of precision why Schapp's assertion is almost certainly untrue:

> At the dawn of the twentieth century, a sizeable number of Hispanic musicians worked in the town's [New Orleans's] clubs and speakeasies. Under their influence Latin syncopations crept into works such as Jesse "Old Man" Picket's *The Dream* (1870), Neil Moret's *Cubanola*, Robert Hampton's *Agitation Rag,* Artie Matthews's *Pastime Rag No. 5* . . . William Christopher Handy, self-proclaimed "inventor of the blues," had traveled to Cuba in 1910 with the U.S. Army, when *tipicas* were in full swing . . . Invented in 1840 by the Belgian Adolphe Sax, the sax was

rare in popular music before Handy in 1909, but Mexican bands had been playing it for years in Louisiana.[52]

A musician and chronicler of music like James Weldon Johnson in *Black Manhattan* (1930) provides another example of this tradition of engaging black music in the form of "Negro as maker of nation's songs" (xiii).[53] Giving voice to the national unconscious, he portrays the influx of Southern blacks into Harlem after World War I due to a labor shortage as an "invasion" in the eyes of New York's white residents, saying the migration resembled the movement of populations from a foreign country. But what, for effect, he makes metaphorical he could have described much more literally. These, after all, were the years of the first sizeable migration from the West Indies – both English and Spanish – which involved a transfer of as many as 50,000 persons, an enormous figure for the time. Although he mentions this transfer in passing, he oddly remarks that they "quickly bec[a]me New Yorkers" without further comment (xiv).

It is impossible to read Johnson's book today without being reminded that the United States is popularly grounded in African-American culture, not simply in the unrewarded and disparaged sense employed by Ishmael Reed in *Mumbo Jumbo*, but in an instrumental one as well. Fighting on two fronts – against the white establishment and the "national interest" – seemed impossibly fanciful to Johnson and others in his era. He does lament, though, the frightful standoff produced by jingoism: "one of the worst effects of the war [World War I] was to draw thousands of aliens out of this country back to their native lands to join the colours" (151). That one of the major early twentieth-century scholars (and authors) of popular music would be so unaware of the Caribbean influence on major U.S. forms is surprising. Johnson's trope of the "foreign within" can be extended, as we have seen, outside U.S. borders; or it can take unexpected forms, as has happened with the treatment of rap music as an invasion by foreigners (see Chapter 1).

Music, violence, discipline

If for Jacques Attali, music is always a re-channeling of ancient rituals of violence – a view that is appealing in part because it cannot be proven – there is a much blunter arena in which his thesis can be tested. From the start, jazz was military. It has been, and still often is, about the army, which is another of the ways to understand what I mean by "imperial jazz."

I have remarked already that military contact with Cuba, Puerto Rico, and Mexico in the late nineteenth and early twentieth centuries was the *sine qua non* of the Caribbean mélange that eventually yielded jazz among other neo-African forms. If these were its conditions of existence, so too were they the cause of its dissemination. Even the PBS jazz documentary points out that one of the earliest great jazz band leaders was James Reese Europe, who enlisted in New York's Negro regiment, the 15th Infantry, under the command of Colonel William Haywood. Very little of the context of Europe's career is explored by Burns, naturally, and the significance of jazz arriving on the European continent at the point of a rifle is never noted.

Haywood approached Europe initially to do a public relations job, asking that he organize the "best damn brass band in the U.S. Army." With the army's help, he called on all the Negro musicians of America, exclaiming "last call, golden opportunity, if you want to do your duty in the present crisis."[54] On hearing the band after it landed in France, General John Pershing (the commander of the U.S. troops that invaded Mexico in 1916) who then led the American expeditionary force in France, ordered the band to be transferred to his headquarters so it could entertain the officers from the British and French armies: "They made such an impression on France that there was an immediate demand for Negro jazz musicians in Paris, and France developed a taste for jazz that is still very strong."[55] Although they recruited fifty musicians, they had trouble filling the clarinet sections. "Then someone suggested Puerto Rico [a recent U.S. acquisition]. Puerto Rican brass bands were famous for their clarinet sections . . . Europe was 'ordered' to Puerto Rico as the Fifteenth Regiment's 'recruiting officer.' Three weeks later he was back with eighteen clarinet players."[56]

However staged, the PBS treatment of this episode in *Jazz* is instructive, not despite but because of its failure to mention the Latin connection. At one point, the voice-over accompanying the Reese Europe scenes quotes from Noble Sissle, a soldier at the time, and later jazzman in his own right:

> With the soul-rousing clash of cymbals, clarinet and cornet players began to manipulate rhythms that no artist has ever been able to put down on paper. Then, as the drummers struck their stride, their shoulders shaking in time, the audience could stand it no longer. The jazz germ hit them and it seemed to find a vital spot, loosening all muscles and causing what is known in American as an eagle rockin' it. And I am satisfied that American music will one day be the world's music.

Figure 7.2 "Lt. Europe Stirring Up the Band."

Uttered with a tone of triumph, the phrase "become the world's music" is ambiguous. From a foreign vantage point, it might reasonably be seen as a threat as much as a prophecy. To imply that this admiring portrait of Sissle's was anything but well-deserved pride in a popular creation of his people being celebrated in the heart of the urbane old world would seem to many to be in bad taste.

But the paradox of jazz lies in its being an imperial brag, an extension of U.S. influence that depended in large part on denying its pan-American character. At the very least, the indisputable record of jazz's Parisian appeal in the interwar decades looks more dubious against this background, since the jazz "virus" would no longer be the story of the irrepressible rise of a novel aesthetic but the circuits of force – and, to put it more bluntly, the systems of cultural propaganda – that made a military argument the French could not refuse. "Jazz," even more clearly here than elsewhere, appropriated an entire musical complex under the name of a Usonian one. This is a point that is never diagnosed in celebrations of "world music," although it has huge consequences for the topic, as we have seen. A country that has begun to assemble foreign possessions by way of military occupation – the consequences of the United States' new imperial ambitions at the beginning of the twentieth century – puts it in a frame of mind that can only be called cosmopolitan. It finds compelling cultural differences in precisely those polities it is busy incorporating into its own polity, and so comes to possess them as well, making them its own.

However, even at the level of musical structure, and in view of the history of its development, jazz had a special relationship to the military – not only for the reasons cited above, or because many of its earlier recruits were soldiers, or because it took wars for a critical mass of musicians from different cultures to meet and mingle (famously, in jazz's case, in the Spanish-American War, in Mexico, and in Haiti). It is rather that the technical expertise needed to perform the demanding instrumental virtuosity could be found above all in military bands. Indeed, the public dissemination of musical style was vastly enhanced by the one kind of musical performances that everyone could hear for free – parades and military marches: "the New Orleans brass band tradition provides another connection to Caribbean and, in particular, Cuban music styles"[57] In New Orleans these bands were typically employed for parade marches and for performing at other set events like political rallies and funerals. "Their repertoire included marches constructed from popular music of the day, such as the tango 'Panama' (1911) and 'La Trocha' (1897), which included a *habanera* bass accompaniment."[58]

Figure 7.3 Regimental band, 13th Minnesota Volunteer Infantry, Manila, P.I.

This pattern of dissemination is very old. Carpentier remarks, for instance, that the first person to understand the rhythmic and melodic value of black Antillean music was not Cuban-born:

> One night in 1836, finding himself at the café La Venus, the excellent Catalan musician Casamitjana (author of Cuban songs well loved in Santiago) witnessed the passing by of a noisy carnival procession, led by two mulatto women, María de la Luz and María de la O., who were singing the *Cocoyé*. On the spot, astounded by the revelation, he wrote down the verses and the rhythms, writing a score for the Regiment of Catalonia band.[59]

Even more consequential, perhaps, is the effect that the military environments of composition had on the orchestration and structure of jazz. The most common meter in jazz is duple, with a regular stress every two beats and a greater stress on the *downbeat* (first beat) of each four-beat bar. As Henry Martin explains, "although four-beat measures dominate jazz throughout its history, a two-beat measure is common in early jazz because of its association with nineteenth-century marching band music. In marches, the two-beat measure corresponds to the left-right stepping pattern with the left foot usually on the first beat of each measure."[60]

The Noble Sissle anecdote exemplified the *uses* to which jazz has been put in military operations – a very different kind of issue from the musical brilliance and integrity of the form evident in its complex development. One of the more striking features of U.S. popular culture in recent decades is the frequency with which its music has become a weapon to punish recalcitrant foreign political opponents and to wreak psychological havoc on dissidents living in traditional societies. The discussion below – a very different take on the idea of imperial jazz – may seem to some too easy, too cheap, and in any case unrelated to the issues we have been considering. I do not mean to overstate their importance, but these examples of music used as a weapon are relevant to the argument insofar as music that has come to assume (for well or ill) a distinctly patriotic character – perceived as indistinguishable from the country's identity, as it were – is routinely deployed by U.S. troops in military settings. In some of these examples, it is not jazz per se that is at issue, but rather cultural products like jazz that have come to be associated with the U.S. national character.

In an article for the London-based *Independent* newspaper in October 2004, Patrick Cockburn described "U.S. soldiers driving bulldozers . . . [who] uprooted ancient groves of date palms as well as orange and lemon trees in central Iraq as part of a new policy of collective punishment of farmers." In a scene reminiscent of the siege of Manuel Noriega's compound in Panama during the invasion of that country in the early 1990s, the bulldozers did their brutal work "with jazz blaring from loudspeakers" just as the soldiers had earlier sought to drive Noriega mad by bombarding his compound with rock music. As one of the Iraqis observed, "they made a sort of joke against us by playing jazz music while they were cutting down trees." At Camp Delta in Guantánamo, similarly, interrogators often found it useful to push prisoners over the edge by incessantly playing acid rock and loud commercials. As if replaying a scene from *A Clockwork Orange*, they would experiment with different kinds of audio tapes to punish and disorient their captives, "a mix of babies crying and the television commercial for Meow Mix in which the jingle consists of the repetition of the word 'Meow.' "[61] According to Neil A. Lewis, "one regular procedure ... was forcing uncooperative prisoners ... to endure strobe lights and screamingly loud rock and rap music played throughout two close loudspeakers, while the air-conditioning was turned up to maximum levels."[62]

Whitney Joiner writes of the consequences of the disproportionate recruitment of U.S. black and Latino soldiers against a background of unemployment and the defunding of higher education. In "The Army be Thuggin' It" she reports that the U.S. Army's African-American events marketing team drives to college and high school campuses, fraternity gatherings, NAACP events, and BET's Spring Bling in a yellow Hummer in a campaign called "Taking it to the Streets," a hip-hop flavored recruitment tour that passes out headbands and customized dog tags.[63] The "Takin' it to the Streets" campaign team "lets possible recruits hang out in the Hummer, where they can try out the multimedia sound system or watch Army recruitment videos." Cartel Creativo, Inc., a Hispanic-owned private company operating out of San Antonio, Texas, has a $380 million contract with the army to perform exactly the same services in recruiting U.S. Latinos. Their strategy, in their own words, is to give a bi-lingual spin to the "be all you can be" slogan, and to "capitalize on the American dream, which is still very much alive with the U.S. Hispanic population."[64]

In a market setting, world music is interesting for being ambiguously placed at a midway point between the familiar and the strange. Its success depends on being both at once. Like the technologies used in communications, plastics, and transportation, musical technologies have often grown out of originally military applications – scientific discoveries made possible only in the heat of war or in anticipation of war. It is in this spirit that the New York Police Department has lately used Long Range Acoustical Devices (LRADs) against demonstrators at the 2004 Republican National Convention. The LRAD, according to Richard Glen Boire, founder of the Center for Cognitive Liberty and Ethics, "produces sound in a way that for most people will be a novel experience." It creates confusion and panic, "it can't be identified, it's an invisible force." Emanating from large black disks like spotlights, thirty-three inches in diameter, it has been used by the U.S. military in Iraq and at sea as a non-lethal force. When used as a weapon, LRAD blasts "a tightly controlled stream of caustic sound that can be turned up to high enough levels to trigger nausea or possibly fainting." According to its founder, Elwood (Woody) Norris, the focused beam of sound "is totally different from the way an ordinary speaker emits sound . . . It's like it's inside your head."[65]

A documentary on VH1 in August of 2004 revealed that U.S. infantry in Iraq, especially the drivers of tanks, strapped on their army-issue earphones along with their night vision goggles in order to surround themselves with the sounds of heavy metal and rap amid sand and battle.[66] "When we rode across the border," said one soldier, "we were listening to Tupac." His friend chimed in, "yea, stuff to keep us in the mood, to keep us motivated." The music made killing easier, displacing them from the reality of what they were doing.

> Music, often pumped through tank and Humvee sound systems into individual helmets, has become a soldier's chief means of personalizing, justifying, heightening and denying the experience of war . . . Americans in Iraq, listen to rap music, especially when going into battle . . . The Army's own psy-ops is said to play AC/DC to energize the troops . . . Another faction – comprised mostly of white men – is loyal to heavy metal, which offers some very literal into-the-breach lyrics set to artillery-like sounds.

Far from isolated incidents, similar evidence of an entire epoch of "not making sense" mounts daily in the war reporting from Iraq and Afghanistan. As the patented export of a U.S.-centered globalism, the popular music industry inevitably reflects the dominant attitudes of the nation. "I heard," writes Eliot Weinberger, that

> some American soldiers had made a heavy metal music video called 'Ramadi Madness,' with sections entitled 'Those Crafty Little Bastards' and 'Another Day, Another Mission, Another Scumbag.' In one scene, a soldier kicks the face of an Iraqi who is bound and lying on the

ground, dying. In another, a soldier moves the arm of a man who has just been shot dead, to make it appear that he is waving.[67]

The anti-social streak in heavy metal, Goth, and certain versions of post-punk emo fits in too easily with Road Warrior apocalypse for it to be surprising that it has been deployed by army tank crews in the thick of war. On the one hand, a shriek from the lower rungs of society – a protest less against a form of life than hope itself – this "crash-and-bang" music is an absolute rejection of meaning that can clearly serve official, institutional purposes just as readily as anti-institutional ones (a point about bohemianism that we raised earlier in this book).

This reduction of musical ecstasy to a mere use-value in the war industry is not a perversion of the musical repertoire of mass-produced popular music but the logical extension of its market life. The divisions within hip-hop that I explored in Chapter 4, for instance, offered an explanation for the triumph of an L.A.-based aesthetic in the rise of an outlaw form. The business ethos that underlies even an essential formal feature like the "boast" – originally a protest against exclusion from economic life – meant that the rollin' in the benzo style had a structural advantage in the media wars over rap's meaning.

How do African-American creative products like rap and jazz become a recruitment tool and battlefield stimulant? This connection may seem glib but in the context of the attractions of an indifferent market it is the expected outgrowth of rap's ideological armature. In a pattern made familiar by the career of jazz, a musical form that sprang to life in New York with multiple outside influences was refined for export in the U.S. urban song industry, later conquering the global airwaves. Although its influence led, as many have commented, to indigenous and wholly unique forms of innovation in every corner of the world (French rap, Japanese rap, Cuban rap . . .), global rap never stops being perceived in the United States as the following of an American lead.

Jazz and *son*

More than any other neo-African music of the Americas, jazz established the ballroom ensemble and concert hall orchestra for the performance of popular song in a setting where the popular was widely considered "serious," respectable, and culturally consequential. Its artistic contributions are inestimable, and its social contribution lay, among other things, in a publicity apparatus that provided openings for many New World African forms both within and outside the United States. The music's plasticity in accommodating the tastes of varied constituencies, although not unique, was especially pronounced in a country as large and diverse as that of the United States.

I argued earlier that U.S. conditions led to a division within the holism of the neo-African aesthetic in jazz's case. Its literary component, and especially its demand for social satire, called forth forms like rap in order to fulfill its musical function. Whether one grants my view or not, there is no question that the different experience of diasporic Africans in the United States had a direct bearing on its music. As many have pointed out, although the United States imported only 5 percent of the slaves, it had one-third of the entire population of Africans in the New World by 1950. As long ago as the American Revolution, only 20 percent of the black population was born in Africa (as opposed to Haiti, say, or Brazil, where a majority was first-generation). Both statistics suggest a relative distance from African belief-systems and cultural practices in the United States which may have been exacerbated by the success of evangelical religion in the American heartland after the "Great Awakening."[68]

In some respects, the color bar was more unforgiving in the United States in the sense that Protestant customs were more dedicated to eliminating the African elements of black culture than had been the case in the Catholic countries of the New World. There is an initial irony, then, in that the vaunted American form of jazz began in the one region of the country that was most traditionally Catholic. The laissez-faire attitudes in New Orleans towards the Sunday slave gatherings at Congo Square could be seen "well into the nineteenth century . . . and were aligned with Spanish and French Catholicism [rather] than with the evangelical English sects."[69] Contributing to this ideological and religious distance from the comparatively close contact with Africa in the Caribbean was the size of the in-land territories to be covered in the United States, and therefore the relative isolation of the minority population. But above all, as I have been arguing, there was the fact of the country's imperial ambitions during the precise period of the rise of jazz – and, indeed, the joint destiny of the one and the other. Degrees of commercialism were not unrelated to this dynamic, and defined the cultural dominant into which blacks as musicians wished to insert themselves. What was most African in the music had been purged from it to the degree that it was filtered through the market sieve in a framework of segregation and an intense, unforgiving populist Christianity alert to pagan deviations. Under these conditions, jazz (unlike the offshoots of *son*) separated itself from its popular origins, severing (or at least restricting) its contact with the blues in an act of smoothing over that fit its commercial setting well.

Musically, these combined pressures led to general features in jazz that are evident in samplings of its most common performance styles over the last six decades or so. For the most part, in contrast to its counterparts in Latin America, jazz has been characterized by a tendency toward mellow instrumental blendings rather than a cacophonous assault on propriety – a structural tendency that has been called "the strait-jacket of four-square common time."[70] Any number of exceptions could be found to this description in the jazz repertoire, of course, but it is nevertheless true that jazz is primarily based on a violation of expectations only within the fundamental regularity imposed by the standard song form. Almost all jazz is composed in four-bar phrases divisible into eight-bar and sixteen-bar sections.[71] The "jazz" typically takes place in strophes in which an individual instrumentalist unpacks, or plays with, the motif drawn from a song with an already existing set of mass-cultural connotations (radio pop, musical theater pieces, and so on – the sort of move evident, for example, in John Coltrane's "My Favorite Things"). The creative obliteration of European norms is still there, and importantly so, in the African-derived gestures of bent pitches, dirty notes, falsetto, melodic inversions, and so on. But three tendencies prevail: the innovation is individual (each "solo" takes its turn), the entire structure is symmetrical (rather than, as in *son*, a fundamentally divided structure that breaks into alien musical territory a third of the way into the song), and the Africanized sound is achieved primarily through sonoric effects on *melody*.

Adorno's argument that jazz destroys subjectivity, or that its improvisations are a forced return to a never-ending same, are partially true. But they are also overstated. I understand these features, though, to be the result not of a musical strategy or an inherent logic of the devices available to a misbegotten concept (as he does) but the severing of jazz from its sources as well as from its rural soul in the blues – a dimension of the problem that Adorno ignores. As jazz moved from juke joint to the Blue Note, it moved from body to mind. If, in certain of its genres, it prompted dance – in the swing era, for example – it placed little burden on the dancer's art, and U.S. commercial dance forms inspired by jazz after the 1920s are strikingly less complex than even the simplest of Latin dance forms. Inventive responses to jazz's mainstreaming did produce its own romp (the theatrical audience-stroking of Cab Calloway at the Cotton Club, for instance) but jazz's trajectory moved it inexorably in the direction of a listener's art where it was tailored to the desires of an audience sitting in the smoky haze of a nightclub. It became the art of the intellectual, white and black, contemplating the demimonde. Duke Ellington's "Black Beauty," for example, is a masterpiece of reducing unexpected musical turns to a highly accessible, even undemanding, sound.

In the United States at least, jazz became in time a manageable difference. In the same country, Latin music was not only linguistically but musically unmanageable. It operated either in a separate, segregated strain in its own nightclubs, playing by the rules of a distinct underground with its own protocols, or as a showcase add-on of the aficionados – a subgenre of jazz that was seen implicitly as a spinoff: jazz with a Latin "flavor." One of the consequences, I am arguing, of imperial jazz is the reduction of the scale of challenge and impropriety in the forms from which it derived, as though Paul Whiteman's desire of transforming the New Orleans sound into something as "precise and predictable as classical music" had rubbed off on the great band leaders of the 1940s and 1950s. Duke Ellington certainly managed to avoid diluting jazz under the pressures of joy-seeking youth in search of danger; and all of bebop and "cool" jazz are still a revelation.[72] Nothing like them exists anywhere for the unpredictability of their melodic imagination or the sheer open-endedness of their liberated structure. But it is hard to deny that Count Basie, Chick Webb, and others were forced to round their riffs, confine their experiments to playing with shades of mellowness, and observe a strict performance etiquette in which each instrument politely takes its turn – a kind of obligatory individuality.

To juxtapose Webb's "Harlem Congo" with a Latin work of the same period and place – say, "Mambo" composed by Webb's own arranger, Mario Bauzá's – is instructive. The former is based on micro-differences of intonation and rhythm whose overall scope is to stay out of the listener's way. By contrast, the latter's intention is violent syncopation and orchestral outrage that achieves a tonal quality in which the instruments are bent to a new measure. The tone is that of pure shock, and the virtuosity is communal: an ensemble played like a single instrument. The melodic elements, although strongly in play, are subordinated to the rhythmic, and every one of the instruments becomes part of the *batería*. It is true that the big-band sound of mambo would have been impossible without the apprenticeship of musicians like Bauzá in the New York jazz circuits of the late 1930s and 1940s where the potential of the ensemble and its many combinations were explored by Latin musicians in the context of a much more developed U.S. performance environment, a larger audience, and more attractive salaries than existed either in Cuba or Mexico. As Acosta puts it, Bauzá "brought jazz conceptions into the aspect of [Latin] harmony, timbre, and orchestration. He sought a greater harmonic and orchestral density than existed in the traditional Cuban groups," and in doing so, revealed dimensions of the big-band sound unexplored by North American musicians.[73] The familiar account of the era from swing to bebop is that a sort of war took place between the rise of the white jazz man (Paul Whiteman, the Dorsey brothers, Benny Goodman, Artie Shaw, Woody Herman) and the more brilliant, but under-regarded, black musicians of the same periods. An entirely different contrast was unfolding, though, between North American jazz and Latin musicians.

To take another example of the contrast, nothing as remotely irreverent as Benny Moré's famous mambo "Babarabitiri" exists in North American big band jazz. No entertainment music could claim to be quite this frenzied or as outrageously and impudently African. In this publicly shared delirium, even as the European instruments are estranged from themselves and forced, like much African-derived music, into mimicry of the voice (here as heavy breathing), Moré brings the African religious elements of the early cantos polemically into the foreground. When he utters the word *"bárbaro"* during one of the instrumental interludes, he is more or less taunting his audience. He is saying, "this is what you think of us" but also "only a sound so unleashed from your restraints can transport me to this higher place."

Some musicians argue that for all its past achievements, jazz has reached its culmination and has stopped developing.[74] This may or may not be true, but there is no question that one of the reasons for its perceived stagnation has to do with seeing its mission as signifying on American popular song, dismantling it in order to rebuild it in a fractured state, rather than aligning itself with deeper and more resonant sources within the culture. In blues, it was simplicity, minor voice shadings, vocal personality, and a repetitive tonal structure based, above all, on sincerity and narrative content that were its replenishing features. Miles Davis, repudiating his association with "cool" jazz in the mid-fifties, understood this point when he "began to evolve in the direction of more loose, emotional, blues-rooted music that paid explicit deference to the black base of jazz."[75]

The market distribution of jazz in the American context interfered with the blues as narrative cry and the creation of a stage-personality based on sincerity – a pressure felt less acutely in the neglected, low-tech creative zones of much of Latin America. What lived on was a rhythmic banality, which left U.S. jazz improvisation looking for its innovations in a very narrow creative space: primarily the voicing given to various instruments.[76] In that sense, Louis Armstrong's scat lacks the surprise that it must have had originally. What it primarily means to listeners today is a "funny" use of voice to simulate trumpet (significantly just the opposite of the typically African practice of using instruments to resemble the voice). In the one case, people move forward by conforming to the instrument; in the other, the instrument takes its lead from the person, against which an instrument is always a failed substitute.

But the fate of Afro-Latin music has always been entwined with the United States, not simply as rival or counterpart but as equal partner with its musical underground. And secular devotion is doubly configured: a neo-African music that stubbornly conserved the past in an unsolemn homage to spirit, using the media of modernity to spread its virus. It was for just that reason revolutionary in the dynamic setting of the Americas, dominated politically by an empire bent on reckless innovation in the name of a modern life that misrecognized itself as progress. This disenchanted race to nowhere, rich with things but poor in soul, found itself in strange and limited ways outmaneuvered by a cultural enemy within, and in plain hearing.

EL PARALITICO
SON

Musica de
M. Matamoros

"EL CONDE LIBORIO"
SOBRE MOTIVO DEL CONDE DE LUXEMBURGO
DANZON

Para Piano

Por Antonio M. Romeu.

Copyright by Anselmo Lopez
Obispo 127 Havana

SOLACE
A Mexican Serenade

1909

Very slow march time

LA CELOSA

Arranged by Elias Barreiro

Ignacio Cervantes

Notes

Introduction

1. Janheinz Jahn, *Muntu: An Outline of Neo African Culture* (London: Faber and Faber, 1961 [1958]). I share the position of Jahn's classic study that "Afro-American culture belongs to African culture . . . and we may consider the two together" (17). These propositions are developed well in John Storm Roberts's *Black Music of Two Worlds* (New York: Praeger, 1972), which explores "neo-African music [whose] elements [are] still totally or very largely African" (19).
2. Focusing on music as the popular outburst of politically subversive youth is very widespread in popular music theory. Examples include Ian Peddie, ed., *The Resisting Muse: Popular Music and Social Protest* (Aldershot, England; Burlington, VT: Ashgate, 2006); George Lipsitz, *Dangerous Crossroads: Popular Music, Postmodernism, and the Poetics of Place* (London, New York: Verso, 1994); Tricia Rose and Andrew Ross, eds., *Microphone Fiends: Youth Music and Youth Culture* (New York: Routledge, 1994).
3. Apart from Thomas Frank's and Maura Mohoney's well-known parodies of pop resistance in *Commodify Your Dissent: Salvos from the Baffler* (New York: Norton, 1997), see also David E. James, "Poetry/Punk/Production: Some Recent Writing in LA," *Postmodernism and Its Discontents: Theories, Practices*, ed. E. Ann Kaplan (London: Verso, 1988).
4. Religious expression by Africans in the New World is extremely varied. The categories would include Revivalist and Spiritualist cults, Religio-Political cults, types of Protestant sectoralism, and Neo-African cults such as *Vodun* (Haiti), *Shango* (Trinidad), *Santería* (Cuba), *Candomblé* (Brazil). It is this last type that concerns me most, since there (unlike in the more Christianized forms) "ritual actions [such] as providing offerings for the gods and the dead, dancing, speaking in unknown tongues, singing, and asking the spirits for assistance" was less about "supernatural phenomena than . . . 'social consensus' " (George Eaton Simpson, *Black Religions in the New World* (New York: Columbia University Press, 1978).
5. Slaves to the New World, moreover, were primarily taken from contiguous areas of the western part of the continent: the Gambia and Senegal area, Sierra Leone, the Ivory Coast and Liberia, the area of present-day Togo and Dahomey, and the Niger delta. In fewer numbers, however, slaves were also taken from the area of Angola and the Cape of Good Hope.
6. Simpson, 58. "In the worship of African deities in Cuba . . . the African elements of Santeria are predominantly Yoruba . . . Yoruba music is played on African types of drums, songs with Yoruba words and music are sung, and dancers are possessed by the orishas" (59).
7. Simpson, 59.

8. The *cabildos*, or mutual aid societies, were set up in Cuba in part to achieve this end, for example.
9. Anne Phillips, *The Enigma of Colonialism: British Policy in West Africa* (Bloomington, IN: Indiana University Press, 1989), 61, 78, 156–63.
10. Simpson, 52.
11. John Miller Chernoff, *African Rhythm and African Sensibility: Aesthetics and Social Action in African Musical Idioms* (Chicago and London: University of Chicago Press, 1979), 41.
12. Ibid., 45, 47. He goes on to note, though, that "most African music is in some common variety of duple or triple time (like 4/4 or 12/8)," a point to which we will return when considering jazz in Chapter 7.
13. Jahn, 149.
14. Chernoff, 49. John Storm Roberts identifies the neo-African features of music even more simply: (1) complex, overlapping rhythms, working in counterpoint; (2) musical instruments and the human voice used percussively as well as in their normal function as the carriers of melody and harmony; (3) music as a communal meditation: the antiphonal structure demands that the lead singer utters a line that the chorus expands and develops (*Black Music of Two Worlds*, 19–68).
15. Of work available in English, some of the pioneers are Charley Gerard (with Marty Sheller), *Salsa!: The Rhythm of Latin Music* (Crown Point, IN: White Cliffs Media Co., 1989); Alma Guillermoprieto, *Samba* (New York: Knopf/Random House, 1990); Vernon Boggs, *Salsiology: Afro-Cuban Music and the Evolution of Salsa in New York City* (Westport, CT: Greenwood, 1992); Rebeca Mauleón, *Salsa: Guidebook for Piano and Ensemble* (Petaluma, CA: Sher Music Co., 1993); and Peter Manuel (with Kenneth Bilby and Michael Largey), *Caribbean Currents: From Rumba to Reggae* (Philadelphia: Temple University Press, 1995).
16. I would like, though, to distinguish my argument from the important recent work on the spiritual aspects of rap and blues, which draws on a similar recognition of the continuing presence of African religious practices in secular musical styles, although in this case melded with less syncretic forms of Christian belief found in established African-American Protestant sects. See Anthony B. Pinn, ed., *Noise and Spirit: The Religious and Spiritual Sensibilities of Rap Music* (New York and London: New York University Press, 2003); and Jon Michael Spencer, ed., *Sacred Music of the Secular City: From Blues to Rap* (Durham: Duke University Press, 1992), especially the essays by Rod Gruver, "The Blues as a Secular Religion," 55–67 and James H. Cone, "The Blues: A Secular Spiritual," 68–97. I have chosen to explore the conflict with Christianity (indeed with monotheism) – a conflict less evident in the U.S. context.
17. This argument has been posed in all of the following studies: Gage Averill, *A Day for the Hunter, A Day for the Prey: Popular Music and Power in Haiti* (Chicago: University of Chicago Press, 1997); Robin Moore, *Nationalizing Blackness: Afrocubanismo and Artistic Revolution in Havana, 1920–1940* (Pittsburgh: University of Pittsburgh Press, 1997); Ruth Glasser, *My Music is My Flag: Puerto Rican Musicians and their New York Communities, 1917–1940*).
18. Vernon W. Boggs, ed., *Salsiology: Afro-Cuban Music and the Evolution of Salsa in New York City*; John Storm Roberts, *Latin Jazz: The First of the Fusions* (New York: Schirmer Books, 1999); Frederick S. Starr, *Bamboula! The Life and Times of Louis Moreau Gottschalk* (New York: Oxford University Press, 1995); Ned Sublette, *Cuba and its Music: From the First Drums to the Mambo* (Chicago: Chicago Press Review, 2004).
19. George Antheil, "The Negro on the Spiral, or A Method of Negro Music," in Nancy Cunard, ed., *Negro: An Anthology* (New York and London: Continuum, 2002 [1934]).

20. I am aware that the term "music theory" refers in musicological circles to theories of composition and tonality. When I use the terms "theories of music" or "music theory," I am referring instead to any commentary on music or theorizations about its social uses or aesthetic values without any other specialist meaning.
21. Régis Debray, *God: An Itinerary* (New York and London: Verso, 2004).
22. Brian Rotman, "Monobeing" [a review of Debray's God: An Itinerary], *London Review of Books* (17 February 2005), 30 (these are Rotman's words).
23. Jahn, 121, 125.
24. Ibid., 149.
25. Edward Kamau Brathwaite, "Caribbean Culture: Two Paradigms" in Jürgen Martini, ed., *Missile and Capsule* (Bremen: University of Bremen, 1983), 9–54. For similar efforts to flip civilizational value, see the Guyanese novelist Wilson Harris's important writing on Limbo in *Explorations,* ed. and intro. by Hena Maes-Jelinek (Mundelstrup, Denmark: Dangaroo Press, 1981), 20–43, 68–83.
26. A fascinating study of the physiology of hearing and the anthropology of listening can be found in Veit Erlmann, ed., *Hearing Cultures: Essays on Sound, Listening, and Modernity* (Oxford: Berg, 2004). My interest in "race" in this book, similarly, is quite different from that found explored in the varied essays of *Music and the Racial Imagination*, Ronald Radano and Philip V. Bohlman, eds. (Chicago: University of Chicago Press, 2000). Unlike many of the contributors to this excellent volume, I am interested in the crossover influence of a secular religion through sound rather than conscious efforts to resist oppression by the staking out of racial territory.

Chapter 1 – World Music Does Not Exist

1. Philip Sweeney, *The Virgin Directory of World Music* (London: Virgin Books, 1991). Sweeney recounts how the term "world music" was coined by record executives meeting in a London pub in order to come up with an identifying category that would give it a niche on the record racks.
2. Amilcar Cabral, speech delivered at Syracuse University, 20 February 1970 (http://historyisaweapon.com/defcon1/cabralnlac.html). For Evora's life, see Véronique Mortaigne, *Cesaria Evora, la voix du Cap-Vert* (Arles: Actes sud, 1997).
3. I would like to thank Lindsey Simms for bringing this film to my attention.
4. Simon Broughton, Mark Ellingham, David Muddymen et al., eds. *World Music: The Rough Guide* (London: Rough Guides, distributed by Penguin Books), 1994.
5. It should be said that Sweeney seems more overwhelmed by the inexorable logic of salesmanship (which he opposes) than he is under the sway of a reductive idea. Although he assumes that popular music "is not art or classical music" (ix) and deliberately excludes "experimental hybrid musics created by Western jazz and rock musicians with African or oriental counterparts" (x), he does include U.S. popular forms under world music – for example, Cajun, Tex/Mex, delta blues, Texas swing, country western, conjunto music and accordion polkas (250–53). Under the "general" category, he also includes gospel, and rap. Indifferent to the imperial dimension, his critique is in full force when it comes to the market. Essentially, world music for him is everything that "is *not* mass-produced corporate pop."
6. Cornel West in Cornel West and Gina Dent, ed., *Black Popular Culture* (Seattle: Bay Press, 1992) refers at one point to the "African-Americanization of global culture." However, he says very little about the African-Americanization that is not Afro-Usonian (Afro-Latin music, for example). There is an assumed monopoly of U.S. black culture in such matters, and that – as Ken Burns's recent PBS

jazz series shows– is oddly, and very inaccurately, patriotic. Stuart Chase alluded to this kind of convergence already before World War II (see Chapter 7).
7. *Attitude: The Dancers' Magazine* 10 (Fall 1994/Winter 1995), 24–39.
8. I am following Frank Lloyd Wright's use of "Usonian" to mean from the United States. In some cases in this book, where context demands it, I still follow convention in using "American" to refer to those from the United States.
9. B. Jennings, "World Music Institute Presents," *Attitude: The Dancers' Magazine* 10 (Fall 1994/Winter 1995), 24.
10. Ibid., 24, 26.
11. Ibid., 27.
12. Deborah Pacini Hernandez, "Dancing with the Enemy: Cuban Popular Music, Race, Authenticity, and the World-Music Landscape," *Latin American Perspectives* 25: 3 (May 1998), 110–25. Pacini Hernandez importantly distinguishes between "world music," which she associates with forms that announce their traditional, rather than commercial, roots, and "world beat" which she associates with "more modernized, dance-oriented products of cross-fertilization," largely "African derived" (112). As my argument suggests, I see the terms (and what they cover) as interchangeable, not only because "world beat" CDs actually include very prominently music from the contemporary Middle East, ethnic Europe ("gypsy groove"), and even the exotic white past (for example, Parisian cabaret music), but because the very substance of the concept relies on multiple elements of difference making up a new unity. In practice, then, world music collapses Pacini Hernandez's useful distinction.
13. *Margarita Mix #2*, Pottery Barn, Rock River Communications, RRC-PB-40 (2002). Along with Putumayo and Pottery Barn, see Banana Republic's *Keepitcool*, Banana Republic, BMG Special Products, BMG Entertainment, DRC12416 (1999).
14. A question that has nevertheless been dealt with admirably by more institutionally oriented studies of musical production. See Roger Wallis and Krister Malm, *Big Sounds from Small Peoples: The Music Industry in Small Countries* (New York: Pendragon Press, 1984).
15. Houston Baker, Jr., *Modernism and the Harlem Renaissance* (Chicago: University of Chicago, 1987), 71.
16. Deborah James in Simon Frith, ed., *World Music: Politics and Social Change* (Manchester: Manchester University Press, 1989).
17. For one of several available accounts of the richness of "diluted" African music in practice, see Jean-Christophe Servant, "The Sound of Music: Rap – Africa Talks Back," *Le Monde Diplomatique*, January 2001.
18. Cheryl L. Keyes, *Rap Music and Street Consciousness* (Urbana and Chicago: University of Illinois, 2002).
19. In March 1996, the major national newspaper *USA Today* argued that "the beef between the rival coasts centered largely on who created the hard-core style of rap music known as gangsta rap, a genre whose graphic language and vivid descriptions of violence have made it one of the best-selling vehicles in recorded music." *USA Today* (10 March), D-2.
20. Timothy Brennan, "Off the Gangsta Tip: A Rap Appreciation, or Forgetting about Los Angeles," *Critical Inquiry* 20 (Summer 1994), 663–693.
21. Nelson George gets into an interesting aspect of the East/West conflict with his exploration of the outstripping of the past in the move from old school to new school on both coasts. Nelson George, *Hip Hop America* (New York: Penguin, 1998).
22. Greg Tate, "Nobody Loves a Genius Child: Jean Michel Basquiat, Flyboy in the Buttermilk," *Flyboy in the Buttermilk: Essays on Contemporary America* (New York: Simon and Schuster 1992), 233.

23. Paul Gilroy, *The Black Atlantic: Modernity and Double Consciousness* (Cambridge, MA: Harvard University Press, 1993), 72.
24. I am thinking here, for example, of the work of Jan Carew, Wilson Harris, José Lezama Lima, Edgar Kamau Brathwaite, and Alejo Carpentier, among others. I take up the specific treatment of these issues of modernity and its discontents in Chapter 5, where I explore Cuban music theory of the last four decades.
25. In contemporary "emo," there is spectacular evidence of the bid to politics in youth subculture – but at the level of mere words. Bands whose music combines moony sentiments, brittle guitar lashings, and raving silences take on names that are like jokes shared with their equally outmaneuvered and powerless fans: Jihad, Living War Room, Slaves, Dillinger Escape Plan, Jimmy Eat World, Honeywell, Native Nod, and Four Hundred Years. In German rap of the 1990s there were groups with names like Massive Tone, *Freundeskreis*, Islamic Force, and Aziza A. (the last two of them from Germany's Turkish minority), which is less surprising, but the same gesture.
26. Fame, however, is regionally defined – an important proviso to the claims of world music. For the Spanish-speaking Americas, Lecuona is typically placed in the company of composers such as Agustín Lara from Mexico or Rafael Hernández from Puerto Rico. Although Lecuona is probably better known abroad, the other two are more famous among Latin Americans themselves. See Cristóbal Díaz Ayala, *Cuando salí de la Habana: 1898–1997, Cien años de la música cubana* (San Juan: Editora Centenario, 1998), 80.
27. His work is recorded on the *London* label in a series called "entartete Musik" ("forbidden music" – an allusion to the infamous exhibit of degenerate painting under the Nazis titled "Entartete Kunst.")
28. James Morton, *Lola Montez: Her Life and Conquests* (London: Portrait, 2007).
29. Bee Wilson, "Boudoir Politics" *London Review of Books* (7 June 2007), 27–29.
30. Ibid., 27–28.
31. Intended as a vehicle for Dolores del Rio, the film was the first Astaire/Rogers combo performance, made when Astaire himself was unknown outside Broadway. This number (which involved a forehead-to-forehead posture for the dancers) became a national dance craze in the United States after the film was released.
32. Doris Day, *Sentimental Journey/ Latin for Lovers* (New York: Collectables, 2001), B00005R1PB.
33. Truth Hurts, "Addictive," *Truthfully Speaking*, Interscope Records (June 25, 2002), B000068TKW.
34. The process of musical creation, level of technological capacity, and distribution for musicians from smaller countries is explored wonderfully in Rober Wallis and Krister Malm, *Big Sounds from Small Peoples: The Music Industry in Small Countries*.
35. Gigi, *Gigi* (New York: Palm Pictures, 2001), PALMCD 2068-2. The CD's language reinforces the idea that Western genres have names but not Ethiopian genres: "Gigi interprets and transcends the romantic poetry of her native Ethiopian vocal traditions to create a true world fusion of jazz, dub, funk, and multiple African and Afro-Asiatic music styles."

Chapter 2 – Surrealism and the *Son*

1. Samuel A. Floyd, "Black Music in the Circum-Caribbean," *Journal of American Music* 17:1 (Spring 1999), 30.
2. Cuban scholarship on the *son*, especially after 1959, is extensive. Among the major works are Samuel Feijóo, *El Son cubano: poesía general* (La Habana:

Editorial Letras Cubanas, 1986) and the evocative and atmospheric photo-essay with biographies (not all Cuban), *Son de Cuba,* with texts by Leonardo Acosta, René Espí, and Adriana Orejuela, intro. by Eliseo Alberto, and photographs by Tomàs Casademunt (Colonia Chapultepec Morales, Mexico: Trilce Ediciones, 1999). Significant scholarly treatment of the form is found, among others, in Argeliers León's excellent *Del canto y el tiempo* (La Habana: Editorial Letras Cubanas, 1984); in María Teresa Linares, *La música y el pueblo* (La Habana: Editorial Pueblo y Educación, 1979); and in Reinaldo Cedeño Pineda and Michel Damián Suárez, *Son de la loma: Los dioses de la música cantan en Santiago de Cuba* (La Habana: Editorial Musical de Cuba, 2001).

3. A good short definition of *son* is provided by Carpentier: "a dance that is sung." Alejo Carpentier in *Music in Cuba,* (Minneapolis, London: University of Minnesota Press, 2001), 229.
4. Cuban music was, with other foreign imports, the rage in Paris from 1922 onward. These "cubanisms" (as Carpentier, then a Parisian-based journalist, dubbed them) entered Europe under the name "*rumba,*" although they had little technically to do with that highly Africanized and improvisational form. Performers like Julio Cuevas, Rogelio Barba, the Tres Hermanos Barreto, and Fernando Collazo frequently performed in such Parisian clubs as La Coupole and Melody's Bar before European and North American film and stage celebrities.
5. For a fuller account of how this took place, see my "Introduction to the English Edition" of Carpentier, *Music in Cuba* (op. cit.), 1–31. Particularly important in this respect was the work of Robert Desnos who collaborated with Carpentier on experimental radio programs for Radio Luxembourg, but a number of the poets and painters of the period were collectors of Latin recordings and frequented the music clubs where Latin music was played.
6. I take up this question in more detail in "Postcolonial Studies between the European Wars: An Intellectual History," in Crystal Bartolovich and Neil Lazarus, eds., *Marxism, Modernity and Postcolonial Studies* (Cambridge: Cambridge University Press, 2002), 185–203.
7. Jacques Attali, *Noise: The Political Economy of Music,* translation by Brian Massumi, Foreward by Fredric Jameson; Afterword by Susan McClary (Minneapolis: University of Minnesota, 1984).
8. A "*tres*" (literally, "three") is a traditional Cuban instrument similar to a guitar with three double strings usually plucked rather than strummed and with a deliberately metallic sound.
9. Argeliers León, "Of the Axle and the Hinge: Nationalism, Afro-Cubanism, and Music in Pre-Revolutionary Cuba," in Peter Manuel, ed., *Essays on Cuban Music* (Lanham, MD: University Press of America, 1991), 279.
10. Anton Kaes, Martin Jay and Edward Dimendberg, eds., *The Weimar Republic Sourcebook* (Berkeley: University of California, 1994), 594.
11. I explore this problem in more detail in "Introduction to the English Edition," Carpentier, *Music in Cuba,* 1–56.
12. Moving some (Salvador Dali, Robert Desnos) to a more open and untroubled embrace of corporate profit-making, and others to leave the arts entirely and declare themselves communists (Aragon and Tzara).
13. In Germany, Walter Benjamin and Bertolt Brecht brought experimental literary work and political commentary to the mass medium of radio; in France, avant-garde formalist techniques were devised for radio by Robert Desnos and Antonin Artaud.
14. Leonardo Acosta, *Otra visión de la música popular cubana* (La Habana: Letras Cubanas, 2004), 10.
15. See, for example, the contributions on radio opera in Kaes, Jay, and Dimendberg,

eds., *The Weimar Republic Sourcebook*; and Bernard Rosenberg and David Manning White, ed., *Mass Culture: The Popular Arts in America* (Glencoe, IL: Free Press, 1957).

16. Ángel G. Quintero Rivera, *Salsa sabor y control: sociología de la musical tropical* (Coyoacán & Madrid: Siglo Veintiuno editors, 1998).
17. Wilson Harris, *History, Fable and Myth in the Caribbean and Guianas* (Georgetown, Guyana: National History and Arts Council, 1970); Kamau Brathwaite, *Middle Passages* (Newcastle upon Tyne: Bloodaxe Books, 1992); Edouard Glissant, *Caribbean Discourse: Selected Essays* (Charlottesville: University Press of Virginia, 1989).
18. See in this respect, Paul Gilroy, *The Black Atlantic: Modernity and Double-Consciousness* (Cambridge, MA: Harvard University Press, 1993).
19. Ernst Bloch, "Venturing Beyond and Most Intense World of Man in Music," in *The Principle of Hope*, Vol. III (Cambridge, MA: MIT Press, 1995), 1058–59.
20. Ernst Bloch, "The Philosophy of Music," *The Spirit of Utopia*, Anthony A. Nassar, ed. (Stanford: Stanford University Press, 2000 [1923], 34–164. My uses of Bloch here are inspired in part by the fact that no philosopher of music has so fully combined a theory of musical form and a theory of modern religious yearning.
21. An idea similar to that of Attali in *Noise*, where he remarks on the homology between the history of tonal music and political economy, "stamping upon spectators the faith that there is harmony in order," 33, 46.
22. Bloch, "Venturing Beyond and Most Intense World of Man in Music," 1059.
23. Marta E. Savigliano, *Tango and the Political Economy of Passion* (Boulder: Westview Press, 1995). "When tango performers and spectators no longer shared a common race, class, and/or culture, tango became exotic for the ones 'up' who were looking 'down.'" 111.
24. George Antheil, "The Negro on the Spiral, or A Method of Negro Music," in Nancy Cunard, ed., *Negro: An Anthology* (New York and London: Continuum, 2002 [1934]), 214–16.
25. Although even here one can learn from Janheinz Jahn's point in *Muntu: An Outline of Neo-African Culture* (London: Faber and Faber, 1961 [1958], 17, that "the African tradition as it appears in the light of neo-African culture may also be a legend – but it is the legend in which African intelligence believes. And it is their perfect right to declare authentic, correct and true those components of their past which they believe to be so."
26. Acosta, *Otra visión de la música popular cubana*, 126.
27. This is the position adopted forcefully both by Carpentier in *Music in Cuba* and by Feijóo in *El Son cubano: poesía general*.
28. Carpentier, *Music in Cuba*, 97. See also Feijóo's chapters on the *fandango* and the *chacon* in *El son cubano*.
29. Feijóo, *El son cubano*, 7.
30. Carpentier, *Music in Cuba*, 229–31. A *botijuela* is a bottle whose sound is created by blowing across the opening; a *diente de arado*, the jaw bones of an ass, played by dragging the stick along the teeth to create a scraping noise; a *marímbula*, a block of wood with thin, flexible metal strips embedded in it that can be plucked with the thumb to make tones; *timbales*, hide drums – similar to the drum sets of modern rock bands – played with a stick rather than the hands; the *tres* is defined above in footnote 8.
31. Samuel Feijóo, *El son cubano: poesía general*, 8: "From the earliest times, 'son' was the word used for any musical air more or less melodic, simple or complex, profoundly or moderately rhythmic. Only slowly did the word come to be seen as indicating a style of dance," a historical fact that underlines its uneasy modulation of the literary.

32. *Maracas* are gourds containing seeds that are shaken to produce rhythmic patterns; *cajón* (literally, "large box"), a wooden box struck with the hands; *bongós,* twin hide drums of different sizes connected by a piece of wood and pinioned between the knees while played with the hands.
33. Although note the following statement by the Santiago-based poet, Marino Wilson, who sees *son* as a twentieth-century genre alone, and who considers the U.S. presence in Cuba strangely unproblematic (quoted in Jory Farr, *Rites of Rhythm: The Music of Cuba* [NY: Regan Books, 2003], 68): "As a poet I receive the spirit of Africa through a Cuban prism. But it's not transmitted through a prism of oppression, which some would have you believe. American blues was born in the South, where historical conditions were quite different for Africans. Even after the Civil War, American blacks suffered terribly. And that suffering went into their blues. But Cuban *son* developed *after* the Spanish lost control of Cuba. There was no longer any slavery in Cuba, and the *son* reflects that. We can't forget that Cuba suffered through two wars of independence in the nineteenth century. But by the beginning of the twentieth century, those struggles were over. The *son* was mostly an ode to love and joy and triumph."
34. Argeliers León, *Del canto y el tiempo* (La Habana: Editorial Letras Cubanas, 1984), 120.
35. Ibid., 136.
36. Farr, *Rites of Rhythm,* 15: Papi Oviedo: "The *son* without *tres* is not *son*. The *tres* carries the rhythm and melody in *son*. Later, when the piano became part of the *conjunto,* the piano played the *tumbaos,* the rhythms that created excitement. But the piano would accompany the *tres*. And the *tresero's* job was to improvise."
37. León, *Del canto y el tiempo,* 136.
38. Ibid., 139–40.
39. Acosta, *Otra visión de la música popular cubana,* 43.
40. Martin Heidegger, "The Origin of the Work of Art," *Basic Writings* (San Francisco: Harper, 1993), 171.
41. Yvonne Daniel, *Rumba: Dance and Social Change in Contemporary Cuba* (Bloomington: Indiana University Press, 1995); Rebeca Mauleón, *Salsa: Guidebook for Piano and Ensemble* (Petaluma, CA: Sher Music Co., 1993; Hernando Calvo Ospina, *Salsa: Havana Heat, Bronx Beat,* translated by Nick Caistor (London: Latin America Bureau, 1995); Peter Manuel with Kenneth Bilby and Michael Largey, *Caribbean Currents: Caribbean Music from Rumba to Reggae* (Philadelphia: Temple University Press, 1995).
42. José Martí, "Lincoln," "Cooper," "Whitman" in *Our America: Writings on Latin America and the Struggle for Cuban Independence* translated by Elinor Randall, with additional translations by Juan de Onis and Roslyn Held Foner; edited, with an introduction and notes by Philip S. Foner (New York: Monthly Review Press, 1977)
43. Vernon W. Boggs, ed., *Salsiology: Afro-Cuban Music and the Evolution of Salsa in New York City* (Westport, CT: Greenwood Press, 1992); Hernando Calvo Ospina, *Salsa: Havana Heat, Bronx Beat*.
44. See, however, Leonardo Acosta's "Los inventores de nuevos ritmos: mito y realidad," in *Otra visión de la música popular cubana,* 86–118.
45. See Cristóbal Díaz Ayala, *Cuando salí de la Habana: 1898–1997, Cien años de la música cubana* (San Juan: Editora Centenario, 1998), 36: "A ti te gusta mucho, Carola/ el son de altura, con sabrosura/ bailarlo sola/ Lo mismo aprisa que despacito/ con tu chiquito, cuando lo bailas/ contenta dices: / Suavecito, suavecito, . . . / . . . Una linda sevillana/ le decía a su maridito/ me vuelvo loco chiquito/ por la música cubana./ Suavecito, suavecito." My translation.
46. Benny Moré and the Rafael de Paz Orchestra, "Bonito y Sabroso (Pretty & Tasty)," *The Best of Mambo,* Vol. 1 (New York: BMG Music, 1992), BL2 3310:

"Pero que bonito y sabroso/ bailan el mambo las Mexicanas/ Muevan las cinturas y los hombros . . . que las Cubanas/ Con el sentido de ritmo/ para bailar y gozar/ hasta parecen que estoy en Habana . . ." (my translation).

47. Trio Matamoros, "Son de la Loma," *Cuba: I am Time* (New York: Blue Jacket Entertainment), BJAC 5012-2: "Mama yo quiero saber/ De donde son los cantantes/ Que los encuentro galantes/ y los quiero conocer/ Son sus trovas fascinantes que me las quiero aprender/ De donde serán, Ay mama/ Serán de La Habana/ Serán de Santiago/ Tierra Soberana/ Son de la Loma/ y Cantan en llano/ Ya Verás/ como no/ Mama ellos son de la loma/ Mama ellos cantan en llano/ Mama ellos son de la loma/ Mama ellos cantan en llano" (my translation).
48. As a wildly popular cover song from the Cuban repertoire, "Son de la loma" has been recorded by hundreds of musicans since the 1920s. However this *loma/llano* (hills/plains) metaphor is particularly pronounced in the elegant version produced by María Dolores Pradera, *Toda una vida* (BMG: 74321 24957-2, 2001).
49. Jerry Masucci, prod., *Los soneros de siempre* (New York: Fania, 1994), JM-679.
50. "Salí de casa una noche aventurera/ Buscando ambiente de placer y de alegría/ Ay mi Dios, cuanto goce!/ En un sopor la noche pase,/ Paseaba alegre nuestros lares luminosos/ Y llegué al bacanal/ En Catalina me encontré lo no pensado,/ La voz de aquel que pregonaba así:/ Échale salsita, échale salsita,/ Échale salsita, échale salsita."
51. Los Soneros del Barrio, *Remembranzas,* featuring Frankie Vazquez, Azucar Music (Rumba Jams), (RJ1014-2), 2002.
52. Celia Cruz, Hector Lavoe, Ismael Rivera, Cheo Feliciano, Ruben Blades, Ismael Quintana, Santos Colon, Ismael Miranda, Bobby Cruz, Pete *Conde* Rodriguez, Justo Betancourt, Sammy Gonzalez, Marvin Santiago, *Los Soneros de Siempre*, produced by Jerry Masucci, Fania (JM-679), 1994. In Betancourt's song: "No creas que porque canto/ Es que me he vuelto loco/ Yo canto porque el que canta/ Dice mucho y sufre poco."
53. Quinto Mayor, *Salsa con Golpe II,* (C11293), Medellin: Codiscos, 2001.
54. *The Best of Ray Barretto* (TCLP 1315), Tico Records, 1974
55. "Por cuenta tuya/ Buscando ambiente major/ Tu estás arrepentido/ Cuesta o cuesta se occupó/ El que se fue (mira) no hace falta/ Hoy me encuentro mejor/ Yo sigo siempre en el goce/ O es en el ritmo soy yo/ (break)/ (chorus) A mí no me importas tú/ Y mente como tú/ Yo sigo siempre en el goce/ En el ritmo no eras tú"
56. *Clave*, in addition to being a rhythm, is also an instrument comprising two thick polished wooden sticks that are struck together to keep the rhythm; the *guiro* is a gourd into which ridges have been cut so that dragging a stick along them creates a rhythmic scraping noise; the *conga* is a tall, deep hide drum played with the hands.
57. Edward W. Said, *Musical Elaborations* (New York: Columbia University Press, 1991), 56.
58. Antheil, "The Negro on the Spiral, or A Method of Negro Music," 215.
59. Ibid., 214–15.
60. Edward G. Perry, "Negro Creative Musicians" in Nancy Cunard, ed., *Negro: An Anthology*, 220–23.
61. Leonardo Acosta, *Elige tú, que canto yo* (La Habana: Letras Cubanas, 1993); Jesus Colon, *A Puerto Rican in New York, and Other Sketches* (New York: Arno Press, 1975 [1961]).
62. "Habanera," in Emilio Casares Rodicio, gen. ed., *Diccionario de la Música Española e Hispanoamericana* (Madrid: Sociedad General de Autores Y Editores, 1999), 178; Carpentier, *Music in Cuba*, 99.
63. Carpentier, *Music in Cuba*, 104.
64. See Gordon Rohlehr's magisterial study, *Calypso and Society in Pre-Independence Trinidad* (Port of Spain, Trinidad: Gordon Rohlehr, 1990). Rohlehr's impressive compilation of calypso history does not as a rule analyze sonority. But when he

turns to musical influences of the 1930s, he writes that "this was the period when folk-song melodies from all over the West Indies – Martinique, Dominica, Guadeloupe, Tobago, Jamaica, St. Vincent, St. Lucia, Barbados and the Grenadines – contributed to the development of Trinidad's Calypso" (60). The Cuban (and given Trinidad's location, Venezuelan) influence are, however, too significant to go unmentioned in this way. To get a sense of the Cuban musical influence on early calypso, see Wilmoth Houdini's "African Love Call" and "Poor But Ambitious" on *Poor But Ambitious* (Arhoolie Productions, Folkloric, 1993), CD 7010; for the Venezuelan influences (especially the use of the Venezuelan *joropo*, a dance in time) see Growling Tiger's "Señorita Panchita #2" on *Neville Marcano, The Growling Tiger of Calypso*, (Cambridge, MA: Rounder Records, 1998), CD 1717 (as well as the instrumental cut #9 on this CD). Growling Tiger performed with the Puerto Rican cuatro player Yomo Toro, and the Cuban flautist Victor Pacheco. The clearest Cuban influences can be found in the New York-based calypsos of Lord Invader. See "Pepsi Cola," "My Intention is War," "No Place Like the West Indies," and "Cat O'Nine Tails" on *Lord Invader, Calypso in New York (1946-1961)* (Washington, DC: Smithsonian Folkways Recordings, 2000), CD 40454.

65. The genealogy of "highlife" music is laid out in detail in *Nigeria '70: The Definitive Story of 1970s Funky Lagos* (London: Afro Strut, 2001), CD 013, B00005R62B (see especially cut #3 on disc 3). See also Tejumola Olaniyan, *Arrest the Music!: Fela and his Rebel Art and Politics* (Bloomington: Indiana University Press, 2004).
66. Díaz Ayala, *Cuando salí de la Habana:* 23 ff.
67. An account of this process can be found in the introduction to Pedro Perez Sarduy and Jean Stubbs, eds., *Afro-Cuba: An Anthology of Cuban Writing on Race, Politics, and Culture* (Melbourne: Ocean Press, 1993).
68. Díaz Ayala, 31–33.
69. An interesting recent essay on this point is Rosalie Schwartz's "Cuba's Roaring Twenties," Lisa Brock and Digna Castañeda Fuertes, eds., *Between Race and Empire: African-Americans and Cubans before the Cuban Revolution* (Philadelphia: Temple University Press, 1998), 104–19.
70. Feijóo, 294.
71. Alejo Carpentier, *The Harp and the Shadow* (San Francisco: Mercury House, 1990), 129.
72. Amiri Baraka (Leroi Jones), "Cuba Libre," *The LeRoi Jones/Amiri Baraka Reader*, William J. Harris, ed. (New York: Thunder's Mouth Press, 1991), 125–60.
73. Jacqueline Rosemain, *La musique dans la société antillaise 1635–1902* (Paris: Editions L'Harmattan, 1986), 74 (my translation).
74. Fernando Ortíz, *La Africanía de la música folklórica de Cuba* (La Habana: Editora Universitaria, 1965), 105.
75. Pierre Mabille, "The Jungle," in Michael Richardson, ed. *Refusal of the Shadow: Surrealism and the Caribbean* (New York and London: Verso, 1996), 205.
76. Joseph Lanza, *Elevator Music: A Surreal History of Muzak, Easy-Listening, and Other Moodsong* (New York: St. Martin's, 1994), 5.

Chapter 3 – Face Down in the Mainstream

1. My title is taken from Outkast's "Mainstream," *Atliens* (La Face: 26029, 1996).
2. Ken Okubo, "On the Musical Work Game: An Essay on the Concept of the Musical Work," *International Review of the Aesthetics and Sociology of Music* 32: 1 (June 2001), 65–92. Okubo even denies that the question "what is authenticity?" makes sense. He prefers, he says, "to show the difficulty (even

the impossibility) of asking such a question with expectation of an appropriate answer" (66).
3. Michael Ventura, "Hear that Long Snake Moan," *Shadow Dancing in the U.S.A.* (Los Angeles: J. P. Tarcher; New York: Macmillan, 1985), 151.
4. As Walter Benjamin, describing what he took to be a fundamental urge, put it: *Ursprung ist das Ziel* ("Origin is the goal"). Or to put it another way, knowing our beginnings is always what we want – our most important goal.
5. The assault on authenticity is derived largely from poststructuralist literary theory. This connection is explicit in K. Okubo's "On the Musical Work Game", 73: The theory of text in Roland Barthes and Julia Kristeva "grasps very strictly the relations between a work, its author and its recipient. The theory of text tells us [that] a so-called 'work' is a place where its recipients ... cross as threads ... The author is deprived of privileged status in a 'work.'"
6. Peter Hill, "Authenticity in Contemporary Music," *Tempo* 159 (December 1986), 7–8.
7. D. Fabian, "Authenticity and Early Music," *International Review of the Aesthetics and Sociology of Music* 32: 2 (2001), 154.
8. David Sanjek, "Ridiculing the 'White Bread Original': The Politics of Parody and Preservation of Greatness in Luther Campbell a.k.a. Luke Skywalker et al. v. Acuff-Rose Music," *Cultural Studies* 20: 2–3 (March/May 2006), 268–69.
9. George H. Lewis, "Lap Dancer or Hillbilly Deluxe? The Cultural Construction of Modern Country Music," *Journal of Popular Culture* 31: 3 (Winter 1997) 163–73.
10. Authenticity, by contrast, is treated at times as a lie. See David Grazian, "The Production of Popular Music as a Confidence Game: The Case of the Chicago Blues," *Qualitative Sociology* 27: 2 (June 2004), 137–58: "In their attempts to manufacture authenticity for the patrons of live music venues, cultural producers devise performances whose formal properties resemble traditional confidence games in which operators, ropers, insiders, shills and marks interact in a cultural ecology of deception and guile."
11. Junior Wells, "Help Me," *Best of the Vanguard Years* (Vanguard Records: 79508, 1998); Bob Dylan, "Song to Woody," *Bob Dylan* (Sony: 8579, 1989 [c. 1965]).
12. Quoted in Jory Farr, *Rites of Rhythm: The Music of Cuba* (New York: Regan Books [Harper Collins], 2003), 15.
13. Zora Neale Hurston, "Spirituals and Neo-Spirituals," in Nancy Cunard, ed., *Negro: An Anthology* (New York and London: Continuum, 2002 [1934]), 224 (223–25).
14. Isabelle Leymarie, *Cuban Fire: The Story of Salsa and Latin Jazz* (London, NY: Continuum, 2002; [in French, 1997]). And in the same spirit, it is significant that Gage Averill in *A Day for the Hunter, A Day for the Prey: Popular Music and Power in Haiti* (Chicago and London: University of Chicago Press, 1997) titles the section dedicated to the era of the U.S. occupation of Haiti (1915–34), which introduced American jazz and Cuban *son* to Haitian urban audiences, "The Discourse of Authenticity."
15. Keya Ganguly, *States of Exception: Everyday Life and Postcolonial Identity* (Minneapolis: University of Minnesota, 2001), 132–33.
16. On the other hand, in "Art and Revolution" (Herbert Marcuse, *Art and Liberation* [London: Routledge, 2007], 169), Marcuse writes of the important theoretical problems posed by the neo-African presence in the Americas: "In [black] music ... the music *is* body; the aesthetic form is the 'gesture of pain, sorrow, indictment. With the takeover by the whites, a significant change occurs: white 'rock' is what its black paradigm is *not*, namely, *performance*."
17. Theodor Adorno (with the assistance of George Simpson), "On Popular Music," Richard Leppert, ed., Theodor Adorno, *Essays on Music* (Berkeley and Los Angeles: University of California Press, 2002), 437–69. Adorno, of

course, famously attacked "authenticity." As the watchword of Martin Heidegger's existentialist followers, the concept is excoriated in Adorno's *The Jargon of Authenticity*. But he is referring there to the truth-value of philosophy secured by the recognition of death rather than fidelity to the social contexts of creation.
18. Rolf Wiggerhaus, *The Frankfurt School: Its History, Theories, and Political Significance*, Michael Robertson, trans. (Cambridge, MA: The MIT Press, 1994), 72.
19. Ibid., 79.
20. Jacques Attali, *Noise: The Political Economy of Music* (Minneapolis: University of Minnesota Press, 1985).
21. Fernando Ortiz, *La música afrocubana* (Madrid: Biblioteca Júcar, 1975). Some of Ortiz's extensive research on the popular music of neo-African cultures includes *Glosario de Afronegrismos* (Habana, 1924), *La clave xilofónica de la música cubana, ensayo etnográfico* (La Habana: Tipografía Molina y Cía, 1935), *La música sagrada de los negros yorubas en Cuba* (La Habana: Estudios Afrocubanos, 1938), and *Los Negros Brujos* (Madrid, 1960).
22. The key terms he mobilizes to capture the second of these meanings is "folk" or "folkloric," terms that have a different meaning in Spanish than English, where they suggest an artificial, showy, or patriotic kitsch performed at state fairs or tourist festivals (or, as Ortiz himself puts it after C. F. Potter, "a living fossil that refuses to die.") To show this distinction, I have usually translated these terms as "popular," "national-popular," or "plebeian."
23. The contemporary Cuban critic who follows most directly in Ortiz's and Carpentier's footsteps in this regard is Carmen Valdés. In *La Música que nos rodea* (Havana: Editorial Arte y Literature, 1984), she tries to pinpoint "the difference between folkloric, popular, and 'high' or 'cultivated' music."
24. Alejo Carpentier, *The Harp and the Shadow*, trans by Thomas Christensen and Carol Christensen, (San Francisco: Mercury House, 1990 [1979]) 17–18.
25. Although indebted to the substantial critical literature on Nicaraguan politics and art over the last two-and-a-half decades, a good deal of the research in this section is original. In 1984 and 1986, as a stringer for *The Nation* and WBAI-FM, I conducted interviews with Ernesto Cardenal, then the Minister of Culture; Luis Enrique Mejía Godoy, a musician and Director of the National Recording Studios; Roberto Cepeda, Co-editor and Film Columnist for *Ventana*, the weekly cultural insert of the newspaper, *Barricada*; Oscar Miranda, Director of Sistema Sandinista, the National Television Network; Francisco Seveño, lead vocalist and songwriter for the rock group, Pancasán; and Carlos Rigby, an English-language poet from the Atlantic Coast. Other comments are based on literary ephemera from newspapers, personal slide collections, mix tapes, and comic books that I assembled between 1982 and 1987.
26. These are precisely the questions taken up by the revolution's leading intellectuals in *Hacia una política cultural (de la Revolución Sandinista)* (Managua: Ministerio de Cultura, 1982). For the view on these matters by a prominent fellow-traveler, see Margaret Randall's excellent series of interviews with leading Nicaraguan women politicians, poets, and activists, *Sandino's Daughters Revisited: Feminism in Nicaragua* (New Brunswick: Rutgers University Press, 2001).
27. Enrique Semo in Armand Mattelart and Seth Siegelaub, eds, *Communication and Mass Culture: An Anthology in 2 Volumes* (New York: International General, 1979–83).
28. Steven White, ed., *Poets of Nicaragua: A Bilingual Anthology* (New York: Unicorn, 1982), and Steven White, ed., *Culture and Politics in Nicaragua: Testimonies of Poets and Writers* (New York: Lumen Books, 1986).

29. David Kunzle, *The Murals of Revolutionary Nicaragua 1979–1992* (Berkeley and Los Angeles: University of California Press, 1995); for the importance of the muralist movements to Latin American politics, and for an examination of the sources of influence on Nicaragua's murals, see Bruce Campbell's *Mexican Murals in Times of Crisis* (Tucson: University of Arizona Press, 2003).
30. To get a clear sense of the conditions of war under which the popular resistance had to operate, see Holly Sklar, *Washington's War on Nicaragua* (Boston: South End Press, 1988).
31. See Elijah Wald, *Narcocorrido: A Journey into the Music of Drugs, Guns, and Guerrillas* (New York: HarperCollins, 2001).
32. Hasta cinco cuadras llega/ su tremendo proyectil/ Pesa diez libras completas/ ocho tiros tiene el clip/ El Garand esta compuesto/ Por tres piezas y estas son:/ caja de los mecanismos, cilindro de gases, y el mero cañón/ Ante todo coloquemos/ de este gran fusil /en alineación bien hecha, de izquierda a derecha, que es mejor así/ Quitemos primero el peine/ hagamos bien la inspección/ Por que a veces bala en boca/ esto nos provoca la peor situación/ *Chorus*: Dentre todos los fusiles/ Este Garand es la ley/ El cañón de su calibre/ tiene trenta zero seis/ Si Ud. quiere desarmarlo/ Sigue al pelo esta instrucción/ Levante bien las dos cejas/ Para las orejas oiga esta canción. (My translation)
33. As Omar Cabezas put it, "the walls were always our accomplices."
34. This hymn is, however, very interesting musically. Each of its three verses varies in length, and the melody, instrumentation, and genre of each verse shifts as well. Its lyrics give a sense of its tone, which is of a very different character from what Ortiz had in mind as the "popular" (as we have been saying). From the deliberately confrontational (although not martial) lyrics of one verse – "The children of Sandino/ never sell out, and never give up (never!)/ our struggle is against the United States/ the enemies of mankind" – to the romantic sentiments of another verse, so characteristic of Nicaraguan poetry : "Today the dawn is no longer a temptation." Both verses draw on well-known quotations from Nicaraguan writers (Leonel Rugama and Tomás Borge respectively). The chorus: "Our people are the owners of their history/ The architects of their liberation."
35. Carlos Mejía Godoy, "El licenciado de pobreza": "Ni estoy leido ni estudiado/ en ninguna sciencia/ pero estoy graduado, por la experiencia/ El curso de alta miseria/ me hizo doctor . . ."
36. Duo Los Compadres, "Págame la caña bien," *Cuba, I am Time* (Blue Jacket Entertainment), BJAC 5012-2: 2002).
37. David McClelland, *The Library Journal*, Temple University Library, Philadelphia, 1995.
38. Ismail Rivera, "Moliendo Café," *Danger: Do not Trespass* (Rumba: CD 55552).
39. Ismail Rivera con Cortijo y su Combo, "El Negro Bembón," *Sonero #1* (Musical Productions: MP-3164, 1990; Sonora Ponceña, *Lo Mejor de Sonora Ponceña* (Inca: SCPCD-1045, 1975); El Gran Combo, *Bailando Con El Mundo* (30 Aniversario) (Combo Records: RSCD 2091): 1992; Joe Arroyo, "Olores," *Colombia '93* (Globo: CDZ 81149, 1993).
40. Alejo Carpentier, *Music in Cuba*, edited and with an introduction by Timothy Brennan (Minneapolis: University of Minnesota Press, 2001), 86.
41. Tommy Olivencia, "Santero," *30 Aniversario* (Universal: 157003: 1999).
42. Mighty Sparrow, "Obeah Wedding," Mighty Sparrow and Lord Kitchener, *16 Carnival Hits* (Ice Records: 9170: 2000).
43. Carpentier, *Music in Cuba*, 144–45.
44. Willie Rosario, "Chango 'ta beni," *Nuevos Horizontes* (Bronco Records: Bronco 128).
45. Issues analyzed wonderfully by Cristóbal Díaz Ayala's, *Cuando Salí de la*

Habana, 1898-1997: Cien años de la música cubana por el mundo (Santo Domingo: Editora Centenario, S. A. 2001), 41–43.
46. Roberto Inglez and his Orchestra, *Come Closer to Me* (from the Savoy Hotel, London) (Vocalion: CDEA 6062, 2001). These arrangements found their way into films such as *Night and Day, Carnival in Costa Rica*, Walt Disney's *Make Mine Music, Easy to Wed*, and *Oklahoma!*

Chapter 4 – Rap and American Business

1. See especially Todd Boyd, "Intergenerational Culture Wars: Civil Rights vs. Hip Hop," interview with Yusuf Nuruddin, *Socialism and Democracy* 18: 2 (July–December 2004), 51–69. Boyd, a West Coast-based critic, is the author of the book *The New H.N.I.C.* [head niggaz in charge]: *The Death of Civil Rights and the Reign of Hip Hop*.
2. See Raquel Rivera, *New York Ricans in the Hip Hop Zone* (Palgrave, 2003). The Latin presence in New York is also attested to in a number of other works on rap, among them Alan Light, ed., *The Vibe History of Hip Hop* (1999); Juan Flores, *From Bomba to Hip-Hop: Puerto Rican Culture and Latino Identity* (New York: Columbia University Press, 2000); Brian Cross, *It's Not About a Salary: Rap, Race, and Resistance in Los Angeles* (London: Verso, 1993).
3. See Cheryl L. Keyes, *Rap Music and Street Consciousness* (Urbana and Chicago: University of Illinois, 2002), xii, 17, 51, 54; Rivera, 13, 37, 51. The Caribbean musical influences on rap are extensively treated in the early chapters of David Toop, *The Rap Attack: African Jive to New York Hip Hop* (London, 1984) (this book has been reissued several times, most recently as *Rap Attack 3: African Rap to Global Hip Hop* (London, Serpents Tail, 2001).
4. Rivera, 57.
5. Juan Flores, *From Bomba to Hip-Hop: Puerto Rican Culture and Latino Identity*, 123.
6. Peter Manuel explores this juxtaposition in "Salsa and Beyond," *Caribbean Currents: Caribbean Music from Rumba to Reggae* (Philadelphia: Temple University Press, 2006), 88–115.
7. Marco Katz, "Salsa Criticism at the Turn of the Century: Identity Politics and Authenticity," *Popular Music and Society* 28: 1 (February 2005), 35.
8. Ibid., 35–36.
9. Apart from Ruth Glasser's *My Music is My Flag: Puerto Rican Musicians and Their New York Communities 1917–1940* (Berkeley, CA: University of California Press, 1995), there are a number of accounts of the rise of salsa in New York: Vernon Boggs, *Salsiology: Afro-Cuban Music and the Evolution of Salsa in New York City* (New York: Greenwood, 1992); Hernando Calvo Ospina, *Salsa: Havana Heat, Bronx Beat* (London: Latin-American Bureau, 1995); and Ed Morales *The Latin Beat: The Rhythms and Roots of Latin Music from Bossa Nova to Salsa and Beyond* (New York: Da Capo, 2003).
10. Peter Manuel, "Salsa and the Music Industry: Corporate Control or Grass Roots Expression," *Essays on Cuban Music: North American and Cuban Perspectives*, Peter Manuel, ed. (Lanham, MD: University Press of America, 1991), 157–81. Manuel notes that standardization, the decline of political content, and the move towards pop stars and romantic ballads were some of these effects.
11. Keyes, 5, 102.
12. Robert Farris Thompson, for instance, writes in *Black Gods and Kings: Yoruba Art at UCLA* (Bloomington and London: Indiana University Press, 1971 (Ch. 3, 4–5) of the Yoruban satiric sculptures of foreigners and criminals, and of the

tradition of "lampooning the barbarian from foreign lands or the indigenous buffoon."
13. Timothy Brennan, "Off the Gangsta Tip: A Rap Appreciation or Forgetting about Los Angeles," *Critical Inquiry* 20 (Summer 1994), 663–94.
14. In *Hip Hop America* (New York: Penguin, 1998), Nelson George later deepened many of these same points, exploring them from new angles.
15. Studies of rap coming from abroad include, Franceso Adinolfi, *Suoni dal ghetto: La musica dalla strada alle hit-parade* (Genova, 1989); Hugues Bazin, *La culture hip hop* (Paris: Descles de Brouwer, 1995); Alain Philippe-Durand, *Black, Blanc, Beur: Rap Music and Hip-Hop Culture in the Francophone World* (Lanham, MD: Scarecrow, 2002); Selwyn Sefu Hinds, *Gunshots in My Cook-up: Bits and Bites from a Hip-Hop Caribbean Life* (New York: Atria, 2002); Tony Mitchell, ed., *Global Noise: Rap and Hip Hop Outside the USA* (Middletown: Wesleyan University Press, 2001)
16. Keyes, 1.
17. Ibid., xii, 83.
18. By the mid- to late-1990s, examples included Skee-Lo, "I Wish" ("I wish I were taller, I wish I were a baller, etc.") about a short kid with ambition, who never gets picked for the basketball squad; LA Nash, "My '64" about a gun fight where the narrators car gets shot up (his '64); Mack 10, "On Them Thangs" about trick cars, driving on two wheels, low-hi riders, etc; K-Dee, "Hittin Corners" about "sun rooftops," "takin' in the scene," "how the players lean"; and Coolio, "Gangsta's Paradise," from the film *Dangerous Minds*.
19. In various ways, all of the following books to some degree treat this aspect of the question: Chuck D., *Fight the Power: Rap, Race & Reality* (New York: Delacorte, 1997); Mark Costello, *Signifying Rappers: Rap and Race in the Urban Present* (New York: Ecco Press, 1997); Betty Houchin Winfield and Sandra Davidson, eds., *Bleep!: Censoring Rock and Rap Music* (Westport: Greenwood, 1999); and Murray Foreman, *The Hood Comes First: Race, Space and Place in Rap and Hip Hop* (Middletown: Wesleyan, 2001).
20. Charen's syndicated piece appeared first as "Much More Nasty Than They Should Be," *Boston Globe*, 16 June 1990, 23.
21. Geneva Smitherman, "'The Chain Remain the Same,' Communicative Practices in the Hip Hop Nation," *Journal of Black Studies* 28: 1 (September 1997), 11–12.
22. Ibid., 12. Herbert Marcuse commented on the significance of "flippin' the script" very early (and prior to rap) in his brilliant analysis of the politics of art in *An Essay on Liberation* (Boston: Beacon, 1969): ". . . a methodical reversal of meaning. It is a familiar phenomenon that subcultural groups develop their own language, taking the harmless words of everyday communication out of their context and using them for designating objects or activities tabooed by the Establishment" 35–36.
23. Paul Delaney, "Amos 'n Andy in Nikes," *New York Times*, October 11, 1993, A31.
24. Erik Eckholm, "Rap Fan Asks Hard Questions about the Music He Loves," *New York Times* (24 December 2006), A16.
25. Joseph Sobran, "Stodgy Detractors are Right: Rap is an Ugly Form of Expression," distributed by Universal Press Syndicate, 1992, *The Milwaukee Journal*.
26. As quoted in Robert S. Boynton, "The Professor of Connection," *New Yorker* (6 November 1995), 71, 35, 116.
27. Toop, *The Rap Attack*, 19.
28. Amiri Baraka, "Greenwich Village and African-American Music," in Amiri Baraka (LeRoi Jones) and Amina Baraka, *The Music: Reflections on Jazz and Blues* (New York, 1987), 184, 181.

29. Ibid., 182.
30. Baraka (LeRoi Jones) in "Jazz and the White Critic" (1963) warns that the efforts of white critics to formalize and institutionalize jazz "technique" distort it beyond recognition (Jones, "Jazz and the White Critic," *Black Music* [New York, 1967], 14). My argument is that rap struggles to be seen *as art* (an obstacle jazz did not have to the same degree).
31. David E. James, "Poetry/Punk/Production: Some Recent Writing in LA," *Postmodernism and Its Discontents: Theories, Practices*, E. Ann Kaplan, ed. (London, 1988), 165, 175.
32. A typical example from KRS-One, the hip-hop philosopher par excellence, appears in Justin Pritchard, "Still the One," *Downtown Resident*, 18–31 December 1993, 15: "Rap comes out of hip hop. Hip hop is our culture. If you destroy hip hop there's no more rap. The illusion is that rap stands on its own. That's bullshit."
33. Yomo and Maulkie, "Mockingbird," *Are U Xperienced?* Ruthless Records, 91760, 1991, and Public Enemy, "Don't Believe the Hype," *It Takes a Nation of Millions to Hold us Back*, Def Jam, 44303, 1988.
34. Cypress Hill, "Hand on the Pump," *Cypress Hill*, RuffHouse, 47889, 1991.
35. Public Enemy, "Contract on the World Love Jam," *Fear of a Black Planet*, Def Jam, 45413; Gang Starr, "Who's Gonna Take the Weight?" *Step in the Arena*, Chrysalis, 21798, 1990.
36. Rap is not unique in this respect. See examples in other popular music lyrics – for example, George Jones and Tammy Wynette's "No, we're not the jet set/ we're the old Chevrolete set/ Our steak and martinis/ is [sic] draft beer with wienies" (George Jones and Tammy Wynette, "(We're not) the Jet Set," *Greatest Hits*, Epic, 34716, 1977). Rap is distinctive because it combines high moral and political seriousness with an otherwise gratuitous rhyming display where posture is the message.
37. For an impressive study of the state of hip-hop in Cuba, see Sujatha Fernandes, *Cuba Represent!: Cuban Arts, State Power, and the Making of New Revolutionary Cultures* (Durham and London: Duke University Press, 2006). See also Melissa Rivière's work in progress based on research collected at the IX Hip Hop Conference held in Havana in the Summer of 2003, which was organized by the Association of Hermanos Sais, a musical entertainment division of the Unión de Jóvenes Comunistas (the Young Communists Union), the Agencia Cubana de Rap (Cuban Rap Agency) and the University of Havana.
38. Marvin Santiago, "Estaca de Guayacán," Chorus: Me llaman el hombre duro/ estaca de guayacán/ Me llaman el hombre duro/ estaca de guayacán// Santiago: Pongo el verde en el maduro/ castigo a los que estan/ Vuelvo a presente el futuro/ yo puedo con superman.
39. Bola de Nieve ("Snow Ball"), "Chivo que rompe tambo," *Cuba: I am Time* (Blue Jacket Entertainment), BJAC 5012-2: 2002).
40. Tate, *Flyboy in the Buttermilk*, 127–28
41. Keyes, 186–209.
42. Common, "Real People," *Be* (2005); Thompson, *Black Gods and Kings*, Ch 2, 2.
43. Melissa Rivière, unpublished dissertation, University of Minnesota, 2003. See footnote 37 above.
44. Or, to take an example from the period I have been considering, take 2Pac, "I Don't Give a !!!!" *2Pacalypse Now*, Interscope, 4403, 1991.
45. Boyd, "Intergenerational Culture Wars: Civil Rights vs. Hip Hop," 51–69.
46. Ibid., 52.

Chapter 5 – Global Youth and Local Pleasure

1. Amiri Baraka, "The Black Arts (Harlem, Politics, Search for a New Life)," *The Leroi Jones/Amiri Baraka Reader* (New York: Thunder Mouth, 1991), 367.
2. Some recent examples are Jory Farr, *Rites of Rhythm: The Music of Cuba* (New York: Regan Books, 2003); Cristóbal Díaz Ayala, *Cuando salí de la Habana: 1898–1997, Cien años de la música cubana* (San Juan: Editora Centenario, 1998); Isabelle Leymarie, *Cuban Fire: The Story of Salsa and Latin Jazz* (London, New York: Continuum, 2002 [1997]); Eric Silva Brenneman, "Havana and Miami: A Music Censorship Sandwich," Marie Korpe, ed., *Shoot the Singer!: Music Censorship Today* (London, New York: Zed Books, 2004), 160–69.
3. For added evidence of the explosion in writing on Afro-Cuban music since the revolution, see the bibliography in Yvonne Daniel, *Rumba: Dance and Social Change in Contemporary Cuba* (Bloomington: Indiana University Press, 1995).
4. A sampling of the Cuban scholarship that documents and theorizes the popular and the Afro-Cuban would include Fernando Ortiz, *La Africanía de la música folklórica de Cuba* (La Habana, Editora Universitaria, 1965) and *La Música Afrocubana* (La Habana: Biblioteca Júcar, 1975); María Teresa Linares, *La música popular* (La Habana: Instituto del Libro, 1970) and *La música y el pueblo* (La Habana: Editorial Pueblo y Educación, 1974); Gloria Antolítia, *Cuba: dos siglos de música (siglos XVI y XVII)* (La Habana: Editorial Letras Cubanas, 1984); Argeliers León, *Del canto y el tiempo* (La Habana: Editorial Letras Cubanas, 1984) and *Tras las huellas de las civilizaciones negras en América* (La Habana: Fundación Fernando Ortiz, 2001); Leonardo Depestre Catony, *Homenaje a la música popular cubana* (Santiago de Cuba: Editorial Oriente, 1989); Olga Fernández, *Strings and Hide* (La Habana: Editorial José Martí, 1995); and Victoria Eli Rodrígez y Zoila Gómez García, . . . *hacienda música cubana* (La Habana: Editorial Pueblo y Educación, 2002).
5. At its most pedagogical, Cuban scholarship is often aimed at non-specialist audiences. Here are three examples: (1) the "*Música Folklore*" series, general editor Angel Vázquez Millares, (La Habana: Ediciones del C.N.C., no date). Among its offerings are *La rumba* (with essays by Argeliers León, and Odilio Urfé); *Danzón* (with essays by Argeliers León and Odilio Urfé); *Música guajira* (with essays by Argeliers León and María Teresa Linares de Leon); *Yoruba, bantú, abakuá* (with essays by Angel Vázquez Millares). (2) "How to" books on popular dances with choreographic illustrations: María Antonia Fernández, *Bailes Populares Cubanos* (La Habana: Editorial Pueblo y Educación, 1974); Caridad Santos García and Nieves Armas Rigal, *Danzas populares tradicionales cubanas: contenido, movimiento y expression* (La Habana: Centro de Investigación y Desarrollo de la Cultura Cubana Juan Marinello, 2002). (3) Primers on the significance of music to larger questions of history and society: José Ardévol, *Música y revolución* [a book on Cuban classical music by a practicing composer] (La Habana: Ediciones Unión, 1966); María Teresa Linares, *La Musica y el pueblo,* (La Habana: Editorial Pueblo y Educación, 1979); and Carmen Valdés, *La música que nos rodea* (La Habana: Editorial Arte Y Literatura, 1984).
6. A special note belongs to the prolific and brilliant contemporary Cuban music and literary critic, Leonardo Acosta, whose wide-ranging knowledge of traditional Cuban forms, of the career of Cuban jazz (and U.S. jazz *in* Cuba), of literature about music and the sociology of music is found in books that are among the most significant in Latin America. A small selection of his important work would include Leonardo Acosta, *Música y descolonización* (Mexico City: Presencia Latinoamericana, S. A., 1982); *Del tambor al sintetizador* (La Habana: Editorial Letras Cubanas, 1983); *Elige tu, que canto yo* (La Habana: Letras

Cubanas, 1993); *Descarga Cubana: el jazz en Cuba 1900–1950* (La Habana: Ediciones Unión, 2000); *Descarga número dos: el jazz en Cuba 1950–2000* (La Habana: Ediciones Unión, 2002); *Cubano Be, Cubano Bop: One Hundred Years of Jazz in Cuba* (Washington, DC: 2003); *Alejo en Tierre Firme: Intertextualidad y encuentros fortuitos* (La Habana: 2004).

7. Examples include Pio Leyva's "Rumba de mi patria," Esther Borja's "Déjame estrechar tu mano," Nino Rivera's "Nuevo Son," Omara Portuondo's "Junto a mi fusil mi son," Ela Calvo's "Cuba que linda es Cuba," Cuarteto d'Aida's "El Cohete Americano," and Celina Gonzalez y Reutilio's "Décimas de la Revolución."

8. Some of the points I make in this chapter have been addressed, recently, by Robin Moore's excellent *Music & Revolution: Cultural Change in Socialist Cuba* (Berkeley: University of California Press, 2006). I wrote this chapter before his book appeared, but find his study the most well-researched and balanced of its kind in English. It brings together information previously available only in many difficult-to-locate individual sources, and (while adding to them) presents to a metropolitan public many of the issues and insights of Cuban scholars like Acosta, Radamés Giró, Carmen Valdés, Reinaldo Cedeño Pineda and Michel Damián Suárez, as well as Cuban scholars working outside Cuba like Cristóbal Díaz Ayala and Tony Évora,.

9. Harold Gramatges, *Presencia de la Revolución en la música Cubana* (Editorial Letras Cubanas, 1983), Harold Gramatges, a composer and essayist influenced by Schoenberg, Stravinski, Julián Carillo, and Debussy, wrote in the 1980s of the need to sing "a grand homage to a free people that recognizes [music] as its national instrument" (8). One of the immediate effects of the revolution was the openings provided in radio CMZ under the direction of the Cultural Ministry for education. With an influx of funds and educational support, Gramatges, Juan Blanco, José Ardévol and Nilo Rodriguez were able in the early years to create two orchestras, one symphonic and the other chamber, with a mixed chorus. Not only in popular music, but in classical, composers adapted techniques from around the world after the revolution, blending them with an Antillean sensibility. Félix Guerrero, Fabio Landa, Enrique González Mántici and Alfredo Diez Nieto all dealt with postimpressionism and atonalism, blending them with popular sources. A noteworthy effort of a similar nature took place in the famous guitar concert of Leo Brouwer in 1978 featuring his fusion of Joplin, Bach, and the Beatles (74).

10. The official sentiment can be seen very clearly expressed in Fernando Ortiz's "For a Cuban Integration of Whites and Blacks," originally published in 1940 but reprinted in Cuba in 1960. In Pedro Pérez Sarduy and Jean Stubbs, eds., *AfroCuba: An Anthology of Cuban Writing on Race, Politics and Culture* (New York: Latin American Bureau, 1993), 27–33.

11. Moore, 64–65.

12. Jesus Colón, *A Puerto Rican in New York and Other Sketches* (New York: International Publishers, 1961), 78–80.

13. Yvonne Daniel, *Rumba*; Peter Manuel, *Caribbean Currents*; Robin Moore, *Music & Revolution: Cultural Change in Socialist Cuba*.

14. Among the better known musicians who fled because they opposed the politics of the revolution are Israel "Cachao" López, José Fajardo, Celia Cruz, Osvaldo Farrés, Ernesto Lecuona, Willie Chirino, La Lupe, and Albita Rodriguez.

15. Taking to heart, perhaps, Nicolás Guillén's poem "Responde Tú" (set to music by Pablo Milanés), which imagines the loyalists chiding the exiles by asking: "You who have forgotten your language, tell me in that mishmash Spanglish of "guell" and "yu," how can you live without being able to speak?, tell me that." ["Tu, que tu lengua olvidaste/ responde tu y en lengua extraña masticas/ el "guell" y el "yu"/.como vivir puedes mudo? responde tu"].

16. Ulf Hannerz, *Transnational Connections: Culture, People, Places* (London, New York: Routledge, 1996).
17. Radamés Giró, "Todo lo que usted quiso saber sobre el mambo . . ." *La Gaceta* (Noviembre-diciembre 1992) 13–17.
18. For an account of Cuba's experiments in high-vegetable diets and organic farming, see Bill McKibben, "The Cuban Diet: What Will you be Eating when the Revolution Comes?," *Harper's* (April 2005), 61–69.
19. Bertolt Brecht, "Emphasis on Sport," *Brecht on Theatre: The Development of an Aesthetic*, John Willett, ed and trans. (New York: Hill and Wang, 1964).
20. See Elena Perez Sanjurjo, *Historia de la música cubana* (Miami: Moderna Poesia, 1986); Marc Cooper, "Semper Fidel," *Village Voice* (1 May 1990), 20–23. See also the video, *Son Sabroson*, directed by Hugo Barroso, (Miami: HBM Productions, P.O. Box 33255-8811) which tells the story of *son* through Miami-based exiles or now dead earlier artists such as Miguel Matamoros and Rita Montaner. For an account of the rise of *son* and its connections to salsa which is more inclusive and less affected by contemporary U.S. political pressures, see *The Roots of Rhythm*, a documentary narrated by Harry Belafonte (Directors/Producers Howard Dratch and Eugene Rosow, KCET Television, Cat. NVG 9436, 1994).
21. Lise Waxer, ed., *Situating Salsa: Global Markets and Local Meaning in Latin Popular Music* (New York and London: Routledge, 2002).
22. Ibid., 23.
23. For a recent anthology that challenges prevailing U.S. views of Cuba see Lisa Brock and Digna Castañeda Fuertes, eds., *Between Race and Empire: African-Americans and Cubans before the Cuban Revolution* (Philadelphia: Temple University Press, 1998), especially the essays by Rosalie Schwartz "Cuba's Roaring Twenties: Race Consciousness and the Column 'Ideales de una Raza,'" and Geoffrey Jacques, "CuBop! Afro-Cuban Music and Mid-Twentieth-Century American Culture."
24. *The Roots of Rhythm* video (op. cit.).
25. Leonardo Acosta, *Otra vision de la música popular cubana* (La Habana: Letras Cubanas, 2004), 123.
26. Ibid., 126–27.
27. Vincenzo Perna, *Timba: The Sound of the Cuban Crisis* (Burlington, VT: Ashgate Publishing, 2005), 7.
28. Ibid., 2; Charles B. Silverman, "Timba – New Styles in Afro-Cuban Popular Music. Evolution or Revolution" www.chucksilverman.com/timbapaper.html; Moore, 315.
29. Acosta, *Otra Visión*, 144.
30. Perna, 4.
31. Moore, among others, documents these initiatives in *Music & Revolution*. See pages 57–106, which cover the early cultural initiatives; the public instruction in, and promotion of, Afro-Cuban musical traditions; the financial incentives given popular artists, and the structures of support for musicians. He also offers an assessment of the state impediments to musical expression during the 1960s and 1970s.
32. To get a sense of how the position against racial and identitarian sectoralism is actually expressed by Cubans themselves, see León, *Del Canto y el tiempo*, 14; and Alejo Carpentier, *Music in Cuba*, "Introduction to English Edition," 30.
33. George Lipsitz, *Dangerous Crossroads: Popular Music, Postmodernism, and the Poetics of Place* (London, New York: Verso, 1994), 31.
34. Ibid., 31.
35. On this point, see Tomás Fernández Robaina, "The 20th Century Black Question," Pérez Sarduy and Stubbs, eds., *AfroCuba: An Anthology of Cuban Writing on Race, Politics and Culture*, 92–108.

36. Perna, 9.
37. Daniel, *Rumba: Dance and Social Change in Contemporary Cuba*; Hernando Calvo Ospina, *Salsa!: Havana Heat, Bronx Beat*, Nick Caistor, trans. (London: Latin American Research Bureau, 1995); Tony Évora, *Orígenes de la música cubana: Los amores de las cuerdas y el tambor* (Madrid: Alianza Editorial, 1997).
38. Jory Farr's *Rites of Rhythm: The Music of Cuba* (New York: ReganBooks, 2003) relies heavily, and almost exclusively, on anecdotes of U.S.-based Cuban exiles. Paquito D'Rivera in one of the books' interviews claims, for instance, that American jazz was outlawed by the revolution as a "dirty word" – that Cuban groups like Irakere had to "hide" it in their music (even though Irakere itself denies this). A more accurate version of the story of the productive exchanges between Cuban musicians and U.S. jazz can be found in Leonardo Acosta's *Descarga Cubana: el jazz en Cuba 1900–1950* and *Descarga número dos: el jazz en Cuba 1950–2000*; Daniel's book is particularly good at describing the way Cubans have freely incorporated U.S. forms: "The young dancers . . . executed the classic style, then proceeded to emphasize contemporary elements of choreography. They even interspersed break dance steps and the moon walk step associated with Michael Jackson and introduced acrobatic double and triple flips" (9).
39. My comments in this section (and the next) on socialist desire and "youth" are based on interviews I conducted during two research trips to Cuba. The first took place toward the beginning of the Special Period (December 1992–January 1993); and the second after many of the changes brought about by the dollar economy and increased tourist investment had made their mark (July 2000).
40. Tomás Guttiérez Alea, dir., *Memories of Underdevelopment*, Black and White, NTSC (New Yorker Films: 14 December 1999; orig. 1973). ASIN 8000005F92.
41. That Castro at the First National Congress on Education and Culture declared that artists and writers must reject "all manifestations of a decadent culture, the fruit of a society or societies that are rent by contradictions" (*Granma*, English edition, 9 May 1971), and that this period in Cuba saw a number of attacks on the film for its soul-searching and perplexity, should not take away from the fact that Guttiérez Alea continued to produce highly critical (and critically acclaimed) films throughout his career with official support – among them *Death of a Bureaucrat* and the sensitive portrait of homosexuality, *Strawberries and Chocolate*. One issue to emphasize here, along with the matter of harassment which is typically the focus, is that the sensibilities unleashed by the revolution itself made Guttiérez Alea's vision in *Memories of Underdevelopment* possible. It is also the case that supporters of Cuba outside the country considered his critically minded films consonant with the revolution itself, and they were widely shown by those demonstrating their solidarity with Cuba.
42. Neil Postman, *Amusing Ourselves to Death: Public Discourse in the Age of Show Business* (New York: Penguin, 1985); Andrew Goodwin, *Dancing in the Distraction Factory: Music Television and Popular Culture* (Minneapolis: University of Minnesota Press, 1992).
43. This startling history is recorded, for example, in Marieke de Mooij, *Global Marketing and Advertising: Understanding Cultural Paradoxes* (Thousand Oaks, CA: Sage, 2005); Stanley C. Hollander and Richard Germain, *Was There a Pepsi Generation Before Pepsi Discovered It? Youth-based Segmentation in Marketing* (Chicago: American Marketing Association, 1992); Alfred L. Schreiber with Barry Lenson, *Multicultural Marketing: Selling to the New America: Position your Company Today for Optimal Success in the Diverse America of Tomorrow* (Lincolnwood, IL: NTC Business Books, 2001). For a critique, see Theodore Roszak, *The Making of a Counter Culture: Reflections on the Technocratic Society and its Youthful Opposition* (London: Faber, 1969).
44. Matt Richtel, "From the Lips of Children, Tips To the Ear of Venture Capi-

talists," *New York Times* (17 December 2006): "Many wealthy, highly connected and well-educated technology investors are taking counsel and investment tips from their children, summer interns and twentysomething receptionists ... 'Children are a secret weapon in my arsenal for making investment decisions,' said Heidi Roizen, a managing director at Mobius Venutre Capital, a Silicon Valley Firm."

45. Thomas Frank, "Why Johnny Can't Dissent," in Thomas Frank and Matt Weiland, eds., *Commodify Your Dissent: Salvos from the Baffler* (New York and London: North, 1997), 31–45.
46. Two small, but concrete, examples of socialist pleasure can be found in Charles Silverman's account of the Cubadisco 2003 events in Havana (op. cit). At one of the concerts he attended, everyone in the theater at one point rushed the stage to show their appreciation for a Benny Moré impersonator. They stayed there throughout the concert, with the bouncers "boppin' [and] the guards nodding." It is difficult to imagine this kind of popular self-expression being permitted at a concert in the United States, where "crowd control" is paramount at music and sporting events. At another point in his travelogue, Silverman admires the public access to the city's beaches. "Imagine a beach skyline in the Caribbean free of any hotels?" he asks.
47. Personal interview, Havana, January 1993.
48. Raymundo del Toro, president of the Cuban American Committee for Peace based in Linden, New Jersey, attested to the effectiveness of the embargo when he reviled Torricelli for "a policy of genocide that seeks to create a Somalia in Cuba," *New York Times* (20 January 1994), A20.
49. McKibben, "The Cuba Diet."
50. For a typical and, if anything, uncommonly blunt example of the genre as it appeared in voluminous quantities in 1993, see Georgia Pabst's four-part series, "Revolution in Ruins," *Milwaukee Journal* (August 1993).
51. Cristina García, *Dreaming in Cuban* (New York: Ballantine, 1992), 117.
52. Written in a French prison in 1883, Paul Lafargue's *The Right to be Lazy, and Other Studies* (Chicago: C. H. Kerr & Company, 1907) posed itself against the discourse of the time that leisure was a "threat to order" and "immoral" (52); Henri Lefebvre, "Renewal, Youth, Repetition," *Introduction to Modernity: Twelve Preludes 1959–1961*, John Moore, trans. (London and New York: Verso, 1995), 157–67.
53. Antonio Gramsci, "Margins" in *History, Philosophy and Culture in the Young Gramsci* (Pedro Cavalcanti and Paul Piccone, eds., (St. Louis: Telos, 1975), 41.
54. From Cuban television, Havana, Cuba, 30 December 1992.
55. Tolerance, in cultural circles, expressed itself most clearly in earlier artistic debates over realism vs. abstraction in socialist societies, where the tolerant view among the stalwarts was that artistic abstraction (like Dionysian excess) is no enemy of socialism. This, after all, was not far from the position of the Cuban leadership itself. In the early 1960s, Fidel flatly announced to his East European allies: "Our enemies are capitalists and imperialists, not abstract art." Quoted in David Craven, "The Visual Arts since the Cuban Revolution," *Third Text* 20 (Autumn 1992), 80.
56. Sujatha Fernandes, "Fear of a Black Nation: Local Rappers, Transnational Crossings, and State Power in Contemporary Cuba," *Anthropological Quarterly* 76: 4 (Fall 2003), 578–79.
57. Ibid., 576.
58. Sujatha Fernandes, *Cuba Represent! Cuban Arts, State Power, and the Making of New Revolutionary Cultures* (Durham: Duke University Press, 2006), 86, 15.
59. John Beverley, *Against Literature* (Minneapolis: University of Minnesota, 1993), 6. After the film's highly successful U.S. release, reviews in the major U.S. media

harmonized with Beverley's assessment, focusing on the appeal of rock among this targeted and disenfranchised sector.
60. Juan José Hoyos, "Esas son las cosas que te da la vida," *Sentir que es un soplo la vida* (Medellín: Editorial Universidad de Antioquia, 1994), 36–37.
61. Angela María Pérez, "La Muerte me tiene miedo" ("Death Scares Me"), *El Mundo*, August 1982. Information about Pérez is taken from an interview in New York, 15 December 1993.
62. See Pamela Mercer, "In the Street Urchin's Dark Haunt, No Ray of Hope," *New York Times* (6 August 1993), A4.
63. [unsigned article], "Vigilantes in Colombia Kill Hundreds in a 'Social Cleansing'," *New York Times* (31 October 1994), A8.
64. Alonso Salazar, *Born to Die in Medellín* (New York: Monthly Review, 1992), 40.
65. John Ross, *Mexico Bárbaro* (6 June 2004), 1–2.
66. Looking only at the major U.S. daily newspapers, 125 stories appeared on Medellín in 1991, the year the film was prominently (and favorably) reviewed in the United States. All but a few of them concerned Pablo Escobar and the Medellín drug cartel.
67. Juan José Hoyos, *Sentir que es un soplo la vida*, 39.
68. Although not a study of music per se, Damián J. Fernández, *Cuba and the Politics of Passion* (Austin: University of Texas, 2000) is relevant in this respect. His goal is to bring the emotions back into the inquiries of political science. The politics of affection govern private life, he argues, but the politics of passion are public and extraordinary (19). His point is that without passion, the revolution would not have occurred. Cubans rely on the politics of affection, *lo informal*, and personal or de-statized relationships to express themselves, and this has led to the expansion of civil society in Cuba.

Chapter 6 – The War of Writing on Music: *Mumbo Jumbo*

1. Lydia Polgreen, "New Haitian Administrator Arrives, Vowing to Restore Unity," *New York Times* (11 March 2004), A10:
2. Ishmael Reed, *Mumbo Jumbo* (New York: Scribner's, 1996).
3. Oddly, Toni Morrison's novel *Jazz* (New York: Plume Books, 1993) does not really fit in this company. She strategically creates a false expectation. The novel draws its title from what may have been jazz's original meaning as "cum" or "jism." A deeply troubled narrative about a woman seeking revenge on her unfaithful husband, who hangs out in disreputable gin joints while she stays at home, *Jazz* is about the self-immolation that results from sexual attraction. The music of jazz plays no significant role in the novel except in its tangential role as the sound of the gin joints.
4. A very good description of such parties can be found in Langston Hughes, "When the Negro was in Vogue," *The Heath Anthology of American Literature*, Paul Lauter, ed., vol. 2, 4th ed. (Boston, NY: Houghton Mifflin, 2002), 1598; 1620–25.
5. Alfred Métraux, *Voodoo in Haiti* (New York: Oxford University Press, 1959), 101.
6. An entire subgenre of rap is dedicated to just such a retelling of the story of Western civilization. A recent example is Rass Kass's "Nature of the Threat," *Soul on Ice* (Priority Records, B000003AB1), 1996. Cheryl L. Keyes, in *Rap Music and Street Consciousness* (Urbana and Chicago: University of Illinois, 2002), discusses this important dimension of rap: "the most widely read cryptic source among contemporary hip-hoppers [is] *Behold a Pale Horse* (1991) by Milton William Cooper, a former U.S. Naval Intelligence Briefing Team member. In

addition to Cooper's book, the historian A. Ralph Epperson's *The New World Order* (1990) is deemed as 'a must read' work by the Zulu Nation ... Both authors basically discuss what is termed 'the illuminati,' the basis of one-world government called the New World Order. The illuminati, or the Illuminated Ones, are described by Cooper as evolving from Lucifer, also known in Kemetic (Egyptian) myth as Osiris, a bright (illumined) star that the ancients believed was cast down onto the earth denoting Lucifer's fall from heaven."

7. "*Mu'tafikah*" – one of the many jokes of the novel – sounds very official, as though referring to an Arabic or African term. But to speak it aloud is to discover Reed's joke: it is meant to sound like "motherfucker" (another clash of the oral and the written).

8. The problem Reed addresses here is perennial – the topic of a short but powerful documentary on the fate of African art consigned to hundreds of wooden crates buried in the basement of the British Museum (Kwate Nee-Owoo, dir., *You Hide Me*, 1972). It expresses itself again in the invasion of Iraq and the plundering of archeological sites and museums there. See Barry Meier and Martin Gottlieb, "An Illicit Journey out of Egypt, Only a Few Questions Asked," *New York Times* (23 February 2004), A1, A12–13. Prices (bounties?) offered by wealthy collectors or private art dealers create an incentive to steal the artifacts and circumvent Egyptian law. See also Andrew Lawler in "Beyond the Looting: What's Next for Iraq's Treasures?," *National Geographic* (October 2003), 58–75.

9. Mr. and Mrs. Vernon Castle, *Modern Dancing* (New York and London: Harpers Brothers, 1914).

10. Although the iconography of *santería* would suggest the appropriate color was "blue" – Yemayá's favorite, as in the old Mitch Ryder and the Detroit Wheel's song "Devil with the Blue Dress."

11. The legendary Egyptian founder of writing, Hermes Trismegistos (a.k.a. "Thoth" the etymological root of Greek "*theos*" or God) is the founder of non-Biblical or "gentile" philosophy and culture.

12. If we imagine that Reed's naming of Gould's troupe "The Harlem Tom-Toms" (an allusion not only to drums but Uncle Toms) is far-fetched, we would be ignoring the fact that even in its details the novel has an historical basis. See Edward G. Perry's "Negro Creative Musicians," Nancy Cunard, ed., *Negro: An Anthology* (New York and London: Continuum, 2002 [1934]): "recently a young woman, whose name is Shirley Graham, completed an opera in four acts called *Tom-Tom*, which was produced during the summer of 1932 by the Cleveland Summer Grand Opera with notable success" (201).

13. This is also the strategy employed in Paul Leduc's extraordinary film *Barroco* (1989) based on Alejo Carpentier's novel *El arpa y la sombra*. The 50-minute film has no words, and yet portrays the rise of Latin music over centuries. We are taken back to the first meeting of the conquistadors and the Tainos where the sounds of the forest, the jangling of armor, the crude wooden flutes of indigenous peoples, the harp transported from Spain hauled along with the cannons – all of these in an awkward and aleatory way begin to be heard alongside one another, creating the possibility of thinking differently about sound.

14. E. A. Budge, *Osiris: The Egyptian Religion of Resurrection* (New Hyde Park, NY: University Books, 1961).

15. Aleister Crowley, *The Works of Aleister Crowley*, vol. III (London: Foyers Society for the Propagation of Religious Truth, 1907).

16. Samuel Noah Kramer, *Mythologies of the Ancient World* (Chicago: Quadrangle Books, 1961).

17. Calvin Kephart, *A Concise History of Freemasonry*, 2nd edition (New York: H. L. Geddie Co., 1964).

18. These observations are repeated in more recent studies like W. Kirk McNulty, *Freemasonry: A Journey through Ritual and Symbol* (London: Thames and Hudson, 1991), 28.
19. Ibid., 176.
20. Donn A. Cass, *Negro Freemasonry and Segregation* (Chicago: E. A. Cook Publications, 1957).
21. McNulty, 12.
22. Martin Bernal, *Black Athena: The Afroasiatic Roots of Classical Civilization*, vol. 1 (New Brunswick, NJ: Rutgers University Press, 1987), 24.
23. Robert Irwin, *For Lust of Knowing: The Orientalists and Their Enemies* (London: Allen Lane, 2006), 107.
24. Bernal, 27.
25. Ibid, 206.
26. Ibid, 31.
27. Ibid, 242. Once again, Reed is drawing on scholarly sources that, although far from universally accepted, are solid and respectable. For the last 7,000 years, the population of Egypt has contained African, South-West Asian and Mediterranean types. According to Bernal, the 1st, 11th, 12th, and 18th dynasties were most likely ruled by pharaohs whom one "can usefully call black."
28. Ibid., 187.
29. Ibid., 12. For further verification of Bernal's point here, see Jack Goody, *The Theft of History* (Cambridge: Cambridge University Press, 2006), especially 13–26.
30. Norman Ian Mackenzie, *Secret Societies* (London: Aldus, 1968), 106–29.
31. Ibid., 118.
32. James Baldwin, "Negroes are Anti-Semitic because They're Anti-White," *Baldwin: Collected Essays* (New York: The Library of America, 1998), 739-48.
33. Crowley, *The Works of Aleister Crowley*, vol. III.
34. V. G. Kiernan, *The Lords of Human Kind: European Attitudes to Other Cultures in the Imperial Age* (London: Serif, 1995 [1969]), 217.
35. Vachel Lindsay, *Collected Poems* (New York: Macmillan Co., 1925 [1913]). For his extraordinary comments on masonry, theosophy and Egypt, see his preface, especially pages xxiv, xxix, xxxii.
36. Lindsay, "The Congo," *Collected Poems*, 178–84.
37. Haiti has long been the source and sustenance of the New World African imagination. See Edward J. Mullen, ed., *Langston Hughes in the Hispanic World and Haiti* (Hamden, CT: Archon Books, 1977), 30; and Milton Meltzer, *Langston Hughes, A Biography* (New York: Thomas Y. Crowell, 1968) for accounts of Hughes's travels to Haiti from Cuba, and his plays, poems, and operas composed about the island. Hughes's great-uncle, John Mercer Langston, had been the American minister to Haiti in the late 1880s.

Chapter 7 – Imperial Jazz

1. Peretti, Burton W. *The Creation of Jazz: Music, Race, and Culture in Urban America.* (Urbana: University of Illinois Press, 1992), 22.
2. Generic "latinidad" is a common feature of U.S. background music. When the Argentinian golfer Angel Cabrera won the U.S. Open in 2007, the PGA tour celebrated the event with a commercial of highlights from his victory against a soundtrack of hot salsa. This faux pas (since salsa is a Caribbean and New York, not Argentinian, form) is analogous to asking for *habichuelas* rather than *frijoles* in a Mexican restaurant.
3. The *Diccionario de la Música Española e Hispanoamericana* defines the *habanera*

as a "genre composed either in a major or a minor key in 2/4 time consisting of two cycles of eight beats each of which is repeated." According to the *Diccionario,* it "probably had the greatest durability of any musical genre, but is also and primarily a 'form' and a 'way of doing' ... rather than a set genre" (177–78).
4. Tamara Martín, *Las Habaneras son de la Habana* (Guatemala: Editorial Cultura, 1999), 4.
5. S. Frederick Starr in his biography of Gottschalk, *Bamboula: The Life and Times of Louis Moreau Gottschalk* (New York: Oxford University Press, 1995), sees the nineteenth-century Cuban composer Manuel Saumell as the initiator of a "lyrical, syncopated music" that stands at the head of the traditions later inherited by Gottschalk, Cervantes, Joplin, and others (184).
6. John Storm Roberts has been tireless in making this kind of case: for example, in *The Latin Tinge: The Impact of Latin American Music on the United States* (New York, Oxford: Oxford University Press, 1999). My discussion of the U.S.-Mexican connection is taken, among others, from his important book, *Latin Jazz: The First of the Fusions, 1880 to Today* (New York: Schirmer Books, 1999).
7. Storm Roberts, *The Latin Tinge,* 23.
8. George Eaton Simpson, *Black Religions in the New World* (New York: Columbia University Press, 1978), 58, 7, 19.
9. Robert Goffin, *Jazz: from the Congo to the Metropolitan,* Introduction by Arnold Gingrich (Garden City, NY: Doubleday, Doran & Co., 1944), 1.
10. Barry Ulanov, *A Handbook of Jazz,* Foreword by Kingsley Amis (London: Hutchinson, 1958), 4–6.
11. Rex Harris, *Jazz* (Melbourne, London: Penguin, 1958), 28 (Harris's emphasis).
12. Joachim Ernst Berendt, *The New Jazz Book: A History and Guide* (New York: Hill and Wang, 1962), 4–6.
13. Martin T. Williams, *Jazz Masters of New Orleans* (New York: Macmillan Co., 1967), xi.
14. Donald D. Megill and Richard S. Demory, *Introduction to Jazz History* (Englewood Cliffs, NJ: Prentice-Hall, c.1984), vii.
15. Henry Martin, *Enjoying Jazz* (New York: Schirmer Books, 1986), 4.
16. James Lincoln Collier, *Jazz: The American Theme Song* (New York: Oxford University Press, 1993), 1.
17. Martin Williams, *The Jazz Tradition* (New York: Oxford University Press, 1993), 3.
18. Alan Axelrod, *The Complete Idiot's Guide to Jazz* (New York, NY: Alpha Books, 1999), 38.
19. Geoffrey C. Ward, *Jazz: A History of America's Music,* 1st ed. (New York: Alfred A. Knopf, 2000), 25.
20. Peter Townsend, *Jazz in American Culture* (Edinburgh: Edinburgh University Press, 2000), 4.
21. Peretti, *The Creation of Jazz,* 23.
22. This chapter was composed before the appearance of Ned Sublette's *The World that Made New Orleans: From Spanish Silver to Congo Square* (New York: Lawrence Hill Books, 2008) – a history of the city, not only its music, that in regard to jazz takes up in our decade what Marshall Stearns began in the 1950s. See following footnote.
23. Marshall W. Stearns, *The Story of Jazz* (New York: Oxford University Press, 1956), 38.
24. Ibid., 42.
25. Martín, *Las Habaneras son de la Habana,* 12. Again, Bizet's famous *habanera* from the first act of *Carmen* was a version of a widely circulating song of the time, "*La arreglita*" (the little arrangement).

26. Irving Schwerke, *Kings Jazz and David* (Paris: Les Presses Modernes, 1927).
27. Isabelle Leymarie, *Cuban Fire: The Story of Salsa and Latin Jazz* (London, New York: Continuum, 1997), 2.
28. Helio Orovio, *Cuban Music from A to Z* (Durham: Duke University Press, 2004 [1992]), 23.
29. Iznaga moved to the United States in 1929 as an accomplished musician who had performed at the Teatro Nacional in Havana the year before. He lived in what is now Harlem, then a Puerto Rican barrio, on 113th Street and Madison, playing in all the five boroughs. An arranger who played clarinet and alto saxophone, in 1937 he became a sideman for the bandleader Augusto Coen.
30. Orovio, *Cuban Music from A to Z*, 24.
31. Leonardo Acosta, *Otra visión de la música popular cubana* (La Habana: Letras Cubanas, 2004), 163.
32. Ibid., 164.
33. Ibid., 165.
34. See on this point Michael Ventura, *Shadow Dancing in the U.S.A.* (New York: St. Martin's; Los Angeles: Jeremy P. Tarcher, 1985). Ventura's excellent chapter, "Hear that Long Snake Moan," bears witness, nevertheless, to American exceptionalism: "What Buddy Bolden started to play was American music. Within thirty years its impact would make an American tune instantly distinguishable from a European tune, no matter how strait-laced the music" (138). The weakness of this approach is evident when he points out that the "brass band was already an American tradition when Sousa marches swept the country in the 1890s" (136), as though that were an early date or as though the brass influence did not come more forcefully from south of the U.S. "South."
35. Cristóbal Díaz Ayala, *Cuando Salí de la Habana: 1898–1997: cien años de música cubana por el mundo* (San Juan: Fundación Musicalia, 2001), 32–33.
36. Gary Giddins in Ken Burns, *Jazz* (Episode One, "Gumbo").
37. See, for example, even an essay on this theme from a much more progressive era than our own: Robert Goffin's "Hot Jazz" in Nancy Cunard, ed., *Negro: An Anthology* (New York and London: Continuum, 2002 [1934]), 238–39: "It is scarcely necessary to repeat that jazz is Afro-American music, developed in the U.S.A. during the war, and attaining its maximum of expression during the period 1920–1930."
38. Richard Wright, *12 Million Black Voices: A Folk History of the Negro in the United States* (New York: Viking, 1941), 127–30.
39. Ibid., 127–28.
40. Thomas Fiehrer, "From Quadrille to Stomp: The Creole Origins of Jazz," *Popular Music* 10: 1 (January 1991), 21–38. Other pioneering work of this sort has been done by Ernest Borneman, "Creole Echoes," *Jazz Review* 2: 8 (September 1959), 13–15; "Creole Echoes: Part II," *Jazz Review* 2: 10 (November 1959), 26–27); and "Jazz and the Creole Tradition," *Jazzforschung* 1, 99–112. I have already mentioned John Storm Roberts above.
41. Christopher Washburne, "The Clave of Jazz: A Caribbean Contribution to the Rhythmic Foundation of an African American Music," *Black Music Research Journal* 17: 1 (Spring 1997), 59.
42. Ibid., 63–64.
43. Ibid., 65.
44. This point about "clave," although found in Washburne as well, is discussed in a number of Latin American musical sources – for example, Rebeca Mauleón's *Salsa: Guidebook for Piano and Ensemble* (Petaluma, CA: Sher Music Co., 1993).
45. See the transcription reproduced in Washburne, "The Clave of Jazz," 70–76.
46. Washburne, "The Clave of Jazz," 75.
47. See, in this respect, Robert G. O'Meally, ed., *The Jazz Cadence of American*

Culture (New York: Columbia University Press, 1998). The volume offers what appears to be the entire spectrum of opinion drawing on a variety of styles and schools from several generations: Sterling Brown on the blues as "folk poetry," Ralph Ellison on "The Golden Age," Bill Evans on "Improvisation," and even "Michael Jordan and the Pedagogy of Desire." But this promise of comprehensiveness is illusory. In a 638-page book, there is almost nothing on Latin music.

48. Gilbert Chase, *America's Music from the Pilgrims to the Present* (New York: McGraw-Hill, 1955), 166.
49. Leymarie, *Cuban Fire*, 2.
50. Ibid., xi.
51. Phil Schapp, WKCR-FM, Monday 4 July 2005, 3:45 p.m.
52. Leymarie, *Cuban Fire*, 78–79.
53. James Weldon Johnson, *Black Manhattan* (New York: Alfred A. Knopf, 1930).
54. The martial context, ignored by Burns and others, is narrated in Samuel B. Charters and Leonard Kunstad, *Jazz: A History of the New York Scene* (Garden City, NY: Doubleday & Co., 1962), 65.
55. Ibid., 68. In Ruth Glasser, *My Music is My Flag: Puerto Rican Musicians and Their New York Communities 1917–1940* (Berkeley: University of California, 1995), the author recalls that the slogan " 'Jazz Won the War!' arose among the music's most ardent fans at the end of 1918" (52). She is referring not only to the role played by 400,000 African-American soldiers but to those "recruited directly from Puerto Rico, [who] were among the pioneers who introduced jazz to France."
56. Charters and Kunstad, *Jazz: A History of the New York Scene*, 66.
57. Washburne, "The Clave of Jazz," 63. Leonardo Acosta, *Elige Tu, que canto yo* (Habana: Editorial Letras Cubanas, 1993), 7. Acosta observes that to say "military band" was for many at the turn of the century redundant. Military bands were for turn-of-the-century performers, "one of the few places that a musician could count on a stable salary."
58. Washburne, "The Clave of Jazz," 65.
59. Alejo Carpentier, *Music in Cuba*, ed. and introduced by Timothy Brennan (Minneapolis: University of Minnesota, 2001), 150–51.
60. Martin, *Enjoying Jazz*, 24.
61. Neil A. Lewis, "Fresh Details Emerge on Harsh Methods at Guantanamo," Saturday, 1 January 2005, *New York Times* Web site.
62. Ibid., p. 2. See also "You Have to See This," *Harpers* 314: 1882 (March 2007), 22: "the detainee was almost unconscious on the floor with a pile of hair next to him (he had apparently been pulling it out throughout the night). Another time, it was sweltering hot and loud rap music played . . . We observed sleep-deprivation interviews with strobe lights and loud music."
63. Whitney Joiner, "The Army be Thuggin' it," *Salon.com* (17 October 2003). The 2003 Army is 16 percent black, compared with 11 percent of the country, and 13.4 percent Latino, compared with 11 percent of the country (3). The Vital Marketing Group has teamed up with rap magazine *The Source*, for a sponsored tour.
64. Teresa Talerico, "Hispanic-Owned Firm Wins U.S. Army Contract" *Hispanic Business.com* (6 October 2000), http://www.hispanicbusiness.com/news/newsbyid.asp?id = 1710&cat = Magazine&more = /magazine/.
65. Amanda Onion, "Listen UP: Unusual Forms of Sound to Emanate from RNC," ABCNEWS.com, reprinted in *Truthout Issues*, 26 August 2004. "Intrepid entrepreneur" Elwood (Woody) Norris, founder and head of American Technology Corp. of San Diego, invented LRAD both as a "crowd control tool" and as a "display audio technology," in which case it is called HyperSonic Sound (HSS).
66. Virginia Heffernan, "Heavy Metal and Rap Amid Sand and Battle," video is "Soundtrack to War," *New York Times* (18 August 2004), 8–18, B3.

67. Eliot Weinberger, "What I Heard About Iraq in 2005," *London Review of Books* 28: 1 (5 January 2006), 8.
68. George Eaton Simpson, *Black Religions in the New World* (New York: Columbia University Press, 1978), 19.
69. Washburne, "The Clave of Jazz," 62.
70. I take this phrase from John Storm Roberts, who in *The Latin Tinge: The Impact of Latin American Music on the United States*, writes: "Many Afro-U.S. rhythmic patterns are similar to Afro-Latin rhythms, for the very good reason of a common heritage, even though the Anglo-Saxon element in the black U.S. music mostly forced those rhythms into the four-square context of common time" (42).
71. Martin, *Enjoying Jazz*, 28–29.
72. But see Frank Kofsky, *Black Nationalism and the Revolution in Music* (New York: Pathfinder, 1970), 109–21. Frank Kofsky has described the attempt to colonize bebop after World War II, and has gone so far as to call it the "secret weapon of the Cold War": "Even the name of the style itself – *cool* – reflected the change. It would never have occurred to anyone who knew the music to refer to bebop as "cool," for bebop was above all a music of engagement, with the feelings of the players, especially its symbolic leader, Charlie Parker, out in the open for all to see. As a style, cool was anything but that; it was the quintessence of individual *dis*-engagement."
73. Acosta, *Elige Tu, que canto yo*, 48. He reports that Chick Webb's band in the 1930s was "one of the great black jazzbands of the period next to that of Count Basie and Duke Ellington" (46). Bauzá played the trumpet and was music director. Together with Webb, they discovered the young Ella Fitzgerald.
74. Martin, *Enjoying Jazz*, 17.
75. Kofsky, *Black Nationalism and the Revolution in Music*, 31.
76. In "Hear that Long Snake Moan" (op. cit.), Ventura argues that in blues "the beat was so implicit that the African, for the first time, didn't need a drum. The hold drum, the drum that is always silent, lived in the blues. One man with a guitar could play the blues and his entire tradition would be alive in his playing" (137). I find this observation inaccurate. The weight over generations of Protestant worship, slavery, and then semi-slavery crushed the drum, and drove the music down different paths. At the very least we might say that Afro-Latin music is the blues plus the drum, dragging the European concert into its own quarter rather than, as in the United States, carving out a space of marginal nobility.

Illustration Credits

Every effort has been made to trace the copyright holder of the images used in this book. Verso and the author would like to extend their gratitude to all of those who have provided permission for their work to be reproduced here.

1.1 Images on Putumayo CD covers © Putumayo World Music, 411 Lafayette, 4th Floor, New York, NY 10003.
1.2 *Flying Down to Rio* (1933), dir. Thornton Freeland, written by Lou Brock and Anne Caldwell © RKO Pictures, Los Angeles, CA 90067.
1.3 *Written on the Wind* (1956), dir. Douglas Sirk © Universal International Pictures.
1.4 Gigi (Ejigayehu Shibabaw), artist photo.
1.5 Koffi Olomide © Africa Hit Music TV 2006.
2.1 The *cinquillo* rhythmic phrase. Alejo Carpentier, *Music in Cuba* (Minneapolis: University of Minnesota Press, 2001), 148.
2.2 The rhythm for the *cinquillo*, the *tresillo*, and the clave and pulse. Samuel Floyd, "Black Music in the Circum-Caribbean," *Journal of American Music* 17: 1 (Spring 1999), 30; Rebeca Mauleón, *Salsa: Guidebook for Piano and Ensemble* (Petaluma, CA: Sher Music Co., 1993).
2.3 The notation of the habanera rhythm in the *contradanza*. Alejo Carpentier, *Music in Cuba* (Minneapolis: University of Minnesota Press, 2001), 158; Ángel G. Quintero Rivera, *Salsa sabor y control: sociología de la música tropical* (Coyoacán & Madrid: Siglo Veintiuno Editores, 1998).
5.1 *National Geographic*, August 1999 © National Geographic Society.
5.2 Pedro Coll, *El Tiempo Detenido: La Habana* (Barcelona: Lunwerg Editores, 1995), 52.
5.3 René Burri, *Cuba y Cuba*, text by Marco Meier, poetry by Miguel

Barnet (Washington, DC: Smithsonian, 1995), 58. © René Burri/ Magnum Photos, 1994.
6.1 and 6.2 Images from W. Kirk MacNulty, *Freemasonry: A Journey Through Ritual and Symbol* (New York: Thames and Hudson, 1991), 66, 72.
6.3 Alfred Métraux, *Voodoo in Haiti* (edition unknown).
6.4 Alfred Métraux, *Voodoo in Haiti* (New York: Oxford University Press, 1959).
6.5 and 6.6 Ishmael Reed, *Mumbo Jumbo* (New York: Scribner's, 1996).
6.7 Image from Vachel Lindsay, *Collected Poems* (New York: Macmillan, 1925).
7.1 Painting by Kdir (Kadir Lopez) © Kadir Lopez.
7.2 "Lt. Europe Stirring Up the Band," cover image from R2C2 H2, *James Reese Europe: Jazz Lieutenant* (Charleston, SC: Booksurge, 2005).
7.3 "Regimental band, 13th Minnesota Volunteer Infantry, Manila, P.I." © Minnesota Historical Society, St. Paul, MN.

PLATES
1 "Son." Argeliers León, *Del Canto y el tiempo* (Editorial Letras Cubanas, Ciudad de La Habana, Cuba, 1984), 149.
2 "Danzón." Argeliers León, *Del Canto y el tiempo* (Editorial Letras Cubanas, Ciudad de La Habana, Cuba, 1984), 285.
3 "Solace: A Mexican Serenade." Scott Joplin, *Complete Piano Rags*, with an introduction by Max Morath (New York: G. Shirmer, Inc, 1998), 187.
4 "La Celosa." Ignacio Cervantes, *Tres Danzas y tres contradanzas* (Habana, Cuba: Editora Musical de Cuba, 1975), 16.

Index

Abakuá ceremony, 66
Abolition, 6
Abreu, Zeguinha, 115
Absolutism, 9
Accreditation, 73
Acosta, Leonardo, 8, 52, 58, 64, 148, 153, 158, 220–21, 239–40
Adorno, Theodor, 90–99, 101, 102; critique of jazz, 238
Aerial bombing, 106
Aeschylus, 197
Aesop Rock, 128
Afghanistan: U.S. invasion, 162, 235
Africa: African music: beat of, 57, 74; social commentary in, 4; capitalism in, 3–4; New World African belief-systems, 191
African-American: immigrants to Cuba, 222; vernacular English, 125
African-American culture: African subtext to, 1–2; counterpart in Latin America and the Caribbean, 191; popcult theory in, 32; popular classicism, 68. *See also* Black American Culture
"African Songs" (Willem Grosz), 35
Afro-Cuban: cultural achievement, 55–56; instruments, 148; migration to Mexico, 74; music, 24, 33–34; antagonistic concept to world music, 54–55; history of, 52–53; relation to jazz, 53, 78; rhythm patterns and jazz, 222; syncopation in, 80
Afro-Cubanism, 150–51
Afro-Cuban Music (Ortiz), 99
Afro-Latin music, 95; classicism of, 14; future of, 241; global spread of, 5–6; religious element in, 66
Agitprop, 110–11
Albanian epic music: narrative content of, 20
Albums, total-concept, 94; replaced by single cut, 140
Alea, Tomás Guittiérez, 162–63
Alexandrian sacred texts, 206
Algeria: *rai* music, 43
Ali G, 128
Alimaña, Juanito, 178
Ali, Muhammad, 127
Allegories, 6
"All Glocks Down," 138
Allman Brothers, 42
All-star wrestling, 130
Alonso, Rodrigo, 176
American culture and tradition, 12, 21

American film, 12
American jazz, 21
American War of Independence: "Battalions of Pardos and Morenos," 221
America's Music: The Pilgrims to the Present (Chase), 226–27
Amharic, 45, 46
Amisen, Fred ("Ferecito"), 41
Amplified music, 84
Amusing Ourselves to Death (Postman), 164
Anacaona, 172
Ancient Model, 197–98
Andalusia, Spain, 61, 77
An Essay on Liberation (Marcuse), 91
Anonymity *vs.* signature, 98–99
Antheil, George, 57–58, 74–75; on 1920–25 trend in music, 8
Anthony, Marc: *El Cantante,* 115
Antolítia, Gloriá, 52, 148
Apis, 206
Appropriation, 128–29
Arab Africa, 66
Arabic popular music, 43
Arab Spain, 66
Aragon, Louis, 51
Arara, 3
Arce, Bayardo, 108
Argentina: tango, 77
Aristide, Jean-Bertrand, 182
Armstrong, Louis, 53, 228, 240–41
"The Army Be Thuggin' It" (Joiner), 234
Arnaz, Desi, 90, 115, 222
Arroyo, Joe, 112
Articulation. *See* "voice"
Artistic freedom: political and commercial constraints, 160–61
Artistry, individual, 46
"Aryan model," 197
"Asi se compone un son" (Ismael Miranda and Orquesta Revelación), 71
Aspiazu, Justo (Don), 220
Assassins (secret society), 201–2
Astaire, Fred, 37
Asturias, Miguel Ángel, 56
Aton, 189–90, 194
Attali, Jacques, 51, 56, 66, 98, 229
Attitude: The Dancers' Magazine, 22–23
Attribution, issue of, 78

Authenticity, 83–84, 89–93, 96; and African spirituality, 113; defense of, 13, 48; defined, 13, 89–90; false, 58, 84–86; and nostalgia, 83; origin myths and, 86, 90; prejudice against, 116
Authoritarian personality, 99
Autobiography of an Ex-Colored Man (Johnson), 80
Avant-garde, 79, 174; anachronism of its popularity, 33; and anticolonialism, 50–53; Ernst Bloch on, 56; European, 50–53; imaginative repertoire of corporate mass culture, 52–53; and radio, 30; social conscience of, 79–82
Avilés, Bartolo, 74
Aztec sacred texts, 206
Azúcar Negro, 158

Babalú (San Lazaro), 66
Babenco, Hector: *Pixote,* 175
Baez, Sonia, 169
Baigent, Michael, 199
Baker, Houston, 28
Baldwin, James, 207
Balkans, 20
Ballroom music, 1, 236
Bambaataa, Afrika, 118, 130
La Bamba, 115
Banera (notation), *85*
Baraka, Amiri, 80, 81, 127–28, 184
Barnet, Miguel, 154
Barretto, Ray, 68, 72, 89, 119
Barroso, Ary, 115
Bartók, Béla, 96
Bata drumming, 23, 69
Battista, Fulgencio, 163
Bauzá, Mario, 68–69, 222, 226, 239–40
"Bay of Pigs" invasion, 152
Beatles, The 90, 94
Beat (musical): literary component to, 120; that is not there, 57
Beat Street (Hager), 117
Beatty, Paul, 80
Bebop, 31, 32, 75, 81, 239
Bebop prosody, 184
Bechet, Sidney, 220
Beethoven, Ludwig van, 94
"Bel airs" (light songs), 80
Benin, 20
Benjamin, Goodwin, 119
Bennet, Arnold, 89
Bennet, Lerone, Jr., 207
Bent pitches, 238
Bernal, Martin, 197, 201
Bernstein, Leonard, 79
Betancourt, Justo, 120
Betancur, Belisario, 178
Bhangra music, 20, 44
Biassou, Jean François, 3–4
Bible, 183, 192, 202; *ff*.45. *See also* Book; Lost texts
Bibliografía Cubana, 148
Biblioteca Nacional José Martí, 148
Big band jazz, 217
Big band *mambo*, 68–69
Biggie Smalls, 30
Big L, 126–27
Biguine music, 74
Billy DeLisle, 121
Black American culture: avant-garde poetry, 80,

208; bohemia, 33, 80; classical composers in U.S. (1829–1880), 76; classical musicians (1800–1840), 74; jazz bands, 222; oral history, 183
Black Islam, 143, 184
"Black Mud Sound," 189, 199, 206, 212
Black Nationalism, 143
Black Panther Movement, 143
Blades, Ruben: *Crossover Dreams*, 115
Bland, James, 76
Blavatsky, Madame Helene, 193
Blige, Mary J., 129
Bloch, Ernst, 56–57
Blues, 1, 14, 21, 84–85, 92, 121, 238; blues-rooted music, 240; delta, 87; Marcuse on, 91; and rock, 43
Boast, the, 118, 134; in salsa, 135–36
"Boat people," 163
Body/mind dichotomy, 238
Boef-sur-leToit (Milhaud), 57
Bogotá, Colombia: murder of "disposables," 177
Bohemians, 33, 54, 75, 76, 77, 79–82, 128; black/red, 52; and *son,* in New York, 67–68, 74, 75, 76, 79–82; subcultures, 81
Boire, Richard Glenn, 235
Bola de Nieve (Ignacio Jacinto Fernández Villa): "Chivo que Rompe Tambo," 136
Bolden, Buddy, 215, 220
Bolero, 64, 69, 76, 149
Bollywood, 43, 44
Bolshevism, 52, 57
Bond, James, 36
Bongo percussion, 61
"Bonito y sobroso" (Benny Moré), 70
Book of Geb, 198
Book of the Dead, 198–99
Book of Thoth, 189–90, 206–7
Bop poetry, 80
Border demarcations, 9
Borges, Jorge Luis, 103
Botijuela, 61
Boukmann (Haitian revolutionary), 3–4
Bourgeoisie, international, 32
"Boutique music," 24–25
Boyd, Todd, 144
Brand New Day (Sting), 43
Brand Nubian, 132
Brando, Marlon, 39
Brass bands, military, 230
Brathwaite, Edward Kamau: on "culture of the circle," 11
Braxton, Tony, 24
Brazil, 3, 57
Brecht, Bertolt, 171
Breton, André, 82
Bridge (song element), 214
Brindis de Salas, Claudio, 151
Broadway, 79
Bronx, New York, 118
Broughton, Simon, 19–20
Brown, Dan, 199–200
Bruno, Giordano, 208
Budge, E. A.: *Osiris: The Egyptian Religion of Resurrection*, 193
Buena Vista Social Club, 8, 58, 153
Buñuel, Luis: *Los Olvidados*, 175
Burns, Ken: *Jazz*, 222–23
Burri, René: *Cuba y Cuba* (photo), *170*

INDEX

Burroughs, William, 79
Bush, George W., 170

Cabildos, 51, 113
Cabral, Emilcar, assassination of, 17
Cabrera, Lydia, on *Reglas de Congo*, 151
Los Cachimbos, 119–20
Cairo, Egypt, 154
Cajón percussion, 61
Calenda, 5
Calloway, Cab, 127, 226, 238
Calypso, 6, 7, 62, 78, 113
Camp Delta, Guantánamo, 234
Candy, John, 115
"El Cantante" (Hector Lavoe), 71
Canto General (Neruda), 64
Cape Verde archipelago, 17–18
Capitalism, pleasure and desire in, 168
Capo, Bobby: "El Negro bembón," 111–12
Cardenal, Ernesto, 104, 105, 108
Carew, Jan, 207
Caribbean: African presence in, 2, 44; dances, 64; social and cultural theory, 34
Caribbean music: and global cultural influence, 56–58
"Carioca" (dance), 37
Carnival, 80
Carpentier, Alejo, 6, 52, 60–61, 77, 113, 148–49, 150, 151, 184, 225–26; novels, 79–80, 101; on two-part rhythmical structure, 64
"El carretero," 71
Carrey, Jim, 115
"Carry Me Back to Old Virginia" (Bland), 76
Cartel Creativo, Inc., 234
Caruso, Enrico, 79
Casa de las Americas, 154, 163
Casamitjana (Catalan composer), 233
Casaubon, Isaac, 196–97
Cass, Don A.: *Negro Freemasonry and Segregation*, 194
Castle, Irene and Vernon, 187–88
Castro, Fidel, 146, 148, 172
Categorization, 29
Catholicism, French and Spanish, 237
Catholic secret societies, 200
Cedar Tavern, New York City, 79
"La Celosa" (Cervantes), 214
Celtic music, 20
Censorship, 79, 106, 147
Center for Cognitive Liberty and Ethics, 235
Central America: contra war in, 157
Cerezo, Vinicio, 108
Cervantes, Ignacio, 76, 213–14, 221, 228
Chaabi music, 24
Chachachá, 58, 64, 69, 158
Chaconne, 60
Chadha, Gurinder, 44
Chamorro, Pedro Joaquin, 105
"Chan-chan," 58
"Chango 'ta Beni" (Machito), 113–14
Channel 16, 138
Charanga (arrangement), 68, 119
Charanga Habana, 158
Charen, Mona, 124
Chase, Charlie, 118
Chase, Gilbert, 226–27

"Cheapos" (record store), 34
Chimurenga, 20
"Chivo que Rompe Tambo" (Bola de Nieve), 136
Chorus, 92
Christianity, 183; African origins of, 183, 200; and Hellenism, 196–97; revival, 7; sensuality and, 200
Christian Right, 135
El Chuchumbé (dance), 71
Chuck D, 135
Cinquillo rhythm, 49, 62, 225; notation, 59, 63
City of God (Meirelles and Lund), 175
Civilizations, comparative value of, 10
Civil rights movement, 6, 144; destruction of, seen as counter-movement, 117
Clarke, John Henrick, 207
Class, 144
Classical music: black composers, 76; Cuban, 148; seriousness of, 92–93; theory and themes in, 94; as world music, 12, 21
Classicism: Cuban, European, and Hindustani, 73–74; in Latin and jazz popular music, 61–63
Classics, Latinized, 115
Clave, 64, 65, 73, 225; notation, 62, 63
Clef Club Orchestra, 76
Clinton, Bill, 135
Clooney, Rosemary, 96
CNN, 135
"The Cocacabana," 114
Cockburn, Patrick, 233–34
Cold War, 35, 163
Cole, Nat King, 2, 3
Coleridge, Samuel Taylor, 76
Collazo, Fernando, 53
Coll, Pedro: *El Tiempo Detenido: La Habana* (photo), 168
Colombia, 13; alienated youth in, 174–81; invasion, 162
Colombia Without Guerrillas, 177
Colonialism, 3, 6, 53, 56, 212
Colón, Jesus: *A Puerto Rican in New York*, 152
Coltrane, John, 228, 238
Commerce: and authenticity, 12, 43, 79, 86–87
Common, 142–43
"Las Communas" (barrio), 177
Communist Youth rally (Cuba), 172
Como, Perry: "Papa Loves Mamba," 115
Concert hall orchestra, 236
Conga (instrument), 73
Congo: Congo peoples, 3; musical styles and rhythms, 48; Olomide, Koffi, 47–48
The Congo (Vachel Lindsay), 210–11
Conjunto (arrangement), 68
Connor, A. J., 76
Conspicuous consumption, 171
Conspiracy theories, 199, 212
Constant, Benjamin, 182
"3 Continents Film Festival" (South Africa), 18
Contradanza, 60, 61, 214; notation, 77; origins of, 76–77
Contras, 105–6
Cook, Will Marion, 76
"Cool" jazz, 239
Cornet, 220
Cornish, Willie, 215
Coro-pregón, 64
Coros de guaguancó, 65

279

Costa Rica, 106
Costume, 50
Cotton Club (Harlem), 207, 238
Count Basie, 239
Counter-monotheism. *See* Secular devotion
Creole ballads, 60
Creole elite, 75
Creole pianists, 78
Critical segregation, 8
Crosby, Bing, 92
Crouch, Stanley, 126
Crowley, Aleister, 192, 208
Crusades, 190, 202
Cruz, Celia, 72–73, 156
Cuadra, Pablo Antonio, 104
Cuba, 156–57; African religious practices in, 54; centrality of as musical innovation transporter, 78; Cuban classical composers, 76, 77, 148; Cuban dances, 64; economic sacrifices, 169, 171–73; educational philosophies, 151; exiles, 163; genuine popular culture in, 165; government restrictions on the arts, 147; government support of the arts, 148–49; hip hop movement, 143; historical background, 23–24; history of music in, 163; influence in sport, 155; international cultural influence, 12, 13, 153–56; isolation of, as source of musical innovation, 23–24, 102; 26 July Movement, 147, 151; middle class, 74; music criticism in, 6; music, global success of, 81; noncommercial musical culture, 79; popular music, 148, 154; prostitution in, 169–73; race relations in, 159; Revolution, 110; and race, 148, 163–64; self-sufficiency in agriculture and biotechnology, 170; slave trade, 3; socialist culture, 155; the "special period," financial pressures of, 172–73
Cuban music: expansion of, 78–79; rap in, 135, 173; rhythms, 68–69; scholarship, 149–50; theatrical performance presentation, 50
Cubism: African forms in, 33
Cubop, 220
Cugat, Xavier, 67–68, 115
Cultural imperialism, 28, 105, 178
Cultural resistance, 177–78
Culture, transgressive, 54–56
Cuplé, 64

Dada, 51, 82; African influence in, 33
Dancehall music, 20
Dance music: African New World, 98; Latin, 53; Spanish New World, 60
Dance numbers, 37
Dancing in the Distraction Factory (Goodwin), 164
Daniel, Yvonne, 152, 161
Danza, 77, 214, 219
Danzón, 69, 75; *cantado*, 64; Cuban derivation of, 77; *de ritmo nuevo*, 64; rhythms, 61; sexuality in, 75
Darío, Rubén, 103
The Da Vinci Code (Brown), 199–201
Davis, Miles, 240
Day, Doris, 41
"The Days of Old," 139
Debray, Régis, 10
Debt coercion, U.S., 159, 161
Decima (verse form), 60
Def Jam, 143

Deities, 3, 66, 113; Afro-Caribbean, 3; Apis, 206; Aton, 189–90, 194; Babalú (San Lazaro), 66; Ezili, 3; Legba (Eshu-Elegba), 3, 113, 193; Ochun, 66; Ogu/Ogun, 3; *orishas*, 66; Osiris, 189, 193; San Lazaro (Babalú), 66; Shango, 3; Thoth, 193, 206; Yemayá (Yemanja), 66, 188
Delaney, Paul, 125–26
Delta, 32
Demythification: neo-African popular culture and, 49–50
Designer radicalism, 165
Desire and pleasure: compelled in capitalist system, 167–68; systems of, 167–68
Desnoës, Edmund, 163
Desquite (bandit), 178
Deuoudray, Halaou, 3–4
Devotion, 66; secularity of, 216. *See also* Secular devotion
Diaz Ayala, Cristóbal, 78, 79
Dictatorship: and surveillance, 103
Diddley, Bo, 127, 130
Did the Blood Scare You? (Ramirez), 104
Digital Underground, 129
Dionysian celebrant on Greek vase (illustration), 205
Dirty notes, 238
DJ Premier, 131
DJ Red Alert, 128
DJs, 128; "scratching" technique, 140
Documentary testimony, 130
Von Dohnányi, Ernst (Ernö), 96
Dole, Bob, 135
Domestic minorities: and transnational majority, 32
Domination, female, 140–41
Double-consciousness, 2
Doubleness, 33–34
Double register, 70
Dr. Dre (gangsta rapper), 123
Dreaming in Cuban (Garcia), 171
Drum, 216
Du Bois, W.E.B., 1–2, 34, 224; *Souls of Black Folk*, 184
Duo los Compadres: "Pagame la caña bien," 110
Dvôrak, Anton: Romany dances, 28
Dylan, Bob, 85, 87

East Africa, 44; origins of humanity in, 191
East Coast rap, 123
Eastern Mediterranean, 182
East/West split, 29–30, 32
"Ebonics" (Big L), 126–27
"Echale salsita" (Piñeiro), 75
Eckholm, Eric, 125
Egypt, 191; myths, 194; pre-dynastic, 182–83, 189, 191
"Egyptian Rite," *193*
Egyptomania, 191, 208
Ejigayehu "Gigi" Shibabaw, 44–46, 45 (photo), 48
"Elements of Western metaphysics as represented by Masonic symbols" (illustration), 195
Ellingham, Mark, 19–20
Ellington, Duke, 46, 79, 220, 226, 228, 239; "Black Beauty," 238–39
Ellison, Ralph: on jazz as an art of individual assertion, 228

INDEX

El Salvador, 179–80
Emigration: economic, 163, 222
Eminem, 132–34
English country dance, 76
Enlightenment, European, 101–2
Entertainment: state of, in U.S., 164
Eroticism, 36–38
Esperanto, 82
Espinoza, Julio Garcia, 154
Ethics, 7
Ethiopia, 44–46, 208
Ethiopian Church, 46
Ethnomusicology, 29, 75
Ethopian groove: dancehall music, 20
European classicism, 21; influence of dance forms, 97–98
Europe, James Reese, 230
Evangelical religion: and slavery, 237
Evora, Cesaria, 16–18
Évora, Tony, 161
Exile: economic, 163
Experience of representation of things, 20
Ezili, 3

Fado music (Portugal), 18
Faílde, Miguel, 69
Falsetto, 238
Fandango, variations on, 149
Fania All-Stars, 24
Far East, 20
Farrakhan, Louis, 130
Farrés, Osvaldo, 35, 41, 115
Fear of a Black Planet (Public Enemy), 94–95
Feijóo, Samuel, 60, 62, 80, 148, 149; research on the *son*, 80
Feliciano, Cheo, 120
Fellow travellers, 51
Female mack, 138–39, 140–41
Fernandez, Sujatha, 173
Fernandez, Vicente, 109
Fernández Villa, Ignacio Jacinto. *See* Bola de Nieve
Ficino, Marsilio, 194–95
Fieher, Thomas, 8; on Afro-Latin roots of jazz, 225
Film and theater: 1920s and 1930s, 12
Fitzgerald, F. Scott, 223
Flavor Flav, 138
Flores, Juan, 118
Florida: Cuban exiles in, 163
Floyd, Samuel A.: on rhythms of the "circum-Caribbean," 49–50
Fly Girls, 141
Flying Down to Rio, 37, 38
Folk epic, proletarian, 112–13
Folk/punk music, 42
Folktales, Afro-Cuban, 151
Fon culture, 3
Foreignness, utility of, 42
Form, musical: as it relates to peoples and world views, 14–16
Foster, Stephen, 185
Four-square common time, 238
France: New World colonies, 59, 219
Frankfurt School (1940s and 1950s), 99; assumptions, 97–98; on viability of authenticity, 90–91
Frank, Thomas: *Commodify Your Dissent*, 165–66

FRAPH, 182
Freemasonry, 184, 194, *195*
"Free Mumia" (KRS-One), 127
French colonial immigration, 60, 220
French Revolution: and Masonic rationalism, 197
Frente Sandinista, 104
"Frente Ventana," 105
Freud, Sigmund, 208, 212
Fritas music, 51, 66
Fuentes, Sanchez de, 75
Funkmaster Flex, 128
Funk tradition, 131
Fusion music, 42–43, 44–45, 139; European and African, 61
Futurism, 82

Gabriel, Peter, 47
Gandhi, Mohandas (Mahatma): *swadeshi* movement, 167
Gangsta rap, 30, 123, 135, 136, 142
Gang Starr, 120, 129, 131
Ganguly, Keya, 90
Ganja-vegetarianism, 31
Garcia, Alejandro, 76
Garcia, Christina: *Dreaming in Cuban*, 171
Garcia Espinoza, Julio, 154
Garland, Judy, 92
Gaviria, Victor, 175–76; *Rodrigo D.: No Futuro*, 174–77, 180–81
Gawwali music from Punjab and Pakistan, 44
Gebrauchmusik, 82
Genius, musical: Ernst Bloch on, 56
Gentrification, 119
Germany: Turkish communities, 135
Gershwin, George, 33; *Cuban Overture*, 75
Ghazal (urdu), 44
Giddens, Gary, 223
Gigi (Ejigayehu Shibabaw), 44–46, 45 (photo), *46*, 48
Gilbert, Elizabeth Rosanna. *See* Montez, Lola
Gil, Gilberto, 27
Gillespie, Dizzy, 220, 223
Ginsberg, Alan, 80
"Girl from Ipanema," 114
Glasser, Ruth, 12
Glissant, Edouard, 55
Globalization: and exile, 162; and socialism, 162; and youth culture, 161–67
Global rap, 236
Gnosticism, 196
God, and technological invention, 10
God: An Itinerary (Debray), 10
Gold Age: Spanish poets of, 60
Goncourt, Jules, 89
Gonzáles, Sammy, 72
González, Celina, 113
Gordillo, Fernando, 105
Gottschalk, Louis Moreau, 78, 214, 219, 228
"Gradas," 105
Graffiti movement, 117–18
Gramsci, Antonio: on collective selfishness, 171
Gran Combo, 112, 119, 156
Grand Master Flash, 127
"Great Awakening," 237
Greece, 182
Greenberg, Clement, 99

Greenwich Village, 81
Gregory, Dick, 130
Grenet, Eliseo, 81
Grosz, Willem, 35
Growling Tiger (calypsonian), 78
"La Guabina," 77
Guaguancó, 37, 58, 68, 72–73, 156
Guantanamera, 114, 149
Guaracha, 61, 73, 149
Guatemala, 108
Guillén, Nicolás, 80, 151, 163, 184
Guinea Bissau, 17
Guiro (instrument), 73
Güiros, 53
Guitar music, 94
Guitarra Armada (Mejiia Godoy), 106–8
Guittiérez Alea, Tomás, 162–63
Gulf region, 20
Guns, 107–8
Guthrie, Woody, 85, 87
Guys and Dolls, 38–39, 42

Habanera, 77, 78, 214–15, 219, 220, 225
Hager, Steven, 117
Haiti, 3, 59, 102; exiles in Cuba, 225, 77; mercenaries, 182; revolution, 4; slave revolt, 59; U.S. occupation (1915–1932), 14, 182
Hancock, Herbie, 46
Handy, W. C. (William Christopher), 188, 215, 225, 228
Hannerz, Ulf, 154
Happiness: as feature of Caribbean music, 73
Harding, Warren G., 80, 182, 185, 186–87
Harlem: black migration to, 229
Harlem Renaissance, 14, 75, 182, 183, 184, 187, 207
The Harp and the Shadow (Carpentier), 80, 101
Harrison, George, 94
Havana, Cuba, 50, 60, 66, 215; golden age of traditional Cuban music, 8; *santeros* of, 69
Havana Film Festival, 154
Hawthorne, Nathaniel, 208
Haywood, Col. William, 230
"Hear that Long Snake Moan," (Ventura), 84
Heather B., 138–39, 140, 141
Heavy metal music: as war tool, 235–36
Heidegger, Martin, 66–67
Heliopolis, 200
Hemmenway, James, 76
Henderson, Fletcher, 225
Hermes Trismegistus, 193, 194–96
Hermetica, 194–95
Hermeticism, 208–9
Hernández, Germán Bode, 149
Herodotus, 197
Heroin trade, 117
Hijuelos, Oscar, 154
Hill, Edwin, 76
Hindemith, Paul, 82
Hip-hop, 118–19; in Cuba, as politically charged, 143; as foreign, 29; involvement of Latinos in, 117–18; Jamaican disk jockeys and, 127; and Latin beat, 118; as lifestyle, 117; lineage and culture of, 123, 126; used as army recruitment tool, 234
History of Greece (Mitford), 201
Hit parade, 35

Hits, types of, 92
Holism, 66, 69, 120, 131
Hollywood, 68
Hollywood films, 39–41; background music, 35–39, 41–42; Latin music and dance in, 36–37, 42
Holy Blood, Holy Grail (Baigent/Leigh/Lincoln), 199
Honduras, 106
Hooker, John Lee, 84
Horkheimer, Max, 90
"Hot 97" (97.1 FM), 137–38
Houdini, Wilmot, 78
Howard, Adina, 140
Howlin' Wolf, 84
Hughes de Payens, 190, 202
Hughes, Langston, 224
Humanity: origins of, 191
Hungarian Soviet Republic, 96
Hungary, 96
Hurston, Zora Neale, 88–89, 219
Hurt, Byron, 125
Hybridization, 19, 27–28, 46
Hyperbole, 134

Ice Cube, 123, 129
Ice-T, 123
Identity, notions of, 86
Idonje, Benson, 78
Iknahton, 194
Immigrants, Congolese, in U.S., 47
Imperial brag, 231
Imperial education systems, 21
Imperialism: and jazz, 213–41, 217, 227, 229–36
Imperial jazz: defined, 215–17
Independent (newspaper, London), 233–34
India, 20; Hindi film songs: trans-regional popularity of, 21; Hindustani classical music, 20; middle class diaspora, 90; Muslim minority community, 44; traditiional musical forms, 44
Indigenousness, black-related, 102, 104
Individuality, survival of (Ortiz), 100
Indie-rap, 124
Inglez, Roberto (Bob Inglis), 115
Intonation. *See* "voice"
Invasion, 102
Iraq: U.S. invasion of, 162
Iraq war, 233–36
Isis, 188. *See also* Yemayá (Yemanja)
Islam, 183
Israelites, 204–5
IX Habana Hip-Hop 2003 conference, 154
Iznaga, Alberto, 220
Izquierdo, Pedro, 156

Jackson Five, 130
Jahn, Janheinz: on Sub-Saharan societies, 10
James Bond movies, 35, 36
James, Deborah, 31
Jazz, 1, 6; as America's art form, 217–41; and authenticity, 216, 223; big band, 217; clarinet, 225; as commodity, 53; Cuban and Haitian origins, 220–21; Cuban influence on, 215; as cultural capital, 217; genres, 32; imperialist promotion and, 14; market distribution of, 240; military influence on, 217, 227, 229–36; New World African music and, 216; North American, 6, 52;

relation to salsa and Cuban *son,* 59; orchestration and structure of composition, 233; perceived stagnation of, 240; performance styles, 238; provenance of, 213–17; and Usonian chauvinism, 217–19, 222–23, 226–27, 230–33; rap music and, 127–28; rhythmic patterns, similar to Cuban music, 225; trombone, 215; trumpet, 215; as war and recruitment tool, 233–36; as world music, 12
Jazz age, 223
Jazz/blues tradition: influence on rap, 131
Jazz criticism, 150
Jazz performance: Afro-Latin presence in, 228
"Jeep music," 125
Jefferson Airplane, 94
Jefferson, Blind Lemon, 92
Jefferson Starship (Jefferson Airplane), 94–95
Jenkins, Jerry B., 212
"Jes Grew" (char., *Mumbo Jumbo*), 185–87, 188, 207
Las Jineteras, 169–73
Jingoism, 229
Johnson, James P., 213
Johnson, James Weldon, 80, 184, 185, 224, 229
Joiner, Whitney, 234
Jones, Keziah, 78
Joplin, Scott, 213–14
Jorrín, Enrique, 69
Judeo-Christian tradition, 54; popular music as rival, 7
Jungle Brothers, 131

Katz, Marco, 118–19
Kaukonen, Jorma, 94
Kennedy, John F., 95
Kephart, Calvin: *Concise History of Freemasonry,* 194
Kerala, India, 162
Kerouac, Jack, 79
Keyes, Cheryl L., 10, 124; on essential nature of rap, 123
Kid Capri, 128
Kidjo, Angelique: Benin rock music, 20
Kiernan, V. G., 209
The King and I (Rodgers and Hammerstein), 35
King, Martin Luther, 31
Kiss-FM, 130, 137
Knights Templar, 184, 190, 194, 201, 2002
Kodály, Zoltán, 96
Kora award (South Africa), 47
Korea: popularity of Western classical music in, 21
Kramer, Samuel: *Mythologies of the Ancient World,* 194
Krenek, Ernst, 57
KRS-One, 120, 127–29, 131
Kung fu movies, 140
Kunzle, David: *The Revolutionary Murals of Nicaragua,* 111
Kuti, Fela Anikulapo, 78
Kwaito music, 18

Labas, PaPa. *See* PaPa LaBas
Lacan, Jacques, 174
La Concha Beach, La Playa, Cuba, 51
Lafargue, Paul: *The Right to be Lazy,* 171
LaHaye, Tim, 212
Landholders, 105

Lane, Frankie, 39, 41
Language barriers, 9
Lanza, Joseph, 82
Lara Bonillo, Rodrigo: assassination of, 176
Largo, 61
The Last Poets, 127
Laswell, Bill, 46
Latifa, Queen, 140, 141
Latin America: African presence in, 1–2; literary and cinematic forms, 154; music, 44
Latin classicism, 119–20
Latin dance: sendups, 41
Latin Headdress gag, 115
Latinidad, 35–36, 37
Latin jazz, 68
Latin music, 114–15; anti-modern outlook, 12; class condescension and, 114–16; commercial success in U.S., 23; in film, 35–37, *38*; has become largest sector of world music, 41; Newtonian time and, 12; recordings, 80; resistance to assimilation, 114–15; U.S. recordings as early as 1898, 222
Latortue, Gerard, 182
Lavoie, Hector, 71, 115
Leavis, F. R., 99
Lecuona, Ernesto, 35, 41, 115, 154
Led Zeppelin, 165
Lefebvre, Henri: *Introduction to Modernity,* 171
Legba (Eshu-Elegba), 3, 113, 193
Leigh, Richard, 199
Leisure activities and lifestyle politics, 26–27
Lennon, John, 94
León, Argeliers, 62, 148, 149; on *fritas* music, 51, 66; on *son* as epic, 61, 62, 63
"Let it Fall" (Lin Qui), 142
Lewis, Neil A., 234
Leymarie, Isabelle, 8, 89, 227, 228–29; on Gottschalk, 220
Liberation theology (Nicaragua), 103
"El Licenciado de la pobreza" (the degree-holder in poverty) (Carlos Meija Godoy), 109–10
Lightnin' Hopkins, 84
Linares, María Teresa, 148
Lincoln, Henry, 199
Lindsay, Vachel, 209, 209–12
Lin Que, 140, 141–42
Lisbon, Portugal, 18
"Listen to the Mockingbird" (Winner), 76
Liszt, Franz, 36
Literary movements, 80
Literature/music: in education, 11–12; lines between, 79–80
Little Richard, 130
Little Walter, 84
2 Live Crew, 123, 125
Lola Montez (Ophuls), 36
Long Range Acoustical Devices (LRADs), 235
Lopez, Israel "Cachao," 69, 156
Lopez, Kadir: painting at "Cuban Art Space" (illustration), 221
López, Ray, 227
Lopez, Trini, 90
Los Angeles riots, 123
Lost texts, 206–9
Louisiana Purchase (1803), 219
Löwenthal, Leo, 90
Lower depths, portraits of, 89

284 SECULAR DEVOTION

Lower East Side, New York, 81
"Lt. Europe Stirring Up the Band" (illustration), 231
Lucumí ceremony, 3, 66
Ludwig of Bavaria, King, 36
Lukács, Georg, 96
Lund, Kátia: *City of God,* 175
Lupe Fiasco, 132

Mabille, Paul, 81–82
Macandal, 3–4
Macfield, David, 105
Machito (Frank Grillo), 153, 156, 222
Mack daddy, 136, 140
Mackenzie, Norman: *Secret Societies,* 201–2
Made-to-order performances, 26
Madonna (musician), 122
Maghreb, 20
Magical realism, 80
Mahler, Gustav, 96
Malcolm X, No Sellout, 131
Malcom X, 95
Malecón (Havana), 169, 171
Male desire, 141
Malone, Dorothy, 39, 40
Mambo, 39, 58, 64–65, 68, 69, 158; revolutionary use of, 110; 1940s and 1950s craze, 23
The Mambo Kings Play Songs of Love (Hijuelos), 154
"Mambru" *(guaracha),* 71
Mandingo, 3
"El Manicero" (Simons), 41
Manuel, Peter, 152
Maracas percussion, 61
Mara Salvatrucha, 179–80
Marcuse, Herbert, 90–91
Marginalization, 51
Marímbula percussion, 53, 61, 73
Marley, Bob, 27
Maroon colonies, 104
"Marroque" (barrio), 177
Martí, José, 68, 151
Martin, Henry: on two- and four-beat jazz, 233
Martinique: *Biguine* music, 74
Marxists, 51
Masons. *See* Freemasonry
Mass culture, 33, 130–31; challenges to, 98–99; critical analyses of, 90–91; debates, 96–97
Mass transportation, 167
Masta Ace, 127
"Master narrative," discussion of, 158–59
Masucci, Jerry, 23
Matamoros, Miguel, 63; "Son de la Loma," 70–71
Matanzas, 60; *santeros* of, 69
Materiality of the world (Heidegger), 67
Maxixe (Brazilian dance), 57
Mayakovsky, Vladimir, 171
Mayan sacred texts, 206
McCartney, Paul, 94
McKay, Claude, 224
McLuhan, Marshall, 99
MC Lyte, 140, 142
Meaning, absence of (Bloch), 56–57
Medellin, Colombia, 175–76; Bellavista prison massacre, 178; murder of "disposables," 177
Media: on rap "gangsta" incidents, 30–31
Media centralization, 118

Medici, Cosimo de, 194–95
Medieval music, 56
Meirelles, Fernando: *City of God,* 175
Mejia Godoy, Carlos, 105, 106, 108–10
Mejia Godoy, Luis Enrique, 105, 106, 107, 109
Melodic inversions, 238
Melville, Herman, 208
Memories of Underdevelopment (Guttiérez Alea), 162–63
Memphis Blues (Handy), 225
Menendez, Milo, 222
Merengue, 152
Messenger gods, 3, 113, 185, 188, 189, 193, 195, 196
Mestizaje (cultural mixing), 6, 28, 53, 73
Metal spoons (as instruments), 67
Meter, 4
Métraux, Alfred, 185, 192
Mexican-Americans, 225
Mexican octets, 215
Mexico, 13; Mexico City, 70; revolution, 215; *telenovela,* 154
M-19 guerrillas, 178
Middle Eastern culture, 20
Mighty Sparrow group: "Obean Woman," 113
Milanés, Pablo, 80, 151, 154, 163
Milhaud, Darius, 33, 57
Military jazz, 229–33
Military occupation, 231–32
Milwaukee Journal, 125
Ministerio de Cultura (Cuba), 148
Minneapolis rap scene, 128
Miranda, Carmen, 115
Miranda, Ismael, 71
Miranda, Oscar, 105
Missa Campesina (Carlos Mejia Godoy), 105, 106, 108
Mitford, William: *History of Greece,* 201
Mixed-race as destiny. *See Mestizaje*
Modern: defined, 84
Modernism: and Afro-Cuban tradition, 50
Modernismo, 103–4
Modernity, Western, 56, 83–84
Monotheism, 10; birth of writing associated with, 200–201
Montez, Lola, 36–37
Montt, Rios, 108
Montuno, 61
Moore, Robin, 152
Morath, Max, 79
Moré, Benny, 69, 90; "Babarabitiri," 240; "Bonito y sobroso," 70–71
Mormonism, 208
Morna music, 18
Morton, Jelly Roll, 53, 213, 223, 226
Moses, 189–90, 204, 206
Motivo, 64, 71
Motown, 43
Moya, Pichardo, 80
Mozambique (dance), 68, 156
Mozambique, Republic of, 162
MTV, 52, 139
Muana, Tshala, 48
Muddyman, David, 19–20
Müller, Karl Ottfried, 198
Multiculturalism, 32
Mumbai, India, 154

INDEX

Mumbo Jumbo (Reed), 182–212, 219; bibliography analyzed, 193–95; literary significance, 191–201; premise of, 182–83, 184; as satire on race relations, 183; synopsis of, 185–90
Muntu, 10
Muralista movement (Nicaragua), 106
Murillo, Rosario, 105
Murrow, Edward R., 152
Museums: as "centers of art detention," 186–87
Music, 5, 10, 101; as army recruiting tool, 234; as cultural influence, 28; folkloric, 100; musical beat and off-beat, 4–5; social symbolism of, 50; sociology of, 92; musical scholarship: Cuban, 147–49, 151; music criticism, 14, 19, 27; as product of a historical experience, 17; total-concept albums, 94; as weapon, 233–36; written, 4
La Música Afrocubana (Ortiz), 99
Música bailable, 121
Música popular Cubana, 81
Music directorate (Hungary), 96
Musicians: in exile, 153; relocation of, 74–75
Music in Cuba (*La Música en Cuba*) (Carpentier), 52, 113
Music technology: for military applications, 234–35
Muslim minority community (India), 44
Muslim sacred texts, 206
Mu'tafikah (in *Mumbo Jumbo*), 186, 188
Mutual aid societies, African American, 51
Mutuashi, 48
Muzak, 35, 82
Myths, 49, 90, 122

NAFTA, 180
Nair, Mira, 44
Naked Gun 2 1/2, 115
Name-dropping, 27
Ñañigos, 3
Napster, 139
Narcocorrido, 107
Narrative music, 20
National anthems, 100
National Geographic: "Global Culture" issue, 166 (illustration), 166–67
Nationalism: as expressed in music, 18
National Recording studios (Nicaragua), 105
Naturalism: literary, 89
Navaja, Pedro, 178
N'Dour, Youssou, 27
Negrismo movement (1920s/1830s), 7, 80, 149
Negro Freemasonry and Segregation (Cass), 194
Negro spirituals, 88–89
Neo-Africanism, 1–2, 113
Neo-African music: defined, 5; forms of, 99, 214; and modernity theory, 57; percussion, and *son* music, 61; political influence of, 3; and rap, 120; rhythms, 59, 60–61; in U.S., 21
Neo-African religion, 74, 113
Neo-Platonism, 196
Neruda, Pablo, 64, 103
New Black Aesthetic, 144
New Orleans, 14, 53, 143, 185, 214, 215, 219; brass band tradition, 232; Caribbean Catholic influence, 216, 219; Cuban immigration to, 163, 222; fictionalized legend of, 8; French and Latin influence in, 216, 219; multidiversity of, 219–20
Newspapers (French and Spanish language), 53

Newtonian time, 12, 53
Newton, Sir Isaac, 196–97
New World: Carribean Catholic influence, 216, 219; U.S. Protestant influence, 216
New World African belief systems, 99, 191. *See also* Neo-Africanism
New World African music, 1–2, 13, 62, 99, 121, 150, 191, 236–37; literature on, 184; as search for lost text of African religion, 14; as sole remnant of mankind's first culture, 183; teaching of, 191; and theory of cultural modernity, 55–56. *See also* Neo-African music
New World dance, 60, 98
New World exploration, 207
New York City, 80–81; Cuban musicians living in exile in, 153, 163; salsa musicians in, 66
New York graffiti movement, 117–18
New York Police Department, 235
New York Syncopated Orchestra, 76
New York Times, 125–26, 182
Nicaragua, 102–11; assassinations, 105; Autonomy talks, 108–9; indigenousness in, 104; national cinema, 106; Sandinista revolution, 13, 103–4; U.S. embargo, 105
Nicaraguan Film Institute, 106
Nieve, Bola de, 92
Nigerian "highlife," 78
Nightclubs, Mexican: and traditional Cuban music of 1920s and 30s, 8
Nightclubs, Parisian: and traditional Cuban music of 1920s and 30s, 8
1920s: film and theater, 12
Nineteenth-century literary realism/naturalism, 89
Noces (Stravinsky), 75
Noise: The Political Economy of Music (Attali), 51, 98
Nommo (magic power of the word), 10
Non-Aligned Nations: Rio Summit, 154
Noriega, Manuel, 234
Norris, Elwood, 235
Nueva trova (folk protest music), 121
Nuñez, Alcide, 227
"Nuttin to Do" (Eminem and Royce), 132–34
Nuyorican musicians, 67–68
Nuyorican Poets' Cafe, 81
NWA, 123

Oakland, Cal., 143
Obando y Bravo, Cardinal Miguel, 108
Ochun, 66
Ogu/Ogun, 3
"Ojos Criollos" (Gottschalk), 214
Old Testament, 207–8; Hebrews of, 208–9
Olivencia, Tommy: *Santero,* 112, 113
Olomide, Koffi, 47 (illustration), 47–48
Los Olvidados (Buñuel), 175
Onomatopoeia, African, 72
"On Popular Music" (Adorno and Simpson), 90–99, 101, 102
Ophuls, Max, 36
Oral language *vs.* written language, 49, 183
Orientalism, 35
Oriente Province (Cuba), 50, 60, 63
Origin myths, 86
"The Origin of the Work of Art" (Heidegger), 66–67
Orishas, 66

Orovio, Helio, 220
Orquesta Revelación, 71
Ortega, Humberto, 106
Ortiz, Fernando, 13, 64, 99–102, 114, 150; on evolution of an art form, 101; exponent of Afro-Cubanism, 151; interpretation of authenticity, 99–100
Osiris, 189, 193
Ospina, Hernando Calvo, 161
Outlaw legends, 122
Oviedo, Papi, 88
"Oye Como Va" (Santana version), 2
Oyelana, Tunji, 79

Pachanga rhythm, 69, 156
Pacheco, Johnny, 72
Pakistan, 20
Palmieri, Eddie, 71, 119, 156; "Azucar," 71
Palos Matos, Luis, 184
Pan-Africanism, v
Pan-African movement: W. E. B. DuBois and, 224
Panama, 234
"Panama" (tango), 232
Pan American Games (1990s), 155
Pancásan, 108
"PaPa La Bas" (char., *Mumbo Jumbo*), 185, 188, 189. *See also* Legba
Paramilitary squads (Colombia), 177–78
Paris: Brazilian music in, 57; jazz in, 57
Paris (rapper), 139, 143
Paris World Music Festival, 45
Parker, Charlie, 79, 228
PBS (Public Broadcasting System): *Jazz* series, 222–23, 226, 230
Peel, Robert, 36
Peña, Juan, 74
Percussion, 61, 64–65; by nonpercussive instruments, 64–65; rap, and Caribbean, 118
Pérez, Angela Maria, 176–77
Pérez, Manuel, 220, 226, 227
Pérez Prado, Dámaso, 69
Performance, 12, 21, 73; Cuban theatrical music presentation, 50; Jazz performance styles, 238, 239; made-to-order, 26; performance etiquette, 239; *salsa* technical demands, 73
"El Periodismo Catacumbas" (Journalism of the Catacombs), 106
Perna, Vincenzo, 158–59
Perry, Edward G., 76
Pershing, General John, 230
Peter and the Wolf (Prokofiev), 95
Peterson, Oscar, 79
Petrovic, Rastko, 51
Phillips, Anne: on communal land tenure, 3
"The Philosophy of Music" (Bloch), 56–57
Phonograph, 79
Piano, technical vocabulary of, 214
Picasso, Pablo, 81–82
Piñeiro, Ignacio, 71, 75, 153
Pisto locos, 174–76, 178
Pixote (Babenco), 175
Plato: *Timaeus,* 197
Playa Girón, 152
Plaza de la Revolución (Havana), 172
Pluralism, 54; in Cuba, under socialism, 163
Poetics, cross-cultural, 55

Poetry: Latin America, 103
Poetry: African social task, 11; black American avant-garde, 80, 208; bop, 80; rap, verbal invention of, 126–27
Pollock, Jackson, 31
Polyphony, 56
Polyrhythm, 60
Polytheism, 194, 200
Poor Righteous Teachers, 120, 129, 131
Pope John Paul II: visit to Nicaragua, 108
"Popular": definitions of, 92, 99–100
Popular culture: definition (Ortiz), 100; global, 164–67
Popular music: as coded revenge, 2; in colonial context, 110–11; and Cuban socialism, 152; harmonics of, 92; Latin influenced, 222; marketed as youth rebellion, 2, 13; seriousness of, 92–93; standardization of, 92, 96–97; studies of, in relation to imperial history and geopolitical arrangements, 55–56; as underground religion, 6
Popular music, Cuban, 147
Popular music in the Americas: Arabic, neo-African and European influences, 1–2
Port-au-Prince, Haiti, 182
Portugal: imperialism and, 17–18; music of, 18
Poster art, 154; Soviet inspiration for, 111
Postman, Neil: *Amusing Ourselves to Death,* 164
Pottery Barn music label: theme titles, 26
Pozo, Chano, 222, 223
Prado, Dámaso Pérez, 69
Press censorship: under Somoza regime, 106
Prohibition, 24, 127
Prokofiev, Sergei: *Peter and the Wolf,* 95
Protestantism, 237
Psychological warfare, 233–36
Public Enemy (group), 94, 129, 130, 140–41; *Fear of a Black Planet,* 131
Public ethics: and institution of slavery, 7
Puebla, Carlos, 110
Puente, Tito, 41–42, 58, 156
Puerto Rico: annexation of, 230; musicians, 152, 226, 230; songs, 111–12
Pulse notation, 63
Punk rock: in Medellín, 174–77; neomodernism *vs.* commercialism in, 129
Punto (verse form), 60
Putumayo record label, 25 (illustrations), 25–26

Qawwalis (Pakistan), 20
Queen Latifah, 140, 141
Que, Lynn. *See* Lin Que
"El Que se Fue" (Sammy Gonzales), 72
The Quiet American, 21
"Quimbara," 72–73
Quintero Rivera, Ángel, 12, 73; on music and Newtonian time, 12; study of *salsa,* 53; on "Tropical Music," 6
"Quitate Tu," 71
"Quizas, quizas, quizas" (Farrés), 41
Quranic religious music: transregional popularity of, 21

Race Man, 144
Race relations: satire on, 183
Racism, 118, 197
Radio, 5; dissemination of jazz, 52–53

Radio art, 95
Radio as technology, 52–53
Radio Havana, 106
Radio-rap, 124
Radio Sandino, 106
Radio stations: commercial R&B, 136–37; operating in Nicaragua, 105–6
Radio technology, 31
Ragtime, 32, 57, 80, 185, 213–15
Rahzel, 132
"Ramblin' Rose" (Nat King Cole), 2
Ramirez, Sergio, 104, 105
Randall, Margaret, 79, 154
Range (octave), 92
Rap, 7, 21, 68, 122–23, 124, 135; Afrocentric, 143; alternative themes for, 143–45; and American business (1960s and 1970s), 117–45; analysis of, 120; appropriation of, 128–29; beats (rhythm), 118; central aesthetics of, 127, 128–29; commercial ambitions of, 32–33, 121–22; commercial packaging and collaging of, 139–40; controversies over, 123, 125–26; DJs, 128–29; fashion trends in, 129; "gangsta" incidents, media exaggeration of, 30–31; lineage of, 126; media promotion of, 139–40; music, 7, 13, 21, 68; nostalgia for, 139; philosophy of, 128–34; politics of, 120–21, 126; R&B fusion, 139, 141; rhyme and voice in, 126–27, 131, 132; sub genres, 31, 62, 135; and verbal dexterity, 123, 131; as vernacular, 62; as war tool, 236
Rastafarianism, 208, 208–209
Ravel: Cuban melodies, 28
Ray, Richie, 156
Raza cósmica, 104
R&B, 5, 13; rap fusion, 139, 141
Reagan, Ronald, 7, 103, 118
Realism, literary, 89
Reconstruction, 6
Record companies, U.S., 79, 222
Recording studios, Western, 27, 47, 87
"Red Sails in the Sunset" (Grosz), 35
Reed, Ishmael, 10, 13–14, 80; on Christianity's concern with miracles and mystery, 199–200; on language/spirit dichotomy, 192–93; *Mumbo Jumbo*, 182–212; writing style, 203–4
Reggae, 5, 131
Regiment of Catalonia Band, 233
Regional hubs, 154
Reglas de ocha, 74
Religion, 147; socialist dogma and, 152
Renaissance: mysticism and, 194
Repetition, 98
Retambo (retambico) dance, 60
Revolutionary Educational Front (FER), 104
Revolution, Nicaraguan (1979–87), 102
Rhyming, 132
Rhythm, 75
Rhythms from Africa: Zanzibar – An Ocean of Melodies (Thompson and Said), 18–19
Rimbaud, Arthur, 33
Rising culture: an alien tradition embedded in, 99
Ritual, 216
Rivera, Ismail, 119; "Moliendo café," 111
Rivera, Raquel, 117
Rivière, Melissa, 143
Rivière, Romaine, 3–4

Roberts, John Storm, 8, 215
Rock music, 21, 94; appropriation of the blues, 43; critique by Marcuse, 91; 1960s and 1970s, 5
Rodrigo D.: No Futuro, 174–77, 180–81
Rodríguez, Arsenio, 222
Rodríguez, Pete "Condé," 71
Rodríguez, Silvio, 154
Rodgers and Hammerstein, 35
Rogers, Ginger, 37
Roldán, Amadeo, 51, 67
Rolling Stones, 165
Romanticism, 87
Roots music, 50
Roots of Rhythm, 156
Rosario, Willie, 113
Rosemain, Jacqueline, 80
Roseñord de Beauvallon, J. B., 220
Rosicrucians, 184
Ross, John, 179–80
Royce Da 5'9, 132–34
Rumba, 5, 6, 7, 8, 37, 58, 72–74, 77, 225; festivals, 154; introduction of, to American jazz, 220
Russolo, Luigi, 82

Sacre du Printemps (Stravinsky), 57, 75
Said, Abdulkadir Ahmed, 18
Salazar, Alonzo, 178
Salazar regime (Portugal): dictatorship and censorship, 18
Sales or non-sales: independence of work of art from, 96
Salsa, 6, 12, 13, 53, 82; the boast in, 135–36; connections to rap, 118–19; definitions of, 68; influence in 1960s and 1970s, 67–68; origins of, 23, 58–59; in *pisto-loco* culture, 178–79; presented as non-Cuban preserve, 156; proletarian labor references in, 112; and religion, political significance of, 113; syncretism of, 64–65; technical and performance demands, 73. See also *Son (cubano)*
Salsa cubana. See *timba*
Salsa performers, 156
Salsa romantica, 71, 156
Samba, 6
Sam, Guillaume, 182
Sanchez, Luis Raphael: *La Guaracha de Macho Camacho*, 184
Sanchez, Sonia, 80, 184
Sanders, Pharoah, 46
Sandinista National Hymn, 109
Sandinista Revolution, 13, 103
Sandino, Augusto César, 104
San Domingo (French colony): slave revolt, 61. See Haiti
San Lazaro (Babalú), 66
Santana, Carlos, 2, 3
Santería, 62, 69, 74, 113–14
Santiago, Marvin: "Estaca de guayacán" ("Beating Stick"), 135–36
Saraband (dance), 60, 78
Satie, Erik, 35; Manifesto (1920), 82
Saumell, Manuel, 76, 228
"El Sauvecito," 75
Sax, Adolph, 228
Saxophone, 228–29

Scat vocalizing, 184
Schapp, Phil, 228
Schiller, Herbert: on leisure, 21
Schoenberg, Arnold, 96
Seattle grunge, 27
Secret societies, 182–83, 184, 200
Secret Societies (Mackenzie), 201
Sectorialism, 158–59
Secular devotion: defined, 2–3, 6, 206–7; music/writing involvement, 183; traditions of, 120
Segregation, 143
Seguidillas, 149
Selena, 115
Self-allusion, 72–73
Self-consciousness, 71
Self, national sense of, 9
Self-reflexivity, 69, 71, 72–73
Senegal, 135
Septeto (arrangement), 68
Septeto Habanero, 75
Septeto Nacional, 153
Seveño, Francisco, 108
Seville Exposition, Spain (1929), 69–70
Sex. *See* Eroticism
Sexteto Habanero, 69
Sex & the City, 41
Shahata, Husni, 215
Shakur, Asata, 143
Shakur, Tupac, 31, 123, 235
Shango, 3
Sheet music publishers, 78
Shorter, Wayne, 46
Siamese bikers rock, 20
"Siempre en my corazón" (Lecuona), 35, 41
Sigler, Vicente, 222
Silicon Valley, 165
Simmons, Jean, 38–39
Simmons, Russell, 143
Simons, Moises, 35, 41
Simpson, George, 90–99, 101, 102
The Simpsons, 41–42
Sinatra, Frank, 131
Single cut, 140
Sirk, Douglas, 39, 40 (illustration)
Sissle, Noble, 230–31
Sistema Sandinista, 105
Sister Souljah, 141, 143
Slavery, 59, 207–8, 215–16, 219; Cuban abolition of (1888), 54, 222; statistics on, 237
Slave trade, 3, 219
Smith, Bessie, 84, 228
Smith, Kate, 96
Smith, Will, 131
Smood, Santiago, 222
Smooth (female mack), 140, 141
Sobran, Joseph, 125
SOB's (Latin jazz venue), 41
Socarrás, Alberto, 220
Social actors, 51
Social cleansing *(limpieza social),* 177
Social danger *(peligrosidad),* 147
Socialism, 80, 96; pleasure and desire in, 161–62, 167–68; pleasures of, 167–68; as resistance to uncontrolled capital exploitation, 162
Socialism, Cuban: Afro-Cuban center, 147; and popular music, 150–51

Socialist-Christian revolution: in Nicaragua, 103, 104, 107
Socialist countries, 162
Social meaning, 87, 90
Sociedades de recreo, 152
"Solace (A Mexican Serenade)" (Joplin), 213–14
Somoza, Anastasio, 103–7
"Son de la Loma" (Trio Matamoros), 70–71; lyrics, 70
Soneros: modern and contemporary, 71–72
Soneros del Barrio, Los, 71, 119
Son montuno rhythm, 69
La Sonora Ponceña, 119
Sonoric mimicry, 184
Son (son cubano), 5, 7, 8, 12, 158; and Cuban middle class, 74; influence on jazz, 215, 219; as literary form, 62–64; musical forms of, 61–69; North Americanization of, 24; origins, 58–60; origins: musical/national, 61–63; ritual element in, 64; social symbolism of, 58–61, 75–76; structure of, 50; surrealism and, 50–51. *See also* Salsa
Soukous, 20, 47
South Africa, 18–19, 135; Kora award, 47; rap, 18
South Bronx: salsa and, 119
Southern Africa, 20
Souza, John Phillip, 185
Soviet Union: fall of, 162; posters, 111
Spain: ballads, 61; colonies, 59; War of Independence against (19th C.), 61; writings of Golden Age (16th and 17th c.), 60
Spain, Golden Age: dances of, 60
Spain, Moorish, 149
Spanish American War, 8, 215, 222, 227, 232
Spanish dances, 60, 64
Spanish popular theater, 19th C., 148
Spears, Britney, 90
Spielmusik (Hindemith), 82
Stacholy, Pedro, 222
Stage persona, 121
"Stagolee" (blues ballad), 121
Standardization: stylization of, 97
Stearns, Marshall: *Story of Jazz,* 219
Sting (musician), 43
St. Louis, 213
St. Louis Blues (W. C. Handy), 215
Storyville, New Orleans, 220
Stravinsky, Igor, 57, 75
Street vernacular, 123
Strophes, 238
Studio technologies, 132
Style Wars, 143
"El Suavecito," 69–70; lyrics, 69
Subtext, African: to culture of the Americas, 1–2
Sufi devotional music, 20
Sugar harvest, 152
Support for scholarly investigations, 148
Support of the arts, 147–56, 159–61
Surrealism, 51–52; African influence in, 33
"Surrealism and *Son*" (Brennan), 12
Sweeney, Phillip, 109
Swing, 32
Symbolism, 42
Symphonic music, 79
Syncopation, 4, 75, 80, 214, 220
Syncopation, Latin, 228, 239
Syncretism, 33–35; neo-African, 216

INDEX

Tango, 57, 77, 110, 111, 177
"Tango [or Spanish-] -bass," 220
Tango rhythm, 78
Tapachula, Mexico, 179
Taraab music, 19
Tate, Greg, 33
Tchaikovsky, Peter Ilyich: Arabic rhythms, 28
Te dió miedo la sangre? (Did the Blood Scare You?) (Ramirez), 104
Television, 55, 79, 106
Terminator X, 95, 131
"Terrorism, war on," 118
Testimonio form, 79, 154
"Tew Ante Sew," 46
Texidor, Luigi, 112
Their Eyes Were Watching God (Hurston), 219
Theme music: Latin, 41
Things, tyranny of: freedom from, 167–68
Thompson, Bridget, 18
Thompson, Robert Farris, 142–43
Thoth, 193, 206. *See also* Legba
Timba (Cuban dance form), 112, 121, 157–60
Timbales, 61
Time: as structured by music, 55
Tin Pan Alley, 1
Tios family, 225; Lorenzo, Sr., Lorenzo, Jr., 227; Luis Tio "Papa," 227
Tizol, Juan, 226
Tomorrows Flavas Today, 138
Tonal clash, 130
Tormé, Mel, 96
Torres, Camilo, 178
Torricelli Bill (U.S. embargo legislation), 169–70
Torture, 234
To Russia with Love, 35
"Trading With the Enemy Act," 24
Tradition: misguided effort to preserve purity of, 27; need for, in post colonial territories, 19
Traditional music, 29; forms, 43; practices, 18–19
Traditional societies: dangers of globalization, 18
Trance, 158
Transculturation, 28
Transnationalism/nationality, 32
Transnational youth culture: in entertainment, 20
Transylvania: metal music, 20
Travel narratives, 10
Tres Hermanos Barretto, 53
Tresillo rhythm, 49, *63*, 225
Tres (instrument), 73
Trillo, Richard, 19–20
Trinidad, 78
"La Trocha" (tango), 232
Troubador modernity, 154
Trumpet, 220
Tshala Muana, 48
"La Tula Cuecho" (Carlos Mieja Godoy), 109
Turf wars: East Coast–West Coast (U.S.), 29–31
Turkey, 20, 182
Tzara, Tristan, 51

Union of Radio Journalists of Managua, 106
United Nations Universal Declaration of Human Rights (1948), 162
United States: conservatism (1990s), 103; foreign policy, 103, 184; ideological outlook on jazz, 217–27, 229–36; Imperialism: and jazz, 213–41; marines, 182; physical violence of, as manifested in rap music turf wars, 32; power politics, 200 (*See also* Secret societies); United States Treasury, 170
United States embargo, 102, 143, 154, 155, 163
United States military: in Haiti, in 1920s, 227; and Mexico, 215; in Mexico, under Pershing, 227; recruitment of black and Latino soldiers, 234
United States military bands: in Europe in World War I: New York 15th Infantry regiment brass band, 215, 230; Puerto Rican Clarinet players recruited for WW I France, 230
University curriculums: post-colonial cultural forms and, 28
Usonians, 20, 24, 30, 32–33, 41; cultural chauvinism of, 217–19, 222–24, 226–27, 230–32

Vacunao (dance), 37, 68
Valdéz, Miguelito, 90, 222
Valentino, Rudolph, 41, 68
Vallejo, César, 103
Vallenato (dance music), 177
Van Sertima, Ivan, 207
Van Vechten, Carl, 187
Varela, Carlos, 172
Vasconcelos, José, 104
Vaughn, Sara, 131
Ventura, Michael, 84, 87
Verde, Cape: national culture, 18
Vernacular religion, 191
Vibrato: in singing, 46
Video programs: rap on, 138–39
Viennese School: minuetto and scherzo in, 97–98
Village Vanguard, 81
Village Voice, 222–23
Villa, Ignacio Jacinto. *See* Bola de Nieve
La Violencia (Colombia), 178
Viva channel, Germany, 28
Vodun. See Voodoo
"Voice": and tonality, 131, 132
Voice of America, 105
Von Vampton, Hinkle (char. *Mumbo Jumbo*), 187, 188–89, 192, 206
Voodoo (vodun), 3, 68, 113, 189, 192, 206, 219; iconography of, 194; images of, *196*

Walcott, Derek, 56
Wallflower Order, 185
War industry, 235–36
"The War of Writing on Music" (Reed), 14
Washburne, Christopher, 225
Webb, Chick, 239
Weber, Max, 74
Weill, Kurt, 33, 57
Welfare, dismantling of, 118
Wells, Junior, 87
Werktreue, 83
West African guitar influences, 46
West Bengal, 162
West Coast rap, 123
Western civilization, 56–57; as conspiracy, 189–90; popular music as alternative history of, 7; as race war, 183
West Indian music, 74
West Indies: migrations to U.S. from, 229

West, Kanye, 136
West Side Story (Bernstein), 79
White Album (Beatles), 94
White jazzman vs. black jazz musicians: from swing to bebop, 239
Whitemen, Paul, 239, 240
White voyeurism, 81
Wiggerhaus, Rolf, 96
Wild Style, 117, 143
Williams, Clarence, 228
Williamson, Sonny Boy, 84, 87
Williams, Wendy, 137
Winley, Paul, 127
Winner, Septimus, 76
Witchcraft *(brujrería)*, 100
WKCR FM, 228
Women in music, 13
Wonder, Stevie, 94
Word-of-mouth: transmission of musical tradition by, 100
Works of art: as commodities, 96
World Health Organization, 180
World Industrial and Cotton Centennial Exposition (New Orleans, 1884–85), 215
World music: basic contradictions of, 16; Cuba's entry into, 69; as cultural capital, 34–35; definitions of, 20–21; as exit from provincialism, 37–39, 41–42; historical vs., commercially disseminated, 12, 43; idea of as marketed vs. its reality, 15–16; in market setting, 234–35; paradoxes of, 16; perceived as Usonian, 24; sonority and structure in, 42–43; trade as backdrop to, 16; what it is not, 20–21
World Music: A Rough Guide (Broughton, Ellingham, Muddyman and Trillo), 19–20
World Music Institute, New York, 22
World music, women in, 44–46, 48
World War I, 229; Negro musicians called upon to volunteer, 230
Wright, Richard, 224
Writing on music. *See* Music, music criticism
Written on the Wind, 39, 40 (illustration), 41

X Clan, 143
X image (from *Mumbo Jumbo*), 204 (illustration)

Yambú, 68
Yemayá (Yemanja), 66, 188
Yo! MTV Raps, 138
Yoruba: culture, 3, 66, 219; religion, 185
Young, Neil, 165
Youth: ideology of, 164–65; seen as force of revolutionary dislodgement, 164–67; as target of market research and advertising, 13, 164–65
Youth culture: penetration of, through music, 55
Youth rebellion, 2, 165; marketing of, 13
YouTube, 139

Zaire, 47
Zanzibar: *Taraab* music blended with rap, 19
"Zero Hour" (Cardenal), 104
Zola, Émile, 89